Your PhD in Accounting or Finance

Produce a thesis to be proud of

and sail through the viva

Chris Brooks

Your PhD in accounting or finance: Produce a thesis to be proud of and sail through the viva by Chris Brooks
Copyright © 2021 Chris Brooks. All rights reserved

PUBLISHED BY FINANCE BOOKS

Cover design by Sheena Brooks

First published, September 2021

ISBN 978-1-915189-03-5

AIMS OF THIS BOOK

This book is specifically written to support PhD students in accounting or finance. I have supervised more than 20 PhDs through to successful completion and examined more than 50 doctoral students. In this guide, I aim to simplify the whole process of conducting doctoral research from the point before you apply right through to the date of the oral exam and beyond.

KEY FEATURES

- Covers all aspects of conducting research and writing a thesis, from finding initial ideas to drafting and polishing the final document
- Focuses specifically on the needs of students in accounting and finance
- Loaded with top tips on how to make quick progress and avoid common pitfalls
- Includes material on how to apply for places on PhD programmes, preparing for the viva voce examination, and publishing your work
- Takeaway messages summarising each chapter
- Access to YouTube videos that map directly onto the key topics covered. Search on the site for Chris Brooks and look for the Finance Books logo or use this URL: https://www.youtube.com/channel/UC0YkHcC4SUgxrpQ6WFPN-Fw, then select the Your PhD in Accounting or Finance Playlist
- Identification of free resources for data, literature and software.

ABOUT THE AUTHOR

Chris Brooks is Professor of Finance at the ICMA Centre, Henley Business School. He was formerly Professor of Finance at the Cass Business School, London. He holds a PhD and a BA in Economics and Econometrics, both from the University of Reading. He has been involved with research for more than 25 years, producing over 150 published papers and books. His interests span a wide range of subject areas including finance, economics, real estate, econometrics, investor behaviour, tax, and history.

Chris has taught undergraduates, postgraduates and executives, and has supervised more than 25 PhD students. He has supervised or examined doctoral students in Belgium, Germany, Mauritius and South Africa as well as all over the UK. Chris was formerly Director of the PhD Programme at the ICMA Centre, and was also Director of the PhD Programme at the Cass Business School when he worked there. His completed PhD students have forged successful academic careers in their own right or now work for major investment banks and other commercial organisations.

Chris is a Senior Fellow of the Higher Education Academy but is probably best known as the author of the first introductory-level econometrics textbook targeted at finance students, *Introductory Econometrics for Finance* (2019, Cambridge University Press), which is now in its fourth edition and has sold over 70,000 copies worldwide.

Contents

II	**Doing the research**

List of Tables

List of Figures

PREFACE

Doing a PhD, or doctorate as it is sometimes known, is a unique experience where you get to choose what to study, how to study it and at what pace. You will produce an extensive research document known as a thesis. Although you will be working within a well-established framework and given support, guidance and encouragement by your supervisor, nobody is going to be continually telling you what to do. The PhD project is also your chance to produce something unique and make a contribution to knowledge.

Conducting research in the process of completing a doctorate can be fun because it allows the investigator to solve a conundrum and possibly reveal a new insight to an issue that has not been done before. It is rarely repetitive since, by definition, academic research involves doing something different than what has been done before, so it can be a gratifying experience. In addition, the process of completing a PhD allows students to identify and study a topic that they are excited about and is instrumental in developing time-management, report-writing, and many other skills.

The phenomenal growth that has taken place in the types and volumes of data available has provided a vast amount of new material to work with, and makes this a fascinating time to be embarking on a research endeavour. New sources of data have arisen due to social media and on-line searching and investing, newsrooms and forums, all of which are conducted electronically, leaving a digital footprint of the activity that could be analysed. Many companies, such as Google, make their data available to researchers in aggregated or anonymised forms, often free of charge. Using such data opens up exciting possibilities for kinds of investigation that were not previously possible, such as examining the disclosures that firms might make through social media before other channels or which types of communications media yield the most significant market impacts.

Technological progress has also made the task of conducting research easier in many ways and more fun. If you get stuck along the way, there will probably be a video on YouTube or a question-and-answer forum that covers precisely what you need. Statistical software can automatically format your regression results to drop into your thesis document, while survey packages can code the results and output them straight into a spreadsheet, both of which will save countless hours of dull and error-prone data-entry.

Why is another book on how to do a PhD needed?

Unfortunately, the nature of modern degree programmes in accounting or finance is such that most are 'conversion courses' requiring no prior knowledge of the subject and covering a wide range of subject matter. This breadth means that depth is sacrificed, and each module only skims the surface of popular topics with textbook-style treatments and no time to delve into the research literature.

Even worse, in the past, virtually all students beginning a PhD would have had the experience of writing an undergraduate or master's dissertation (or both). Thus, moving onto a PhD would be a matter for them to 'up their game' in terms of the scale and intellectual level of their research, but they would already have all the raw ingredients and know the process. Yet nowadays, it is quite common for students accepted onto doctoral programmes to have no research experience whatsoever, their prior learning confined to taught modules alone. The task of completing a doctorate is still entirely feasible for such students, but it will be a steep learning curve in the first year with many new skills to learn and a new way of thinking to get to grips with.

In my view, none of the extant textbooks really hit the mark for a PhD in accounting or finance. They are either too high-level and lacking in practical details, or they are mainly aimed at another field. There is so much variation in research approaches across disciplines that a book written for English literature or biology students won't cut it for someone in our subject, which sometimes considers itself a science and sometimes a social science. We are, therefore, fortunate that the subject area draws its methods from both and embodies a range of approaches so that quantitative and qualitative research are employed. Nonetheless, the methods used and the conventional writing style in accounting and finance are somewhat different from those in other disciplines. Most existing 'how to do research' books are written by sociologists or professors of education using an approach and a language that are at variance with how researchers in accounting and finance think and write.

In addition, many extant books on doing a PhD are simply too abstract. I skimmed through several of them as I was preparing this manuscript, and I wondered whether students would be able to apply what was written in those books to their situation and chosen topic. I scratched my head wondering what messages a PhD student was supposed to take away and how the material would help them do better research and write a better thesis.

By contrast, this text aims to cover the nuts and bolts of the research process, and where intangible concepts are used, clear examples and applications to the accounting or finance context are provided. The focus is squarely on the practical aspects of conducting research and writing about it. In some cases, I have used illustrative examples from my own (usually co-authored) research. While this is perhaps somewhat self-indulgent, it does ensure that I know the material well, and I don't have to be concerned about infringing someone else's copyright.

For whom is this book written?

The book is aimed at anyone contemplating applying for or in the process of doing a PhD in accounting or finance. It might also prove useful for those studying in cognate areas such as economics, business studies or management. I have tried to adopt an informal and engaging style as far as possible, and readers might also observe that I have used gender-neutral pronouns in the plural ('them' and 'they') when discussing an unspecified person even when I am referring to one individual.

The book covers all facets of the process, right from writing a proposal and making applications through to how to prepare for the viva voce exam and publish work from the thesis at the end.

Where relevant, some aspects of this text are drawn from my earlier book, *First Class Research: A guide to your research project or dissertation in accounting and finance*, modified as appropriate. Even though the audiences for the two books are entirely different (taught undergrad or master's versus PhD students), both are written assuming no prior experience of research and therefore they need to cover some of the same ground.

Outline of the remainder of this book

The book is divides naturally into three parts. The first combines chapters involved with activities prior to the PhD commencing: namely, what doctoral research is all about, different kinds of research that can be conducted, choosing the topic and applying for places on PhD programmes. The second part collects together the chapters on various aspects of the process of actually doing the research, including what to expect from your supervisor, how to organise your time efficiently, reflecting on any potential ethical concerns and conducting the literature review. The final part examines the latter stages of thesis completion (writing up and polishing the document) together with a comprehensive discussion around the – usually dreaded – viva voce exam. It also provides suggestions on how and where to present and publish work from a thesis and finally, how to apply for academic posts for any readers crazy enough to want to do so.

More specifically, each individual chapter in the book develops as follows. Chapter 1 covers the essential background information needed to make an effective choice about whether to apply for a PhD, and if you do, what the experience would be like and what you would be aiming to produce. This includes a treatment of what research is, how it might differ between the taught programme and research degree levels and the differences between the kinds of research conducted by academics and practitioners. The various stages involved in completing a PhD, from the first day of the course until the oral exam at the end, are presented and elucidated. This chapter also encourages you to consider, at this very early stage, what a good thesis might look like, and what examiners will be looking for.

Chapter 2 provides a brief introduction to the philosophy of research as it is conducted in social sciences, with a specific focus on accounting and finance. A distinction is drawn between the positivist tradition of the empirical study of large datasets and the interpretivist approach using interviews and case studies to extract detailed information within specific contexts. Various approaches to classifying research and learning are discussed, providing useful frameworks that make it easier to understand where different types of research fit within the body of knowledge.

Chapter 3 examines a wide range of issues around the choice of PhD topic to investigate. This is the first, and in many ways most important, challenge and making a bad decision can render the entire process thereafter much less rewarding – both emotionally and in terms of the quality of the finished product at the end – than it would have been if more careful consideration had been given at the outset. Tips on where to look for inspiration and the kinds of research areas that might be acceptable are presented alongside coverage of some of the aspects that can go wrong and how to avoid that outcome.

Chapter 4 continues the work begun in chapter 3 by covering all aspects of how to write a PhD proposal, which is a vital ingredient in the application process for PhD programmes. The chapter discusses in detail the document structure and sections likely to be required, including how to write a Gantt chart or timeline.

Chapter 5 completes part 1 of the book and broadens the focus established in chapter 4 to consider the application process more widely. This chapter provides suggestions on choosing how and when to apply, and what other materials will be needed in addition to the proposal.

The second part of the book begins with chapter 6, which discusses two skills that are essential to develop for a smooth and stress-free experience. The first is organising yourself and managing your time, while the second involves dealing effectively with your supervisor. Forming a solid and productive working relationship with them is paramount given that they will be your primary point of contact and source of guidance for several years.

The ethical issues that can arise in the production of research are covered in chapter 7. The chapter examines the Data Protection Act and discusses the ethics approval process that students are likely to have to go through if their research uses live subjects rather than anonymised secondary data. There then follows a detailed examination of plagiarism, including what it is, how it is detected, and how to avoid it. Other issues are examined around ethical behaviour in research, including falsification of data or results, the importance of accuracy and honesty, and how to prevent conflicts of interest.

Chapter 8 is the first of two that cover an essential component of all dissertations, namely the literature review. This chapter examines how and where to find the source material to incorporate in the review, including accessing journal articles, books, websites, working papers and PhD theses. It also offers suggestions on how to ensure the quality of your reading material, how to focus your search if there is too much literature, and how to read quickly.

Chapter 9 then proceeds to discuss how to pull all of the material together to write the literature review. It discusses issues around both style and content, including suggestions for structure, how to write critically while at the same time presenting a balanced argument, and how to cite existing work appropriately. The chapter ends with a discussion of some of the flaws that weak literature reviews could contain and how to fix them.

Chapter 10 completes part 2 of the book and discusses the investigative aspects of a PhD, namely the methods and data. It explains how the choice of research methods is made and examines how to incorporate theory into a dissertation in accounting or finance, including discussing from where relevant theories come. The chapter continues the focus on the investigation to present the various types of data that can be employed in research, distinguishing between primary and secondary data types.

The final part of the book begins with Chapter 11, which is the first of two chapters on writing the thesis document. It begins by discussing the differences between the style of writing employed by academics and those used in other walks of life. Tips are provided on how to make your writing entertaining as well as informative, and the chapter also outlines how to structure the thesis and what material should be placed in each section or chapter of the dissertation.

Chapter 12 continues the thesis document theme with a consideration of the further issues regarding refinement and polishing of the draft prior to submission. Suggestions are provided on how to deal with feedback or comments from supervisors and others, and how to get the most from it. The chapter proposes ideas for improving the thesis structure and narrative, along with tips on how to respond if your draft is significantly under or over the official word limit. The chapter ends with a checklist of aspects to tick off before final submission.

The viva voce (oral) examination, which many students fear, is the subject of chapter 13. The key aim is to allay any concerns about the process by explaining how it works and that the odds of success are stacked in the candidate's favour. All aspects of the viva are discussed, including its purpose, how to prepare for the event, what to expect and what outcomes could occur.

The two remaining chapters cover matters that are not direct parts of the PhD degree but are nonetheless essential for students to consider well before they complete their programme. The first of these, in chapter 14, explains the importance of disseminating your work and building your reputation by presenting papers at conferences and submitting papers to journals.Practical suggestions are given on how to design the slide deck, deliver the talk, and deal with questions and feedback. The chapter then moves on to discuss how to draft papers for submission, how to select the appropriate journal, and what process will be used to evaluate your study.

The book finishes with chapter 15, which covers the career options that are open to PhD graduates in accounting and finance, with a particular focus on academic posts. It provides some tips on how to apply, the kinds of questions likely to be asked at interviews, and what universities are going to be looking for in today's highly competitive job market.

Preparing and applying

1. INTRODUCTION

Learning outcomes: this chapter covers

- ✓ Some reasons for doing a research degree
- ✓ The skills needed to complete a PhD successfully
- ✓ The difference between academic (scholarly) and practitioner research
- ✓ The requirements for a PhD thesis

1.1 What is a PhD, and what is it for?

A PhD is an advanced programme of research that ends in the production of an extensive document known as a *thesis*, and, if successful, the candidate will be awarded the title of Doctor of Philosophy. The person can then use the title 'Dr'. In the UK, a PhD typically takes between three and four years full-time (or up to six years part-time) to complete. There are several primary reasons why people choose to spend such a significant amount of time doing this, listed in the following subsection.

1.1.1 Why do a PhD?

1. To gain entry to a job that requires the qualification
2. To study a subject in-depth for several years
3. To develop skills as an independent researcher
4. To produce new knowledge that might be useful for the economy or society

5. To remain a student for as long as possible

Some jobs have possession of a PhD as a minimum requirement, and this includes academic jobs in universities (even those involving only teaching), as well as research roles in consultancy firms, investment banks, central banks or market regulators. More detail will be given on career options in chapter 15, but to have any chance of successfully applying for such roles, a PhD is needed.

A second, arguably even more important reason for conducting a PhD is to satisfy your intellectual curiosity. Researchers identify and solve puzzles, which help our understanding of how things work and why. As I will discuss at various stages in this book, doctoral research is a long, and sometimes lonely process with numerous ups and downs, and only a deep fascination for the subject under study will carry the researcher through to the end. It provides a unique opportunity to study a subject in-depth for a several years with relatively few interruptions.

Third, if you elect to do a PhD, the process of working on it will help you obtain or strengthen several key skills that would be hard to acquire elsewhere. These are often attributes that employers value more than subject-specific knowledge, and completing a PhD will enable you to evidence that you have acquired these competencies. The following is a non-exhaustive list of the key skills that you could acquire:

- Independent thinking – not only do you decide what research problem to work on and how to tackle it, but you will also be primarily responsible for resolving any issues that you face
- Time management – the doctoral project is yours to organise from the start until the end. Although there is a support structure in place, you will be responsible for the workflow and keeping progress on track
- Critical synthesis of a body of existing work – you choose what to read, how to summarise it, and, most importantly, how to identify the flaws in what is already written
- Identification of opportunities and 'gaps in the literature' – partly leading on from the previous point, once you have filled your head with knowledge about a particular topic, you will be in a position to see where the limitations are – what is missing, where existing research is lacking, and where you could potentially contribute
- Data collection and organisation – you might need to use some detective work to identify the types of data you need, matched to your doctoral project's aims and methodology. You might be conducting surveys, interviews, or experiments, and doing this validly is a specialist competence in its own right. Wherever the data come from, they will almost certainly need cleaning and organising in a spreadsheet to get them in an appropriate form for analysis
- Statistical modelling – quantitative data investigation including econometrics and other approaches are specific skills that will hopefully be covered in other aspects of your programme, but this might be the first instance where you need

to select the appropriate techniques and use them in a context that you have chosen rather than being provided with all of the steps

- Report structuring and writing – organising all the parts of the research output and adopting a sound writing style that engages the reader and explains the findings clearly is another valuable skill

These skills are all required to successfully complete a PhD, which is why writing one is such a worthwhile experience. Thesis topics need to be highly specific because the available resources – your finances, time, knowledge of the field, skills in data collection and analysis, and the amount that you are permitted to write, will all face some constraints. Working within these boundaries is another important aspect of the process.

The doctoral dissertation might also be the only time during your life where you have genuine freedom to choose what, when and how to study (within some fairly loose constraints). Most PhD students are free to select their own topic, unless they tied down by a sponsorship agreement that comes with strings attached. It is an intellectual challenge involving a comprehensive array of required attributes. The proof that you have acquired those talents will arise from the thesis document you produce that will remain on your shelf for a lifetime.

Even though doctoral students and academics generally have the freedom to research whatever they choose, their outputs can have many benefits for the 'real world' outside the academy. For instance, to offer just a few illustrations, university researchers work on many topics of practical importance in accounting and finance such as:

- Environmental accounting
- Dealing with tax avoidance
- Revising and updating accounting standards
- Supporting the efficient running of multinationals with timelier information
- Imputing values for work conducted by the public sector
- Ensuring that banks have sufficient capital to avoid financial distress
- Building portfolios with desired risk characteristics
- Designing new approaches to pension saving
- Determining whether an asset market contains a speculative bubble

Thus, another reason to conduct a PhD is as a first step on a journey to producing knowledge that has genuine practical value to solve some of the issues faced by accountants and financial market participants.

A final reason why people might opt to study for a PhD is so that they can remain in education and put off the point where they join the workforce (or, in some cases, return to their home country) for as long as possible. The academic lifestyle embodies considerable latitude: PhD students can sleep all day and work at night in their pyjamas if they wish. They can write at the desk in their department, at home on the sofa or at Mount Everest Base Camp – this freedom is cherished and invariably unavailable to those working outside the academy. For such individuals, PhD study offers a useful holding stage providing them with new skills and knowledge while they decide that they want to do in the longer term.

1.1.2   Reasons not to do a PhD

The previous subsection provided an extensive list containing some excellent motivations for doing a PhD, but in the interests of balance, it is also worth showing the other side of the coin. Doing a PhD is not easy, and there are numerous reasons to choose a different path and do something else with your life:

- The cost – as discussed above, the total fees at a UK university for doing a PhD are likely to exceed £15,000 for UK-based students and perhaps £50,000 for those from overseas. When you throw in the cost of living over a three to four year period, this will amount to an extremely large cost. Even if you are fortunate enough to receive a scholarship that covers tuition fees and living expenses, you need to consider the foregone income that you could have earned if you had been working rather than studying. PhD graduates typically earn more than those starting work with only a master's qualification, but this is not always the case

- Doing a PhD entails living with significant insecurity for a prolonged period. When you begin, you will have only a little idea what you will be working on and how you will tackle it, and probably no idea what you will do after completing in three of four years' time. Can you handle it? Although, as I discuss in chapter 13, the chances of failing are actually very low if you persevere, the risks relate to how you get to the end and how quickly

- Successful completion requires putting in a lot of hours. Particularly if you aim to complete within three years, you will need to get used to working in the evenings and at weekends as well as during the day time. In theory, a PhD can be completed in three years of full-time study (at 37 hours per week) but in reality most students need far more hours than that

- The PhD is a lonely experience. Working on a thesis is a solo endeavour, and while you will make friends among other students and have support from the department and especially your supervisor, the vast bulk of the work will be done by you alone. You will need to learn to be resourceful and solve your own problems

- You need to be self-disciplined. Although having the freedom to determine your own working patterns is one of the greatest virtues of PhD study, for those who cannot organise themselves it is a disaster. If you are the sort of person who stays in bed until somebody steals the covers and leaves your essays until the night before they are due, you will really struggle to stay on top of a PhD, which has so little structure and so few deadlines

- You will be working on the same topic for several years. This requires patience, staying power and a deep fascination with the subject to retain your interest over such a long time period

- If you cook a meal, write a poem, or even build a shed, you get to see the fruits of your labours very quickly, but with a PhD you will have virtually nothing to show for your years of work until right at the end
- You need to be able to deal with criticism. Getting feedback on your work from your supervisor, conferences, examiners, and eventually journal referees, is an integral part of growing as a researcher and improving your work. But it can be brutal: despite the time and effort that goes into conducting research and writing it up, others will try to dismantle it in a five-minute critique. Their negative comments may or may not be valid, but to be successful as a researcher, you need to be able to learn from critical suggestions rather than taking them to heart
- Many PhD candidates aspire to obtain a full-time position as a lecturer / assistant professor when they complete. But while the number of doctoral students registered in accounting and finance has grown significantly over the past two decades, the number of academic jobs available for them to apply to has not. Therefore, competition for posts is now extremely intense, with the result that even good candidates are having to take part-time or temporary roles with heavy teaching loads after graduation; chapter 15 provides an extensive discussion on how to apply for academic posts

Before making the decision to start putting together your applications, or taking up the place on a programme if you have already been offered one, reflect on the lists of pros and cons above and make sure that your motivation and commitment to getting the qualification are sufficiently strong to overcome the disadvantages.

Is there a difference between a thesis and dissertation?

The words *dissertation* and *thesis* are often used synonymously and will be used interchangeably in this book to refer to the document that is produced and submitted for examination. Similarly, the words *PhD* and *doctoral research* will be used interchangeably here.

1.1.3   What is it like to do a PhD?

If you have never been involved with research before, it will be an entirely new experience. Some students will have completed research projects as undergraduate or master's students, but for the remainder, the closest they will probably have come is when they have written an extended essay or mini-project. There, they will likely have had to identify their own sources, summarising a little published research, and possibly conducting some empirical modelling. There are three main differences between that and a full PhD dissertation, however:

1. The scale of the undertaking: this doctoral project will be very much bigger, taking far longer to complete and requiring considerably more investigation and writing
2. The freedom you now have to organise everything yourself: the topic, the

aims, the methodological approach, the timescale, and the writing style

3. There is a requirement for PhDs to have an original contribution. This will be discussed further in section 1.4

1.1.4   Is a thesis in accounting or finance different?

To what extent is a PhD in accounting or finance different from one in another field? The basic definition of research, and the core ingredients that every thesis should embody, are universal will transcend subject boundaries. An appropriate structure, straightforward writing style, appropriate document length, a review of the relevant literature, rigorous data analysis and appropriate conclusions will all be expected of all PhD research, whatever the field.

There are, however, several features of accounting and finance as subject areas that distinguish them from other fields. First, as discussed in chapter 2, they straddle the sciences and social sciences, and hence they draw methods from both sides. The most common structure adopts the form seen in scientific papers, although case studies or interviews are also used, and would lead to a style more akin to a sociology or history piece.

What differentiates accounting and finance from the sciences, however, is the importance of the narrative in our subjects. As described in detail in chapter 11, having a solid story to tell based on theory is essential for a high-quality thesis. On the other hand, the results would be written up more dispassionately and probably at less length in the sciences.

1.1.5   Skills needed to complete a good PhD

Some students will start from the premise that they will never be able to write 70,000 words (a typical length for a PhD thesis) on the same topic and will be nervous that they do not have the skills to complete it to the required standard. But my experience suggests that even if you have never written a document of that length before, it is far more likely that you will struggle to keep the length of your thesis down to the limit than not being able to write enough. For comparison, this book is approximately 140,000 words long.

You don't need to be super-intelligent to do good research, nor do you need to be a brilliant writer. Of course, both of those attributes would be helpful, but much more important characteristics are:

- Possessing a genuine interest in learning something new and having an inquisitive mindset
- Having a willingness to put in many hours over a long period of time and to prioritise the PhD over activities that might be more fun or more financially rewarding in the short term
- Being an all-rounder with a mixture of skills, including organising, writing, analysing, programming, etc.
- Remaining doggedly determined to finish and being able to overcome the

many issues that will occur along the way rather than becoming disheartened and giving up

- Being confident in working alone without frequent guidance, albeit within a supervisory framework that operates at arm's length

If you do not enjoy working on the thesis and find it a chore, you are much more likely to do a poor job or even give up altogether. No student will find pleasure in every aspect of the process – for instance, some people love writing but hate dealing with data and doing quantitative analysis, others vice versa. Consequently, try to focus your energy on the parts that you enjoy the most and make them as big a part as possible of the whole activity. You have the scope to select the kind of study that makes the most of your interests and abilities, as discussed in chapter 3.

1.1.6 How does a PhD differ from an undergrad or master's dissertation?

Traditionally, it was understood that an undergraduate programme would provide a general education across a field, with a master's qualification building upon the subject matter that was already covered to offer more in-depth, specialist knowledge. In that sense, we might expect that a research project at the master's level ought to be more detailed and at a higher intellectual level, embodying smarter and more novel ideas, more sophisticated models, more depth in analysis, etc. But over recent years, business schools have seen the growth of 'conversion' master's, where no or little prior knowledge of the subject is required for entry onto the programme. While there will be variation across universities, in this context, the level of master's dissertations has arguably slipped so that the expectations for undergraduate and master's courses are now probably fairly similar.

When the term 'master's' is used in this book, it refers to a taught postgraduate (MSc or MA) programme, usually of 9- or 12-months' full-time duration. A 'traditional' UK one-year master's programme involved nine months of taught courses and exams followed by a three-month summer dissertation. In these cases, the research component will be at most a third of the whole programme's credit weighting and possibly as little as 15-20%.

However, many universities also offer MRes or MPhil degrees, which are more specialist research-based programmes. The MRes is partly a taught programme that is likely to involve some modules specifically supporting the project (for example, in research methodology or the philosophy of research). These will probably be assessed separately from the dissertation itself. But an MPhil is a pure research degree where only the final thesis is assessed, which would generally be of two years' full-time duration. An MPhil will usually contain less investigative work than a PhD, and will have weaker requirements concerning the contribution to knowledge. The holder of an MPhil is not entitled to call themselves 'Dr', however.

There are several key differences between the research you might have conducted for a taught (BSc or MSc) programme in accounting or finance and the PhD requirements. Naturally, the difference between an outstanding master's project and a weak doctoral thesis will be less than between an average project and an excellent thesis, but in general, there are some crucial aspects that you would need to up your game on:

- Originality – a PhD must make an original contribution to knowledge, discussed in more detail in section 1.4. A good master's student project might also possess such novelty, but this will be the exception and is usually not required to obtain a high passing mark
- Length – a student project might typically be between 8,000 and 15,000 words long, whereas a PhD is likely to be 60–90,000 words, so perhaps five times longer altogether
- Sophistication – a PhD needs to have evidence that the work contained within it is of sufficient quality to be publishable in a peer-reviewed journal. It needs to use cutting edge techniques consistent with current best practice in the field
- Depth of analysis – the investigative work in a PhD must be rigorous, with the data examined in considerable depth rather than just skimming over the surface. There will likely be numerous robustness checks to ensure that the results are as reliable as possible
- Timeframe – typically, a research project will be of three months' full-time duration as part of a taught programme, whereas PhD registration is generally at least three years full-time and five or six part-time

1.1.7 PhD by published works

Some universities offer the opportunity for candidates to complete a PhD by prior publication. This sort of route is aimed at people who have already amassed a set of publications through their career. For instance, this might be someone who has worked in a central bank or as a practitioner-researcher who could demonstrate through their publications that they possess the required attributes of being an independent researcher producing work of an acceptable standard. This route to getting a PhD is also sometimes taken up by senior scholars who joined the academy many years ago before possessing a doctorate was an entry requirement.

In such cases, the individual would usually register for a PhD for a short period (such as one year), during which time they would draft an introduction and literature review that aimed to draw their existing contributions together and put them in the context of the current body of knowledge. This review chapter would then be submitted for examination along with the published papers.

The requirements for such a PhD in terms of the candidate's knowledge and skills and the quality and originality of the work they have produced are the same as for a more conventional PhD. However, this route would be inappropriate for the vast majority of PhD candidates since they will not possess a body of existing publications upon which they can draw. Note that a PhD by prior publications is not the same as producing a PhD in the form of a set of publishable (not published) papers, which is an increasingly common thesis structure in accounting and finance, as discussed in section 11.4.

1.1.8 Does PhD research need to be original?

For an undergraduate or taught master's degree dissertation, it is unlikely that the project would be expected to have a significant original contribution. At best, it will probably be an enhanced replication study that re-analyses an existing problem with a new dataset or a very slightly different empirical approach. This situation is unlike a full research degree, such as a DPhil or PhD, where making a clear and evident contribution to knowledge will be an absolute requirement for getting the qualification. A PhD cannot comprise a series of replication studies, as it must contribute to knowledge – see section 1.4.

1.1.9 Practitioner research compared with scholarly research

If you compare an article published in an academic journal with a report written by a management consultant or a researcher working for a bank or auditing firm, you will notice several systematic differences between them. As well as differences in the writing style, which will be discussed at length in chapter 11 and chapter 12, there will be variations in the purpose and nature of the research itself.

Academic research tends to be primarily interested in solving puzzles – in other words, determining why a particular phenomenon occurs or explaining the factors that affect the extent of that phenomenon. Such research does not necessarily need to have any specific use outside of the academy and is sometimes called blue skies, curiosity-driven, or basic research. Note in passing that the term 'basic' does not imply that the investigation is simple or intellectually low-level; instead, it means that it is not yet applied or focused on a particular practical problem. In such research, there will be an emphasis on the rigour, validity and reliability of the findings. Contrast this with practitioner research, where the focus will be on producing something directly useful to the organisation. Here, the study's drafting is directed to demonstrate the value of the approach with the robustness of the findings merely a secondary consideration or not of interest at all.

For instance, in the asset pricing branch of finance, academics have given a considerable amount of attention to documenting and explaining pricing anomalies, where systematic patterns are found in stock returns. Their research efforts have been directed primarily at trying to explain the anomalies, why they might have occurred, whether they are still present in various other settings, and whether risk-based or behavioural explanations are most plausible.

On the other hand, a practitioner writing on this same subject would be more concerned with how big the returns might be to a trading strategy that sought to exploit the anomaly and how risky such a system would be, together with details about the transactions costs of implementing it. In essence, their focus would be on whether they could make money from the research, and if so, how

Table 1.1: Potential sources of support if things go wrong

Person	Type of problem they can solve
Friends, siblings, classmates	Feeling isolated, lacking motivation, general problems with progress
Your supervisor	High-level issues, serious problems with data collection or falling behind
Classmates, PhD students	Problems accessing data, faulty computer code
University statistical services	Problems running or interpreting quantitative models
Library services	Finding or accessing prior literature, help with databases
PhD administrator	Uncertainty about the format or deadline for thesis submission
Study skills team	Help with organising your time or with writing

much. However, these technical aspects would probably not be of much interest to academic researchers since they would argue that this information would not help our understanding of how financial markets work or why they operate in that fashion.

Research programmes that have a strong practice-basis, such as those that are part of an MBA or DBA, and research projects that firms sponsor, will need to combine elements of both the practitioner and scholarly foci. Their studies would need to simultaneously satisfy the two audiences by producing work that is both useful and rigorous, which is quite a challenge – see also subsection 1.3.3.

1.1.10 Establishing your network

Doing research can be a lonely experience, and for researchers at all levels, there will be instances when they feel stuck and unsure how to proceed. At such times, they will call upon someone in their network for help and support. Similarly, for your research process to be as pleasant and smooth-running as possible, you will also need a network. You are more likely to remain on track if you have already considered who is in your network and to whom you can turn for different types of problems rather than letting them build up or curtail your progress. Making a mental list such as that in Table 1.1 could be useful.

More generally, other PhD students conducting their research in your cohort can be a precious source of support since they are likely to be facing many of the same issues as you at roughly the same time. Discussing your work with them (even though the topic will probably be different) could provide suggestions relating to the PhD itself and help diminish any feelings of isolation that are a common aspect of doing research.

1.2 What are the stages involved in completing a PhD?

Each student will progress at their own pace, with some taking time to select their precise topic and review the literature while others quickly go through the early stages but then hit some issues with their data collection that slow them down. But we could characterise a *typical* doctoral student journey as follows, and each of these aspects will be discussed in considerable detail in subsequent chapters of this book:

Skeleton timeline towards PhD Completion

Year 1

- Registration, organisation, 'gearing up'
- Taught course attendance, coursework and exams
- Literature review
- Refine proposal, timeline and action plan
- Seek ethical approval if needed
- Begin data collection for 'project 1'
- Skill acquisition as required (data collection, programming, running surveys, writing, teaching, etc.)

Year 2

- Data collection and analysis for project 1
- Completion and drafting of chapter(s) for project 1
- Scope out project 2 and begin data collection and analysis
- School presentations

Year 3

- Complete data analysis and drafting for project 2
- Undertake all work for project 3
- Conference presentations
- Aim to submit a paper based on a chapter to a journal

Year 4

- Possibly not needed if all stages are completed in year 3
- Polishing and drafting the entire thesis document
- Incorporate supervisor comments and other reader feedback
- Submit thesis
- Undertake viva voce exam
- Make any required modifications and graduate

The first year primarily involves setting everything in place so that the remaining steps progress as smoothly as possible. Establish your timetable, consider access requirements or other constraints, and seek ethics committee approval if it will be needed. Also, reflect on any training needs at this point to speed up the later stages – e.g., sourcing electronic literature, data collection, coding or econometrics.

Year 1 will be the literature review phase that is discussed in detail in chapter 8 and chapter 9 of this book. It also involves refining and honing your research questions and finalising your methodology so that you obtain the appropriate data.

The second and third years will be mainly taken up in completing the PhD's investigative work, which will comprise the most time-consuming aspects. If you are using secondary data from existing databases, it should be reasonably straightforward to download everything you need. Still, it might take a while to become familiar with the interface and get the information into the correct format for input into a spreadsheet or statistical package. On the other hand, if you elect to use a survey or interviews, the data collection could take considerably longer. Analysis will generally be conducted using spreadsheets and statistical software, but as well as generating the results, it will take significant time to interpret them and reflect on what they mean.

The final stage is the part that that many students dread the most – where you start to collect the pieces together and write the first draft. If you have been writing up the aspects of the thesis as you got to them, this stage will progress more quickly, but it is still common to leave all the writing until the end.

The checking and polishing stage is a crucial aspect despite many students believing that they have pretty much finished already, and so it is the subject of an entire chapter of this book. If there is a requirement to submit a (now rather old-fashioned) bound hard copy (or two copies), then you will need to allow time for printing and binding at the end as well.

1.2.1   The PhD registration, upgrade and review process

Prior to completing and submitting the thesis, compared with taught programmes at the undergraduate or master's level, there are relatively few stages where you will be required to 'jump through hoops', but there will still be several. All of these will be about ensuring that you have the skills and knowledge that you need to successfully complete the thesis and helping you to stay on track regarding the work's timing and quality.

At registration, you might have to complete a 'learning needs analysis form' or something equivalent. This document will ask you a series of questions that encourage you to reflect on the skills you already have and what new ones you might need to do the research specified in your proposal. The skills might include subject-specific knowledge, investigative or writing skills, presentational techniques, and so on. You might need to agree on a plan for skills development with your supervisor.

Unless you already have a research master's degree (i.e., an MRes in accounting or finance where there was a significant dissertation and research methods courses, not a standard master's) or some other exemption, it is also highly likely that during the first year of PhD registration you will be required to complete several taught courses. The modules could include one or two on approaches to research in the social sciences or 'the philosophy of social science research' or something to that effect.

Students are frequently put off by the titles of these modules, failing to see the relevance of such material, and keen to just get on with their research. In many ways, that is a pity since if taught well, they can be enlightening, helping students to put their ideas and approach into a wider context. For those who have been focused squarely on one methodological approach (for example, using only quantitative analysis of data or just considering discursive research material - see chapter 2 for a detailed discussion of these), attending an 'approaches to research' module could also open your eyes to the wide range of other techniques that are available for addressing research problems. This breadth of vision is valuable as, perhaps, the only opportunity you will have to reflect on the subject matter at a high level and explore other approaches to research than the one you will primarily use.

It might additionally be the case that you are required to improve your subject-specific knowledge with more advanced taught courses in areas such as accounting theory, corporate finance or financial economics. You could also have to take one or more 'methods' modules in either quantitative methods (econometrics or statistics, data analysis, etc.) or qualitative methods (such as interview and survey design). You will probably have to undertake coursework and exams in these subjects, securing a passing mark, in order to be able to proceed onto the next stage of the programme.

Typically, when students begin a PhD programme, technically, they are registered for an 'Unspecified higher degree' or an MPhil rather than a PhD. Their status will then be upgraded to that of PhD student upon demonstration of satisfactory progress. This step is sometimes known as 'confirmation of registration' and will usually occur at the end of a student's first year or during the second year. Although the precise requirements will vary between institutions, successful completion of taught courses, the production of a detailed literature review, a more focused and informed research proposal than was submitted at the application stage, and possibly some finished investigative work are likely to be needed.

After that, your progress will probably be formally reviewed on an annual basis, via a report that you will complete detailing what you have done over the previous year and plans for the next, submitting a completed chapter, and possibly giving a research presentation at a PhD student workshop. Your supervisor(s) will also be asked to submit a report detailing your progress over the previous year.

Aside from this, you will have considerable latitude to organise your own work and proceed at your own pace, and therefore it is essential to get and stay well organised, setting yourself deadlines as discussed in chapter 6.

1.2.2 Part-time registration

Although the majority of students are registered on full-time research degree programmes, some are engaged in part-time study. In such cases, the total number of hours of effort expected will be the same as for a full-time schedule but spread over a longer timeframe – for example, five or six years rather than three. This long horizon may encourage a feeling that there is time to spare, but part-time study is usually even more challenging as the student needs to balance academic study with employment (possibly full-time) or significant family responsibilities.

There is also the danger that the momentum full-time students are able to generate when focusing on their PhD is not achievable for part-timers, so that the latter are never able to really get going with it. Therefore, if you are registered on a part-time programme, it is even more important to establish a schedule towards completion and to endeavour to stick to it since the consequences of falling behind are direr: competing time demands will mean that it is not possible to work intensively at the end to catch up.

If you are registered on a full-time programme but are now doing outside, paid work for a significant number of hours per week, it is worth considering applying to switch to part-time registration, which would stretch the period available to complete your dissertation and buy you considerably more time. But be careful – having a job for more than a few hours per week during term-time registration for a full-time degree programme is probably against the rules.

Another difficulty relates to part-time students' scope to visit the campus and engage with their supervisor and fellow learners. Full-time students are generally based at, or close to, their universities for the entire duration of their studies. On the other hand, part-time students might be located a considerable distance away from their university and only visit infrequently for classes or pre-planned supervision meetings, which can engender a sense of isolation. Consequently, part-time students need to make additional efforts to embed themselves into the academic community at their university, taking every opportunity to engage with their supervisor, other academic staff and students. Not doing so risks losing out on the development of the social and support network that is so vital for PhD candidates, as well as missing out on the scope to learn from other students.

1.3   Other aspects of a PhD programme to consider

1.3.1   Doctoral training

The nature and structure of doctoral training programmes have been changing in European universities over the past decade. Traditionally, such training was limited to a module or two on the philosophy of social sciences research, with students invited, but not mandated, to 'top up' their skills in the quantitative or qualitative methods they intended to use. They would typically begin their research with a literature review from day one of registration.

More recently, training requirements for new PhD students have become far more extensive and formalised. It is now common for them to attend various taught modules in the advanced economic theory that underpins much of finance alongside training in methods, with a stipulation that they must take the exams and pass the modules before being permitted to focus on their research. In the US, the intellectual and mathematical level of the taught courses is high, with an elevated failure rate. The structure in European universities is becoming increasingly like that in the US, and the reduced time for research in the first year (with candidates not really getting going at all with it until year two) naturally implies that PhDs are taking longer to complete. What was previously a three-year (or so) registration period has become four years, which is a significant problem for institutions since the maximum PhD registration period is usually four years full-time. Therefore, if students routinely take four years to complete their doctorates because the first year is lost to taught courses, there is no buffer for those who encounter difficulties with their research and require more time. The situation has left UK universities trying to justify somehow extending the clock, without admitting that students have not finished on time, such as by granting retrospective suspensions so as not to damage their completion statistics.

In some ways, the switch from the broad-based training on social science research methods of the past, often attended with students from other fields such as sociology and psychology, is regrettable. While the focus on advanced economics and formal quantitative modelling has helped to ensure a rigorous standard of empirical work, it has also had a homogenising effect. In accounting in particular, this has further encouraged a move away from qualitative methods to the ubiquitous use of large secondary databases. This technical work has a vital role to play in advancing knowledge of course, but the European tradition of also engaging in more reflective critical analysis using a wider range of methodological techniques is in danger of becoming lost.

Students of finance in particular often dread broad-based social sciences research methods modules, not appreciating their relevance (although this is also in part due to the abstract way in which they are commonly taught by specialists from other fields) and preferring instead to concentrate on more practical skills in quantitative methods or programming that can be directly applied to their research topic. This is unfortunate since the PhD provides a valuable opportunity for students to broaden their horizons and become aware of research methods and subject matter from other fields. Indeed, given how busy academics tend to become immediately post-PhD completion, this is likely to be the only such opportunity.

My recommendation is to take up and try to get the most from any such opportunities you have during your PhD registration. It might well be that this training will enable you to view the literature on your topic through a wider lens or even make use of one of these other approaches in your own work. Knowing where knowledge comes from, what are the different approaches to gathering knowledge, and how research can be classified is worthwhile to be aware of and this understanding will stay with you throughout your research lifetime.

1.3.2 Can you get departmental funding for research expenses?

Many PhD programmes will provide a financial contribution to their participants' research expenses. This could, for example, be £1,000 per year for each of the first three years of registration, which is a typical figure across UK universities. These funds can be spent on training courses, conference attendance, the purchase of data, the costs of running surveys, software, etc.

While this sum is considerably more than many students will have access to, and is much more than was available when I was a PhD student, evidently it will not go far. One conference outside of Europe could easily use up an entire year's allowance. Consequently, it is worth considering your likely research costs right from the time you are deciding on the topic and methods. Unless you have considerable funds of your own, purchasing expensive specialist data or software is likely to be infeasible. If the costs you believe that you will incur might be higher than this (e.g., expenses involved with conducting a survey, travel for conducting interviews, purchasing a specialist database), it is worth asking your supervisor if the department will offer additional financial support. But be prepared for a negative response, which means that you will have to partly rely on your own resources and probably keep any outgoings to a minimum and select your methods accordingly.

1.3.3   Sponsored or independent research?

Sometimes, a university or department has strong connections with firms and they are able to offer their PhD candidates the chance to work on pre-specified thesis topics with a 'sponsor'. Alternatively, if you can make such connections yourself by linking your dissertation to your job or an association you have with an external organisation, there are potentially several benefits:

- The sponsoring firm is likely to provide research ideas and give suggestions from a practitioner angle throughout the registration period
- A sponsored PhD will provide the candidate with an inside knowledge of the types of research issues that are faced in the industry, thus ensuring that the thesis topic is relevant for practitioners
- The sponsoring firm may provide access to specialist or proprietary data, which will enable research on unique and otherwise infeasible topics
- Additional funding might be available for research expenses
- The organisation might make use of the research findings, providing additional motivation for the student and possibly useful publicity
- Vitally, working on a sponsored thesis could provide the opportunity of permanent post-PhD employment with the firm if the candidate does a sufficiently good job and impresses the firm

For the reasons listed above, most candidates would jump at the opportunity to work closely with a firm in this way, but it is important to be aware that sponsored research also has several disadvantages. A potential drawback of working in such a partnership is that by linking your research with an outside entity, there might be tensions between what the two parties (your university department and the external organisation) want to see from the work. The organisation might wish you to examine something of practical value to them and which they can put to use directly. They might also prefer the work to be written in an entirely non-technical language that non-academics can easily understand. But your supervisor and examiners will want to see a thesis written in the style of an academic paper, using scholarly language with an emphasis on the contribution to knowledge rather than to practice.

Unfortunately, in reality, the kinds of research that are of primary relevance in the industry are frequently (although not universally) of less relevance as topics for scholarly enquiry and vice versa. In important ways, the objectives of the firm providing the funding and the university department may be conflicting. To provide a typecast illustration, a project that compares several technical trading rules and evaluates their profitability could be of interest to a hedge fund, but a lot of scholars would suggest that such a topic has already received sufficient treatment and that identifying trading rules that make money for investment banks does not embody a constitute a contribution to knowledge. Therefore, they would argue that this topic would be poor for a PhD thesis.

There is a danger that by trying to please two separate audiences, you will satisfy neither of them. Remember that, first and foremost, the PhD is an academic exercise and so this should always be the primary consideration if there are tensions between what would constitute a good quality thesis that is highly likely to pass and what an external party wants.

Corporate sponsors of research might also place restrictions on your scope to publish work from the thesis, or on your opportunities to discuss it freely at scholarly conferences if the findings are commercially sensitive and the firm wishes to keep them secret for as long as possible. Such a blockage on dissemination could scupper your chances of securing an academic post after graduation at the same time as other students are raising their profiles and obtaining several published papers from their theses.

Furthermore, most schools cannot offer such sponsored PhD projects, and even those that do have sufficient opportunities for providing them to only a fraction of the PhD year group. In summary, if you have the chance of a sponsored project, consider the offer carefully as there could be numerous benefits. But also ensure that you would still be in the driving seat and that your research would be of scholarly interest in addition to practical value since, ultimately, the purpose of registering for a PhD is to get the qualification. Or consider that you might have to take the time to produce two different versions of the work, one for each of the academic and practitioner audiences.

1.3.4   Can you undertake a group-based research?

It is often more fun and easier to work on a project with other students. As you will have seen (or soon will see), the majority of academic publications (papers and books) are multi-authored by teams of academics working together rather than sole-authored by individuals studying alone. There are several reasons for this: principally, working with others allows much faster progress and permits authors to cover their weaknesses by focusing on the parts of the research process they enjoy and at which they are best. The same would be true of PhD projects, of course.

However, ultimately, the PhD qualification must be a solo endeavour and you would have no choice but to work primarily by yourself. It would still be allowable and indeed desirable to discuss ideas with fellow PhD students, offering each other support with technical issues (e.g., problems getting data or estimating models), and reading each other's drafts. But you would need to select individual topics, do your own reading, conduct your own analysis, and write the thesis yourself.

1.3.5   Where to get help when you get stuck

Sometimes, you might hit a stumbling block with the research – not a complete disaster but merely a minor hitch but one which nonetheless prevents you from pushing full-steam ahead with the task at hand. Hitting a wall is most likely to occur with the investigative work, such as the statistical analysis not working correctly, bugs in your code, issues with a survey, and so on. If this happens, where should you go for help? An obvious response could be your supervisor, but you may prefer to avoid contacting them too often for fear of using up all of the available supervisory time or goodwill on relatively minor matters. So what other options are available?

Other PhD candidates – both in your department and elsewhere – can be a precious resource for doctoral students. They tend to be 'closer to the empirical work' because they are involved with the fundamental aspects of the research process, such as data gathering and programming that your supervisor may have left behind long ago. As I have worked through my career, I have tended to spend an increasingly large proportion of my time reading, writing, and doing administration. This has left less time available for doing data analysis. On the other hand, since PhD students are earlier in their careers, they are usually more up to date with the latest databases, literature sources, and programming languages than academic staff members. They typically hang around in the department more than the faculty, so they are easier to find and therefore frequently worth seeking out for help.

Another group of people who might be able to help with certain aspects of your research are 'post-docs', variously known as post-doctoral research assistants or research fellows. However, they are relatively rare in accounting and finance compared with the natural and physical sciences, where they are employed in large numbers. Post-docs are usually full-time junior staff researchers who will have already obtained (or be very close to getting) their PhDs, and thus they will have developed relevant skills and knowledge. As for PhD students, they can be a valuable resource, but their help will be voluntary and should not be taken for granted.

Finally, a considerable amount of relevant information and support will be available on the internet through blogsites and forums. If the problem is with data handling, statistical analysis or coding, there is likely to be a forum dealing with precisely that topic. Whichever statistical or coding package you use, there will probably be a forum for it, for example, searching for 'EViews forum' correctly brings up the EViews forum as the first hit.

For programming languages including R and Python, it is possible to get paid expert 1:1 support from organisations such as Codementor.[1] There is also a database of more than 20 million questions with responses regarding code debugging and other issues on the Stackoverflow site that can be searched by theme, package or keyword.[2]

While you might obtain useful advice from others, remember that your supervisor is ultimately formally charged with the responsibility for supporting your progress, so their guidance should be taken as definitive. If you are facing a more substantive issue, it is they whom you should be contacting.

Sometimes, PhD students can feel totally overwhelmed when conducting their research and writing the thesis seems like a massive and unmanageable task. Conducting and writing a piece of research is always a significant undertaking, especially for those who have not done so before and consequently, many students initially approach it completely lacking in confidence. Rather than thinking of the PhD as a single enormous problem, deconstruct it into a series of small ones. Follow the stages given in your department's guide on how to do a PhD, and try not to think too many steps ahead. So long as you follow the process in a sensible order and according to the required timescale, you will reach the endpoint by the deadline. Establish a routine, set up a work plan with timescales, and tick off each milestone as you achieve it.

As well as working on your thesis you could follow up on resources to strengthen your self-confidence and build your resilience. There are plenty of free sources to support this on-line including YouTube and various websites including the Skills You Need[3] and MindTools[4] among many others.

1.4   Requirements for a PhD

What features does a thesis need to embody to be acceptable and for the student who wrote it to pass the degree? Further details on the assessment process and what happens after submission of the thesis are presented in chapter 13, but at this preliminary stage, it is still nonetheless worth knowing what you would be aiming at. Although to some extent the outcome of the assessment process will depend on the expert judgement of the examiners, there should be an absolute standard applied to all PhDs and a set of common characteristics which an acceptable thesis will contain:

A contribution to knowledge

A thesis must make *an original contribution to knowledge*. This means that the work should have produced some entirely new findings that are not available in any existing study, either published or unpublished. To those who are new to academic research,

---

[1] https://www.codementor.io/browser-bugs-experts
[2] https://stackoverflow.com/questions
[3] https://www.skillsyouneed.com/ps/confidence.html
[4] https://www.mindtools.com/pages/article/resilience.htm

this might appear an unassailably high threshold, but the original contribution can be quite narrowly defined. Sources of originality can come from many angles. For example, a PhD may employ standard techniques with data arising from a different country, market or asset, or it could derive a novel technique or apply an established design in another sphere of interest. The following are examples of situations where an original contribution can arise:

1. Testing a new theory or idea
2. Using a different dataset to test existing theories
3. Using a different empirical model to test an existing theory
4. Taking a concept or approach used in one field and applying it in a different domain (transdisciplinary research)

Although your thinking and writing will be framed by what you have read, you will need to develop and demonstrate your own ideas, rather than just producing a 'rehash' of someone else's work. In that sense, any good dissertation will have an element of originality, i.e., a 'contribution to knowledge'.

As well as studying a new phenomenon, or a different market to those examined in existing research, another way to make a novel contribution is to re-examine an established problem that was previously not tackled well. Most commonly, a research study can be compromised by an inappropriate or flawed methodology. This issue could be pretty fundamental, such as using secondary data where there was a need to get out and ask people questions directly, or it could be that less-than-ideal models or datasets have been used, rendering the findings tenuous. You might spot this either from the descriptions of the methods used in the papers or where the results simply don't look right. In such cases, your research could follow broadly the same path as the existing study, but fixing what was done wrong and examining the extent to which the findings differ.

Awareness of where the work fits within the wider field

Students must demonstrate, both in the thesis document and in their verbal discussion during the viva, that they are aware of the wider literature in their chosen research field and they can see where their contribution fits in this body of work. The thesis will usually include an extensive and appropriately organised review of the relevant literature which allows the candidate to demonstrate the research gap that their investigative work will help to fill.

Ability to establish and pursue an appropriate investigation

The regulations for obtaining a PhD will require the candidate to specify a set of aims or questions and then establish an agenda to address them. This will involve determining and employing the most efficacious research methods, developing new theory or collecting relevant data, producing results and analysing and interpreting them, and finally drawing appropriate conclusions.

Evidence of publishable quality material

One of the criteria that universities often stipulate that examiners should consider when deciding whether to recommend the award of the degree is whether there is evidence of 'publishable quality material' in the thesis. In some ways, this criterion is merely a summary of the others since if it evidently contains originality, is well-written with a good structure and engages with the existing literature, some of the thesis contents should be publishable. Note that this does not mean any of the work must already have been published, or that it needs to be suitable for publication in its present form, or that every investigative chapter must be publishable. The thesis is not intended to be a collection of ready-made journal articles, and so if some parts require restructuring, reordering, pruning, extending or redrafting before a journal might seriously consider publishing the work, that should still be fine.

It is important to note that a PhD is unlikely to constitute a brilliant piece of research. Although it should be solid, of good quality, and meet the criteria listed above, it will almost invariably represent a modest contribution to knowledge. Instead, it is best thought of like any other qualification – as a means to acquire a set of skills and to demonstrate that they have been mastered. Even brilliant scholars typically do their world-beating research after completing their thesis, not during it.

Chapter takeaways – top tips for success

- ⊛ Conducting a PhD will provide you with many transferrable skills in demand by employers
- ⊛ Successful completion of a thesis depends more on putting in the hours and dogged determination than being super-smart
- ⊛ A thesis is primarily a document aimed at academics and it will not necessarily cover a topic of practical importance
- ⊛ Most PhD students take almost four years to complete their thesis, with the first year increasingly being taken up by taught modules
- ⊛ Undertaking broad training in the methodology of social science research will help you to gain a broad perspective on the research in the field that would be valuable throughout your future academic career
- ⊛ A PhD must make a novel contribution to knowledge
- ⊛ Take sponsorship for your research if you can get it but be aware of the disadvantages

2. APPROACHES TO RESEARCH

Learning outcomes: this chapter covers

✓ The difference between scholarly and everyday research
✓ Different philosophies of research
✓ The distinction between positivism and interpretivism
✓ How to classify research and learning
✓ The difference between inductive and deductive research

2.1 What is research?

The Cambridge dictionary defines it as the 'detailed study of a subject, especially in order to discover (new) information or reach a (new) understanding.' This general definition of the word embodies the fact that in everyday parlance, deliberately searching for information to find something out that you did not already know would fit under the research umbrella. If you scoured the internet to find the best type of mortgage for you, given your circumstances, this constitutes research because you did not previously know that information, but after investigation, you will.

However, the academic (or 'scholarly') definition of research is somewhat narrower, such as 'the process of investigation leading to a new contribution to knowledge.' This statement embodies the idea that academic research involves learning something new to everybody, not just new to you. In other words, you would be generating new ideas that could not be found anywhere else in the world before, and hence the example of finding the best mortgage would not fit within the scholarly definition of research. Scholarly research is a strategically planned, systematic and highly organised search for new knowledge. It provides routes to formally testing and evaluating new ideas to determine whether the data support them. Sometimes, research that is new to everyone is termed primary research, whereas when you learn something that others already know, it is called secondary research.

The main purpose of research is to understand the physical, natural and social worlds in detail. This relates to physical or natural occurrences, such as the climate, the migration of birds, or crop yields, but it also involves social experiences, including human behaviour and decision-making. Once scientists or social scientists have firm knowledge about a phenomenon, this can lead to a range of related objectives for further research, including:

- Explaining why these phenomena occur
- Categorising events or occurrences as being of one type or another
- Evaluating the efficacy of various courses of action to control or mitigate something happening (e.g., preventing flooding or stock market bubbles from occurring)
- Forecasting what is likely to happen in the future

Research is important because, although we rarely see it being conducted, its findings influence our everyday lives in so many ways. As well as obvious examples such as the development and testing of vaccines against diseases, product development and choices of which government policies to implement are also frequently supported by research.

2.2   Types of research

There are various ways to typecast and classify research, and this chapter will now examine two approaches to doing this. Being able to categorise research output is useful when trying to identify how your work fits into the bigger picture, and it also helps other researchers when they come to evaluate a particular piece of work.

2.2.1   Four kinds of research

The book by Hussey and Hussey (1997) provides a helpful classification of research into four types (although a similar framework is presented by many other authors):

1. Exploratory
2. Descriptive
3. Analytical
4. Predictive

In some ways, this typology also describes how the body of work on a particular topic develops chronologically.

Exploratory research refers to the process of scholars working in a new area where the current extent of knowledge is meagre, no structure has yet emerged, no formal research agenda has been developed, and it is too early to identify any theoretical framework or hypotheses. Such studies will aim to gather evidence that will subsequently be used (probably by other researchers) to develop further and formalise the ideas. Exploratory research usually adopts a case study or observation approach to data collection and analysis, with formal quantitative models rare. This type of research tends to be unstructured, and therefore, while the originality will be evident since the topic area is new, it tends not to fit into an established framework. It may also be accused of lacking the rigour of the other types of research and hence is riskier and less common in accounting and finance.

Descriptive research adds structure to exploratory research, where data about the phenomenon under study are gathered and documented systematically, and the new research area begins to develop some form and establishes concepts. This research may even extend towards a typology (i.e., a classification) of the phenomenon under study. There will be little analysis or depth at this stage, so this is a similarly risky type of research in accounting and finance. While it is more structured than exploratory research, it may be considered somewhat superficial, answering 'what'-type questions rather than 'how' or 'why' a particular phenomenon occurs.

The distinction between *description* and *analysis* is crucial in accounting, finance and economics. When you describe your data, you are merely pointing out interesting features or explaining how the data are, not why they take the values they do, which would be analysis. Similarly, when you describe a phenomenon (such as stock markets tending to rise in January) or a piece of research, you are merely reporting an observation or rephrasing an argument that someone else has already made. But when you analyse it, you are attempting to explain why an event happened, how a piece of research relates to others, and whether the findings are valid and robust.

The majority of doctoral research projects in accounting and finance fall under the analytical umbrella. Such research takes a further step from descriptive research in that it tries to understand and explain why a phenomenon occurs or how it has occurred. This extension might involve developing a theoretical or empirical model that consists of specifying causal links between the variables of interest and possibly establishing a set of testable hypotheses. Analytical research is prevalent in accounting and finance because it can lead to profound insights, and it involves a rich and rigorous examination of a phenomenon. However, there are limitations such as a frequent confusion between correlation (two variables tending to move together) and causality (movements in one variable cause movements in another).

Finally, *predictive research* involves taking existing findings and trying to use them to determine whether they plausibly also apply in other places or situations without actually collecting data and testing the latter. In essence, this class of research involves a reapplication of prior knowledge to create additional insights. Many PhDs will have a predictive element, although this frequently occurs after conducting analysis rather than as a stand-alone endeavour.

2.2.2   A Framework for Classifying Learning

Another way to think about research is from the perspective of what you have learned through the process rather than the type of research being undertaken. The famous Bloom's classification (sometimes known as Bloom's taxonomy) does this, establishing a 'ladder' with six rungs, each building on the level beneath it. The ladder classifies a researcher's level of familiarity with and understanding of a particular topic. Sometimes the classification is instead conceptually represented as a pyramid rather than a ladder. Bloom was an educational psychologist, and his original scale had three aspects, although only the cognitive one is widely employed in teaching research methods. The ladder is sometimes expressed in the following terms:

Knowledge – being able to remember a particular piece of information, probably without being able to understand or explain it. This bottom rung on the ladder relates to being aware of fundamental concepts and ideas.

Comprehension – not only knowing information but also understanding what it means so that you could explain that meaning to someone else. You could also summarise the information and arrange it in different ways. This level is the minimum required to conduct a literature review, which would not be possible while only at the lowest rung on the ladder (knowledge).

Application – here, you could take information and apply it in different contexts. Hence, this level moves beyond only a conceptual understanding towards being able to use the knowledge in various settings to solve real problems.

Analysis – this involves being able to explain why certain things happen based on linking pieces of information together and identifying causal relationships.

Synthesis – where pieces of information are chosen for a purpose and combined to generate new knowledge and understanding.

Evaluation – the highest level of attainment in the knowledge space embodying the ability to reflect on information and other research to form a viewpoint or verdict on it and to provide recommendations about the best course of action.

Note that the taxonomy should not be taken to imply that only evaluatory research is worthwhile since that is not the case. A good piece of work will demonstrate that all rungs on the ladder have been mastered to a lesser or greater extent.

2.3   The philosophy of research

Numerous books on how to do research begin with one or more chapters on the philosophy of research and different high-level approaches to research. The texts use esoteric words such as ontology and epistemology, positivism versus interpretivism, and so on. These are the foundations upon which the 'house of knowledge' is built, and the ideas relate to how knowledge is gathered and interpreted and what methods are used to obtain it.

You would probably be able to complete a very successful thesis by just pushing ahead with the research, applying the knowledge that exists and slightly extending it by working within that framework but remaining blissfully unaware of these concepts or how they underpin research structures. It is certainly not necessary for PhD students to know a great deal about the philosophy of research, and it is unlikely that you will need to explain the rationale for your choice of methods using the specialist terminology described here; you would be able to discuss why you chose the approaches you did using a more informal language.

But having an understanding of these ideas will help you to be able to classify research (yours and others') and to understand how the research paradigm adopted by the investigator leads to a research design that will favour some particular methods over others. Paradigms are broad categorisations approaches to research, and within a paradigm, researchers will share a consistent way of conceptualising and framing their investigations, and using a common set of methods.

Knowing this material will also help you evaluate research, reflect on which methodology might be most appropriate to tackle a specific problem and how different approaches can yield alternative insights. Therefore, this chapter now discusses two of the key concepts in this area – ontology and epistemology – and how they relate to the kinds of research conducted in accounting and finance. A concept can be defined as an idea that is represented by a brief statement, which is often operationalised by attempting to measure it with a specific variable.

Ontology is concerned with what knowledge exists ('what is out there to know?') while epistemology is about the theory of knowledge and the knowledge gathering process ('what can we find out and how can we find out about it?') Knowledge can be defined as a set of justified true beliefs or true statements, and given this definition, it is clear that knowledge is always changing. Ontology is important since it defines how we believe the social world is, and a particular epistemological position and the associated research methods follow from it.

There is more than one ontological view of the world, and the two key ontological positions are objectivism and subjectivism. Objectivists, also referred to as foundationalists believe that there is one reality that exists independent of the person experiencing it, whereas subjectivists (sometimes known as constructivists or antifoundationalists) contend that each reality is invented by the person observing it. Therefore, that person's view of 'how things are' is socially constructed and hence all knowledge is subjective.

These different perspectives lead to different foci for gathering knowledge. Objectivists focus on individual decision-makers, aiming to understand how and why they make choices (their motivations) and what are the consequences. Subjectivists, on the other hand, start from the core premise that analysing individuals would be fruitless and instead the focus from the outset should be on groups and the dynamics between them. The concepts of social capital, trust and power are key to this approach.

Epistemology is the part of philosophy focused on how knowledge is generated and the techniques we consider best to produce it. Epistemology is sometimes called the theory of knowledge. Two contrasting epistemological approaches are the starting points for thinking about knowledge creation, known as positivism and interpretivism, which are linked with the objectivist and subjectivist ontological positions, respectively.

The positivist and interpretivist epistemological philosophies are also sometimes termed research paradigms, and they are diametrically opposed, which means that many researchers would argue they cannot be combined in a single study as they are not compatible. They are rooted within fundamentally different premises, and the key distinction between them arises from how researchers gather knowledge under each paradigm. In other words, the research approaches, including the methods and data collection, are very different, and the main features of each will now be discussed.

2.3.1　Positivism

Positivism is arguably the oldest philosophical approach and dates back to Aristotle, although it is often suggested to have been invented by Auguste Comte (1880) and John S. Mill (1881) in the nineteenth century. It is also associated with the French philosopher René Descartes and the French sociologist Emile Durkheim, amongst others. Sometimes positivism is known as the 'scientific approach' to research since it is the methodology for knowledge creation employed in the natural and physical sciences. Its proponents argue that research in the social sciences should be conducted in the same fashion.

Models are usually at the heart of the positivist approach, and might be defined as representations of the real world that simplify it but still aim to retain its essence. Models are established to describe the relationships between relevant variables and the directions of causality based on a theory. Models are frequently written using mathematical equations, although this does not have to be the case. Setting up a model facilitates the proposal and testing of hypotheses.

According to positivists:
- Research should focus on observable and verifiable phenomena and avoid engaging in conjecture or supposition
- They claim to take an unbiased view of the world when conducting research
- Research seeks not only to understand how the world is, but also to explain why with the aim of ultimately making predictions
- Cause and effect arise and can be captured in a model, and hence the empirical method of collecting and analysing data follows
- Proposing and testing causal relationships is a key objective of research
- There is a congruence between what we observe and how things really are
- They are concerned with facts and not with judgements or values
- The key approach is to use theories to generate testable hypotheses, which are then applied to data

- The methods should be 'scientific' (using mathematics, statistics and large databases and involving repeated sampling)
- Assumptions might be required to test theories or implement models
- Researchers should be unbiased in their views about their research and should be at a distance from their data or test subjects

Positivism was the dominant paradigm for social research as well as scientific exploration up to the 1960s. Until that point, most researchers in the social sciences believed that it was the appropriate epistemological position for all fields of enquiry, while philosophy had also become primarily focused on concrete questions to which there should be an answer.

But in sociology, the consensus around the pre-eminence of positivism started to collapse in the 1950s and continued thereafter. There were several reasons for this decline, including its reliance on some knowledge as being given or certain and the difficulty in answering particular kinds of questions about human behaviour using a hands-off approach with statistics. There was also concern that too much weight was being placed on the outcome of hypothesis tests, whereas in reality, if a hypothesis is rejected, it could be because it is wrong or merely that one of the assumptions built into the theory behind the hypothesis does not hold.

2.3.2   Interpretivism

The concerns outlined at the end of the previous section led to the growth of an alternative epistemological approach, interpretivism, which has a much shorter history. It is in many ways the opposite of positivism, and indeed, it is occasionally referred to as 'antipositivism.' Although some of its ways of working have been around much longer, the development of interpretivism is often credited to German sociologists such as Karl Marx, Georg Simmel and Max Weber.

Interpretivists believe that:
- There is a clear distinction between the natural and social sciences so that the two need entirely different approaches to gather knowledge
- Judgement and fact cannot easily be separated, and therefore all knowledge is tentative
- Purely objective analysis is impossible since all research is a function of the opinions and attitudes of the researcher who conducts it
- Usually, the emphasis is on documenting and understanding phenomena and not on explaining them using causal analysis
- The approach is based on observation, case studies, interviews, etc.
- Detailed investigation of small datasets is preferred over arm's length analysis of big data
- The context of research is important so that a different researcher in a slightly different environment may obtain starkly varying results
- Assumptions are not needed as the researcher can observe what is happening

The interpretivist researcher understands that findings cannot be independent of the investigator's views or the manner in which the research is conducted. So this dependence is explicitly acknowledged as interpretivists observe each phenomenon in action within its own environment and typically use qualitative techniques as will be discussed in chapter 10.

Positivists would retort that the interpretivist approach to obtaining knowledge is *ad hoc* and unscientific. However, the latter argue that the additional insight gained from a close examination of phenomena and events in their own environments makes a different and more valuable contribution to knowledge that outweighs the lack of replicability or generalisability. The debate about the efficacy of each paradigm continues. Nowadays, positivism has a much more modest role in modern social science research, yet it is still endemic and represents the usual paradigm forming the approach used in virtually all research in finance and economics, with some accounting research fitting under each umbrella.

2.3.3 Critical realism

Between the two extreme epistemological positions sits critical realism, also known as 'post positivism', and as constructivism, realism or pragmatism, which seeks to bridge positivism and interpretivism by both understanding and explaining phenomena. A pragmatist would support strands of the positivist and interpretivist arguments, seeing the value of both large-scale statistical analysis and a fine-grained micro-examination of individual cases. Thus, a wide range of research methods are conceivable, and these should be chosen dependent upon the nature of the phenomenon under examination and what the investigator wants to achieve. Pragmatists believe that the same methods can be used in the natural and social sciences but that an added interpretation is required in the latter case. They support mixed methods research and are willing to use whatever research design is best suited to the particular task at hand. In some cases, that will be a sophisticated econometric analysis of aggregate secondary data, but in others, it could be one-to-one unstructured interviews with key individuals in an organisation.

Critical realism retains the key ideology of positivism but recognises that analysis can never be truly objective or certain, so that we should merely hope to obtain a close approximation to the truth rather than its totality. It is a relatively recently developed perspective compared with positivism and interpretivism, drawing ideas from both. Critical realists believe that there is a truth that holds irrespective of how people view it, but how people see this reality can be distorted. These distortions arise both because people cannot gather all relevant information (e.g., they can only gather imperfect historical recollections rather than seeing for themselves what happened in the past) and since their pre-conceived beliefs heavily influence their perspectives. In that sense, reality is, therefore, still to a degree socially constructed, as interpretivists argue.

There are also several other paradigms that are again variants of the two primary types, but these are beyond the scope of this chapter and rarely employed for research in accounting or finance and so are not further considered here.

How will you know which ontological or epistemological position to adopt? Rather than trying to answer this question directly, my suggestion would be to focus on your research aims, which will lead naturally to a particular design and a set of methods, as discussed in chapter 10. Incorporating such a statement of your research design will imply that you will have selected a specific epistemological approach, although you will have done so indirectly, and you probably do not need to refer to it directly in your dissertation. But having some idea of where your design sits within the range of possible approaches to knowledge creation will help you put it into perspective.

2.3.4 Critical accounting and finance

Critical accounting is a well-established focus of research beginning from the premise that existing accounting approaches and models are insufficient for explaining the linkages that accounting systems have with the wider society, influencing matters such as organisational structures, equality of power and resources, environmental issues. Critical research in accounting has been the subject of numerous PhD theses in the field. By contrast, there is a lack of a robust critical stream in finance, which has been argued to be linked with stagnation in the discipline and its failure to develop the tools required to study the 'grand challenges' that the world faces. It has also been pointed out that finance theory scarcely changed at all in the shadow of the global financial crisis.

A small body of critical work has emerged in finance, primarily focused on discussions of the lack of linkages between scholarly finance and practice, the excessive use of mathematics in the field, and the absence of qualitative research. On the asset pricing side of finance, models such as the capital asset pricing model, arbitrage pricing theory, and options pricing formulae based on the Black-Scholes approach still predominate nearly half a century since their initial development (see Brooks et al., 2019 for a detailed discussion of some of these issues and their consequences). In a series of studies, Frankfurter and McGoun (1999, 2001) argue that a key reason the established models in finance are so enduring despite their flaws is the existence of barriers to developing new types of models. For instance, they discuss how the word 'anomalies' is used to trivialise the findings against an established financial theory or paradigm (such as the efficient markets hypothesis), even if such evidence is overwhelming.

Kuhn (1962) defined an anomaly as something that goes against an established paradigm, 'Discovery commences with the awareness of an anomaly, i.e., with the recognition that nature has somehow violated the paradigm-induced expectations that govern normal science. It then continues with a more or less extended exploration of the area of the anomaly. And it closes only when the paradigm theory has been adjusted so that the anomalous has become the expected' (p.52).

In most scientific disciplines, anomalies result in the development of new, better theories that can explain them, but in finance, the word has been given a lesser, insignificant and even trivialising interpretation. In this field, an anomaly is usually considered merely an odd result that does not fit in with the expected pattern, so an unimportant phenomenon and something that is probably spurious. It is an interesting paradox that an increasing array of anomalies has been discovered in finance, which have persisted for many years, and yet they still remain anomalies with the current paradigm undented. Frankfurter and McGoun argue that it is impossible to adequately capture human behaviour with a set of mathematical equations and that an entirely different approach is required.

Another important difference between accounting and finance as disciplines is the strong links between accounting academics and practising accountants, in particular through the professional associations. These bodies involve academics in standards setting and provide funding for academic research and conferences. The same is not true in finance, where the links between scholarly research and the industry are tenuous. Addressing the lack of connections between academic finance and 'city finance' in the financial services sector, Keasey and Hudson (2007) use the metaphor of a house without windows, to describe finance theory, arguing that its academics do not engage with the industry or investor. They never ask investors, fund managers, and other practitioners why they made their decisions, instead preferring to infer this information from anonymous market data. As a result, the context in which decisions are made is lost. According to Keasey and Hudson, maintaining a distance from real financial market issues keeps the subject safe from questions of its validity and relevance, and findings that go against the theory are labelled as 'puzzles' to be explained in future studies. This approach both maintains the core ideology but also generates new research agendas for continuing within the established paradigm.

It is valuable for doctoral students to reflect on the role that critical accounting and finance, broadly defined, have in the development of knowledge in their disciplines, even if their PhDs are focused on developing research within existing streams. But more generally, an acknowledgement of the failings of existing theories and models can pave the way for improved approaches that work better.

2.3.5 'Scientific revolutions'

A relevant question to ask when examining how the literature in a particular field develops over time is, 'if all knowledge is tentative, and could later be demonstrated to have been wrong, how does a subject move from one set of widely held beliefs to another?' The American philosopher, Thomas Kuhn (1962), suggested that a field's progress does not follow a continuous path, but there are periods where it develops rapidly and others where it stagnates. He also argued that once a set of ideas – what he called a paradigm – becomes established, it shapes future study as other researchers follow in the footsteps of the tradition developed by those previously working on the same topic.

Even though the ideas might be widely understood to be right at a particular point in time, if, in fact, they did not represent 'true knowledge', then an increasing array of evidence against the notions will emerge. These cases that do not fit in with the established patterns are termed anomalies. Initially, and for a potentially considerable time, any challenges to the established doctrine may be dismissed out of hand, and the anomalies are considered by those working in the mainstream of the field as inconvenient and perhaps even irrelevant statistical coincidences. But eventually, a particular set of ideas may come to be viewed as inadequate as the number of anomalies, and the weight of evidence against the current perspective grow so substantial that they can no longer be summarily dismissed.

The paradigm then faces a crisis with new ideas that could potentially resolve the puzzles that have been created put forward. Kuhn argued these new viewpoints might arise through a 'revolutionary scientist' who is perhaps more junior than those who developed the previous paradigm, and they will therefore not be so wedded to it. There will subsequently be a regime change to a completely new way of thinking about the particular issues that Kuhn termed a 'paradigm shift', which is an expression that is still in widespread use today. An interesting implication of the occurrence of such paradigmatic breakdown and reconstruction is that the total amount of knowledge does not rise monotonically over time, since shifts involve a requirement to reconsider what we previously thought we knew and for puzzles that we believed were already solved to be reopened. So it is as if the global stock of knowledge is on an upward trajectory but with temporary declines as it is continually re-evaluated.

In economics, the move from the dominance of Keynesian thinking towards neoclassical, supply-side economics is often provided as an example of a paradigm shift. To offer an illustration of this process of shift in finance, from the 1970s through to the 2000s, it was widely considered by scholars that financial markets were broadly efficient with prices incorporating relevant information rapidly in most cases. This ties in with the risk-based view of how assets are priced, which purports that investors will be rewarded with higher expected returns for taking on additional risks. Thus, on average, the returns on riskier asset classes are higher than those on lower risk classes (equities outperform bonds, which outperform Treasury bills, etc.)

This era represented what Kuhn would term a period of 'normal science'. However, the global financial crisis of c.2008 spurred a period of 'extraordinary science' in Kuhn's terminology, where new ideas were entertained that previously would not have been taken seriously. The new approaches that emerged are based on the principles of behavioural finance and adaptive markets rather than neoclassical economics. It is possible that a scientific revolution will emerge, but the new ideas have still yet to fully take hold, and the majority of the previously existing models are still in widespread use. The paper by Gippel (2012) provides a highly readable and accessible treatment of this topic.

A particular point of concern among behavioural researchers, which leads them to criticise orthodox finance theory, is the vast array of assumptions required to operationalise most of the models employed. For example, the striking list of suppositions stated before deriving the capital asset pricing model (CAPM). Those who adopt an interpretivist perspective might argue that such models are doomed to failure because the assumptions are demonstrably unrealistic (e.g., perfect capital markets, no short sales constraints, all agents have full information).

However, positivist researchers, dating back to Friedman (1953), have argued that the plausibility of model assumptions is not relevant, and a theory or model with questionable suppositions will still be valuable if it can explain observed outcomes. Indeed, they would argue that the more unrealistic the assumptions the better, since this helps to make theories the simplest they can be so that models can abstract further from the complexities of the real issues. These concerns with the requirement for assumptions so that positivists can do their research led to the development of phenomenology in the 1960s and 1970s, which argued that our understanding of the world flows from the assumptions we make rather than reflecting how the world actually is.

2.3.6 Inductive versus deductive reasoning

Research following the 'scientific approach' involves beginning with a theory formulated into a set of testable hypotheses that are then evaluated using data. This ordering is known as deductive reasoning, or sometimes as a 'top-down' approach, which is prevalent in finance and much accounting research, and is associated with the positivist paradigm discussed above. The deductive approach involves a structured and formalised approach to analysis.

The converse, known as inductive reasoning, involves starting with empirical data, examining it carefully and then formulating a theory based on what is observed. Hence, according to the inductive approach, the data come first and the theory after as an output of the process, and vice versa for the deductive method where theory is an input. As a result, inductive theories make few assumptions since nothing is taken for granted about the entity under examination, and the researcher begins with a blank page. Inductive research is usually associated with the interpretivist paradigm. The distinctions between inductive and deductive research are summarised in Table 2.1 and explained in further detail in chapter 10.

In practice, most research involves at least a little of both approaches. Researchers using the scientific method might modify and improve their theories after seeing their empirical results, even though sometimes the work is written up to appear as if the theory was fully formulated before the empirical work began. Likewise, inductive researchers might have some initial ideas (perhaps based on previous research) and will not start their investigation with an entirely clean slate, although they will not have fully formulated a theory at the outset.

It might also be the case that researcher X develops a theory based on observing some data (an inductive approach), but then researcher Y reads the resulting study written by X and then takes that theory as a starting point for a new empirical analysis.

Table 2.1: The differences between inductive and deductive research

Characteristic	Approach	
	Deductive	Inductive
Alternative name	Scientific approach	Grounded theory approach
Epistemological position	Positivist	Interpretivist
Assumptions	Could be numerous	Not required
Standard research methods	Surveys, secondary data analysis	Case studies, interviews
Standard sample size	Large	Small
Order of steps	Formulate theory ↓ Test theory empirically ↓ Theory is supported or refuted by the data	Empirical observation ↓ Formulate theory to explain observed behaviour

Is this now a deductive theory? Therefore, in reality, the distinction is blurred, and most theory development is a mixture of both induction and deduction.

2.3.7 Grounded theory research

The grounded theory approach to social science research is attributed to Glaser and Strauss (1967) and is linked with inductive reasoning. It is, in some ways, the antithesis of the conventional scientific method. According to the latter, a theory is developed or implemented first, and it is then 'shown' to the data, with the theory either refuted or supported by empirical observation. Grounded theory does the reverse, where researchers begin *a priori* with observations. They explore the data (or situation) first and then use it to develop a theory that evolves along with their surveillance and is said to be grounded in the data – hence the name. According to the grounded theory approach, a theory emerges as a tentative step to putting assorted findings into a coherent framework and explaining them. It does not begin with a set of pre-determined testable hypotheses, nor would there necessarily even be a literature review before the investigative work begins.

In the management field, broadly defined, the deductive approach to research where the theory comes first is sometimes known as structured research since the prior theory places structure onto the process of organising the investigative work and guides how it should be done. In reality, while most research in accounting and finance claims to use the scientific methodology, it is common to refine the theory in the light of the empirical evidence, which would be a hybrid of the two approaches.

Further reading

- There are numerous textbooks on the philosophy that underpins social sciences research, although many of them are specifically aimed at educational research. More general texts that might be of interest to students of accounting and finance include Hollis (1994), Howell (2012) and Williams (2016)
- Birks and Mills (2015) and Urquhart (2012) both provide focused and accessible introductions to grounded theory research
- In my view, there are no textbooks on critical accounting that are relevant for beginning PhD students, but the paper by Laughlin (1999) is a useful introductory starting point available for download from Research Gate,[1] while on the finance side, readers might be interested in the paper I co-authored, Brooks et al. (2019) that is available from SSRN.[2]

Chapter takeaways – top tips for success

- ✻ Know the difference between academic research and the everyday use of the term
- ✻ Be aware of the differences between positivist and interpretivist approaches to conducting research
- ✻ Be able to explain the four types of research (exploratory, descriptive, analytical and predictive) and know where your research will fit within this classification
- ✻ Think about Bloom's classification and whether your familiarity with your research topic will cover all the rungs on the ladder
- ✻ Decide whether your research will be of the inductive or deductive type
- ✻ Ensure that you understand the importance of theory for conducting high-quality research and decide what conceptual or theoretical framework will underpin your study

---

[1] https://www.researchgate.net/profile/Richard-Laughlin/publication/235306328_ Critical_accounting_Nature_progress_and_prognosis/links/55b8d90b08aed621de07b426/ Critical-accounting-Nature-progress-and-prognosis.pdf
[2] https://papers.ssrn.com/sol3/papers.cfm?abstract_id=2936544

3. CHOOSING THE TOPIC

Learning outcomes: this chapter covers

✓ Where to begin thinking about topic selection
✓ Whether a PhD has to be 'useful'
✓ How to turn a broad area into a focused idea
✓ How to select a good topic rather than a bad one

3.1 Introduction to choosing your topic

Once you have made the decision to do a PhD, before you can nail down the research methods to use, you will need to have narrowly defined exactly what it is that you want to study. In some ways, it is a misnomer to talk of a 'choice of topic stage' since the majority of PhD dissertation topics will continue to evolve right until the point that the investigative work is completed. Therefore, a first point to note is that you should not be concerned about being somehow boxed in by what you write in your research proposal. You can and probably will end up producing something somewhat different, even though it will usually be in the same general area as the proposal.

Armed with some knowledge about what research is and how it is structured, this is the first of two chapters that aim to steer you in the right direction regarding the subject to undertake your research on (this chapter) and how to write up your initial ideas into a plan document (the next chapter).

Selecting the topic is arguably one of the most, if not the most, crucial part of the whole process. You will be spending a significant amount of time on the dissertation – probably somewhere between three and four whole years, so the topic must maintain your interest for that long, and you need to choose carefully. Being able to generate novel yet feasible research ideas is a valuable skill that even many career academics never fully master. It is not easy, and for those who are new to research with little prior reading completed, it is even tougher.

You need to select a sufficiently challenging topic that it will push you to learn and achieve more than you have before and will allow you to showcase your abilities across a range of aspects. But on the other hand, it needs to be within your scope given the time available and not be so out of reach that it leaves you floundering, permanently worried, and making no progress.

If you find the subject boring, then reading and writing about it will be a chore from beginning to end, and your lack of passion for it will probably show through in your writing. If your response to this statement is that you find all research dull or that none of the topics within the subject is enjoyable, then it is better not to start a PhD and instead do something else with your life.

As taught student numbers in accounting and finance departments have grown over the past two decades, supervising their projects has become more challenging for the staff. In some instances, departments have responded by making the project optional where it was previously compulsory or by reducing its scope. This is unfortunate because it means that many students applying for a PhD and writing their research proposals are stabbing in the dark as they have no first-hand experience of research and they have not been introduced to it in their taught modules.

If you have the opportunity to examine previous successfully completed PhDs in the department, then do take this up as it will give a clear idea of what you are aiming at and might spark some inspiration. Of course, the topics might not also be an appropriate choice for you but still, you can get useful ideas on the kinds of subjects that could be chosen, how a completed document might look, what sections are included and in what order, and how the work is formatted and presented.

3.1.1   How are research ideas generated?

Where do research ideas come from, and why do research agendas develop in the way that they do rather than proceeding in some other direction? Since the majority of academics have the freedom to establish their own research priorities, there are forces analogous to Adam Smith's 'invisible hand' at play. Therefore, the body of research produced results from the collective decisions of all of the scholars in the field regarding their choices of topics to work on (and not to work on). This laissez-faire attitude to the development of research agendas begs the question as to whether the incentives are right to encourage academics to engage in 'the right kinds of research' and push the boundaries of knowledge back as far and as fast as possible, as was touched upon in subsection 2.3.4.

Similarly, you will also have the opportunity to select the subject you wish. This freedom to work on whatever topic you choose makes coming up with a research plan even more challenging. When designing your own scheme of work, it is useful to consider where established academics might find their inspiration.

In some ways, developing the initial ideas is the most fundamental part of the research process and arguably the hardest. Since it is difficult to see this part of the process in action or to know how decisions are made, there is very little evidence on this. No academics write about how they came up with their research agendas or why they selected the topics they did. One of the few such studies is by Sandberg and Alvesson (2011), who develop a typology of how research questions are formed. They examine the wording of the introductory sections of 52 articles published in four leading management journals and identify that an approach they term 'gap-spotting' is dominant. This technique involves examining the existing literature and identifying aspects of the research continuum that have not yet been thoroughly investigated. – in other words, trying to find a gap in the literature that the researcher can fill. While their study was conducted in the context of general management journals, the issues they examine are equally prevalent in accounting and finance. Sandberg and Alvesson (*op cit.*) identify several types of gap spotting:

1. Confusion-spotting – this happens where there is already existing research available on the topic but showing conflicting results. The new research would then aim to reconcile these competing perspectives.
2. Neglect-spotting – Sandberg and Alvesson (*op cit.*) argue that this is by far the most common kind of gap-spotting and happens when there is no research on a particular area or topic. They sub-divide such research into two types:
   - A particular aspect of the research has been overlooked despite the existence of studies in the area more broadly construed
   - A whole area is under-researched
3. Application-spotting – occurs when techniques and theory are already there, but the new research seeks to apply them to a novel problem

Gap-spotting is a relatively low-risk strategy for generating research ideas, and it can lead to rigorous and valid research. However, Sandberg and Alvesson suggest that robustness and validity are not sufficient to create exciting or significant research, and the issue is that gap-spotting rarely leads to great advances. By definition, this approach adds to and builds upon what is already there, and thus new contributions of such research will be incremental and will not break the mould.

What alternative strategies exist for generating research ideas aside from looking for gaps in the knowledge base? One possibility is known as 'problematisation', based on a concept developed by the French philosopher Michel Foucault. It involves trying to think in a radically different fashion instead of simply following what is already known. In this way, the assumptions underlying existing theories are questioned in significant ways. The conventional lines of reasoning are broken by reconsidering established positions where the suppositions are troubling by turning the received wisdom into something problematic. Problematising requires a willingness to adopt unfamiliar theoretical positions that may cut across traditional methodological boundaries.

In reality, most academics in accounting and finance adopt a gap-spotting-type approach to research rather than aiming for something more radical and it makes sense for PhD proposals to do likewise. Numerous other suggestions for where to get inspiration are given in section 3.2.

3.1.2   Defining a contribution

It is essential for research papers as well as PhD theses to articulate clearly their novel contributions. The 'contribution' describes aspects of the work new in this particular study that were not known before. This is also important because papers submitted for possible publication to journals are likely to be rejected if the editor cannot identify what is new. Similarly, a PhD thesis must also make a contribution to knowledge (see section 1.4).

It is worth noting that many scholars would view contributions as 'socially constructed', which means that what constitutes a contribution will differ between research communities. An idea becomes a contribution when it is regarded as important by members of the scholarly community.

How do writers identify and explain their contribution? Problematisation is implicit in numerous studies as a way for the authors to articulate their contribution. They do this by first showing deference to existing studies by re-presenting and organising the existing knowledge to make a context for the contribution. Second, they subvert or problematise the literature to provide a location and motivation for the current effort. It is as if the authors build up the quality and importance of the research area and prior studies before knocking them down by turning against these existing works and identifying their flaws. Authors then feign surprise that their research questions have not been addressed before because they are an apparent omission from the literature and very important to know about.

I now provide an example of where the contribution is defined in a studies that I have co-authored, taken from Brooks, Prokopczuk and Wu (2015), which is a study that tested for whether there were speculative bubbles in commodities prices. A pre-publication version of the paper is available from the University of Reading repository.[1] It is quite a long excerpt, but it usefully illustrates how a piece of research can be positioned and its contribution defined:

> 'The prices of many commodities experienced a spectacular run up during the period leading into the recent financial crisis. Gold prices, for example, rose by c.500% between 2000 and 2011 before losing a third of their value by 2013. Standard economic theory suggests that changes in price levels will be governed by the laws of supply and demand, but it is unclear

---

[1] http://centaur.reading.ac.uk/39235/1/third_CB_Feb2015.pdf

whether such extreme price swings over protracted periods can be justified fundamentally, leading to suggestions that they may arise from speculation.

. . .

Since commodities are core inputs to the production process or are consumption goods, the roller coaster-like behavior of their prices has also been argued to have real consequences. In particular, there have been concerns that price spikes have adversely affected the social welfare of consumers, especially those in developing countries since households there spend a relatively high proportion of their incomes on basic food and energy. Many commentators in the media explicitly laid the blame for the price rises and increased volatility squarely at the door of speculators, arguing that investment banks and funds were immoral to engage in strategies that may have pushed up food prices. While newspapers called for commodity speculation to be banned altogether, in a more measured response, governments and regulatory bodies have argued for it to be restricted, including a requirement for transparency in the reporting of speculative trades and the establishment of strict position limits. In 2006, a US Senate Permanent Subcommittee Staff Report claimed that traditional supply and demand forces could not fully explain the price increase that began from the beginning of 2000. Later, the United Nations also blamed food price rises on trading in agricultural commodities rather than the actual food stocks in physical markets, arguing that "Over $400bn (of paper money) is traded – that's 20-30 times the physical production of the commodity", and calling for tighter regulation of investors to limit the formation of commodity bubbles.

. . .

It is clear that a formal evaluation of the possibility of bubbles in such series is warranted and yet there have been surprisingly few studies (discussed in detail below) that have done this. A speculative bubble is argued to exist if there are systematic, persistent and increasing deviations of actual prices from their fundamentally justifiable values. Among existing empirical studies, there is no clear conclusion that can be drawn so far as to whether commodity price series have been characterised by speculative bubbles or not.

. . .

We extend this emergent literature that investigates putative speculative bubbles in commodity markets in several important ways. First, we employ a much longer run of data than existing studies – our sample spans over forty years going back to the late 1960s. We would argue that it is not possible to robustly test for speculative bubbles in series that do not cover more than one price cycle. Second, we employ a much broader range of commodities than the one or two individual series used in the majority of existing studies. Such a comparative approach will enable us to much better tackle the issue of whether commodity markets have become financialised since if this is the case we might see bubbles in many commodity markets even where their underlying demand has risen less strongly. Third, and perhaps most importantly, unlike equity and real estate markets where the appropriate type of cashflow used to construct the fundamental measure is clear (dividends and rental income respectively), for commodities it is not immediately obvious how we should analogously construct the fundamental price. Existing studies have employed convenience yield in this vein, but this series may itself be contaminated with a bubble since its estimation is based on the actual price. Therefore, we follow a second approach and obtain the fundamental value by exploiting the relationship of commodity prices with a set of macroeconomic factors that are widely believed to capture commodity demand. Finally, we employ a direct test for bubble presence based on a regime-switching specification, which, by actually specifying a model for the dynamics of the bubble and the underlying price series, provides more diagnostic information than the indirect technique based on recursive unit root tests employed in most extant research in the commodities arena.'

Note the style that we use here, which is quite typical for this genre, although, of course, there are numerous other ways that the research could be introduced and motivated. We first explain why testing for speculative bubbles in commodities is important by discussing how much price volatility had arisen and also pointing out the impact that this can have for users of commodities and especially food purchasers in developing countries. Second, we highlight that despite how essential this is as a research topic, there are very few existing studies. Finally, we outline several ways in which our research differs from prior studies. Ideally, these variations will cover several different aspects of the investigation: the research questions, the data and the models.

3.2   Where to start looking for research ideas

So, where do you start? My first suggestion is that is advisable to stick within the remit of the research areas covered in the department(s) to which you are applying, since if your proposal is focused on a topic outside of its scope, the chances that it will engage some supervisory interest is much diminished. Working on a subject you have studied on a taught module will use your existing knowledge and reduce the amount of groundwork you have to undertake initially. More generally, it is possible to approach the task of topic selection strategically, thinking about your strengths and weaknesses and focusing the choice to make the most use of the former and the least of the latter.

Alternatively, you could treat the PhD, in part, as a learning experience, and use it as a way to maximise opportunities for that. For example, if there are particular new

Figure 3.1: How to focus your ideas to select a topic

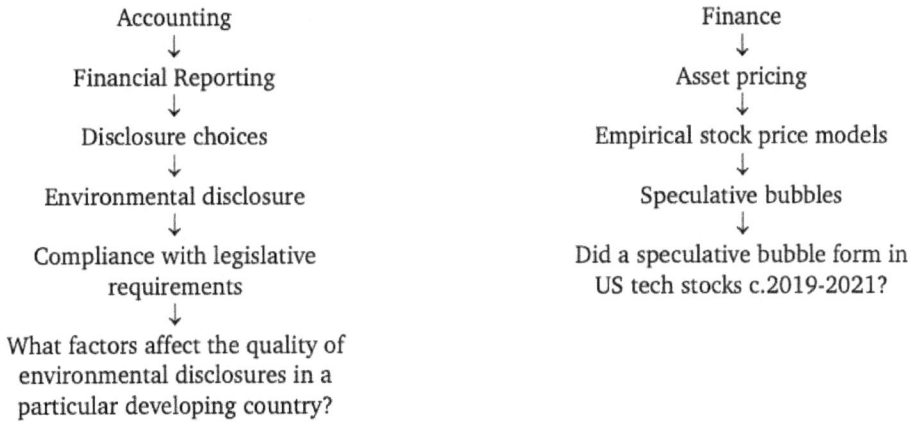

Accounting	Finance
↓	↓
Financial Reporting	Asset pricing
↓	↓
Disclosure choices	Empirical stock price models
↓	↓
Environmental disclosure	Speculative bubbles
↓	↓
Compliance with legislative requirements	Did a speculative bubble form in US tech stocks c.2019-2021?
↓	
What factors affect the quality of environmental disclosures in a particular developing country?	

quantitative techniques or programming languages that you feel could be valuable for your personal or career development, then select a topic that will require those skills and provide you with a concrete motivation to develop them. Be realistic, though, about the extent to which you can learn entirely new techniques in the time available, given that you would need to develop your knowledge to a fairly advanced level and you also have to do the research and write it up.

Clearly, you will need to make a preliminary topic selection in order to be able to draft a proposal before you apply. Preparing well at this stage and selecting the idea judiciously will pay dividends at a later stage. You need to choose something that will hold your attention, is challenging but feasible with your skills and time constraints, and is likely to generate good quality academic research. Making this selection will probably require extensive information retrieval and detailed thought and reflection, which will take time.

Sometimes a student will have a very focused idea from the outset – if it is something they always wanted to study, or if someone else has presented them with an 'oven-ready' idea that they can just get cracking on. But in most cases, it is a process of starting with an expansive area and gradually narrowing down the perspective until an idea that is manageable within the available timeframe emerges. In this case, there are several stages in the process:
- Define a broad area for research
- Narrow this to pinpoint a research problem
- Articulate the research problem in a statement
- Separate the statement into several practicable aspects
- Draft the statements into a set of research aims, questions or hypotheses

Focusing your ideas beginning with a very broad idea and successively narrowing it down until you have a workable title could operate as in Figure 3.1 for particular ideas in accounting and finance, respectively.

When you have pinned down a broad topic area for your research, one way to think about converting your general ideas into a manageable plan is to transform them into a question or set of questions because, ultimately, the whole purpose of research is to provide answers to problems.

If you have a broad area in mind but not yet a specific topic, it is worthwhile to proceed by reading introductory-level treatments of that topic. It is advisable not to dive straight into the latest, cutting-edge thinking since the level of assumed knowledge and detail will be too great. Trying to penetrate such work at this stage might be off-putting and may give the incorrect impression that you will never understand any of it and need to choose a different, less challenging field.

Instead, start with an introductory-level treatment such as a textbook, lecture notes, or even Wikipedia. Although the source is much maligned by scholars and should never be the only point of reference, it is often a good starting point since it is quick, free, and easy to access. Wikipedia will provide you with basic, foundation-level knowledge from which you can build by moving to gradually more specialist and advanced treatments once you are determined that this is the topic for you. Even if the Wiki pages suffer from some omissions or contain some inaccuracies, that does not matter at this stage if you are starting from the position of having very limited prior knowledge.

Have a browse through some recent editions of relevant journals and practitioner magazines. Browsing used to be a much different experience in days gone by where it was common to wander into the library and peruse the physical copies. Nowadays, the journals are all on-line, but browsing can still be useful. If you go to your university library's website, you should be able to search the e-journals available to find those in the subject area you are interested in (e.g., management accounting, quantitative finance, etc.). There are many accounting and finance journal lists available on the internet, including the Academic Journal Guide, which is very comprehensive (see chapter 8 for a discussion of this and more detail on how to search for and download the papers).

Another useful tip is that most journal articles end their concluding sections with an 'ideas for further research' paragraph, which does precisely what the name suggests, where the authors provide a list of new research ideas that lead on from what they did (and did not do). Obviously, there are no guarantees that these ideas are sound or even feasible, and if the article is old, the suggestions may have already been taken up subsequently by those authors or other researchers. Looking at this concluding paragraph in high quality, recent studies might provide you with some suggestions, although to be able to go down this route, you would need to know which studies' conclusions to look at. This issue is discussed in the remainder of this chapter and chapter 8.

3.2.1 Where to look if you have no ideas whatsoever

Inspiration for topic choice may come from several sources, so if you have absolutely no idea what to study or where even to start looking for a topic, initially cast your

Table 3.1: Subject areas in accounting and finance

Accounting	Finance
Management accounting	Bonds and money market securities
Financial accounting and financial reporting	Investments and asset pricing
Tax	Derivatives and financial engineering
Business finance / financial management	Corporate finance
Business strategy: an accounting perspective	Ethics for finance
Critical accounting	Mathematical finance & econometrics
Quantitative techniques for accountants	Risk management
Public sector and charity accounting	Portfolio management
Social and environmental accounting	Alternative investments
Governance and ethics in accounting	

search net very wide and see what you can catch. The following headings provide some ideas.

Successfully completed PhDs
Your department might have a library of previously completed PhDs – either in a display cupboard somewhere in the department or on-line in an intranet folder. The vast Ethos thesis collection, available on-line from the British Library website is also worth looking at – see subsection 8.3.5 for details.

Consider the subject areas that interested you the most
One way to begin thinking about what to study is to make a list of all of the modules covered in a degree programme in accounting or finance and deciding which of these you find the most interesting. Although this will not provide you with a research topic, it will at least allow you to select a research area, which then makes the choice of the topic more straightforward since you will have a better idea of where to look and who to ask (journals, books, academic staff and existing PhD students in that subject area). A list of subject areas in accounting and finance could be as given in Table 3.1, not listed in any particular order.

If one area from the list above is particularly appealing, it is worth spending time talking to the corresponding module(s)' instructors to gain their advice on the exciting and plausible topics in their subject areas.

A related avenue to explore for research ideas would be to re-examine a topic that you have already studied in a taught module. For example, one where you have done some reading and written an assignment or project that interested you and for which you scored a high mark, indicating a solid understanding of the material. However, if you go down this route, take care not to self-plagiarise from what you have already written (see chapter 7).

Practitioner magazines and hybrid journals

Academic journals are often not ideal as sources of inspiration for new PhD candidates since they are so great in number, and the articles are frequently esoteric and spanning such a wide-ranging subject matter that it is hard to know where to look.

Journals aimed at practitioners or hybrid journals spanning both academic and industrial environments can be more useful for beginner researchers since they deal with practical problems in accounting or finance and tend to be more accessible than squarely academic papers. Care is needed since some of these are more magazine than journal, and your research topic will still need to fit within the scholarly framework for research discussed in subsequent chapters of this book. But examining recent studies published in these outlets might spark some exciting ideas, and the list below contains a few suggestions for such journals, although note that some charge subscriptions to view the full article unless the outlet is included in your university's bundle.

Accounting practitioner journals
- Accounting Horizons[2]
- CPA Journal[3]
- Journal of Accountancy[4]
- Strategic Finance[5]

Finance practitioner journals
- Financial Analysts Journal[6]
- Journal of Alternative Investments[7]
- Journal of Asset Management[8]
- Journal of Fixed Income[9]
- Journal of Portfolio Management[10]
- Journal of Risk[11]

Practitioners

If you know any accounting or finance practitioners, it could be valuable to chat with them and try to find out about the problems they face in their roles that might be amenable to academic research. If they are working in an area of interest to you as

---

[2]https://aaahq.org/Research/Journals/Accounting-Horizons

[3]https://www.cpajournal.com

[4]https://www.journalofaccountancy.com

[5]https://sfmagazine.com

[6]https://cfainstitute.org/en/research/financial-analysts-journal

[7]https://jai.pm-research.com

[8]https://www.palgrave.com/gp/journal/41260

[9]https://jfi.pm-research.com

[10]https://jpm.pm-research.com

[11]https://www.risk.net/journal-of-risk

a potential future career, this could serve two purposes. Even better, if you already have some relevant experience from the industry, you might be able to identify an exciting subject that has practical relevance from your role there.

Forums

Numerous web-based interest groups have established discussion forums, and by looking at the threads on these, you will get a good idea of the kinds of practical issues people are writing about. For example, in finance:

- Citywire has an investing forum where members discuss ideas and challenges on that topic[12]
- The Wilmott Quantitative Finance forum[13]

There are also forums in accounting such as:

- Accountant Forums[14]
- Proformative[15]
- Accounting Web

By linking it with the relevant academic literature, it might be possible that you can turn one of these questions or responses into a dissertation topic.

An internet search

As I will discuss in chapter 8, internet searches can be enormously valuable, but of course, before you can find any ideas you need to know the keywords to insert, which is a bit of a catch-22. If you have some vague areas of interest, you can try those combined with 'hot topics in ...' or 'trending topics in ...', or if all else fails, 'current topics in finance' or 'current topics in accounting'. Hopefully, you will find something among the lists on the websites generated that excites you.

A word of warning, though. If you type 'research ideas in accounting' (or the same for finance), the top hits are all supplied by essay mills encouraging students to plagiarise their entire dissertation (see chapter 7). They provide services to write projects for students alongside a list of very vague and unhelpful titles.

Ask your research project supervisor, another academic or a current PhD student

These ideas speak for themselves. If you conducted a research project at the undergraduate or master's level, your supervisor for that endeavour might be willing to suggest some ideas around the investigations on which they have been working, even if your intention is to apply to other universities. Similarly, if you have got to know any PhD students in your current department, they might be happy to discuss the topics that they or their peers are working on. Start by asking them about their research, though, before turning the conversation to trying to extract their ideas for your thesis

---

[12]https://moneyforums.citywire.co.uk

[13]https://wilmott.com/

[14]https://www.accountantforums.com

[15]https://www.proformative.com/questions

Read a financial newspaper or look on a finance website

All of the financial media have websites, and many of them also have news apps that can be downloaded onto your phone or other device (CNBC, Yahoo!, MarketWatch, Bloomberg, etc.) The content on these can be accessed for free (although you might have to register) and contain a vast amount of current financial news on various topics updated frequently. As above, it will be important to consider such topics from an academic perspective and an idea taken straight from a newspaper would probably not make an appropriate PhD thesis idea.

Videos

Podcasts and YouTube videos can also be useful as an entertaining way to generate ideas. A surprisingly large number of intellectually grounded presentations are available in this way, including 'TED-style' talks, which are short performances from expert speakers on a vast range of topics. These can be found on subjects that you are interested in via a keyword search.

Reflect on your skills and interests

An alternative approach to selecting a topic would be to reflect on what interests you and what you are good at. Before formally specifying the subject of your thesis, it is worth considering your skills and interests and what you hope to get out of the process (aside from being able to call yourself Dr.):

- How good is your maths and do you like algebra? Some people enjoy deriving models while others prefer to be engaged in qualitative research
- Are you good at data analysis with statistics?
- Can you write code (e.g., in Python, R, C++ or Visual Basic)?
- Do you enjoy writing long, detailed arguments, or would you prefer to focus more on numbers and models?
- Do you like manually collecting data (e.g., through surveys or interviews), or would you prefer just to download it from a website?
- Are you aiming at a particular career path and would like to study something supporting that objective?

Your responses to all of these questions will help steer you towards certain types of research and favour specific approaches to research over others, although they might not help with choosing the precise topic.

Many students find maths and statistics both problematic and uninteresting. In that case, a qualitative approach might be preferable: methodological choices are discussed in detail in chapter 10.

A different way to generate new research ideas is to start with one or two articles (they could be published in journals or working papers, but practitioner pieces or magazine articles might still be suitable) that you enjoyed reading, and you thought were quite inspiring. Then try to identify ways that the research methods in those studies could be varied. For example, the sample period covered or country focus could be changed (e.g., if the research applied a new model to US data, you could use UK data). Or the models employed could be altered or compared with some alternatives.

Although this type of approach might not lead to an inspiring outcome because it would be very much based on something already written, it is a safe option that is more likely than others to lead to a solid piece of work. Here, you would be following in the footsteps of an established and successfully completed study, which can be used as a template to guide all the stages of your research. Sometimes, what starts off as almost a replication study gradually morphs into something quite original as the new research ideas develop in the mind of the investigator as they are conducting the study. In that case, the first empirical piece in your thesis would be closely related to an existing paper, allowing you to hone your skills in a low risk context before moving on to something more challenging for your second investigative chapter.

3.3   Other issues regarding topic selection

This section discusses several other relevant issues regarding topic choice that have not already been covered in this text.

3.3.1   A controversial subject or something from the news?

When selecting a topic, it is probably advisable to avoid a highly controversial area, such as investigating financial fraud, market manipulation, or auditing failures. While these are all fascinating and important subjects in need of scholarly inquiry, they are likely to be extremely challenging for new researchers with particular difficulties to obtain sensitive and confidential information. There would be much more scope for something to go wrong, leaving you with very little to write about. All in all, selecting such an idea is probably not worth the risk given what is at stake, and highly controversial research can be left until after you have already got the PhD qualification and will have less to lose if the research doesn't work out.

You may gain some inspiring ideas based on current events that are taking place in the financial markets or the wider economy. However, choosing to work on something that is currently very newsworthy and popular also involves some additional issues. Such a topic might well generate significant initial interest, but it is also likely to date quickly. For example, any research related to covid-19 (covid-19 and stock returns; covid-19 and dividend pay-outs; the impact of culture and wealth on the spread of covid-19, etc.) is very much in vogue at the time of writing this book (spring 2021). But such research will probably be of considerably less interest in a year or two's time, and there might even be a backlash where people are bored with it and it is considered largely pointless.

It might also be more challenging to frame the research aims of a news-generated topic within an existing scholarly paradigm than a more conventional and less currently fashionable topic; there will likely be less existing evidence to review and upon which to base your investigation. The risk is then that your work is more likely to end up as something akin to a descriptive report rather than an academic study, and the former would probably not meet the requirements for a PhD.

3.3.2   Interdisciplinary research

You might have ideas from other fields (such as maths, history, psychology, or operations research) that you have studied as part of your current or previous degree programme – a so-called transdisciplinary or interdisciplinary approach.

Exciting research can be produced in situations where concepts and approaches are drawn from another subject area and applied to accounting or finance, although they can be challenging to identify and carry through to completion as this sort of research by definition does not involve continuing an established 'formula-following' path. You may be able to think of such a cross-disciplinary idea based on the material that you studied from another subject as part of your previous degree programme or that you have read about. Behavioural finance is an excellent example of this, where ideas and concepts drawn from psychology (such as the impacts of personality and emotions on investment decision-making) are employed to good effect for addressing relevant problems in finance.

While finance has increasingly taken ideas from psychology in the development of the fashionable field of behavioural finance, the same has not occurred in accounting, which has more commonly adopted numerous concepts and theories from sociology.

3.3.3   Does PhD research need to be 'useful'?

Your research does not have to have an apparent practical outcome. Often, the work that scholars consider as having the most merit has no immediate usage outside the academy, but instead, it develops new concepts or methods or pushes forward the way they think about a particular topic. It might be that you would prefer your research to have implications for policy or practice and for it to be useful to some external group (practitioners, regulators, policymakers, retail investors, etc.). But this is not usually a requirement for a PhD dissertation, and you need to be aware that there might be a trade-off if you sacrifice rigour or originality to make your work practical and accessible.

Selecting a topic with high practical relevance, or one motivated by a practitioner problem, could lead to a novel thesis, but it will not hit the academic target and be awarded a PhD if it does not pose intellectually challenging as well as real-world-relevant questions. Making it a credible piece of academic work can be quite a task to achieve since it is sometimes the case that the nature of real-world research is hard to squeeze into a scholarly framework.

3.3.4   Narrowing a broad idea to a manageable topic

Once you have determined the general subject area, the next step is to narrow this down into a topic that is sufficiently self-contained that it can be tackled within around three years' full-time or the equivalent. It is crucial to check that the research aims are not so vast that they cannot be adequately addressed during the doctoral registration period. The PhD should only be aiming to solve a manageably small problem.

If your idea originated from an examination of the literature or other relevant media (a 'bottom-up' approach), you would already be aware of some of the existing work on the topic, and it is then a matter of honing and refining the suggestions.

But if your idea was presented to you by someone else or came to you without examining any of the existing research that came before it, you will need to 'back-fill' this aspect before you can write and submit a proposal as discussed in the next chapter. For instance, you will need to consider:

- How much work has already been done on this topic? Is it a mature area with numerous studies dating back decades or a relatively recent or specialised research focus? What are the pivotal studies on this subject?
- What did existing authors conclude about this topic? What data and methods did they use? What were their research aims or questions?
- Given your response to the previous question, are you aiming to do something a little different, or is it the case that a very similar study has already been completed? If so, it would be worthwhile to consider modifying it somewhat to differentiate your plans from what was previously done.

More discussion of these issues will be presented in the following chapter.

3.3.5   What is a replication study, and would it make a good PhD?

A replication study, as the name suggests, is one aiming to recreate the analysis already undertaken by existing research with a view to confirming or refuting the previous findings. While a pure replication, where a new piece of work aims to do precisely something that has been done already, is a useful starting point for a PhD, it would be dull and definitely insufficient if it constituted the entire dissertation since by definition it would not make the required contribution to knowledge.

However, there is an asymmetry: if you were able to demonstrate that an existing study (especially a widely cited piece by a well-respected author) contained systematic errors, and you were able to identify the source of those errors, it could be a fascinating and valuable exercise. But the more likely outcomes are that either your results will match those of the original authors, or they will not match because you (not the other author) made a technical error in the implementation. These eventualities are evidently less desirable. Such a topic would then be unoriginal and uninspiring if you had 'copied' the design and methods, even if the writing was all in your own words.

Many empirical research projects begin with replication but then extend it somehow – for instance, by updating the sample period or applying the same approach to a new country or asset market or adding a new variable into a regression model. This strategy is reasonably low risk and often a sensible one that can form the basis of a good piece of work. But if you are considering beginning with such a thesis topic, it is worth determining how the replication will be extended subsequently to introduce novelty into your research.

3.4   What can go wrong with a choice of topic?

Once you submit your proposal alongside the rest of your application (see chapter 4) and if you are successful and subsequently register on the programme, you will be allocated a supervisor. In your first meeting with them, there should be an opportunity to receive feedback on it before commencing any further work. This early critique will avoid wasting additional time if the idea that you have focused on is somehow inappropriate. Naturally, things can and do go wrong in many different ways, but there are several particularly common pitfalls to avoid when selecting a topic and it is more probable that you will run into difficulties further down the line where your initial idea is:

- Too vague and thus not feasible
- Clever but cannot be implemented due to lack of data
- Really a method rather than a research topic
- Journalistic or populist and not appropriate for a scholarly study
- Too broad in scope to be completed in the available time
- Too sophisticated or in too distant a field for you to have a reasonable chance to achieve it in the available time given your background and prior education
- A replica of an existing study

Although there is much more work to be done before any data you collect are analysed, it is crucial to think before doing anything further about what data are required to complete the research. Many interesting and sensible ideas for research fall flat owing to a lack of availability of relevant data. For example, the data required may be confidential, available only at a considerable financial cost, or too time-consuming to collect from many different paper sources. Before finally deciding on a particular topic, make sure that the data or any other required resources will be available.

Similarly, ensure that the methods you propose to use are feasible within the timescale, skills and your budget. For instance, it would be impressive but challenging as part of a PhD to learn how to use archival material written in medieval Latin or implement a national-scale survey. Are you sure you can achieve that? If you have doubts about the feasibility of your research ideas after you have enrolled on a PhD programme, discuss them with your supervisor, who will be able to advise on whether you need to scale back your ambitions. If you aim too high but find it impossible to complete the work within the registration period, it could be a disaster.

After you have an initial topic for the PhD, be confident in sharing it with others to get feedback at this earliest possible stage. Even if the idea is not fully developed at this juncture, or you are concerned that it would not make such a great thesis, prospective supervisors, their academic colleagues, and other students will have suggestions on how to improve it. Even if the response is that the conception is not workable into a valid PhD topic, it is much better to be aware of its infeasibility at this stage before expending any further effort on it so that you have time to consider something else.

3.4.1   After selecting a topic, can you change it?

Occasionally, candidates request a change in topic between applying for a place on a PhD programme and learning the outcome. This can create confusion or a bad impression and so it is better to be confident in the research area you include in your application proposal, but if you subsequently change your mind, wait until you are allocated a supervisor and meet them after enrolment to discuss it.

But what happens in the much more common scenario whereby you apply for a place on a PhD programme with a proposal on a particular topic but after registration and upon further reading, you come to realise that the idea you had is boring, impossible to achieve or has already been done? If you want to make a minor change to your PhD dissertation's focus, it should be fine just to go ahead and do so. Almost all dissertations change direction slightly during the course of their completion as the student learns more about the topic, collects the data, and works through the investigation.

But suppose you wanted to change the topic substantively after having already taken up a place and started work on your PhD – for example, from how intra-company pricing transfer values are determined to how international bodies can ensure that companies make consistent carbon disclosures across countries. That would represent a complete change of direction rather than a slight adjustment of emphasis. In that case, you should seek your supervisor's approval first. Otherwise, they might be somewhat irritated that you hadn't bothered to communicate with them on such a substantive issue.

Worse, when students commit severe acts of plagiarism or purchase their entire dissertation from an essay mill, it is sometimes difficult to get a project 'made to order' on precisely the desired topic, so rather than follow through with their proposal specialism, they take whatever is on offer in an entirely different area. Hence an unexpected and radical shift of topic at a later stage could arouse considerable suspicion that the work is not yours.

Chapter takeaways – top tips for success

⊛ Reflect on your skills and interests to help you select an appropriate topic
⊛ Choose your topic carefully – a poor choice will lead you to some avoidable issues later down the line
⊛ Notwithstanding the previous point, be aware that it is likely you will be able to change your topic later after registration on a programme (with approval from your supervisor)
⊛ Ensure that your research idea is challenging and sufficiently well-defined to be feasible

Chapter takeaways – continued

⊛ Your thesis does not have to cover something directly useful to practitioners

⊛ A PhD must include an element of original contribution and do some research that nobody else has done before

4. THE RESEARCH PROPOSAL

Learning outcomes: this chapter covers

✓ What a research proposal is
✓ How to draft a research proposal
✓ The elements of a successful proposal
✓ How to design a Gantt chart or timeline

4.1 What is a research proposal?

The research proposal is a brief (typically between one and six pages) document that shows the universities to which you apply what you intend to write your thesis on, how you will do it, in what sequence and over what timescale. It could be thought of as a pitch or a project bid for what you plan to work on. The proposal will include information on the study's scope, the methods and data you will employ, and possibly some discussion of the risks to successful completion or ethical issues that need to be considered.

Although very much shorter than the final thesis, the proposal still needs to be written in the same formal, scholarly style. It needs to have a clear, logical structure, be of the appropriate length, and including all of the required information. The purpose of this chapter is to discuss all aspects of the proposal writing process, including tips to make it as strong and effective a document as possible.

A first consideration is in terms of the approach you should use to drafting the document regarding the appropriate level of technical detail and the level of knowledge assumed of the reader. On this issue, it is usually best to write it for an 'intelligent non-specialist.' In other words, draft the proposal for someone who knows the field (broadly defined) but not the precise topic. If, for example, you are writing a dissertation on responsible tax, you can assume that the reader is also an accountant of sorts, but not that they are a tax specialist. If the department to which you apply has a member of staff with expertise in this area, it is likely that they will be asked to comment on your application and whether they might be interested in supervising it. However, the department might not have such a specialist, and in any case, the Director of the PhD programme, who will conduct a preliminary sift through all the applications, will likely not be a tax expert. This is why the proposal should not assume that the reader has a narrowly defined subject-specific knowledge.

Requirements regarding the research proposal vary substantially from one university to another. The extent to which the proposal is a primary means to evaluate the candidate will also vary: in some cases it will be essential that it is of high quality in terms of both the ideas and the writing otherwise the applicant will be rejected. In other instances, the department will concentrate primarily on the applicant's credentials, so that they are mainly focused on the candidate's intrinsic qualities rather than the proposal. In that case, once the applicant has been accepted and registered, their allocated supervisor would work with them to improve the proposal or rework it entirely.

Even if the proposal is not important as a selection tool, putting in the time to draft a good one will lay the groundwork for a smoother ride through the rest of the process. It is also likely that the proposal will be the first point of contact between you and your supervisor, and if it is incomplete or evidently hastily written, it will create a poor initial impression.

The research proposal allows the department to have an early view of whether your thesis is likely to meet the required standards. If you are accepted onto the programme, the academic staff can then provide suggestions on how to get it up to scratch (or, indeed, they might recommend trying again with another idea). The document will allow your supervisor to ensure that your PhD idea is feasible to complete within the timescale and given the resources that you have available and what you have learned on previous degree programmes. The proposal should also demonstrate that you have considered whether any ethical issues are likely to arise in your research and, if so, how you will deal with them.

Writing proposals is useful not only because it is usually a required step in the application process, but also because the act of writing it will make you:

- Read and summarise a little of the existing literature carefully
- Think about the novelty of your idea and how it fits into the body of previous research
- Assess the plausibility of the proposed methodology
- Think about where the data will come from

- Determine whether the idea is too big, too small, or of just the right size
- Consider whether there are likely to be any ethical issues to be concerned with
- Establish a timetable to completion and think carefully about how long each stage is likely to take

A further benefit of having to write and submit a proposal is that it imposes some initial structure on the process and forces you to start thinking about the research from a very early stage. Otherwise, you might have been tempted not even to begin working on it until you are already on the programme, which would cause considerable delays before you were able to begin the investigation. There might be a particular proposal form that you must complete, or more likely, you will be expected to draft your own document within a pre-defined set of parameters.

Once you submit your proposal with your application and you are accepted onto the programme, the allocation of a supervisor will likely be based on your chosen topic. If you subsequently make a radical switch to an entirely different area, then your designated supervisor may no longer be the most appropriate subject expert. Yet changing to another supervisor might not be permitted, and it would cause significant confusion and disorder if many students similarly changed their minds and tried to switch supervisors. Hence, the best strategy is to choose as carefully as possible from the outset and to put as much effort and information into the proposal as you can. It is often the case that the proposal, if detailed, will transform naturally into the outline of the thesis since the structure is quite similar. It's as if the proposal forms the skeleton for the entire document.

Once you begin the PhD and meet your supervisor, you will likely receive detailed feedback on the document to guide you going forwards. The more developed the proposal's content, the more effective can be that feedback, which will give you a stronger foundation to progress the work.

The proposal should be tailored to the audience and the word limit, so you should find out straight away what the requirements are and work within them. If it is a struggle to write the proposal, this is a bad sign that the research ideas are not sufficiently sharp, and it might be that you need to do more reading and thinking before having another go at it. The motivation and intended contribution are probably the most important parts of the proposal and should be given sufficient time and space accordingly. Students sometimes get too focused on the technical details (e.g., where they will get the data from, or even including a mathematical derivation of the quantitative model that they are going to use); this is not necessary at this stage and should be left for once you have started work on the PhD.

You might wish to circulate your proposal among selected prospective supervisors to get their comments and suggestions. You could then incorporate the feedback to improve the document's quality prior to submitting your application. Many academics will be reluctant to offer comments to students who have not yet applied, however, so be prepared for a number of polite excuses if you elect to make such requests.

The key attribute of a good proposal is to start with a good research idea, and once you have this straightened out, you can draft the rest of the proposal fairly quickly. As discussed in detail in chapter 3, some students will already have the core idea from the outset, but in other cases, it will only emerge slowly after a long period of reading and discussion. In some ways, students who take longer to get their research idea are in a stronger position from then on as they will have done quite a lot of digging and will consequently have become familiar with the topic and the existing literature. On the other hand, those who had their research idea 'handed to them on a plate' or where it arrived in a flash of inspiration will need to catch up with what is already written on the topic.

4.2 What should the proposal contain?

Schools will vary enormously in their requirements here, so read the rubric and deliver what is requested. But in general, provided that there is sufficient space, all good proposals should include several key elements:
- A descriptive title
- An executive summary or abstract
- A general motivation section – why is the general area attractive?
- A brief review of the relevant existing literature with enough detail to demonstrate your familiarity with the core material
- A clear statement of the objectives and the research questions or hypotheses
- A brief description of the methodological approach to be employed (e.g., quantitative analysis of data, development of a conceptual model, conducting experiments) and of the data sources if relevant
- A statement confirming that you have considered any ethical issues and whether the investigative work will need ethics committee approval or not (see chapter 7)
- A discussion of any anticipated risks to successful completion
- A brief timeline of significant milestones and when they are expected to be completed
- A list of references cited in the literature review part or elsewhere in the proposal

A suggestion for possible lengths for each section is given in Table 4.1 for examples of proposals that are three pages and eight pages long. Of course, these are just general guidelines, and an excellent proposal could nonetheless depart significantly from these suggestions. I will now discuss each of the sections required of the proposal in a bit more detail.

4.2.1 The title

You need to select a working title for the proposal – this might not be the title of your final thesis of course, but it should nonetheless provide a reasonable idea of what

Table 4.1: Possible research proposal lengths for each section

Element	Short proposal (pages)	Long proposal (pages)
Summary	–	$\frac{1}{3}$
Introduction	$\frac{1}{2}$	1
Literature review	$\frac{1}{2}$	2
Research objectives and questions	$\frac{1}{2}$	1
Methodology and data sources	$\frac{1}{2}$	2
Ethical issues	$\frac{1}{3}$	$\frac{1}{3}$
Risk assessment	–	$\frac{1}{3}$
Timescale	$\frac{1}{3}$	$\frac{1}{2}$
References	$\frac{1}{3}$	$\frac{1}{2}$
Total	3	8

you are planning to do. It should be concise (perhaps a maximum of 12 words or a shorter title followed by a sub-title totalling not more than around 15 words) and explain what the research is about. Although a well-considered title might remain relevant for the final document, you would not be required to stick rigidly to it. It is not worth agonising at this stage as your research could move in any number of directions that you cannot predict when writing the proposal. Just draft a title that makes sense given the ideas that you have now.

4.2.2 The summary

This section would be a single paragraph of around 100-150 words that gives the reader the gist of your ideas - including the topic, the research questions, the methodological approach you will use, the geographical coverage or period covered (if relevant), any data or resource requirements, and what you are expecting to find. For a shorter proposal, this section would usually be omitted altogether as the entire piece is essentially a precis so that the abstract would be a summary of a summary.

4.2.3 The introduction

This section will first set the scene for the topic to contextualise the material you will discuss below. You would then cover the motivation, which is a statement of why this study is needed. This will usually involve establishing the background and then identifying a gap in existing knowledge that your research will fill. You would then explain what you want to do (only in broad terms at this stage), why it is exciting and what is the significance of it and for whom. Will your work be mainly aimed at other academics, developing new knowledge that other researchers could take forwards, or will it be directed predominantly at practitioners or policymakers? What is the need for the research you intend to produce? This section has to persuade the reader that the study will be relevant, worthwhile, and exciting.

4.2.4   The literature review

The review does not have to be exhaustive at this stage, covering everything already written on the topic. It just needs to be suggestive and sufficient to convince the reader that you can see where your ideas will fit within the knowledge base and that you are reasonably confident that you are not merely repeating work that is already out there. Note that many (most?) research proposals are 'review heavy' – that is, they contain too much review and background information with not enough space devoted to the actual research that will be conducted and how. The latter is the core of the proposal (and will be the core of the thesis) – the literature review is just context setting, albeit necessary background.

Even if you have done a lot of reading, focus on the most important and relevant articles in the review parts of your proposal. If your literature review is more than around a third of the proposal, you should consider cutting it down to include only the most pertinent sources or discussing each piece in less detail. The rest of the material is not wasted because it can be saved for discussion in the literature review of the actual thesis, where you will have considerably more space to devote to it.

While the review does not need to be extensive at this stage, the more legwork you do now to see what is out there, the less will be remaining to do once you start on the actual PhD. And the better position you would be to hit the deck running with the investigative part at an early stage rather than spending a great deal of additional time later on review work, which many students find the least interesting aspect of the research process. Conducting a thorough review from the outset also diminishes the chances that you subsequently discover an existing paper that already accomplished exactly what you have done.

4.2.5   The research objectives

This section is at the heart of the whole proposal and outlines what you aim to study and achieve from the work. It can either be in the form of a set of questions or hypotheses or a group of aims and objectives. Be succinct and clear on what these are. Although your research objectives will likely change as you get deeper into the PhD study, thinking carefully about them now will help you clarify the methods and data aspects and ensure that these parts of the proposal are coherent.

You will need to identify a way to explain your ideas for the investigation. This can be in one of several ways, or a combination of them, where you provide:
  • A set of statements about what you plan to do, or research aims
  • A set of research questions

- A set of hypotheses

Any of these are acceptable, and they can be viewed as equivalent ways of expressing the same ideas. It usually works best to have multiple research questions, aims or hypotheses. Even if you have one core aim, try to break it down into a set of sub-aims, which will make the task of addressing it more manageable, even though you probably do not have each part of the core aim fully worked through at this stage. Having several aims will also make the purpose appear more substantive and facilitate having separate pieces of analysis that collectively make enough to constitute a PhD. Perhaps 2–4 aims is about the right number; more than that would seem excessive and infeasible to address in detail given the time constraints in the proposal document. Using a fictional example to illustrate, you could write the part outlining one of your research objectives as follows:

'The overall aim of my thesis is to investigate the impact of the tone of earnings announcements on UK companies' share prices. In the first empirical chapter, I will analyse the relationship between the sentiment expressed in the reports and changes in the share price within a window from 20 trading days before to 20 days after the announcement. I will also examine the impact on the volatility of stock returns and trading volume during the event window. I will draw out the implications of the findings for the way in which companies can express their earnings reports to encourage particular market reactions.'

When expressing your aims in writing, there are many key verbs that you can use to describe what you wish to do (and if you have several aims, try not to use the same word repeatedly but make use of its synonyms), for example: assess, calculate, compare, compute, contrast, determine, evaluate, explain, explore, identify, investigate, summarise, propose, understand.

Ideally, the aims will cover all aspects of the investigative work from the initial part to the conclusions where you would draw together the findings and propose policy recommendations. So the first aim could use words such as describe, summarise, or understand (with regards to the data or phenomenon under study). The second aim or aims could use words such as: explain, assess, or investigate, as this is the part where you would be trying to determine why something happened using causal relationships. The final aims could then relate to the broader implications of your findings, such as identifying recommendations for firms or regulators or investors, and so on. Note that there is no need to include general aims that would apply to every PhD irrespective of the subject matter (e.g., 'I will review the literature', or 'I will summarise my findings'). Of course you will do that since all studies do, and these are requirements, so there is no need to list them.

In principle, a researcher following a positivist scientific approach should specify the research aims first and then proceed to collect the data and analyse it, as discussed in section 2.3. However, in reality many researchers get some data, play around with it, see if they can generate some impressive results, and then try to 'retro-fit' a set of aims or a theoretical model that can explain what they observe. Although, strictly, such an ordering of the steps can lead to issues around data mining, finding spurious relationships, and misattributing the causes, it is common practice in accounting and finance research. And realistically, provided that your drafting is careful, nobody will know when reading your work that the output was generated first and the aims were written after. Therefore, in reality, you will be able to modify your research aims at a later stage when you have had the opportunity to dig deeper into the literature, collect your data and begin the investigative work.

4.2.6   The methodology and data section

This section will probably be brief and merely outline the approach you will use at a high level. You only need to present enough detail to show the reader that you have thought about how you will attack your research questions and to inspire sufficient confidence that you are knowledgeable about your chosen methods. These will probably be tentative at this stage to be updated and refined as you read more and start the investigative work later. As for the aims and title, you will not be forced to stick rigidly to the methodological approach and data sources you specified in the proposal. Returning to the example used above, the kind of structure you could use here is as follows:

> 'I will obtain daily share price and trading volume data over the past five years on all listed stocks that are or were members of the FTSE100 using Bloomberg. I will estimate the daily returns to each stock use a rolling window to calculate the standard deviations of returns as a measure of volatility. I will download the earnings announcements from the Dow Jones Newswire database. The sentiment analysis will use a dictionary of positive and negative words based on the approach developed by Loughran and McDonald (2011). The sample will be split into sub-groups based on whether the sentiment is positive, negative or neutral. An event study will then be used with a 40-day window centred on the announcement with the abnormal returns examined and compared for each group.'

Note that, unless your proposal is very short (a page or two), you would need to provide more detail than this on your methods and data collection. The amount you write on this aspect should be proportionate to the overall length of the proposal along the lines of the suggestions in Table 4.1 above.

4.2.7   The timeline

This part needs to demonstrate to your prospective supervisor that you have thought about the feasibility of the work in terms of how long each stage is likely to take and in what order you expect to undertake the steps. It is useful to be compelled to think about this, and although your supervisor won't hold you to meeting the exact dates for each section, it will help establish a framework so that you can gauge your progress as you proceed through each stage of the research. Think about the tasks to be done for the timeline, which could comprise the following list assuming that the thesis involves three investigative studies:

Preparation and training
1. Meet with supervisor to discuss submitted proposal and assess any training needs
2. Undertake training programme and advanced subject matter modules
3. Begin detailed literature gathering
4. Commence the first draft of the literature review
5. Complete the draft of the literature review and submit it to the supervisor for comment
6. Discuss whether ethical approval is needed and, if so, complete and submit the form

Study 1
7. (Re)formulate research aims or hypotheses
8. Determine methods to be used
9. Consider data requirements
10. Check data access and availability
11. Download data or conduct survey (including the pilot), interviews or experiments
12. Conduct preliminary data analysis and produce descriptive summaries
13. Conduct principal data analysis and create results tables
14. Write first draft of study 1
15. Send draft of study 1 to supervisor and others for comments

Study 2
16. Repeat steps as above for study 1
17. At the same time, continue polishing draft of study 1
18. Present study 1 at conferences

Study 3
19. Repeat steps as above for study 1
20. At the same time, continue polishing draft of study 2
21. Present study 2 at conferences
22. Consider submitting study 1 to a journal for possible publication
23. Polish study 3

'Writing up stage'
24. Write the first draft of the entire thesis document
25. Send draft to supervisor and others; modify in the light of the comments
26. Prepare study 2 for publication
27. Present study 3 at conferences
28. Undertake final checking, polishing and submission of the draft
29. Await and prepare for viva exam

Table 4.2: Sample timeline for a PhD

Task	Year of study	Months	Time taken (months)	Detailed summary of the step
Attend training modules	1	Oct-Jun	9	Attend any taught subject matter modules, philosophy of research, develop key skills in coding, data collection etc.
Literature review	1	Oct-Jan	4	Gather reference list; detailed reading; draft review; comments from supervisor
Reformulate research proposal	1	Dec-Feb	3	Rewrite proposal based on literature reading and feedback from supervisor
Study 1	1–2	Mar-Nov	9	Complete all aspects of the first investigative chapter, including data collection, analysis and write-up
Study 2	2	Dec-Aug	9	Complete all aspects of the second investigative chapter, including data collection, analysis and write-up
Study 3	2–3	Sep-Mar	7	Complete all aspects of the third investigative chapter, including data collection, analysis and write-up
Complete & refine the draft	3	Apr-Sep	6	Write introductory and concluding chapters, and then the abstract; complete first draft; proof-read and get feedback from supervisor and others; polish, make final changes and checks

30. Prepare study 3 for publication
31. Undertake post-viva corrections, if any

This list probably involves more detail than is necessary, in particular in the later stages, but it should provide some suggestions as to what to put in your proposal timetable and it needs to be personalised. There are several ways to construct a timeline, which could be anything from a brief and straightforward list to a formal flow diagram or Gantt chart. A basic list-type structure (including only the primary headings) would be as depicted in Table 4.2, assuming that you aim to complete the thesis in exactly three years.

A Gantt chart (named after its inventor, Henry Gantt) is simply a chart demonstrating how a project (or in this case, a PhD) will be structured and the timescale over which it is expected to progress. It shows the same information as the table above but in a slightly different format, and an example of the chart is given in

Table 4.3.

Things will likely go wrong at some point, and therefore it is advisable to build some slack into each stage. Producing a Gantt chart is quite a useful exercise even if you are not formally required to submit it, since it encourages you to think about how long you expect each aspect of the PhD to take and in what order to carry out each task. Once you have completed the thesis, you could then compare the chart you produced before starting with the outturn; I would guess that every aspect will have taken longer than you had anticipated.

4.2.8 Other sections

While the list above probably covers everything that the majority of proposals would include, there are several other aspects to consider writing something about:

- Can you identify (albeit you are at a preliminary stage) any practical issues that you might face in progressing the research (e.g., difficulties in getting respondents to engage with a survey) and note them down to get early suggestions on how to avoid or mitigate these problems? This is a forward-looking risk assessment demonstrating that you have considered potential hitches you may face, although, of course, many different things can go wrong and hence it is impossible to predict most of them.
- Will you need to undertake any specific training or development to achieve what you want to – for example, learning a new quantitative or interview technique? Again, noting this down will maximise the chances that you are pointed in the right direction to receive the support required, and it will create a favourable impression that you have carefully considered all of the issues from the outset.
- Will you need ethics approval, if so, for which parts of the work and why? If you are using only secondary data from a third-party website (e.g., downloaded from FAME or Bloomberg), then a simple statement that you have considered any ethical issues that may arise and you believe that no ethics committee approval will be necessary would be sufficient.

4.2.9 What can go wrong with a proposal?

Proposals tend to vary much more in terms of their quality than theses, simply because students treat the former with a wider variation in seriousness, owing to them usually not being assessed. And as discussed above, proposals are hard to write since many students have had no prior experience of undertaking independent research, let alone on the topic they intend to study for their PhD.

Some applicants put a minimal amount of effort into their proposals, barely writing a few lines off the tops of their heads, while others agonise for weeks and produce a detailed and polished document. However, when students put in the work to draft a proposal but which is nonetheless still weak, it is usually one of the issues in the following list that applies.

Task	Year 1												Year 2												Year 3											
	O	N	D	J	F	M	A	M	J	J	A	S	O	N	D	J	F	M	A	M	J	J	A	S	O	N	D	J	F	M	A	M	J	J	A	S
Attend training	■	■	■																																	
Literature review			■	■	■	■																														
Reformulate proposal						■	■	■																												
Study 1					■	■	■	■	■	■	■	■	■																							
Study 2														■	■	■	■	■	■	■																
Study 3																									■	■	■	■	■	■						
Complete & refine draft																															■	■	■	■	■	■

Table 4.3: Sample basic Gantt chart for a PhD

- Weak structure or poor writing style
- No originality in the idea or no imagination
- The research idea is either trivial or too all-encompassing and thus not feasible
- The idea is highly practical but not amenable to scholarly study
- Too much literature review or the review is out of date
- No consideration at all given to data collection and whether this is likely to be too costly or time-consuming
- A requirement to obtain confidential information or 'buy-in' from interview participants who will have no incentives to be involved
- Too much detail on the models to be used, including derivations and pages of algebra
- The writing is rambling and repetitive
- Failure to cite fundamental studies or inaccurately reporting them
- Too many or too few references

Some of these problems relate to the structure or style of the proposal document while others track back to the research aims or choice of topic. Evidently, a high quality proposal can only be constructed on the basis of clear research aims and issues with writing the document can reveal more fundamental problems with the underpinning research ideas that need to be addressed.

Until you finally get the go-ahead from your supervisor to begin working on a specific topic, it is worth having a 'plan B up your sleeve'. As well as your fully worked up proposal that you have spent the time to craft into the required format and level of detail, you should also have a back-up idea that you could turn into a workable proposal fairly quickly if plan A falls flat for some reason (e.g., your supervisor suggests abandoning it, you cannot get the required data, or you realise it will be too arduous given the constraints). That way, although you would lose some time when having to work up the second idea to the development stage of the first, all will not be lost.

However, once you begin working on the PhD, if you encounter difficulties with your primary choice of topic, in the first instance, it is worth considering whether you can modify rather than abandon it. Changing the idea slightly implies that most of the reading you have already done will continue to be relevant. Beginning with something totally different is a more drastic action meaning that much of your previous work may have been needless, setting you back and wasting valuable time investigating another idea. At that stage, however, you will be able to discuss the options with your supervisor and thus be given support and guidance to make an informed choice about whether a change of topic is necessary or desirable.

Further reading

Many specialist texts exist on writing research proposals, but most are aimed at established academics who need to apply for funding rather than PhD students. Those written for the latter include O'Leary (2018), which provides a straightforward introduction, and the more comprehensive books by Denscombe (2019) and Punch (2016).

Chapter takeaways – top tips for success

- ❊ If you are required to submit a research proposal as part of your PhD application, first investigate what is needed in terms of the length and level of detail
- ❊ Ensure that your proposal is not 'review-heavy' where the literature review part swamps your own ideas and proposed methods
- ❊ The most important part of the proposal is the statement of research aims, questions or hypotheses
- ❊ Make preliminary decisions on the methods and sources of data that you will employ
- ❊ Draw up a timeline or Gantt chart. Even if this is not formally required, it will be helpful as a way for you to establish informal deadlines to determine whether you are on target or not
- ❊ Ensure that your proposal is as detailed, well-thought-out, and polished as possible since it can be used as a template from which to begin the actual PhD

5. YOUR PHD APPLICATION

Learning outcomes: this chapter covers

✓ Deciding where to apply
✓ Looking for funding
✓ What is needed in an application

5.1   What are the requirements to get on a PhD programme?

Before spending a significant amount of time preparing the materials for PhD applications, it is worth first reflecting on whether you are likely to meet the entry requirements. Each university website will clearly state their typical entry requirements, and these will vary somewhat between departments even within a university. The minimum entry requirement is likely to be an upper second class undergraduate degree an a relevant discipline (i.e., a subject closely related to what you intend to study for your PhD). For non-native English speakers who have not already undertaken a degree in English, there will probably be a language requirement of an IELTS (International English Language Testing System) score of seven or more.

5.1.1   Do you need a master's before beginning a PhD?

In the natural and physical sciences, it is standard practice for PhD students to be recruited immediately from a bachelor's degree, but in accounting and finance (along with other business and management fields), it is usually required to have an MSc degree first. The majority of applicants will have undertaken one-year taught programmes rather than a specialist research master's.

However, it is normal to apply during the master's year rather than waiting until the end, in which case you might receive an offer for a PhD place conditional upon achieving certain results at the MSc level. Waiting until you have completed the MSc might imply missing the following session's entry and a gap of up to a year before the PhD begins.

Note that it is almost never necessary to have a specialist research master's (an MRes or the equivalent) in order to apply, since appropriate research training will be provided in the first year of the PhD programme. Any applicants who do have such a master's, however, would probably be able to gain exemption from these training modules, allowing them to make faster progress with their research in the early stages after registration.

5.2 Where to apply

If you have decided to apply for places on PhD programmes, selecting the university is a major decision since you will be studying there for perhaps four years full-time, and the qualification will be yours for a lifetime. The first consideration is how many applications to make. Unfortunately, it is unlikely that you will be able to do this sequentially – in other words, making one or two applications, seeing the outcome and then deciding whether to make any more, since each institution is likely to take too long to reach a decision and leaving you insufficient time to approach other places before their deadlines. Therefore, you will need to make several applications more or less concurrently.

As described in section 5.5, to maximise your chances of success, you should tailor each application to the school, providing details about why you want to apply there that are unique to them. This process will be time-consuming and will limit the number of applications you can make, but it is better to do a handful of good ones than many that are rushed and poorly considered. Perhaps six to eight applications would be an appropriate number: fewer limits your opportunities while many more could be a waste of everyone's time. Obviously, if, having reviewed the entry criteria, you would consider yourself to be at best a marginal candidate, you would need to submit more applications to have a reasonable shot at getting an offer. It can be useful to spread your applications among schools with different levels of competition. This means targeting some applications at institutions that are less competitive, where you feel that your credentials well exceed the entry requirements, some applications at schools where you meet the entry requirements and you feel that your CV is at about the right level, and perhaps also sending one or two aspirational applications to highly prestigious schools where you feel that, realistically, your chances of success are slim but you would love to attend if you got the opportunity.

For many people, the first consideration when selecting the schools to which to apply will be the geographic location: where in the world do you want to be? Numerous accounting and finance schools around the world offer PhD progammes in English, and there will be a perhaps surprising degree of homogeneity across countries in terms of the structures of the programmes and what is expected of candidates. You can therefore afford to cast the net widely and consider more than one country. If your focus is the UK, you could begin with a list of universities, then narrow it down to those in a particular area if you prefer to, for example, be in or close to London. UCAS, which is the organisation through which undergraduates apply, have a useful map, which not only provides a list of UK universities, but also shows where they are in the country.[1]

Aside from the location, there are numerous other factors to consider when determining where to apply and, if you are successful at several institutions, which offer to accept:

- Research focus – do they conduct the kind of research you are interested in? Being in the right subject area is arguably the most crucial factor of all. If a particular school has little interest or expertise in the topics you want to study, it might be best to look elsewhere. Having a shared focus in a particular area will make your progress more certain and provide the best experience. Think about the subject matter and the methods that faculty employ in their own research in terms of theory versus practical implementations and secondary data analysis versus qualitative research

- Prestige and value of 'the brand' – in an ideal world, your doctoral research quality should speak for itself, irrespective of where you studied. But in reality, potential employers will use the ranking of your institution as a proxy for the quality of your research and you more generally. This situation is analogous to how scholars use journal rankings to evaluate the quality of a paper that they have not bothered to read. From that perspective, it makes sense to aim for a well-respected school or university but note that sometimes the school's rankings and the university's could be quite different. For instance, according to the Complete University Guide (accessed March 2021), Robert Gordon, a university in Scotland, was ranked 27th in accounting and finance but 72nd for the university as a whole. This demonstrates that rankings need to be interpreted with caution, are ambiguous and at best a rough guide to the prestige of a university. Many of the ratings include elements that are largely irrelevant for doctoral study, such as undergraduate student satisfaction, so focus on research quality. But don't get too hung up on the rankings – the quality of your supervision will be more important in determining the strength of your thesis than the status of the university or school, and supervision will not necessarily be better at more prestigious schools

- Availability of scholarships – funding their own studies for three or four years, including tuition fees and living expenses, will be an unviable proposition for

---

[1] https://www.ucas.com/file/172566/download?token=bwGYCgS9

the vast majority of applicants. Some schools have generous (albeit usually also highly competitive) scholarship schemes, covering tuition fees and paying a tax-free bursary; see the sub-section below for further details

- Availability of data or other specialist facilities – some institutions, particularly larger schools with bigger budgets, will have access to comprehensive databases such as Compustat, FAME, CRSP, etc. If your research requires access to such data, you will have no option but to ensure that you register at a subscribing institution

- Opportunities for paid teaching or research assistant roles – some universities make extensive use of PhD students to support their teaching or faculty research activities. This paid work can not only provide a valuable source of funds but also worthwhile work experience to bolster a CV

- Completion statistics – it is hard to assess the 'performance' of PhD programmes, but one way to evaluate the quality of the training, supervision and support is to examine the so-called completion statistics. These measure the proportion of students completing within four years and the proportion withdrawing or leaving with a lesser degree. Clearly, these statistics will be influenced by a range of factors, some of which will not relate to the programme's quality, but they will nonetheless provide an indication of whether there are serious issues with the PhD programme in that school

- Links with industry – some accounting and finance schools have particularly strong links with the accounting profession or the financial services sector. The faculty in such institutions are more likely to be engaged in research with a practical focus or undertaking consultancy projects. If your ultimate career objective is to join the industry rather than remaining in the academy post-graduation, having access to these contacts would be valuable

- Success in 'placements' – another way to measure a PhD programme's quality is according to the success that its graduates have in finding posts at other prestigious universities, central banks, regulators or companies

- Network of other PhD students – if the school has already established a strong cohort in your PhD area, not only will doing the research be more fun, but you will also have an easily accessible support network to rely on for everything from where to get data to where to get the best takeaways

- Taught modules access or requirements – some programmes, particularly at larger and more prestigious schools, have strict requirements in terms of taught modules that you must attend and pass during the first year (or two) of PhD registration. Depending on your background, interests and aspirations, this might be something you would value, but on the other hand, you might see it as a distraction that stops you from making quick progress with your research. There could also be a requirement to achieve a certain mark in each module, which comes with the risk that you could be removed from the programme if you don't make the grade

5.3 Financing your PhD

The fees for PhD programmes vary substantially, and while the annual figures are less than for some master's programmes in accounting and finance, the costs are nonetheless still high. At UK universities, students from the UK can expect to pay £4–5,000, while for overseas students the fees are likely to be within the range £15–20,000, although they could be as high as £25,000 for some of the most prestigious universities. These figures are annual, so while you might get a discount in year 4, you would pay this sum for at least three years. Fees per annum for part-time registration are roughly half their full-time equivalents, but spread over twice as many years.

It is advisable not to begin a PhD unless you are fairly confident that you will have sufficient funds to complete it: for instance, don't enrol if you just have enough savings to cover one year of tuition and living expenses in the hope that something will 'just turn up' to cover the costs in the second year. Usually, universities allocate scholarships that cover the entire registration period, not part of it, which means that you are almost never going to be awarded a scholarship in the second year if you didn't already receive one in the first. Part-time registration combined with outside employment to cover the costs might be a possibility although it has several disadvantages as discussed in subsection 1.2.2.

Some PhD studentships are advertised with scholarships that cover tuition fees plus a sum to finance living expenses of around £15,000 per year (tax-free and not counting towards taxable income). Some useful information is available at FindAPhD.[2] Scholarships can either be funded by an external body (such as the Economic and Social Research Council, ESRC) or by the university from its own resources. A university-funded scholarship might come with some teaching requirements or the expectation that recipients would act as research assistants for faculty members.

Scholarships are competitive, prestigious, and lucrative (compared with self-funding), but there is an important aspect to consider before applying. There are broadly two types of scholarship. The first is where the school seeks to recruit an excellent candidate with a submission on any topic of interest to colleagues. In such cases, the applicant would be free to select their own research focus so long as it is in an area where there is some supervision expertise across the faculty.

A second situation is where the school advertises opportunities for funded studentships on particular topics where the research objectives, methods and so on will have already been specified. Here, the candidate would have little scope to modify the agenda and would effectively be working on a topic of someone else's choosing. The benefit of this prescribed approach is that it removes the requirement for the student to identify their own topic, research aims, and so on, thus diminishing the scope for problems to arise due to the selection of an inappropriate subject focus. However, this situation is also very limiting: by pre-selecting the research area,

---

[2]https://www.findaphd.com/funding/guides/research-council-studentships.aspx

the student will not develop the transferrable skills associated with defining their own research agenda, which would have necessitated a significant amount of groundwork, reading and thought. Having had their thesis topic handed to them may come back to haunt the candidate later in their career if they complete the thesis but are then expected to develop their own research ideas, which they had not become accustomed to doing before or during their doctoral registration.

More importantly, working to someone else's research agenda can imply that a student ends up spending three or four years on a topic about which they have barely minimal interest. Working on a subject that you are not passionate about would be a tragedy, for the freedom to pursue your own curiosity is one of the major benefits of scholarly research, and being denied this opportunity would diminish the value of doing a PhD at all. When students inevitably face challenges with their study, it is an underpinning fascination of the subject that provides the strength to continue.

In summary, choosing a PhD scholarship on a narrowly defined, pre-selected subject might be initially appealing but could lead to problems and frustrations further down the line and therefore requires careful consideration.

5.3.1   Where to find funded PhD opportunities

Most institutions use their PhD programmes as a source of revenue, and therefore obtaining a place on the programme is usually not that challenging for suitably qualified applicants. So students with at least an upper second class undergraduate degree plus a merit-level pass (or an expectation of getting this if it is still in process) and a competently written (even if uninspiring, unoriginal or not entirely thought through) proposal are likely to receive several offers. While most applicants will have a high chance of securing a place on a given PhD programme, obtaining funding is far more difficult. Most accounting and finance departments will have only one or two scholarships to award per year from among, perhaps 20-50 applicants of whom 10-20 could have been offered places. Therefore, if a candidate needs to be good to get a place, they would need to be outstanding to have a reasonable chance of obtaining a scholarship. Such applicants are likely to have:

1. A first class undergraduate degree and a distinction at master's level (ideally from a prestigious university)
2. An excellent proposal – novel, engaging, and well written
3. A desire to work on a topic of particular relevance to the department
4. Made a connection with a prospective supervisor who acts as a champion for the application

It is possible that paid teaching or research assistant work will be available for PhD students in your department, but you should not rely on this as a source of income unless you have a contract or written assurance that such opportunities will definitely be offered to you.

Here are a few possibilities from the internet. Some of them will have opportunities that vary through the year, dependent upon which institutions are advertising at the time you are looking, and obviously, many will only advertise on their own website and not more widely. I would suggest looking at the sites for any schools you are particularly interested in to see what is available. Some scholarship-holders received them from an external agency or a corporate sponsorship, but the majority obtained them from within the university department – either from its own sources or from research council funding via the department.

- A list of funded accounting PhDs in US schools on the World Scholarship Forum website[3]
- A list for both accounting and finance, mainly covering the UK but also in other parts of Europe at FindAPhD[4]
- Several possibilities at UK universities on jobs.ac.uk[5]
- Several banking and finance scholarships, updated on a rolling basis on ScholarshipAd[6]
- One or two finance PhD scholarships, updated on a rolling basis, on the European Commission website[7]

5.4 When to apply

In the UK context, even though universities might continue to accept applications from self-funded students right through the summer for entry in September at the start of the next academic year, any funding is likely to be well gone before that since competition for it is so intense. It is usually the case that universities receive their best applications quite early in the cycle, which is no coincidence because high calibre students are often well-organised.

Some institutions will wait until a deadline (e.g., in March or April) and then review all the scholarship applications at the same time, while others will use their historical experience to assess them on an individual basis as they come in, and therefore any scholarships could be taken well before the official deadline. The danger for institutions that wait until later in the year is that their best candidates may have already been given and accepted an offer elsewhere. Consequently, the best time to apply is from October to January for entry in September, although it is still worth applying even if you miss that window. Don't apply before October for admission in the following September (effectively more than a year in advance) because this will cause confusion with applications for the current academic session. If you apply for a PhD while you are currently registered for a master's, the drawback

---

[3]https://worldscholarshipforum.com/phd-scholarships-for-accounting-students/

[4]https://www.findaphd.com/phds/accounting-and-finance/?20goD0

[5]https://www.jobs.ac.uk/search/?keywords=&location=&placeId=&activeFacet=subDisciplineFacet &resetFacet=&sortOrder=1&pageSize=25&startIndex=1&academicDisciplineFacet%5B0%5D= business-and-management-studies&subDisciplineFacet%5B0%5D=accountancy-and-finance&jobTypeFacet%5B0%5D=phds

[6]https://www.scholarshipsads.com/category/subject/banking-and-finance/

[7]https://euraxess.ec.europa.eu/jobs/606921

of doing so early in the cycle is that you will have completed little of it, and so the university to whom you are applying will have fewer performance measures from your master's on which to base their decision.

5.5   What will your application contain?

Your PhD application will probably comprise several elements:
- A CV or application form
- Copies of your transcripts or degree certificates
- At least one academic reference from your previous or current programme(s)
- A proposal
- A cover letter or personal statement

You can do relatively little to improve the first three components of your application, so you should focus on the final two, and these are the main aspects that differentiate outstanding candidates from good ones. Of these, the proposal is by far the most important, the hardest to write, and was the focus of the entirety of chapter 4 in this book.

The application form or CV

If you have some relevant work experience (such as doing some administrative or organisational work or customer service), this might have a minimal positive impact. Most importantly, the university will probably require at least an upper second-class honours degree in a relevant subject, plus usually a master's pass at the merit level. Realistically, to have an excellent chance to obtain a scholarship, you would need a first-class undergraduate degree and a master's distinction.

Although they are frequently told not to do so, PhD student recruiters often use the prestige of the applicants' prior universities as a proxy for the quality of their education, and so the more esteemed the institution that you studied at, the lower grade might be accepted for admission onto a PhD programme and the higher the chances of success.

The CV might be replaced by a specific application form that you are required to complete for each institution. Naturally, you should invest the time in drafting this as carefully as possible and in a way which casts your skills and experiences in the most favourable light. If you are currently attending a taught programme, the careers service in your university or school might be able to provide advice or feedback on your CV or application form.

The references

The number of references required will vary between institutions but is likely to be two or three. Clearly, given that the PhD is a university qualification, academic references will carry more weight, although one of the referees could be a current or former employer, especially if you have been away from education for some time. Ideally, given that it is the closest thing to doing a PhD you could have previously experienced, one of the referees will be your current or former research project supervisor, who could then discuss how you tackled the project and the relevant skills that you developed. Another referee could be your personal tutor or the convenor of a module where you performed particularly well.

Students tend to believe that a reference from a more senior academic (e.g., a full professor or a head of department) would hold more prestige and impress the selection panel, but in my view this is untrue for a PhD application (it might have more validity when applying for academic posts, though). More important is that you find someone who is going to use a lot of superlatives when describing your work than someone famous who will write something bland. Always check with your referees that they are willing to provide a reference before putting their names forward. Also, find out whether the institution(s) you are applying to want the references submitted with your application or the school will ask for them subsequently directly from the referees.

Some referees will be happy for you to see what they have written, but in general, the reference is a confidential document between the person writing it and the place to which they are sending it. In principle, in the UK under the Data Protection Act you can request to see your references from the places to which you have applied. But if you make such a request, it is likely that they will inform your referee(s), who might be unhappy and unwilling to provide further references. It is best to select your referees carefully and then trust that they will write the most favourable reference that they can whilst remaining honest.

If one or more of your applications is successful and you take up a place there, drop your referees an e-mail to let them know and thank them again for their support. Not only will this courtesy make them glad that writing the reference was worthwhile, staying in contact with them could be valuable if you might need their help again in the future. One day, you could be a fellow academic alongside them so don't lose a valuable contact.

The personal statement

The cover letter or personal statement (depending on the requirements of the admissions process in that institution) needs to be more general than the proposal and avoid overlapping too much with it. It should be no more than a page long, and it should briefly summarise your background and achievements, explain the programme that you are applying for and why. You need to explain your motivation for wanting to do a PhD and perhaps mention your longer term career ambitions. The cover letter or personal statement both need to be brief – a maximum of one page (single-spaced) will be sufficient.

Make sure that you personalise each application to that school, explaining why you think it will be a fantastic place to study. In other words, what is it that attracted you to this school – for example, a specific research specialisation, the facilities and data access, or are there particular members of staff in that area? This activity will be time-consuming but worthwhile as it will be much more impressive than a generic

'Dear Sir / Madam'-type letter that only writes about you and not the school.

Your application will also need to demonstrate commitment and resilience. The academics reading your application will be aware of the importance of these attributes in determining which students will succeed and which will throw in the towel part-way through.

In addition, as part of the selection process, you may be required to attend an interview – either in-person or on-line. The purpose of the interview will be to assess your level of spoken English (if you are not a native speaker) and what kind of person you might be to work with, as well as asking questions about:

- Your motivation to do a PhD
- Your knowledge of the subject area
- Your career ambitions
- Your skills in relevant related areas (e.g., programming)
- Whether you are familiar with the school, its staff and its characteristics

At the most prestigious schools, preference might be given to those who state that their career intention is to obtain a job in the academy. Having their PhD studentd aiming for a lectureship (assistant professorship) post is desirable for the institution because a characteristic of schools that is assessed in ranking measures and accreditations is the successes they have had in 'placing' students at other prestigious universities.

The outcome of your application

Once you hear from the department to which you applied, which might take a couple of months or even longer, hopefully it will be a conditional or unconditional offer. If you are currently in the process of sitting for a master's degree, the PhD offer might be conditional upon you receiving at least a pass with merit overall.

But if your application for a place on the PhD programme is rejected, don't be too disheartened. Check the standard entry criteria again on the university web site and see if your qualifications and background fit the bill. If they ask for an upper second class undergraduate degree while you have a lower second, that could be the reason. Whether this is the case or not, you could ask for feedback on your application by writing a polite e-mail to either the Programme Director or Programme Administrator – explain that while you were disappointed and of course you respect their decision not to offer you a place, you would appreciate receiving some feedback on why you were rejected since this will be invaluable in helping you to make future applications to other institutions stronger. If they do provide a rationale for their decision and it is that your qualifications were not good enough, consider applying to other universities with less stringent requirements. On the other hand, if the response is that the proposal was not sufficiently strong, or did not spark any supervisory interest, it is worth going through it again to see if you can strengthen it or, if time permits, begin again with a different idea. Try to get an opinion and detailed comments from a member of staff, current PhD student or post doc at your current or most recent university before you apply elsewhere.

Usually, if you are rejected from a particular institution, you will not have the chance to reapply, at least not for that academic year, whatever the reason for rejection, so you will need to get over it and move on to seek other opportunities.

If you get the occasion to visit a university from which you have received an offer (or if it is feasible to attend an in-person interview), I would strongly recommend taking up the possibility. If you do undertake a PhD there, you will be spending a great deal of time in the school and finding out as much as you can about it and getting a feel for the place will help you make an informed choice. You would obtain a much better idea of the extent of facilities for PhD students (working environment and desk space, computer and data access, etc.) by looking directly rather than at pictures of them. You could also chat informally with current PhD students and staff about the environment and ethos as well as their research to see if there is common ground with your interests.

5.5.1 Do you need to find your own PhD supervisor?

The issues around PhD supervision are discussed at length in section 6.3, but the one that will concern you at the application stage is whether you need to look for your own supervisor. In most cases, technically the answer to this question is 'no', since your application materials would be circulated to all prospective supervisors in the department after you have submitted them. Any member of staff who expressed an interest would then follow up, probably by contacting you to arrange a discussion or interview.

However, in my experience, one of the primary reasons that PhD applications do not succeed is because there is no interest from potential supervisors in working on that topic. This could be because they view of the proposal as being of insufficient quality, indicating perhaps that the student might not have the skills to do good research, or the focus specified in the proposal is not one that fits within their sphere of expertise. If one potential supervisor feels that the topic is not in their area of specialisation, there might be others whose research interests are more closely aligned with those of the applicant. However, if there is no 'fit' between the proposal topic and any of the faculty in the department, this might suggest that the focus proposed by the candidate is too esoteric or not appropriate for PhD study.

Even if there is no formal requirement to identify your own supervisor before applying, if you can identify one who is interested in what you propose to study and you can strike up an e-mail exchange with them, your chances of subsequent admission on to the programme are substantially increased. For this reason, once you have selected a list of university departments that you intend to apply to, it is worth going through the faculty list and identifying relevant faculty members who cover the same broad area that you intend to conduct your research in. Some applicants focus only on senior academics, but as discussed in section 6.3, these people are likely to be inundated with similar e-mails and so your chances of success are substantially increased if you also contact faculty at the associate professor / reader / senior lecturer and assistant professor / lecturer levels.

It is advisable to contact people sequentially within each institution and wait for their replies, avoiding the temptation to spam the entire department. Academics talk to one another and if you do write to a large group in one go, they will find out and be irritated, and that will likely be the end of your chance of admission there. Even when a department is taking new students (which they usually will every year), this will not imply that every member of staff is available – it is usually left to each individual academic to decide whether they wish to take any new PhD students, and if so how many and which ones. Sometimes staff members state on their websites whether they are accepting new PhD students and, if so, on which subjects, which will avoid you wasting time writing to those who are already up to their capacity limit.

When you write to a member of staff for the first time, choose your wording carefully and seek to create a good impression. Ensure that you initially address them formally using their correct title (Professor, Dr, etc.) depending on their level of seniority. Explain who you are and what your interests are. It's fine to say that you have read some of their work and that you found it inspiring but be sincere and only mention it if you really did look at it and it is relevant to your proposed topic. Ask whether they are accepting any new supervisions for the next academic year. If their response is not, you could ask for recommendations of which among their colleagues you could contact instead. Most academics will reply to your e-mail, but don't be despondent if some don't as they probably receive many such contacts, and even if you don't initially get much interest, persevere and keep writing to others.

Chapter takeaways – top tips for success

⊛ Be aspirational but realistic in your choices of schools to apply to. Thoroughly research each one before submitting an application

⊛ Scholarships are particularly competitive so apply early and seek opportunities for paid teaching or research assistance

⊛ Take time on your proposal and cover letter, ensuring that the latter is personalised for each school you are applying to

⊛ Although you do not need to identify a supervisor before applying, your application stands a better chance if you have already established a rapport by e-mail with a prospective supervisor

Doing the research

6. YOUR TIME AND SUPERVISOR

Learning outcomes: this chapter covers

✓ How to stay focused
✓ How to build your network
✓ How to manage your time
✓ What you can and cannot expect from your supervisor
✓ How to handle your supervisor

6.1 Time management

6.1.1 How much time is needed?

Effective time management is probably the most valuable talent you will need to master to complete the thesis to the best of your ability. This is an essential skill for the long-term because so many aspects of work and life are improved if you can organise yourself, stay on track, and plan ahead.

Before you get deeply into your research, it is worthwhile to consider that an MPhil should constitute two years' of full-time study and a PhD three years', and the volume of work in the completed thesis must be at least commensurate with this amount of time. In other words, if you are supposed to have spent approximately three years on the PhD overall (including reading, data collection, analysis and writing), will your completed thesis give the impression that you spent that long on it?

An essential aspect of the time-management involved in doing research is to develop self-discipline. One of the most exciting features of conducting research is that you will have considerable latitude to run the doctoral project at your own timescale and in the order you want. This freedom also brings a responsibility to pace yourself and to make progress continually. If you leave it until the last minute, it will be infeasible to complete the required study, investigation and writing in a few weeks or even months. Initially, the amount of time you have available to complete the PhD will seem vast, but the weeks and months will simply fly by. Programmes include this amount of time for a reason – because that is approximately how long a typical student will need. So you need to get started straight away and regularly work on the thesis until it is completed.

Equally, it is important not to put in so many hours from the outset that you burn out. Think of the registration period as a marathon, and to get to the finishing line, you will need to pace yourself. If you set off too quickly, you will tire and run out of steam. On the other hand, if you stop off for a series of long breaks along the way, you won't get to the end either.

The supervision of PhD dissertations is very 'hands-off' so that nobody will be standing behind you on a day-to-day basis telling you what to do, meaning that you must motivate yourself to make gradual progress with the work to stay on track and complete on time. In particular, successfully finishing requires a certain amount of mental resilience – not only to keep working on it when there always seem to be other calls on your time but also to keep plugging away at it when things seem to be going wrong. It would be easy to lose heart and give up in such circumstances, so every completed dissertation implies a certain amount of dogged determination and triumph in the face of adversity on the part of the person who wrote it.

Since there are so few real deadlines during the entire PhD registration period, you need to set some artificial ones and try to stick to them. And as you progress towards the final stages, always make sure that you aim to finish well before the official deadline to allow for a careful last check through and have some slack in case things go wrong.

The guidance on what to do and when is likely to be at arm's length, and hence you need to impose your own structure to avoid falling behind and feeling a lot of stress as you rush at the end. Most aspects of a university degree have a framework where you are answerable to someone (usually a tutor or essay marker) within a fairly narrow time window, but the PhD programme is much less structured, and hence you will need to learn to become answerable to yourself. In some ways, the situation is akin to being self-employed, where you have to establish your own goals and be disappointed with yourself if you fail to achieve them.

The best approach is to start working on the PhD right away and set aside regular time every week to make progress with it. If you are registered full-time, treat the PhD like a job and make sure that you work on it at least five days most weeks. Draw up a rough timeline to completion like the ones discussed in subsection 4.2.7 and try to stick to it. It is also useful to build in some slack at the end for unforeseen problems with the research itself or with other work that unexpectedly eats into your research schedule. Don't overestimate what can be achieved in the time that you have. It is better to complete a solid PhD on time than to attempt something earth-shattering but only get part-way through it.

To obtain the most out of the PhD while keeping your stress at an acceptable level will require you to work efficiently. This means that you will need to focus on what is required in order to impress the thesis examiners, something that this book is explicitly designed to help with. You will want to minimise the amount of time you waste with pointless or fruitless work.

You will also need to be able to prioritise, which means that at certain points, any urgent tasks arising are completed first, and important work on your PhD dissertation may have to wait. Some people find that making lists of all the jobs they have to do, and keeping the list up to date, helps them to set priorities and ensure that nothing gets forgotten or falls behind.

6.1.2 Avoiding procrastination

Everyone goes through periods in their working lives where they tend to procrastinate. Procrastination means finding any and every excuse not to undertake an important task, putting it off as long as possible. Completing a PhD thesis is no exception, and there will be numerous instances where you will be at risk of procrastinating – for example, by doing some housework or tidying a cupboard rather than getting started on drafting your literature review. It is as if you convince yourself that you cannot focus on this big and important task until every small and insignificant distraction is out of the way. Procrastination can manifest itself in many different ways, including:

- Prioritising unimportant tasks that could have waited (or not been done at all)
- Spending excessive amounts of time planning how you will tackle various aspects of the PhD rather than just getting on with them
- Starting work on a particular dissertation-related task but never making any progress
- Focusing on trivial aspects such as the font size or page layout rather than the substance of the writing

Procrastination often arises from a 'mental block' where you can't bear to think about doing a particular task because the intellectual exertion required is so considerable. It is essential to tackle outbreaks of procrastination before they eat away at significant portions of the available time. Procrastination usually occurs at points where the effort needed is the most considerable, or the task is deadly dull such as:

- The very beginning of a new aspect of the research, and you don't know where to start
- Any aspect involving writing, as this is the part of the whole task that students typically find the most challenging (and least enjoyable)
- Tackling a massive pile of papers to read and summarise for the review

- Gathering or cleaning the data, which might be time-consuming and monotonous
- Formatting the tables and improving the presentation
- Reading through and polishing a rough draft

The trick to resolving all of these issues is simply to get started. Worrying too much about planning and setting the perfect conditions for progress mean that you delay beginning the task and lose valuable time. Invariably, once you have started, you will discover that you make much quicker progress than you expected. And improving an existing spreadsheet, programming code, or draft is a much more straightforward and less painful task than beginning from scratch.

Another trick to make progress and avoid blocks is to plan a system of rewards for yourself and resolve not to take a treat, such as a trip to the pub/cinema/clothes shop, until you have reached your self-established target, which might be to write 2,000 words of the introduction to an empirical chapter. Don't delay, start right away.

In addition to mental blocks, a further reason why students sometimes progress slowly is their hesitance because they experience 'imposter syndrome' where they doubt their own ability to complete the thesis. Such feelings are pervasive, and if this happens to you, remember that you were accepted onto the programme, and therefore you must have possessed the requisite skills and qualifications. You have also made it through the programme this far, and thus you have credibility as a PhD student.All of your classmates will be going through the same steps, and no doubt many of them will be feeling the same trepidation. As you progress through the tasks involved, your confidence will grow.

6.1.3   Organise your time

Some aspects of the PhD process require more focus and mental effort than others. For instance, interpreting results, writing and debugging code, and writing the abstract all need intense concentration. Try to time the tasks to conduct the most demanding parts when you are at your best cognitively and the least distracted. Other aspects, such as formatting tables, inputting results, completing and checking the reference list, require less mental effort and progress with these tasks can still be made when you are somewhat tired or distracted (e.g., waiting for a train or plane). These sorts of tasks can also be dipped in and out of rapidly without the need to 'get in the zone' and so can be accomplished during short stretches of otherwise dead time. Having a tablet or laptop computer rather than just a desktop will help make this possible since you can then work outside of the home and on the move. Never spend time idling when you could be making progress with some aspect or other of your thesis.

When you are extremely busy at various points in life, the only way to simultaneously stay on top of everything is to work harder than you were previously accustomed to. One way to fit more into the day is simply to make the day longer by, for instance, getting up an hour earlier or going to bed later, depending on whether you are an early riser or a night person. Although, of course, maintaining sufficient sleep is important, getting into the habit of not lying in bed will help you to schedule more work time; once the dissertation is submitted, you will be able to revert to your previous pattern.

Finally, if you are really struggling with a particular aspect of the work or your motivation more generally, seek help from your supervisor, other students, or a university study skills advisor. They will all be well used to dealing with these sorts of issues and geared up to provide support.

Mix it up

Some people naturally have a high boredom threshold and can continue with the same task for a prolonged period without losing enthusiasm or focus. But others experience task fatigue when they have had enough of what they are doing, and their productivity and concentration start to decline. To avoid this, try to mix the tasks so that you can make progress with several aspects more or less concurrently – for example, by writing up the methodology section at the same time as running statistical models to analyse the data. While they are related, the two tasks require different skills and can therefore be interspersed to limit monotony.

6.1.4   Get motivated and get organised: Some initial tips for success

The PhD is likely the most significant undertaking of your life so far and the most time-consuming, so get motivated and organised. As well as the time management ideas presented above, you might find that working with music in the background helps you concentrate and avoids boredom. It also drowns out other people's noise, although some people nonetheless prefer silence.

I do believe, though, that seeing moving visual images while trying to read or write is a distraction. The radio, Spotify or Amazon Music, etc. are ok but switch the TV, computer games and YouTube off. Also, turn off the notifications from every app on all your devices to have as few disturbances as possible while you are working.

As well as establishing a timeline, think about where, when and how you will study for your PhD. The more ideal the conditions you can create, the better the quality of the work produced.

Where

Find somewhere comfortable, in a place you won't be disturbed, where there are not too many distractions, and you feel creative. That might be the library, in a garden (weather permitting), or by the window in a coffee shop. It might even be sitting in the lounge on the sofa or at the desk in your room – whatever works for you. Wherever you work, make your study area clutter-free, which will help you think more clearly. Remember, a tidy desk is a tidy mind.

When

Setting aside regular, timetabled hours is more likely to lead to good progress than irregular blocks. It is best to treat your research as you would a lecture series or a paid job – prioritise it, drop it into your calendar, and fit other things in your schedule around it. If any non-essential activities clash with your allocated research time, then refuse them; when any time is lost from the research schedule, try to replace it somewhere else during that week. Like preparing for participation in a sports event, while missing one training session almost certainly won't affect your ultimate performance, skipping one workout is the beginning of a slippery slope to getting out of the habit altogether and falling far behind.

How

Research is not a process that moves in a straight line with a constant rate of progress. Sometimes things will go awry, and you will waste hours chasing down an alley that leads nowhere. There will also be instances where you are stuck and unsure of how to proceed. Be prepared for these occurrences and don't become disheartened over minor setbacks. Other days, something you anticipate being tricky and time-consuming will turn out to be much more straightforward than you expected. The good days and the bad will balance out to some extent.

Try to anticipate in advance when you are likely to face delays in waiting for other people to complete tasks, including waiting for your supervisor to read your proposal or comment on drafts of the document, waiting for responses to your survey to come in, or when you have to book access to a terminal for data collection. Rather than having dead time when you are not able to make any progress, you could aim to do other work during those periods, such as brushing up on your coding skills or engaging in further reading or writing.

6.1.5   Paid teaching and research assistance

Conducting paid work alongside your thesis registration is a valuable way to earn extra money, develop your skills and knowledge, expand your network of close contacts, and make a worthwhile addition to your CV. This work could involve teaching small group seminars, marking essays or projects, or acting as a research assistant for an established staff member (collecting data, estimating models, gathering references) or on a funded project. There are several ways that you can make the most of these opportunities:

- Ensure that you do not spend so long conducting additional work that you get behind with your PhD. This is a significant danger, and it would be a disaster if you ended up bumping close to the maximum registration deadline. Remember that you are likely to earn far more as a full-time employee with a PhD than as a part-time paid helper without one
- Try to limit paid work to those tasks that will not only provide financial support but will also strengthen your skills and CV. Having some relevant

work experience can make your subsequent job applications stronger as a more rounded prospect than someone with a pure educational background

- If you are asked to become involved with a project outside of your PhD as a research assistant, see whether you might also be able to make a 'higher level' intellectual contribution to the work so that you would be given a co-authorship of the resulting output. A further co-authored piece would be enormously valuable if you were applying for an academic post

6.1.6 Don't take an internship part-way through your PhD!

It seems to be increasingly common for students to decide to take time out part-way through their doctoral studies to undertake either paid employment or an internship. This is particularly true of students who are aiming at a career in central banks or the private sector. Such opportunities might appear enticing to obtain work experience doing something interesting and applying some of the ideas and skills that you amassed so far by working on your thesis. The organisations are also typically highly enthusiastic about hiring PhD-level interns, for these candidates are evidently enthusiastic, highly qualified and can do valuable work.

However, in my view taking such an internship is both unnecessary and counter-productive. Taking six months or a year out from your PhD will mean that you will lose momentum with your research and an such an extended break is likely to diminish the quality of the work when you return to it. If you have hit a wall with the investigative part of your studies or your enthusiasm is waning, it is better to take a week or two of holidays to relax than take a year of poorly paid employment. Internships rarely leave the post holder with any spare time to also make progress with their thesis, and so this inevitably sits on the shelf until they return to university. There is also a significant danger that a prolonged period away from study makes it likely that the former student will never return to complete their studies, and while they will have learned many new and valuable skills along the way, all the efforts they made before leaving will not lead to a formal qualification.

Internship roles are usually very poorly paid, with the remuneration just a token (and the pay will be taxable, unlike a university scholarship) sum that is barely enough to live on so it is preferable to wait until completing the PhD and seeking employment as a doctoral graduate rather than a doctoral candidate. Having prior work experience is far less important for someone with a PhD than for a master's graduate, as it is such a high-level, specialised qualification. My advice is therefore that once you have begun a PhD, leave full-time employment for after you have finished the thesis.

6.2 Some other organisational tips

6.2.1 Keep copies of everything

It is crucial to become accustomed to keeping more than one electronic copy of all of your files in case the primary version becomes lost or corrupted, and indeed, make backups of the backups and backups of the backups of the backups.

Be careful with version control, however, which means, in particular, not dragging a file in the wrong direction from one storage location to another so that you write over a new version of it with an old one. This is a disaster if it happens since there is probably no way to retrieve the more recent version unless you happened to have another backup of it already. One way around this is to rename the file every time you open it by, for example, including the date in the filename such as 'phd110221' would be the thesis draft as of 11 February 2021. This would ensure that you do not write over a file with an older edition, but you need to be vigilant that you always begin working on the latest prior version – a concern that does not arise if you keep the same filename and write over it. Whichever approach you use, ensure to use the latest version and not write over it or lose it.

Your university might have some free cloud storage space that you can use, which is ideal for backups since it cannot get lost or corrupted like a flash drive might. If not, or if you require more space to store data, code and documents, several commercial cloud storage options are available. Many of these operate a 'freemium' model, offering a modest amount of space for free, with the opportunity to purchase more if required. For example, at the time of writing, the following are examples of some of the free services available, although there are many others (use a search engine to find them):

- Apple iCloud provides 5Gb, which integrates seamlessly with Apple products and hence is ideal for Mac users[1]
- Google Drive provides 15Gb (shared with other Google products such as Gmail), and an app can be installed to facilitate transfers[2]
- Degoo provides 100Gb[3]
- Mega provides 50Gb, and an app can be installed to facilitate transfers[4]
- pCloud provides 10Gb, and an app can be installed to facilitate transfers[5]

Of course, there is nothing to stop you from making use of the free allocations from several providers and separating your files among them.

You should retain all of your notes, data spreadsheets, code, statistical output, intermediate drafts, and so on until after the point when you sit the viva voce. Doing this has at least three benefits. First, it will help to safeguard against any corrupted files or version control problems. It will also offer a fall-back in case you need

---

[1] https://www.icloud.com

[2] https://www.google.com/drive/

[3] https://degoo.com

[4] https://mega.io/start

[5] https://www.pcloud.com/lifetime-storage/?ref=1120

to check something, or you made some changes that you later realise rendered something incorrect when it was previously correct. Second, it would also provide a line of defence if you were to be in the situation where your department alleges that you have not done the work in your dissertation yourself. Third, if you conduct further research post-PhD, it is highly likely that some of your former data files or code will come in handy in your new projects.

6.2.2 Get your writing abilities up to scratch

All universities will offer some forms of writing support, either using on-line resources or via face-to-face sessions organised through their student services division. If you feel that your writing skills are not up to the job, it is worth enrolling in one of these – not just to improve your dissertation's quality but also to develop your aptitude for writing more generally.

You could use the requirement to complete the PhD as a reason to invest the time to upgrade those skills that could be strengthened and that you are likely to continue to use during your future career plans. Any relevant skill or knowledge gaps need to be addressed as early as possible during the dissertation registration period since, by the time these attributes are required, it may be too late to develop them.

6.2.3 Developing resilience

Inevitably, some aspects of your PhD will work out less well than you might have hoped, particularly relating to the data collection and analysis. For instance, if you anticipated getting 150 participants in your survey, but you ended up with only 52 usable responses. Or if you were aiming to conduct some fundamental analysis by manually going through all current FTSE100 constituents' accounts, but it took longer than you expected so that you only achieved half that number. Or you might have had a brilliant idea for an empirical model only to find when you estimate it that none of the coefficients is statistically significant and some have the wrong signs.

These kinds of issues are all part and parcel of academic research, and your examiners will appreciate this. You have no choice but to make the best of your data and results, whatever they are and to make the best of your writing, even if this is not your strongest skill. You are partly being assessed on how effectively you went through the process of conducting research and writing it up, not just how strong your findings are. Provided that your results are sufficiently plausible, none of these difficulties above with data or results would be disastrous. And with time and possibly a proof-reader, you could considerably improve the standard of exposition in the draft to deal with supervisor comments, as discussed in section 12.3.

Another situation where you might feel discouraged is if you believe that you have produced an excellent piece of work, only to receive scathing criticism from your supervisor or someone else who reads it. The greater the effort you have put into the draft up to that point, the more bruising such disparagement will be. More detail is given on this point in section 12.3, but the main message is that you must take it on the chin: pick yourself up, dust yourself down and carry on, trying to learn from the feedback.

More generally, there are some excellent free resources available on-line that discuss how to build your mental resilience so that you cope well with minor setbacks and learn to take them in your stride. These include:

- The American Psychological Association[6]
- Greater Good Magazine at Berkeley[7]
- A more detailed report at the Chartered Institute of Personnel and Development[8]
- An article specifically on building 'academic resilience'[9]

6.3   The role of the supervisor and what to expect

Supervisors have a crucial role in the development and progress of their PhD students and therefore this extensive section is devoted to a detailed discussion of their roles and responsibilities. The supervisor is sometimes referred to as a thesis advisor.

6.3.1   How do you choose your supervisor?

The short answer is 'you don't' since, almost invariably, you will have little opportunity to select your own supervisor. The process is usually that submitted application materials are circulated among all relevant faculty, and any showing interest is likely to become the supervisor(s), with the allocation of PhD students to supervisors resulting from the subject area and availability of the latter. Consequently, at the application stage, the supervisors will self-select rather than being chosen by the candidate.

Another opportunity you might have as an applicant to influence the process is choosing the subject area for the research proposal. If you select a topic related more closely to one particular individual's research, they would likely be a relevant supervisor. However, there is still usually no compulsion for a particular academic to agree to supervise a specific applicant, even if the former's research interests most closely relate to the latter's application.

It might be possible for you to affect who is likely to become your supervisor by writing, prior to your application, to individual members of staff with whom you would like to work. If you have struck up a useful e-mail exchange with them, they might pick up on your application when it is processed and request to the Director of the PhD programme that you are assigned to them.

It is best not to be overly concerned with who your supervisor might be or to experience supervisor envy, even if another PhD student's supervisor is much

---

[6]https://www.apa.org/topics/resilience/

[7]https://greatergood.berkeley.edu/article/item/five_science_backed_strategies_to_build_resilience

[8]https://www.cipd.co.uk/Images/developing-resilience_2011_tcm18-10576.pdf

[9]https://www.editage.com/insights/7-secrets-to-help-you-build-academic-resilience

more senior and more famous than yours or appears to be much more supportive. Supervisors are usually allocated based on their availability and coverage of the topic (admittedly with a certain element of randomness in the process), but most of the time, there is no scope for students to select a different supervisor or request a change unless something has gone seriously wrong. It would cause chaos, not to mention considerable embarrassment, if students were permitted to demand a particular supervisor on a whim.

All supervisors have their strengths and weaknesses. Although it is stereotyping somewhat, more senior academics will probably have more experience of the process and better knowledge of what constitutes a good thesis; but they might also be more aloof and less able to provide guidance on the detailed aspects of data collection and programming, for instance. So think positively, try to build a strong working relationship with the supervisor you have, and make use of their skills, whoever it is.

How many supervisors?

It was traditionally the case that UK and European students would have had a single supervisor throughout their registration. But more recently, universities have been requiring that there be two named supervisors for every student, in a nod towards the US model of supervision committees. Having two supervisors broadens the supervisory team's expertise and ensures continuity if one of them leaves the university or becomes otherwise unavailable. This approach also allows junior faculty to get on the job training in how to be a supervisor by going through the process as a second or back-up supervisor and following the lead of the more experienced, academic initially before becoming a primary supervisor in the future once they have accomplished a successful completion in a secondary role. A PhD supervision team including one party who is senior and accomplished with another who completed their own PhD more recently can work very well.

Occasionally, students have more supervisors where they initially had two but then the candidate's research moved direction or they started to use a particular methodological approach that their current supervisors are not experts in. Yet having more than two supervisors seems an overkill and a waste of a precious resource. It is not necessary for a member of staff to be formally named as a supervisor before they would be willing to help with specific aspects of a student's research.

6.3.2 Models for supervision

Different supervisors take varying approaches to the task of PhD supervision, and you have to follow their lead and fit in with their model for the process. Many different models for supervision will be acceptable within the department's general guidelines, so, to some extent, you have little choice but to 'go with the flow' and conform to the approach to the process that your allocated supervisor adopts.

One style is where the supervisor closely guides the student, meeting often (possibly weekly), and providing frequent feedback with quite detailed suggestions on how to proceed and what to work on until the next meeting. In this context, the

PhD student is almost treated as a research assistant, with the supervisor providing guidance on the development of the research agenda from the outset, which will likely be on the topics that the latter usually works on. Student and supervisor work closely together, publish work from the thesis together, and any applicant interested in covering a different research area would be encouraged to seek a different supervisor.

The other approach to supervision is more *laissez faire*, where supervisors leave it to the student to take the lead in requesting meetings when needed. Students are given much more freedom and they are responsible for driving the research forward, establishing milestones and dealing with issues as they arise. Such supervisors might be willing to consider supervising students on a wider range of topics that might not tie in closely with their own research interests. Under this model, the supervisor would only be more proactive if there were grounds for concern that the student was making insufficient progress or that the work was heading in the wrong direction. At other times, students are left to find things out for themselves and perhaps even make mistakes at times as part of the learning process.

Both approaches have their advantages and disadvantages: in the first case, the 'hand-holding' allows less scope for things to go wrong and wasted time floundering. It should ensure that the research conducted is rigorous and of an appropriate standard. But the close direction could also be argued to prevent the student from developing as quickly as an independent researcher by following their own ideas and learning from the errors they make along the way. This might leave them lacking these valuable skills after PhD graduation as they begin an academic career where they are expected to rapidly develop a research agenda that is distinct from that of their former supervisor.

6.3.3   What will your supervisor do?

Your supervisor will be your primary contact point throughout the entire process, providing support and guidance from the first day of registration right through to dealing with post-viva corrections. They will fulfil a range of related roles, and you can reasonably expect that your supervisor should:

- Be knowledgeable about the broadly defined subject area
- Provide comments on your proposal in an initial meeting and on drafts of your chapters and the entire thesis as each document is completed
- Supply suggestions for sources of data and literature
- Offer advice and suggestions at any point where you need them
- Respond to your e-mails in a timely fashion and be available to attend scheduled meetings
- Point you to additional learning resources to enhance your skills and knowledge
- Write you a reference for a job or further study

Do not be concerned if your allocated supervisor has research interests in a different part of accounting or finance than your proposal's subject matter. Academics are used to working across different areas and will be experienced in supervising a wide range of research topics. Their breadth of knowledge will be an asset, not a liability, and their primary role is to supply high-level guidance rather than detailed subject-specific technical information (which is mainly your job to source elsewhere).

6.3.4 When to meet your supervisor(s)

After you initially register and begin the PhD programme, your supervisor will probably set up an initial meeting to discuss the proposal and any issues they foresee. You might have already made contact with them at the application stage and received initial feedback on the proposal then. But for many students, post-registration will be the first time that they meet their supervisor. The latter will provide some suggestions for additional reading or approaching the topic from a different angle. The feedback could be more severe – for instance, that the idea is unworkable, too risky, too ambitious or not feasible within the time available, in which case you may be invited to have a rethink and draft a revised proposal. The supervisor will also discuss your work-plan and whether it is realistic and likely to allow you to finish within three to four years.

After that, as mentioned above, the frequency with which students meet with their supervisors varies enormously. Some students will meet their supervisor at least weekly for the entire duration of their registration, while for others it could be once every month or less. It is therefore worthwhile for the two parties to have an informal discussion at the earliest possible stage to agree how often meetings will take place and whether they will be regular and timetabled or will only be organised upon the student's request at stages when they are in need of further guidance. Of course, students can contact their supervisors at any stages of the process as the need arises.

In my experience, it is still worthwhile to continue to engage with your supervisor whether you believe that you are making good progress with your research and so not needing any guidance or hopelessly behind and feeling embarrassed. They will be able to help (possibly a lot) whatever your current state of progress with suggestions for improvement or new directions.

6.3.5 How to deal with your supervisor

Always keep e-mails to your supervisor friendly but reasonably formal. It is probably polite to address them as 'Dr X' or 'Professor Y': find the correct title and use it (with Professor being the more senior one, so employ that if the person also has a PhD) the first time you make contact with them or any other members of the academic staff. However, you will likely revert to first-name terms when you have got to know them a little better. Some academics take themselves more seriously than others, so it is best to err on the side of formality to ensure that no offence is caused.

Supervisors will differ in terms of their approach to the process, and you will have no choice but to dance to their tune. You can only find out how your supervisor works after you have experienced it. Some will be willing to be flexible about when you meet with them and will respond promptly to your e-mails, even in the evening and at weekends. Others might take a day (or longer) to respond, and you might have to wait a week to have an appointment to see them. Unfortunately, even if they take several days or more to reply to an e-mail, and they are not available to see you for two weeks despite arranging an appointment, there is little that you can do except to ensure that you make up for this tardiness by being even better organised and more efficient yourself so as not to fall behind schedule or waste time waiting for their replies. Hopefully, they will make up for lack of timeliness with particularly useful input, providing high-quality ideas and comments.

Relatedly, some supervisors will be more friendly and supportive than others. Some might ask you about your post-university career ambitions, your family or hobbies as part of polite conversation, while others will want to get straight down to the task at hand. Again, whether you have a more expansive chat with your supervisor or brief interactions based only on the PhD will depend on their preferences, and it is simplest to conform to that.

Ideally, a supervisor will always be encouraging, combining criticism and suggestions for improvement with praise for what went well. However, some supervisors will focus exclusively on the aspects of your thesis needing work, passing over any parts that are already strong. Hence, an overall balance of negative comments on a draft should not be taken to imply that the work is weak and will fail the viva examination. If you are concerned that the tone or balance of comments indicates serious flaws, you should go back to your supervisor and ask them directly if that is the case. But always reflect on the negative comments, take them on-board and re-work the draft accordingly.

Overall, though, one supervisory experience cannot be compared with another, so do not be concerned if your supervisor appears less impressed with your work than other students' supervisors are with theirs. Some academics supply harsh comments as it is in their nature to do that while others might do the reverse. You would only need to be concerned in the unlikely event that the comments were unfounded or incorrect.

Supervisors are usually juggling a range of different roles, so it is vital to use their time effectively. It is a waste of your supervisor's time, which they will find irritating, if you:

- Turn up to meetings late repeatedly or without a very good cause
- Don't prepare, so you have no questions to ask, leaving the supervisor to drive the meeting
- Ignore the advice you are given
- Take offence at mild and well-intentioned criticism of your work
- Expect your supervisor to undertake tasks that are not part of their role
- Leave everything until the last minute and then expect your supervisor to treat your e-mails and requests as urgent

If, for some legitimate reason, you know you will be late for a meeting or delayed in submitting a piece of work, out of politeness, drop your supervisor a note to let them know so that they can adjust their schedule accordingly. Don't just fail to turn up or send a pointless message the next day about what happened. Supervisors will have heard numerous imaginative excuses for late work or failure to attend meetings over the years, so the best strategy is to be refreshingly honest. If you overslept or forgot an appointment, be very apologetic but don't be tempted to lie as it won't wash and would further damage your reputation and working relationship.

As mentioned above, the frequency with which academics check and respond to e-mail varies enormously, so when e-mailing your supervisor, do not expect an instant response and always wait at least a few days before sending a reminder unless the matter is urgent. I met a student once who set e-mails to resend automatically every hour until they got a response! As you can imagine, that technique was not popular with academic staff, and the student was soon persuaded to adopt a more patient approach.

Ensure that you pre-arrange meetings with your supervisor where possible or drop by during their office hours, which are set times that each academic commits to being available to see students without an appointment. Avoid just turning up out of those hours unless it is an emergency since your supervisor will be expecting to spend time on other activities rather than seeing you, and so you may receive a less warm welcome than if you had timed your visit more carefully.

When you are due to meet your supervisor, make sure you are well prepared for the discussions. Think beforehand about what you want to achieve from each meeting and plan in advance a list of questions you want to ask. Try to direct the flow of the session yourself to get the outcome that you want. If there are awkward silences with your supervisor having to take charge and question you on how you are doing, the meeting will be less useful to you than it could have been.

Your supervisor's role is to push you forwards from where you were, and so the further you are already into your research, the more in-depth guidance you will receive. Your supervisor might be able to suggest where to start looking for existing research on your chosen topic or which class of models would be appropriate to analyse the data. But it would be a much better use of the time you have with them if you have already nailed down these fundamental aspects to leave the meetings free for a more detailed discussion. In general, your supervisor should be commenting on your ideas rather than establishing the ideas from scratch. If you find that they are driving the agenda, you need to be more proactive and forward-thinking in future.

Your supervisor will probably get to know you better than any other staff member so they would be an obvious choice to ask for a reference for a job or further study applications when you leave. That makes it all the more vital that you create a good impression throughout and try your best.

If (or when) you hit difficulties with the research, your supervisor should always be there to offer suggestions or steer you towards another colleague or resource that might be better placed to help. Never be afraid to seek guidance when you need it. This could be for a specific narrow task, such as operating a piece of software or trying to get your head around what should go in an abstract. Or you might require support with something more substantive, such as not knowing where to start or feeling overwhelmed by the enormity of the task ahead. Although you would usually not expect your supervisor to show you how to use a statistical package or to act as a counsellor, they will be aware of some resources that are available if you cannot identify any yourself.

It is sometimes said that supervisory time is a precious and finite resource, so you must use it wisely. If you waste too much, it may be used up just when you need it the most. An essential aspect of dealing with your supervisor is to demonstrate some independence in your learning. While they are there to help you, they should not always be the first point of contact when you hit a problem or there is something you cannot understand. Show some resourcefulness and investigate other ways to solve problems before turning to your supervisor – a vast amount of information is available on the internet through YouTube videos, forums and blogs. It is probably the case that other PhD students will be having or will have had similar types of problems, so you can also rely on them as a mutual support network.

Your supervisor will have the primary responsibility for providing support and guidance towards the completion of the dissertation. While they will be doing so within a well-established framework, it would be unwise to put them into a negative frame of mind about you and your work by continually bugging them over relatively minor issues that you could have dealt with yourself. A supervisor who has needed to spend much time telling you in detail what to do or solving problems that you encounter could become increasingly evasive and unwilling to provide further help.

It is worth reflecting on what you cannot reasonably expect from your supervisor, as well as what you can. In most cases, your supervisor will not:
- Provide you with an 'oven-ready' research topic
- Provide you with data or code
- Fix your code or statistical programs when they don't work
- Show you how to write any part of the thesis
- Correct your spelling and grammatical errors

Concerning all these points, your supervisor might have suggestions for where to look or how to sort out the issues, but the primary responsibility in all cases is yours.

What to do if you fall out with your supervisor

Try your hardest not to fall out with your supervisor! Fortunately, this is an infrequent occurrence. As a supervisor for over 25 years, I don't think I ever had a serious dispute with any of my research students, although I considered some of them rude, and some were more fun to work with than others. As a new researcher, you need all the help you can get to obtain the most you can out of the experience and maximise your grade. Most supervisors are consummate professionals, and so they will still provide support and guidance even if you have a bad working relationship with them.

But in such circumstances, they might not be willing to go beyond the minimum level that could be expected of them. It would also make the whole experience much less pleasant than it otherwise could have been for both parties.

Suppose that you had a massive argument with your supervisor at your previous meeting but now you are stuck with something and need help. What should you do? Unfortunately, it is common to make remarks in a heated conversation that are ill-advised and later regretted. Usually, the best advice initially would be to try to smooth over any difficulties, to apologise if you are at least in part to blame for the breakdown of communications and see if you can get things back on track. If this is really not possible, or you have tried this, but it was to no effect, then it would be wise to make an appointment to see the PhD Programme Director – this is the staff member who is responsible for organising all aspects of doctoral studies and probably the same person who allocated the students to supervisors. You can explain the situation to them and follow their advice. They might be able to have a word with your supervisor to see what the issue is and how it could be resolved.

If this still fails to produce a resolution, the PhD Director would be able to arrange a change of supervisor. But this would be absolutely a last resort. A change of supervisor is a drastic step only to be taken if all else fails, such as a long-term absence on their part or a serious disagreement resulting in a complete breakdown of your working relationship with them. Changing supervisors is disruptive and awkward for all parties and, therefore, only worth considering if you are near the start of the process rather than close to completing the thesis. In the latter case, it would be preferable just to make the best of the situation.

What to do if your supervisor is not responding to e-mails

As stated above, some supervisors routinely respond in a timely fashion to e-mails, while others assign checking and replying a lower priority. But what should you do if it has been some considerable time (e.g., more than a week) since you wrote to your supervisor and they have not replied, even after you sent a polite reminder? In the first instance, it might be advisable to try some other way to contact them. The most obvious way would be to drop in to see them during their surgery or office hours. Check with other academic or administrative staff whether the supervisor has been away or off sick, which would explain their non-response.

If your supervisor has not responded because you argued during the previous meeting, or you have been contacting them daily since registration, then you will probably have to consider that you have used up all of the available supervisory resources, and you will need to find other ways to address the difficulties you now face.

If it has been more than a week since you sent a reminder e-mail to your supervisor and your efforts to contact them through other channels have also failed, and your need for support is urgent, it is probably time to reach out to the PhD Programme Director. Alternatively, you could seek help from another member of staff or a PhD student.

6.3.6 Other sources of support

A vast array of sources of support and guidance is at your disposal, each of which is discussed at various points in this book, including friends and classmates, other academic staff, forums and discussion boards. Having discussions with experts on the subject matter – not only your supervisor but also other academic members of staff – can be valuable in providing additional ideas and suggestions. But since you cannot over-use their time, you should refrain from contacting them until you have done enough background research that you could have an informed and worthwhile conversation.

Current or former PhD students can be another invaluable asset in helping you to overcome the issues that arise as you work on your research. But suppose that no other doctoral students are working on the same topic as you in your department. In that case, it is also worth considering whether you can develop an e-support network by looking for students at other universities studying in similar areas. For example, people often post questions to forums and chatrooms; you could do the same, and it is surprising how commonly academics and other experienced researchers reply to these and offer their expert guidance and suggestions for free.

If you are struggling with a particular aspect of your doctoral project work, the more clearly you can explain what the issue is, the more targeted help your supervisor or others will be able to give. And the more initiative you have already taken to sort out the problem before contacting them, the keener they will be to offer support because they will appreciate that you have sought alternative solutions rather than over-relying on them.

6.3.7 Should a record be kept of supervision meetings?

Ideally, both parties should make notes of every meeting – the time, place and duration of the meeting, what was discussed, whether there were any deliverables or targets agreed, what would be the next meeting's date, and so on. Taking minutes of the meeting will not only act as an aide-mémoire and ensure that suggestions are acted upon, but it will also help to avoid any subsequent misunderstandings or disputes which can protect both the student and the supervisor if things go wrong.

However, I must be honest at this stage that while such record-keeping is good practice, I have never done so, either when I was a student or, for a much longer period, as a supervisor. I believe that life is too short, and the academy already has so much paperwork that we can no longer function as teachers or researchers, but no doubt many colleagues would regard such a perspective as old-fashioned. I am sure that the day will soon come where meeting logs will be a requirement for both students and their supervisors. If you are willing to take the time to do that, it would be a worthwhile activity. At the least, you should note down any key action points arising from the meeting – the note taking is your responsibility rather than your supervisor's.

Further reading

- If you struggle to manage your time, the book by Carroll (2012) might be useful, and Redfield (2020) provides practical tips to stop procrastinating
- There are numerous self-help resources for people to deal with stress and build their mental resilience. The books by Johnstone (2019) and Wilson (2020) are good starting points
- There are also numerous books on how to enhance the supervisor-supervisee relationship, although most are written from the perspective of the former. Tanggaard and Wegener (2016) is a good example that includes a student perspective.

Chapter takeaways – top tips for success

⊛ Treat your PhD like a job and aim to work regular hours
⊛ Build in breaks, days off and holidays but expect to work long hours for part of the time, including evenings and some days at the weekend
⊛ Take relevant, part-time roles as a teaching or research assistant as opportunities arise, but ensure that they do not crowd out your PhD progress
⊛ Organising yourself from the outset and preventing procrastination are essential
⊛ Keep backups of everything using free cloud storage
⊛ Treat your supervisor's time as precious, and don't waste it
⊛ Don't expect your supervisor to provide you with a fully formed topic idea or check your spelling
⊛ Seek help when you need it, but make use of a range of sources of support

7. ETHICAL ISSUES

Learning outcomes: this chapter covers

- ✓ What are ethics
- ✓ Why ethics are important in research
- ✓ How to apply for ethics approval
- ✓ What is plagiarism
- ✓ How plagiarism is detected
- ✓ How to avoid plagiarism
- ✓ What is the fabrication of data or results
- ✓ Mitigating conflicts of interest

7.1   What are ethics, and how do they relate to research?

When research is conducted, it will have a direct or indirect influence on other people. Ethical considerations are about reflecting on and preventing any adverse effects that your research could have on others. 'Ethics' is an inclusive term that encompasses various aspects of behaviour when conducting research work, writing it up, and publishing it. Ethics refer to a set of moral principles and a level of integrity that should be adhered to in the process of doing research, incorporating a set of actions that researchers should take and a corresponding set of things they should not do. Honesty and objectivity in all aspects of the research process are viewed as essential.

All academic work should conform to specific standards of conduct, and as someone at the start of their research journey, it is worthwhile for you to be aware of these debates and rules and get into good habits. Given that the outputs from their endeavours are usually made public, researchers have several responsibilities that include ensuring their results are accurate and can be trusted by others. Consequently, like most other books on how to do a PhD, I have devoted a whole chapter to this subject.

Although there is a moral aspect to behaving with integrity in research, there are also important practicalities to consider since falling foul of the rules can lead to severe problems. Ethics is not pure science, and different people will hold different ethical standards in several of the 'grey areas', with some researchers believing that a particular practice is acceptable while others strongly consider it unacceptable. Yet there is also a common set of beliefs that most researchers hold about what is tolerable and what is clearly not. This chapter will now flesh out some of these issues and discuss the ethical problems and dilemmas that can arise in various aspects of the process of conducting and writing up research.

There are typically fewer ethical considerations in accounting and finance than in other fields within business and management owing to the predominant use of secondary data, which will become apparent below. But there are nonetheless some key areas where ethical issues can arise if:

- Your research could harm someone – for example, if participants are made to feel embarrassed or stressed
- Someone is unexpectedly deceived in the course of your research
- Someone's right to privacy has been breached
- Someone has been involved with your research without their consent
- Someone's information has been used in a way that they did not agree to
- You are dishonest in reporting the methods or results
- You face and do not mitigate any conflicts of interest that arise
- You do not properly treat copyrighted materials and data

It would be impossible never to bump up against any of the principles listed above in the course of conducting and writing up research. For example, it would be a legitimate topic to examine how investors' trading behaviours alter during times of market volatility and whether women are better at handling the resulting stress than men. In the process of setting up an experiment to test this, it would be impossible to achieve the aims without putting participants in a stressful environment to see how they react. While making people feel stressed, especially if it is deliberate, would usually be considered wrong, in this case it is justifiable as an integral and necessary part of the research design. It would, however, be important to mitigate the effects as much as possible, to make people aware of what could happen during the research so that they are able to make an informed judgement about whether to participate or not, and to have a clear plan to support any participant who became excessively traumatised.

This example illustrates that there are few absolutes when dealing with ethics, and there should always be a careful consideration of whether the ends justify the means and how the potential for harm, along with any risks, can be minimised.

The use of deception in research studies requires particularly careful consideration, and is specifically mentioned in the list above and on ethics approval forms for several reasons. First, sometimes if a participant in an experiment is aware of precisely what the researcher is testing and looking for, it will influence the way that the former acts, thus damaging the validity of the findings. Therefore, in order to have the potential of obtaining valuable findings, it is necessary to be at least somewhat economical with the truth for some experimental research. Second, if a participant is deceived and later finds out that this was the case, they may feel hurt in a way that would affect their willingness to participate in any future experimental studies. Even if they consent to participate a second time, the previous deceit may influence the way that they perform next time, making them behave warily and viewing the researcher with suspicion, even if there is no deception involved in the second study.

Having a set of guiding principles and rules on ethics for research programmes, enforcing them, and educating students about them is vital because unethical research can cause harm to others in numerous ways. It is obvious to see how damage could be done by the examples in the list above, but more subtle instances of unethical research practices can still be detrimental to others and thus should be avoided. For example, if one researcher is dishonest in reporting their findings, other scholars (including students) could waste precious time following the original researcher's methods. It is also possible that practitioners or policymakers seeing the published findings might make decisions based upon them that, had the results been stated accurately, they would not have done. Following the conclusions or guidance from flawed research could lead to lost revenues, unnecessary risks, inappropriate policies, and so on. Everyone needs to have confidence in the veracity of what is written in the scholarly research literature so that it can be relied upon and used without the need to question it, and for that reason, amongst many others, all researchers must take the responsibility to behave ethically.

Beyond the academy, behaving ethically and demonstrating that rigorous standards are in place are viewed as increasingly important in both accounting and the financial services sector. The majority of professional qualifications in accounting and finance (ACCA, CFA, etc.) will include at least one module on ethics, and this material will include a discussion of research ethics. The requirement to formally demonstrate that these issues are covered on the syllabus has arisen as a result of the reputational damage that was done to firms, and indeed to the entire industry, as a result of high-profile cases of accounting fraud, including Enron in the US and Tesco in the UK, amongst many others, and financial scandals involving money laundering and LIBOR rigging at big banks.

The likely consequences within the university of being caught behaving unethically are discussed below. But it is also important to note that a potentially even more disastrous outcome for you in the most serious cases can occur where a form of unethical behaviour is noted on your student record. If this happened, it might make it harder for you to obtain a position in an accounting firm or a bank, particularly if the academic staff member writing your reference feels compelled to point it out. If there is any mention of improper behaviour, many firms would not want to take the risk of hiring that person, and they would have plenty of other candidates from which to choose in today's highly competitive recruitment market. Therefore, the most serious unethical practices could result in lost job opportunities as well as potentially putting the PhD in jeopardy.

7.2   The ethics approval process

Since dealing with these issues is tricky, especially for new and inexperienced researchers, with the possibility for significant damage if things go wrong, all universities are required to have a robust process in place to ensure that research is conducted ethically. Usually, there will be a formal university-level committee charged with the responsibility for ensuring that all research undertaken at the institution (whether by staff or students) upholds high standards of ethics. But day-to-day matters concerning ethics will frequently be delegated to a school- or department-level committee. This committee's primary responsibility will be to ensure the 'ethical propriety' of any research that uses 'human subjects or human personal data', in other words, research based on people or individual, identifiable data about people.

Naturally, ethics approval processes fall most heavily on areas where the potential for harm to participants is the greatest. Such fields include medical research, where the most egregious examples of unethical behaviour include situations where ill patients have been deliberately discouraged from seeking treatments (see Dooley, 1995, for examples). Consequently, additional checks are required for medical topics, but these will not be relevant for the vast majority of researchers in business schools or social science faculties and so are not considered further here.

The approval process would usually be that any students (or staff members) considering conducting research that uses human subjects or personal data would be required to complete a form that explains how they will collect, store, and use the data. Any research that will use, for example, surveys or interviews, will usually need to go through this process. The committee will have the discretion to disallow the proposed research from taking place or require modifications in its design before the study can begin. These safeguards are in place to protect the reputation of the university and the researcher.

In the worst-case scenario, unethical or very badly designed research could cause severe embarrassment to a participant, such as if some of their personal information was (either deliberately or accidentally) made publicly available. The harmed person would then have grounds to take legal action against the university (and possibly against the individual researcher).

When proposed research goes before a committee such as this, they will want to be reassured that it will be conducted in a way that minimises the scope for any problems to occur. For example, when a survey will be performed, the committee will want to see evidence that:

- Survey participants will have given their consent to participate, using a form of the type below
- Participants will have the right to withdraw at any point during the survey, and then any information they had given up to that point would be deleted
- All data will be stored securely; only you or your supervisor would have access to it
- The data will only be retained for as long as it is required and then destroyed
- The nature of your investigation will not offend or cause worry among survey participants
- Only information required for the research will be collected
- The information will be stored, and the results presented, in a manner that protects the privacy of individuals (e.g., in an anonymised or aggregate format)

Vulnerable groups, such as children or people in hospitals, have additional protections. Including them in an interview, questionnaire, or experimental design is likely to require additional layers of scrutiny and possibly even a police check to ensure that you are not banned from working with such people. This is known as a Disclosure and Barring Service (DBS) check in the UK. Given the onerous, time-consuming and costly (there is a fee) nature of these authorisations, it is best to stick to using non-vulnerable adults as subjects in your investigation, if you are using 'live subjects' at all; for PhD research in accounting or finance, doing otherwise is unlikely to be relevant and worthwhile.

It is crucial not to begin any primary data collection using surveys or interviews until you have gone through the ethical approval procedure and been given the go-ahead by your supervisor. If there are any issues with your approach or the questions you ask, it could land you in big trouble if you have not been through the due process to obtain authorisation to proceed.

However, research that uses only secondary data will probably not need such scrutiny because it is either at an aggregate level (e.g., for a whole market) or is anonymised from the outset. Therefore, there is nothing sensitive or personal about the information, and there would be no potential harm to individuals if the data were leaked or lost. If, on the other hand, your research methods involve undertaking surveys, interviews, or experiments, then ethical approval will probably be required.

Usually, to obtain ethics approval will require the researcher to complete a form and submit it to a designated person who might have the authority to make a decision if the case is straightforward, or they might refer the document to a committee, who will then consider it at their next meeting. Sometimes, obtaining ethics approval can take several weeks, and therefore you should discuss this with your supervisor at the earliest possible opportunity to ensure that your progress is not held up in waiting for

Figure 7.1: Sample ethics approval form

Research Ethics Approval Form

Name of Student:
Title and level of the student's degree programme:
Title of project:

Brief summary of the project aims and methods (c.150-300 words)

Is the research externally funded? If so, please provide details:

How many participants do you intend to recruit, and through what channels?

Please confirm that each of the following issues has been considered (tick the boxes)
Security of storage of research data
Confidentiality of research participants
The disposal of data upon completion of the research
Assuring participants of the right to withdraw from the research at any point
Whether participants will be reimbursed their expenses
Whether participants will be paid for their time or receive any other benefits
Whether participants will be permitted access to the research findings
Whether any aspects are likely to cause offence or concern among participants
The signing of consent forms for all participants
To the best of your knowledge, participants will have the capacity to give free and informed
consent because they are under 18 years of age or in the sense of the Mental Capacity Act 2005
Whether any participants have a special relationship with the researcher that could affect their
ability freely to give informed consent
Whether any aspects of the research could compromise the personal safety of the researcher or
participants

Please outline any further ethical issues that may arise in the course of your research and how you will deal
with them:

Will the research involve any deliberate deception? If so, please provide details and explain why it is
necessary:

- I confirm that I have completed this form honestly and made all known and relevant information
  available to the Research Ethics Committee. I also confirm to keep the Committee updated if any
  changes to the above take place after approval has been given.
- I understand that it is a statutory requirement that any researcher who will be working with children or
  vulnerable adults undertakes a Disclosure and Barring Service check prior to commencement of the
  research.

Signature: Date:

Figure 7.2: Sample consent form

Consent to Participate in Research

I am a PhD student in the accounting department at the University of the Skies. I am conducting a study of how management accountants in manufacturing firms feel about environmental disclosure requirements. This research has been given consent to proceed by the University's ethics approval process. Your signing of this form confirms your willingness to participate.

Sharing your honest opinions will provide me with the best chance of conducting a valuable study. The survey is anonymous, and no individuals will be identified. I will not collect your name, e-mail address or any personal details about you. Individual results will be kept confidential between myself and my supervisor. Demographic questions (for example, your age and marital status) are asked where it is helpful for the study to analyse this information. The raw data will be kept in files that are password protected; these will not be shared with third parties.

Your participation in this survey is entirely voluntary. You are free to exit the survey at any point, and you do not have to answer any questions that you do not want to. However, please note that incomplete survey data will not be used for analysis, and once you click 'submit', your responses will be entered into the database without identifiers, and it will not be possible to withdraw them.

Once you have completed the survey, you will not be required to do anything else, and you will not be contacted again. If you wish to receive further information about the project at any stage, you may contact me by e-mail at <Your e-mail address>.

Thank you for your participation.

Name: Signature: Date:

this process to occur. A sample of the kind of form that you might have to complete is given in Figure 7.1.

Consent forms

If you are conducting surveys, interviews or experiments, as well as obtaining ethics approval from your department, you will need to ensure that all participants complete a consent form. This document constitutes written proof that respondents are fully aware of the nature of the research, what their information will be used for, how it will be stored, and who will have access to it. This is known as giving 'informed consent', whereby participants not only agree to be involved, but they are given full information that allows them to choose between participating in the research or not in possession of all the facts. These documents need to be signed (either in hard copy or electronically) and then stored until the thesis has been completed and examined, at which point they should be destroyed along with any other sensitive information. A sample consent form is given in Figure 7.2.

Legal risk

A further ethical consideration is that you do not expose any of your participants to 'legal risk'. In other words, you must design your survey or interviews so that you are not asking any questions that could encourage them to reveal that they had engaged in any unlawful actions, such as taking payments in cash to evade tax or overstating damage in an insurance claim to enhance the pay-out. Doing so could put them and you at risk. If you became aware of such illegal activity, would you have a duty to report it to the authorities? And if you felt that you had no choice but to report the person, how could you reconcile that with the promise you had made to all survey participants that their information would remain confidential to you and your supervisor? The best way to avoid such a situation is to design surveys and interviews carefully to ensure that participants are never asked any questions that would relate to illegal activities.

Anonymity

If you are conducting case studies or interviews, you should offer your participants a guarantee of anonymity and take care that they cannot be identified from the way that you report their roles or other characteristics. For example, if you attributed a quotation to 'the CEO of an accountancy software firm based in Reading and established in 2008 with an annual turnover of £5m', it could make it reasonably straightforward for readers to identify whom you are talking about. This could cause embarrassment or worse if the CEO had said something in confidence that could cast them or their company in a bad light.

If you have any doubts about the integrity of what you are doing and whether it could contravene any rules on confidentiality or data protection, for example, then do not continue until you have sought guidance from your supervisor or another staff member experienced in similar kinds of research and the ethical issues it can lead to.

7.2.1   The Data Protection and Freedom of Information Acts

The Data Protection Act (DPA) 1998 and Freedom of Information Act (FOIA) 2000 are two pieces of legislation that apply to the way that data are handled and who has access to information. Although these are both laws that apply in the UK, similar regulations hold in many other countries. The DPA was amended in 2018 to reflect a pan-European set of common rules (General Data Protection Regulation, GDPR) that has been in place since then. Following the UK's departure from the European Union at the end of January 2020, there have been further, minor changes in the legislation, but the core principles remain the same. The technicalities of the current modifications are quite complex but nicely summarised by in a document by the ICAEW.[1]

The DPA places a requirement on people who work with personal information to comply with certain principles regarding how the data are collected, stored and disposed of. Hence, the rules relate to the same issues that ethics committees are concerned with, which is why the Act is discussed here.

---

[1] https://www.icaew.com/insights/viewpoints-on-the-news/2021/jan-2021/data-protection-now-the-uk-has-left-the-eu-january-2021-update

The DPA stipulates that any information relating to individuals is used only for the specific purposes it was collected for and that it is only employed and retained where necessary. If the information is going to be stored for a prolonged period, it should be updated, and once it is no longer required, it should be destroyed. The data must also be stored securely to prevent possible access by anyone who does not have permission to do so and to protect the information from theft or misuse. Sensitive data such as health status or sexual orientation is treated even more seriously, and there can be severe penalties for a 'data breach' where such delicate information is accessed by those without authorisation.

The Act also grants individuals the right to know of and see any information held about them in computerised and some hard copy records. Individuals can additionally require data held about them to be corrected or deleted. Once an individual makes a request to see this data, they must be provided with it, and a request for it to be deleted must be actioned within a specific timeframe.

The FOIA is another relevant piece of UK law that it is valuable to be aware of. The DPA relates to all organisations, whereas FOIA relates only to organisations in the public sector (e.g., national or local government, universities, schools, hospitals, the police, etc.). The FOIA requires these organisations in the UK to supply upon request any information they hold, not just relating to specific individuals but regarding any of the organisation's activities. The idea behind establishing this law was to engender more transparency and trust in the public sector and increase accountability through openness about the organisations' activities. For example, it might make it easier for any unnecessary waste or poor performance to be brought to light and then challenged if outsiders were given the right to demand access to information that the organisation holds.

Public sector institutions can refuse to comply with an FOIA request in certain circumstances. For example, if the request would take an excessive amount of time to process, if supplying the information would breach someone's right to privacy, or if the data requested would damage a commercial interest. But the default position is that all information demanded should be supplied.

Knowledge of the DPA is useful because if you will be handling individual data (e.g., from surveys or interviews), you will need to comply with the legislation, although doing so will be built into your university's ethical approval process. The FOIA is probably not a piece of law that will apply to you; rather, it might be something you would want to make use of if, for example, you were interested in university or government finances. Making FOI requests can be a valuable source of data that are not publicly available, providing essential input to case studies written about public sector bodies. A substantial amount of detail about the FOIA is available directly from the Information Commissioner's Office.[2]

---

[2]https://ico.org.uk/for-organisations/guide-to-freedom-of-information/what-is-the-foi-act/

7.3 Plagiarism

7.3.1 What is plagiarism?

Even when researchers conduct all of their investigations using secondary data and do not need to seek approval from an ethics committee, there is still one crucial area where they need to consider ethical principles. That is how to handle copyrighted material, how to include ideas and wording from existing studies, and more specifically, how to avoid committing plagiarism.

In essence, plagiarism refers to the act of attempting to pass off another person's work as your own. The term plagiarism covers a whole spectrum of offences, right from copying a few phrases or sentences upwards to something far more serious. The most egregious example I have ever seen was where a student took an academic working paper from the internet, replaced the name on the front with their name and submitted it – so literally, the entire piece was a direct copy from just one source. The student's first name and surname were the only two words they had written themself! Other severe cases involve taking large slabs of text from various sources and splicing them together.

It does not matter whether the source of the material is published work, an unpublished working paper, a letter, or a blog. If you copy some of someone else's words or ideas without acknowledgement that they are not yours, then that is plagiarism.

It is also plagiarism if you get another person to write some or all of your thesis for you, and you do not acknowledge in writing that they did those parts of the work. This is true if a friend does the job for you or if you pay an on-line 'essay mill' to do it. An essay mill is an essay- and project-writing service where, for a fee, the company will employ someone to produce a fully completed piece of work for you to your specification. This can be anything from a short essay to a full PhD thesis, priced according to the level and amount of work involved. The company will hire many writers, covering a range of subjects, and who could be based in any location.

If you use an essay mill, you run the risk that the person who wrote your thesis for you might commit plagiarism and then what would your defence be? That you didn't realise because you did not write it? Supervisors can often identify that something 'smells fishy' about a paper if written by someone else since they will be aware of their students' skills and backgrounds. In particular, it will be easy to spot if the study is written in pristine English, yet the student who allegedly wrote it struggles to write e-mails fluently. Of course, there could be a perfectly reasonable explanation for any anomalous or unexpected features of the work. But if you have cheated in this way and then some irregularities have been detected, it will be a very tricky situation from which to escape.

Equally as worrying, the quality of the work arising from essay mills comes with no guarantees, and you have no idea whether the person who penned it is really a subject expert who can write well in English. Given the illicit nature of the transaction, if they do a lousy job and the work is not of sufficient quality for a PhD to be awarded, you will not have any comeback. How will you discuss and defend the thesis in the viva if you did not write it? That the work was conducted by someone else will become immediately obvious to your examiners, and conducting such a check is one of the main reasons for having an oral exam, as discussed in chapter 13.

Not only is it dishonest to get someone else to do your research for you, it is unethical, and perhaps the most severe form of cheating. Conducting research for and writing a PhD are valuable learning experiences, and by merely buying the finished product, you will learn nothing. The chances of being caught out are high since your supervisor will expect to see you and your progressing work periodically, and so will be surprised in the extreme when you appear to go from zero to a finished product overnight.

Note that it is not only wrong to copy someone else's writing without attribution, it would also be considered plagiarism if you used someone else's ideas written in your own words, but you gave your reader the misleading impression that the ideas were yours. Of course, it is fine to use prior studies when developing your own research – after all, that is how humanity makes progress, and the body of knowledge grows. But this must be done while at the same time acknowledging existing authors whose work shaped your own.

Plagiarism can be deliberate, where the researcher knows that they are copying someone else's material or ideas without attribution, but they do it anyway. Plagiarism can also be accidental: inadvertent plagiarism can occur if you read an existing piece of work and then later draft a section in the dissertation, including that information. As you are writing, you might believe that you are making up new sentences, but you are actually transcribing your recollection from what you had read. In that case, you did not intend to copy someone else's work, and perhaps you did not even realise you were doing it.

7.3.2 The consequences of plagiarism

When universities uncover plagiarism by their students, the consequences can be severe. Plagiarism is dishonest; it is cheating and will, if detected, result in a severe breakdown of trust between a student and their supervisor, with the former's reputation in the department permanently tarnished. The practice is viewed extremely dimly, and it dramatically damages the credibility of the researcher.

It could also be viewed as a breach of copyright and an act of fraud because the perpetrator is implicitly claiming to own the copyright to some ideas or writing, which in fact, they don't. Consequently, in theory, a plagiarist could be subject to legal action by the person whose work they have plagiarised, although this is unlikely unless the former was making money from it.

As a result, it is treated as a severe offence and will usually result in disciplinary action. The penalties for plagiarism are likely to vary depending on the extent of it in the work. A PhD student is likely to be given a verbal warning and told to redraft the offending material for relatively minor cases. In more extreme situations where large amounts have been copied, the offender is likely to be given a formal written warning that will be added to the student's records. In its most severe form for a serial plagiarist who has done so and been caught several times, the result could be that they are required to leave the university altogether with no qualification awarded.

Even in the unlikely event that you get away with intentional and substantial plagiarism in the course of your studies, it could come back to haunt you later in life, particularly if you become famous. There are numerous examples of high-profile figures who were stripped of their qualifications when allegations of plagiarism were made against them, sometimes many years after their degrees were awarded. In most cases, they were fired or forced to resign from their roles. Some interesting examples are listed on the City University New York website.[3] There are some particularly notable cases:

- Annette Schavan, formerly German Minister for Education, was stripped of her doctorate when accused of plagiarism by Heinrich Heine University in 2013. See for example an article on the BBC.[4]
- Ursula von der Leyen, who was at the time German Defence Minister, was accused of plagiarism in her doctoral thesis in 2015, again reported in another BBC article.[5]
- Tony Antoniou was Dean of Durham Business School in the UK when he was accused of having plagiarised his DPhil Thesis at York, even though the alleged incident had happened almost two decades previously, as reported in an article in the Financial Times.[6]

7.3.3 Some spurious excuses for plagiarism

Given that the potential penalties for those who plagiarise and get caught are so severe, with modern software routinely in use at universities making detection highly likely (see the next section), why do students still plagiarise work? There are various reasons that students might give, none of which justifies the act:

'I don't know what plagiarism is as nobody explained it to me'

Students often argue that they lack an understanding of what plagiarism is. But this is extremely unlikely to be accepted as an argument since all universities now go to great lengths to explain it – not just in PhD training modules but probably also in the student handbook and all over the website. Even if you never bothered to look at your department's student handbook or its internet pages, for sure there will be sections on plagiarism in both. Ignorance is no excuse.

---

[3]https://www.baruch.cuny.edu/rio/research_misconduct_examples.htm
[4]https://www.bbc.co.uk/news/world-europe-21395102
[5]https://www.bbc.co.uk/news/world-europe-34376563
[6]https://www.ft.com/content/bb122680-87d0-11dc-9464-0000779fd2ac

'I want to use my own words but I am not a native English speaker'

The whole point of doing a PhD degree in English is to learn how to write in the language, and this is a valuable skill that, once learned, you would have for life. Any negative consequences of poor grammar are likely to be much less severe than those for plagiarism. It is wrong to believe that you would be better off to copy someone else than to miswrite it yourself. Besides, as I will discuss below, it is perfectly acceptable to employ a proof-reader to go through your work at the end to fix up the grammar. Modern software such as ProWritingAid and Grammarly is handy in helping to improve the standard of written English too, particularly if your level is already reasonable, although if the drafting is very poor, these apps will struggle to make it better. In the latter case, using a proof-reader (a person rather than a package) would be recommended.

'I left everything until the last minute, , so I just copied it'

If you left working on the PhD because you were sick, or you had too many other things to do such as teaching or other paid work, it is not legitimate to suggest that you didn't have the time to write in your own words. If you were genuinely sick or there was an exogenous reason why you could not do the work, your school will have a process where you can put in a claim to get more time (e.g., an extension of registration or a retrospective suspension) due to extenuating circumstances.

7.3.4   Plagiarism detection

Just as the scope for plagiarism and the ease with which it can be undertaken have grown with the development of the internet, so too has the capacity for identifying the places where it has occurred. Turnitin is a piece of software that detects plagiarism.[7] It is used ubiquitously in UK universities and has also been adopted in many other countries. It claims to be 'the world's most effective plagiarism detection solution.' The software incorporates a vast database containing electronically available books, web pages (both current and older), newspapers, and journal articles. It also retains all of the essays and projects written by students that have previously been uploaded into the system. Of course, it does not contain literally every source globally, and its coverage of older content that is only available in hard copy format is very patchy, but overall, the database is incredibly comprehensive. Therefore, whenever you lift material from published sources, working papers, or previous student work, the chances of being discovered are exceptionally high.

The software works by producing a 'similarity report' that gives an overall match of the current work to all existing sources in the database (e.g., 12%), which is then broken down into the percentage attributable to each source. When the software is producing a similarity report, it is useful to exclude both quotations and the reference list, for these can sometimes provide spurious matches that considerably increase the recorded similarity without actually constituting plagiarism. Also, tiny matches, or

---

[7]https://www.turnitin.com

where there are technical terms that are hard to rephrase or prevalent phrases, should be ignored. For instance, 'I will now proceed to examine the results' or 'Engle (1982) developed the autoregressive conditional heteroscedasticity model,' have probably been written thousands of times and saying that again is not plagiarism.

Some schools will establish a threshold for the overall similarity index (e.g., 15% or 20%) with anything below deemed acceptable and anything above needing further investigation. Nevertheless, the reviewer needs to read through the report and see whether the matches are predominantly from short, randomly located groups of words or concentrated on one or two big blocks. The latter would usually be considered to be much more likely to constitute plagiarism than the former.

If students have lifted chunks from an existing source without quoting them directly, but this is interspersed with some of their own writing, this is sometimes known as 'paragraph plagiarism' or 'paraplagiarism'. Although arguably less serious than copying entire pages or sections, this would nonetheless be viewed as breaking the rules and treated accordingly. You have still committed plagiarism if you copy someone else's phrases, whether intentionally or unintentionally, even if some of the material is yours.

It is essential to cite the sources of all ideas, even when you successfully paraphrase the work into your own words. Failure to add a citation and include that paper in the reference list at the back of the dissertation is still plagiarism. While this sort of plagiarism where ideas are taken is less likely to be detected by the software than reusing someone else's words, it could still be spotted by your supervisor or examiners.

Some people try to cheat the software – for example, by playing with the characters so that the letter 'a' is replaced by a foreign language character that looks very similar but is not. They hope that the software then cannot read any of the words, and so no matches will be recorded even in cases of severe copying. Superficially, this might work, but the perpetrator will be in big trouble if the marker spots the attempt at deceit, and a matching score that is too low (0% or 1%, say) will be very suspicious. Genuine pieces of work that students have written themselves will never have similarity scores of zero since the program will always identify some phrases that match by chance with those written before by someone else. Therefore, a score of, say, 2%-8% is normal and usually of no concern.

Should students use plagiarism checking software?

An interesting question is whether students should be permitted to use the software themselves to pre-check their papers or whether it should be reserved exclusively for universities to employ after the work has been submitted. Some people might argue that it is inappropriate to let students use the software as a way to learn how to paraphrase by doing it wrong and then making the minimum amount of modification required to fix the issue, continually putting marginally changed drafts into the software until a version emerges that passes the plagiarism test.

However, others would argue that looking at the similarity report is the best way for students to identify any plagiarism, even if inadvertent, in their work. By doing so, they would learn how to improve, thereby reducing the likelihood of a formally submitted piece failing the plagiarism detection test. This argument seems to trump any philosophical objections, so most universities now allow students to submit an early version of their work to the Turnitin site and examine the similarity report. You should, therefore, always take up this opportunity if it is permitted in your department even if you are confident that your thesis is free from plagiarism.

The Premium versions of Grammarly[8] and ProWritingAid[9] also embody plagiarism checkers. Although they are less comprehensive than Turnitin since they do not include previously submitted student work, they would be better than nothing to use for pre-checking if Turnitin is not available. There are also other plagiarism checking sites such as Quetext,[10] which has a free version that allows the user to upload a short piece and a 'pro' version that allows much longer documents to be tested for a monthly fee.

7.3.5   How to prevent plagiarism

It almost goes without stating that serious and intentional acts of plagiarism can be easily avoided by simply redrafting the material in your own words and including a citation. However, unintentional and less severe cases are more likely to occur and should still be avoided since even minor plagiarism could cause issues, including losing your supervisor's confidence and goodwill or receiving a warning. Frequently, students are concerned that they might inadvertently commit plagiarism in their work, but provided that you follow the reasonably straightforward guidance below, it is extremely unlikely to happen.

Obviously, the crucial point is to ensure that all the thesis material is written in your own words unless it is in quotation marks. In essence, this means paraphrasing existing authors' arguments, and doing so successfully requires skill and practice as it must be done manually for every piece of text. It is fine to use a thesaurus to search for synonyms, but you need to stay in control and decide where to use them and replacing a few words at random with substitutes is not sufficient to avoid plagiarism.

There are now on-line paraphrasing websites that will produce a reworded version for you when you enter a block of text. Using one of these is probably still plagiarism unless you state that a paraphrasing site created this aspect of your draft since the modified version will still not be written in your words, albeit it is also not in the original author's words. I tried inserting a paragraph from a paper I had written into such a website, and the outcome was incoherent. It was almost comically bad, which gave me considerable reassurance that as a writer I cannot yet be replaced by a robot. Therefore, I strongly recommend against using an automated paraphraser.

Making careful notes from existing sources is vital, and in particular, ensuring

---

[8]https://www.grammarly.com

[9]https://prowritingaid.com/

[10]https://www.quetext.com/pricing

that you record any material that you note down directly without alteration and which parts you have already put into your own words so that there is no subsequent confusion. Also, make your summaries on each study not too long after reading them when the author's phraseology is relatively fresh in your mind. In that case, if you are in any doubt about whether what you have written is too close to the original source, you can always check since you know where it came from.

A minor rearrangement of a piece of text with the replacement of a handful of terms with their synonyms is not sufficient to avoid committing plagiarism, even if you cite the source of the ideas. Paraphrasing successfully requires making your version of the information considerably different from the original. To be able to do so will also demonstrate an understanding of the material since a non-expert would find this hard to achieve.

Ensure that you use appropriate referencing and quotation marks throughout for material copied from any source, published or not. Referencing has two primary purposes: first, to give credit to the originator of ideas and knowledge, and second, to ensure that other researchers can identify and follow up on the sources of those ideas to learn more about them. Any ideas taken from existing work should refer to that source unless they are already 'common knowledge'. If you are in any doubt about your ability to avoid plagiarising or the issue concerns you, ask your supervisor.

7.3.6 Avoiding plagiarism: an illustration

Here is a sample of text from a paper that I co-authored (Brooks, Fenton, Schopohl and Walker, 2019), taken directly from the original source:

> 'The two worlds of scholarly finance and of financial market finance have never been closely linked. It is therefore interesting that the legitimacy of finance as an academic discipline and indeed its apparent intellectual strength, which we document in this section of the paper, have been able to develop over the past two decades despite its tenuous connections with real world financial markets. Moreover, as we discuss further in section 5, the advent of the global financial crisis barely dented the self-image of finance academics or raised questions concerning the validity of finance as a scholarly field of enquiry. This has arisen as a result of the separate socially constructed environments in which academic finance and the financial services sector operate, with the former gaining and retaining its legitimacy from internally generated metrics such as "elite" journal publishing and citation factors.' (p.27).

Now I will present three different redrafts of this, but it should be noted that there are, of course, many ways that the work could be summarised effectively, and so the illustrations below are by no means unique.

Version 1

'Academic finance and financial market finances have always been closely connected. It is consequently fascinating that the validity of finance as a scholastic field and moreover its seeming intellectual vigour have grown over the past 20 years in spite of its weak linkages with the actual financial world. Also, the onset of the global financial crisis hardly made a difference to the self-image of finance scholars or made them reflect on the legitimacy of finance as an academic subject. This situation was caused by academic finance and the financial services sector being in distinct, socially constructed environments. Academic finance gets and keeps its validity from inward-looking performance measures, including publication in the top journals and citations.'

This version has managed to undertake some paraphrasing, but there are still several serious issues. The first and most important problem is that there is no reference to Brooks et al. (2019) as the source of the original ideas. Second, the structures of the original version and this paraphrased one are too similar, with the ordering of the material being retained. The simple substitutions of one set of words for some synonyms are not sufficient to avoid plagiarism or for the writer to demonstrate their understanding of the material.

Version 2

'Brooks et al. (2019) suggest that academic finance and the financial services sector have both grown over the past 20 years but independently of one another. They further argue that 'the advent of the global financial crisis barely dented the self-image of finance academics or raised questions concerning the validity of finance as a scholarly field of enquiry. This has arisen as a result of the separate socially constructed environments in which academic finance and the financial services sector operate' (p.27) because academics and practitioners focus on different objectives, with the former being pre-occupied with getting published in the top journals. '

This version is not plagiarised since it has been significantly rewritten from the original version except for the part in quotation marks, and it is clear that this part is attributed accurately to the original authors. However, to have such a long quotation in a relatively short summary is probably not ideal and might be considered 'excessively derivative'. It would have been better for the writer to have redrafted this aspect into their own words.

Version 3

'Brooks et al. (2019) suggest that academic finance and the financial services sector have both grown over the past 20 years but independently of one another. They further argue that the global financial crisis did not affect how academic researchers felt about the strength of their discipline, which appeared to remain strong, because academics and practitioners focus on different objectives, with the former being pre-occupied with getting published in the top journals. '

This version is an accurate and succinct summary of the original passage that is free from plagiarism.

A few additional anti-plagiarism resources

A wealth of resources is available on the internet, too (although beware that some websites sell plagiarism checks at high prices, which is not worthwhile if you have university access to Turnitin) – including:

- A useful introductory treatment at Wix[11]
- A description with video and examples at Scribbr[12]
- A suite of interesting videos on a site sponsored by Turnitin[13]
- Finally, numerous other videos on YouTube can be found by searching using keywords such as 'how to avoid plagiarism.'[14]

7.3.7   Self-plagiarism

As the name suggests, self-plagiarism occurs when an author recycles some material they wrote previously and uses it again somewhere else without attribution to their prior work. Unfortunately, experienced academics are sometimes guilty of this too. A typical scenario is when they publish a paper that applies a particular method or model, and they then use the same model elsewhere but using a different market or context, copying and pasting the description of the methods and using a very similar template and literature review for the study.

Although considered less grave than copying someone else's words, self-plagiarism is still often taken seriously by university departments. In research studies, it occurs when students include material that they have already submitted for another assignment, albeit a considerably expanded version. Self-plagiarism is fairly easy to catch since it is likely that the earlier assignment will now be in the Turnitin database, and so the new work will find a significant match to it. If you elect to study a different topic for your thesis than anything else you have done before, even accidental self-plagiarism will be impossible; if not, then be careful to use entirely different wording for the two pieces of work. Treat your own previous work as if it was written by someone else and paraphrase from it rather than copying directly. Most universities will have a rule, either explicit or implicit, that the same piece of work, or parts of that work, cannot be submitted for more than one assessment.

7.4   Falsification of data or results

Alongside plagiarism, the fabrication or falsification of results is considered another serious academic malpractice that could apply equally in accounting and finance as

---

[11] https://www.wix.com/wordsmatter/blog/2020/02/ways-to-avoid-plagiarism/

[12] https://www.scribbr.com/plagiarism/how-to-avoid-plagiarism/

[13] https://www.plagiarism.org/collection/videos

[14] https://www.youtube.com

in the sciences. Falsification essentially means making up or modifying your results to fit better what you wanted to find or so that the findings are easier to explain using an existing theory.

For instance, you might be criticised if your survey sample size was small because you could not persuade many people to complete it. So, to get around this, you might write that you had 123 participants instead of the real figure, which was 23. Or you had expected a negative relationship between two variables in a regression model because this is what previous studies had found, so you simply change the sign on your parameter estimate from positive (which it actually was) to negative.

Both of these are examples of falsification of results, which is terrible scholarship and not acting with the integrity expected of researchers. Not only is it cheating, but it also defeats the purpose of all the effort that you had put in to get the results in the first place. More practically, making up results is hard to do thoroughly and systematically, opening up the possibility for inconsistencies that lead your supervisor to become suspicious because things don't look right. There are many ways that made-up data or results could be spotted, including when:

- The results look just too good to be true
- The results appear inconsistent with each other
- The proportions of each data type look wrong (e.g., you appear to have more large firms in your sample than exist in that country or market)
- It is infeasible for a student with that background to have conducted such a comprehensive or sophisticated analysis in the time available
- The results presented could not have been generated by the models described in the methods section

As discussed above, plagiarism is extremely likely to be detected as automated software has such a comprehensive database. But while detection is somewhat more challenging for falsification since to do so would require a keen eye and some detective work on the part of the reader, you might still be caught out. If that happened, the consequences would be dire, perhaps even more so than plagiarism, depending on how egregious it was.

Universities tend to treat plagiarism or falsification cases harshly because their reputation is at stake as well as yours. They would not want someone who had cheated in that way to complete their programme and obtain a transcript or degree certificate giving the misleading impression to the outside world that the student had successfully mastered all the skills required to undertake a high-quality piece of scholarly research.

PhD students falsifying data or plagiarising their theses will disappoint their supervisors and family or friends if they found out, but more high-profile misdemeanours will have a more significant and wide-reaching impact. Unethical or otherwise poor-quality research eats away at the respect that people both inside and outside the academy have for it. Most famously, a study published *The Lancet* (which is a top medical journal) by Wakefield *et al.* (1998) claimed to have found a link between the measles-mumps-rubella (MMR) vaccine and autism. Yet, it was later reported in the national newspapers in the UK that the study's data had been falsified. The journal subsequently retracted the study, and Wakefield was struck off the medical register – see, for example, Deer (2011), for a discussion of some of the issues involved. The publicity surrounding the original research was so considerable that it damaged confidence in the vaccine and reduced the percentage of parents willing to get their children inoculated. When it was later revealed that the findings were fake, it then cast doubt in many people's minds about the veracity of other scholarly research findings, in some ways bringing the entire academy into disrepute. If this high-profile and important study published in a top journal could not be trusted, then how many other academic studies – not just in medicine but in any discipline – could be similarly worthless?

The lesson here is to avoid falsifying data, don't misrepresent your findings, and don't draw firm conclusions when the results do not warrant it. Even though you are unlikely to be vilified in the way that Wakefield and his co-workers were, it would be the first step on a slippery slope that could nonetheless have severe consequences for your academic progress.

7.5   Other ethical issues

Although the MMR vaccine data falsification seems shocking and evidently wrong, representing a serious fraud, many ethical dilemmas are more subtle than this, with the choice to do or not to do it being less clear-cut. Here are a few examples to reflect upon.

1. Suppose you have a new theory for explaining the cross-sectional variation in asset returns. You collect data for the period 1960-2019, but you find by chance that the approach only works for the period 1960-2015 and then it breaks down. Do you report all the results or just those for the first part sub-sample? If you report all the results, in essence, your study will be proposing a novel model that appears not to work. On the other hand, if you report the earlier sub-sample results only, they will appear much more potent (although the information will look dated if it stopped in 2015). But are the improved findings worth the deceit?

   The situation is arguably less serious than a falsification of results since the findings for the period to 2015 are genuine. However, it would still constitute dishonesty by omission rather than commission, meaning that while you did not make up the results, they are nonetheless misleading if presented on their own.

   A model only working for part of the sample (either for a specific time only or for certain firms and not others or certain countries and not others) is a common occurrence, and therefore this is a situation many researchers face. One approach, and arguably the best one, would be to present both sets of results and then supply a reassuring explanation (backed with evidence) as to why that is the case. Understanding why a model works in some instances but not others is a significant contribution to knowledge but challenging to achieve, causing many researchers to take what they believe to be the easy route, which is to bury the bad results and only present the good ones. Hiding some data or results just because they are inconvenient is unethical.

2. More generally, you should always be transparent in the way you write up what you have done. Failure to report certain aspects of your methods is a questionable research practice. Being transparent means both stating all the steps you took (even if they might appear 'dodgy') and not stating you did something when you didn't do it. For instance, if your raw data included several outliers (e.g., where prices were zero or where something had gone demonstrably wrong with the recording process and you had to make some adjustments), then explain that. If both the reason for the problem and the way that you dealt with it are justifiable and make sense, then the perceived quality of your work will not be adversely affected. Indeed, it might be the case that previous researchers had already documented the issues that you are now facing, and so it would a sign that something was suspicious if you had not also encountered them.

If, ideally, you would have cross-checked something but you did not get the opportunity to do it, do not be tempted to pretend that you had. Do not make up any missing results (although it is acceptable to interpolate or extrapolate to cover missing data points if that is necessary and provided that you explain clearly what you have done and why). Making up results (even some of them) would constitute falsification of information.

3. Deliberately failing to state the assumptions you needed to make to conduct your analysis or deliberately using inferior or invalid techniques because they are more straightforward to implement would also be dishonest. It could bias the results or present a misleading picture of the findings to unwary readers.

7.5.1 Accuracy and careful investigation

Another crucial aspect of the research process is that the investigator should be careful throughout, paying attention to detail and doing everything possible to ensure accuracy. Some of the most severe problems that can arise if researchers deliberately falsify or misrepresent their findings have been described above, but troubling issues can still occur if researchers make accidental errors due to sloppy procedures or a lack of care.

Research findings must be reliable and trustworthy, so you should try to get into the good habit of double-checking every step, engaging in robustness examinations wherever possible. Accuracy extends beyond any empirical work to also cover how your thesis is written, so you should take care to ensure that the statements you make throughout the draft are clear and unambiguous. If you ask them, your supervisor or other readers of your drafts will be able to look for unclear or poorly worded explanations.

7.5.2   Conflicts of interest

Conflicts of interest may result when a student has 'multiple relationships' with a person or organisation. They can occur in research where the participants are friends or family members of the researcher, for example, and so cannot be expected to provide entirely unbiased, independent responses.

Conflicts of interest can also sometimes arise in sponsored research, such as if a bank were to fund research on competition in the UK customer lending market. This funding could give rise to a conflict of interest because a bank would probably prefer to see the findings come down on one side of the debate (that competition in banking is already working well and that no further regulatory intervention is required). Similarly, drug companies often fund research into tests of the side effects of newly developed medicines in the context that if such side-effects are found and documented, the new drug will probably never be utilised, and the vast sums spent on its development up to that point could be wasted.

Within the academy, a journal editor would face a conflict of interest when one of their PhD students submits a paper for possible publication there or when a Head of Department works as a consultant for a company that develops learning materials that the academic's department purchases. Another example of a conflict that could arise is when the admissions tutor for a particular academic programme is a family friend of one of the applicants.

In all of these examples, the person or organisation making the decision conducting the research has more than one interest in the outcome, which could affect their judgement at various points in the research's progress or in making other choices.

Conflicts of interest are dangerous in research since they could encourage the investigator to design the study or present the findings in a particular, biased way in order to satisfy another party. In other situations, a resolution would be to separate the conflicted individual from the decision-making process, (e.g., the admissions tutor passing responsibility for assessing the family applicant to another member of staff).

Evidently, however, you cannot be isolated from your own research. Therefore, you should reflect on any conflicts of interest that you might face in conducting your research and writing it up and, if they arise, how they could be mitigated. For an unsponsored PhD, these are likely to be minimal, but where they exist, they should be discussed with your supervisor and stated in the ethics approval form in the interests of transparency. This step is called 'disclosure' of a conflict. Some useful resources to learn more about conflicts of interest and how to manage and avoid them:

- The National Academic Press has a helpfularticle on conflicts in the context of medical research, where such issues most commonly arise[15]

---

[15]https://www.nap.edu/read/1821/chapter/7

- A further discussion with examples at the US Office of Research Integrity[16]
- A detailed and more general discussion by Curzer and Santillanes (2012) is available from Research Gate[17]

This section has presented several ethical dilemmas that PhD students may face, and in deciding how to act, the critical question is always, 'do the ends justify the means, is behaving underhandedly worth it, and would you take the risk?' In each case, behaving unethically can have severe consequences, and it is essential to know where such actions can arise and how to avoid them.

Further reading

- All books on conducting a PhD or other research will include one or more chapters on research ethics, but there are also more specialist texts entirely devoted to this topic, including Hammersley and Traianou (2012), who discuss some of the debates and dilemmas involved in conducting research
- If you are particularly concerned about plagiarism, two short books focused on this issue that explain ways to avoid it and how to reference correctly are by Williams and Davis (2017) and Lancaster (2019).

Chapter takeaways – top tips for success

- ⊛ Be aware of how essential it is to conduct research ethically
- ⊛ Consider whether your research will require formal ethics approval and if so, apply as early as possible
- ⊛ Know the Data Protection Act 1998 (if you are in the UK, but similar legislation will be in place in most countries) and reflect on whether it has implications for your research
- ⊛ Understand what plagiarism is and how to prevent it
- ⊛ Be familiar with plagiarism checking software such as Turnitin, and use it to check your work prior to submission if permissible
- ⊛ Try to minimise or mitigate against any conflicts of interest that could arise in your research
- ⊛ Ensure that your investigative research is carefully and accurately conducted, with no data or results falsified

---

[16] https://ori.hhs.gov/education/products/ucla/chapter4/Chapter4.pdf
[17] https://www.researchgate.net/publication/225294925_
Managing_Conflict_of_Interest_in_Research_Some_Suggestions_for_Investigators

8. FINDING THE LITERATURE

Learning outcomes: this chapter covers

✓ What a literature review is
✓ Why you should review the literature
✓ The types of material that can be examined
✓ Where to look for possible sources of material
✓ How to read an academic paper

8.1 What is a literature review?

A literature review may be defined as a document that presents a thorough examination and organisation of the existing knowledge that has arisen from established researchers' work in the field of interest. When writing a literature review, you will learn to find and recognise the information relevant to your topic and how to evaluate the quality of each piece of research. You will be able to identify the most important contributions and 'synthesise' the body of knowledge. Synthesising means that you can work across the existing studies, classify them, draw out the common threads, and put them into a framework. By synthesising the literature, you will be making a new contribution by combining studies to create new interpretations of existing research and possibly viewing it from a different perspective than the original authors.

Notice the difference between a summary and a synthesis. A summary is just a shortened version of the original piece, although it should still be written using different words. It will not provide any novel insights compared with the existing work. A synthesis, on the other hand, will use more than one source and will generate fresh ideas. It is clear from the discussion above that a literature review is not merely a list of papers or a collection of summaries; it is much more than that.

In years gone by, taught modules would often require students to delve into the primary literature (i.e., journal articles and research books) but nowadays, courses increasingly rely solely on textbooks and other standardised materials. This teaching approach means that their PhD will be the first time many students are exposed to the research literature. This brings with it numerous challenges – tasks that are all covered, in order, in this chapter or the next:

1. Deciding what kind of material you need to read and on what subjects
2. Where to find the material, ensuring that you uncover any relevant sources but not wasting time looking at studies that are not germane
3. Trying to decipher the language used in the studies to get a grip on what the authors are writing about and how it relates to your research
4. Organising the material and crafting it into a well-written and well-structured literature review of an appropriate length
5. Ensuring that the referencing is done correctly and producing the reference list in a suitable format

When you first begin to search through the sources, the sheer volume of material can appear overwhelming, but much of it will either be irrelevant or part of a parallel stream of work with little incremental value so that it can be skipped over or read cursorily. With experience, you will be able to rapidly identify the sources that you need to note the existence of, those that need to be read thoroughly, and those that can be ignored. The review task then becomes not quite as daunting as it might have first appeared, and you could make rapid progress.

Doing the searches to find the relevant work, reading it and then writing the review are all time-consuming activities that might take, perhaps, up to a fifth of all of the time available to complete the thesis. It needs to be done thoroughly, of course, but on the other hand, don't spend so long seeking, reading and summarising the literature that you leave insufficient time for your investigative work.

With some thought and thorough planning, the review can be completed successfully without too much stress, but there are broadly two primary ways that it can go wrong. First, if you do not search in a sufficiently systematic fashion, and you end up missing key studies relevant to your research. Not spotting these will be a problem if you end up needlessly repeating what others have done or written, especially if your examiners are aware of these other pieces. Second, if your exploration is so broad that you cannot identify the crucial studies to incorporate so that you include too many and your review drifts, lacking focus. Reading this chapter thoroughly should help you avoid those issues and many others of a more minor nature.

8.2 Why should you review the literature?

A core objective behind getting students to write a literature review is that they should demonstrate their understanding of and ability to synthesise a specific branch of existing work *in depth* (note the emphasis here). Therefore, you should avoid covering such a breadth of material that you have no time, energy or words remaining when it comes to the part of the literature relating to precisely your chosen topic so that you only skim over the surface. Although the literature review might begin very broadly, it needs to quite rapidly narrow down to the specifics of the research matter directly covered in the investigative part of the dissertation.

Before you begin the investigative part of your thesis, it is always vital to review the existing literature thoroughly. As you will have spotted, every research article in a journal or research monograph will contain a literature review aspect. Likewise, all PhD theses need to incorporate such a review, which will not only support the generation of ideas and put the proposed research in an appropriate context, but may also pinpoint particular aspects that are likely to cause problems. You cannot identify where the gaps are in the body of knowledge until you have read much of it in that area.

The primary reason researchers (both students and staff members) always begin a new project by reviewing existing studies is to inform their work and to help them sharpen the research questions they want to consider. It allows them to see where their research aims fit within the range of research that has already been done. A second key reason is to ensure that their ideas have not already been employed by someone else and that the new study is not a partial (albeit unintentional) replication of a previous study.

As you are reading for the literature review, it will lead you to develop lots of new ideas, and it might even encourage you to question whether the subject in your proposal is still the right one to pursue. If, upon digging deeper into the literature, you want to change your research aims or even the whole topic, should you do so? This is a tricky question since you will be learning fast as you become more immersed in the body of knowledge, and, naturally, the information obtained will help you refine your aims and polish your ideas.

But it is usually advisable not to drift too far from the original topic – your department may not allow it, and you don't want to be in the position of unnecessarily throwing away all of the study that you have done so far. If you have already gathered data or code, will that have to be scrapped too? If you have already sought ethical approval, would that still be valid, or would it have to be resubmitted? These are delicate issues that have to be weighed carefully when considering any non-trivial revisions to your original proposal topic.

In addition to the content of each study that you read, another aspect to reflect upon is the style that the authors have used, both in terms of the structuring and flow of material and how the arguments have been phrased. Think about which literary techniques you feel work best, are easiest to follow and most pleasant to read, which will help you make decisions about how to organise your writing throughout the PhD when you get to that stage.

Even if the ideas you have for your research are highly practical and motivated by a real-world problem, it is nonetheless vital that you embed your work in the existing literature. You will therefore need to reflect on which parts of the literature best fit with your research area and try to identify and explain the linkages. Failure to achieve this is likely to result in a poor quality review that appears disjointed from your investigative work.

Conducting a thorough review of existing papers will make sure that you use contemporary techniques incorporating the latest thinking in the research area since carefully reading through existing studies will help you identify the methodologies that other authors have most commonly used to tackle their research questions. You will be able to assess the approaches that worked best and those that were less successful, which will support you when you subsequently come to begin your investigative work.

8.3   What should you read?

The review should cover not just empirical applications in your topic area but also discuss the theoretical frameworks that have been adopted in the relevant literature and the methods used to test them. Conducting the literature review will provide you with suggestions for these aspects of your research too. In order to conduct a thorough review, you will need to examine a range of different kinds of sources, including both published and unpublished material. The former will comprise journal articles, books and book chapters, while the latter might include lecture materials, websites, PhD theses, blogsites and working papers. Each of these sources will now be discussed.

8.3.1   Lecture notes and textbooks

Lecture notes and textbooks can be a useful place to start reading on a particular topic because they usually provide a more accessible and logically ordered treatment of the material than articles. Notes and books typically begin right from the beginning and use a consistent notation and terminology throughout that are easy to pick up rapidly. On the other hand, space is at a premium for journal articles, and as a result, there is a tendency to cut straight to the methods and models used in the paper, assuming that the reader is already familiar with a set of other studies that had previously been published on the topic. Different journal articles might also use varying ways of writing the same phrases or equations, and the differences in terminology can cause considerable confusion for someone new to the research area. Textbooks often contain many references to the original research literature, enabling you to build your bibliography in key areas rapidly.

However, while textbooks and course materials are indeed a good starting point, they should not be the only or predominant source that you use since they tend to date fairly quickly, and so they might not contain the latest thinking in more recent issues of the leading field journals. Textbooks will almost certainly be too basic or too broad and lacking in detail concerning the specific subject you are working on to constitute your primary references. If your reference list contains many texts, especially if they are aimed at the introductory level, it will make your work appear rather amateurish.

Alongside textbooks, research monographs should also be mentioned here. Unlike texts, they will likely contain original research material that the author has chosen to publish in a book format rather than as a (series of) journal article(s). Research monographs are ubiquitous in the arts and humanities but less common in accounting and finance, and they are harder (and often more costly) to get hold of than journal articles. Accessing research books will be discussed in the next chapter.

8.3.2 Journal articles

Journals, or periodicals as they are sometimes known, are published at regular intervals – often quarterly but sometimes monthly or at another frequency. They contain several articles (typically 6–12) in each issue, each of around 10–30 pages in length. The articles will comprise the research of (predominantly) academics working in the field, which has been submitted to that journal. The issues are usually published both in-print and on-line, although the latter is now the primary mode of access.

Each journal tends to have a specialisation in terms of the type of work published there (empirical work, informed opinion pieces, theoretical models with a lot of maths, review papers, etc.). Journals also vary systematically in terms of the articles' style and length, and sometimes the viewpoint (such as being pro-auditor or pro-regulation in the tax avoidance debate) expressed in the journal so that other perspectives are rarely if ever presented in that outlet.

Periodicals with 'Letters' in the title publish short articles (e.g., *Economics Letters, Finance Research Letters*), which provide a brief and, therefore, quick-to-read treatment for the reader. However, the lack of words means that they cannot develop their arguments with the same depth as regular journals, limiting their use as sources for research students.

In accounting and finance, most scholars consider publication in the leading journals to be more prestigious and valuable for their careers than writing books (even research monographs) and therefore, they draft all of their best ideas into journal papers. Fortunately, most journal articles are easy for students to obtain electronically and free of charge, provided that their university library subscribes to that journal, either by purchasing it individually or through a 'bundle' deal – see section section 8.7 below. The other feature of journal articles is that, at 6,000–12,000 words, typically, they are mercifully short and so can be read relatively rapidly compared with books (which are likely to be of the order 80,000–150,000 words).

Journal articles will probably constitute the principal source of material for your literature review, although this will depend on the topic to some extent. If you are working on a very current subject, such as fintech or cryptocurrencies, many studies will be so recent that they may not yet have been published. Also, given the practical nature of the topic, much of the research will have been conducted by practitioners who tend not to publish their work in journals.

Why do some papers become popular?

Some papers in the literature are considered 'seminal'. These are influential studies that almost everyone working on the topic refers to in their research. Such work will have changed how people have thought about a problem (so-called 'pivotal' studies), or it will have had a major influence on policy or practice. The researcher might have been introducing a new idea or at least one unique to that subject area. Literature reviews can sometimes be written to highlight such studies, with all of the others following on from that, and reviews should always mention any seminal papers in the area.

Occasionally, it is hard to identify the seminal studies when you are new to a research area. But if you notice that many recent authors are citing a particular study, it is probably worth you finding, reading and referencing the work too since this indicates its importance.

Sometimes journal articles become widely cited not because they are seminal but rather since the work is published in a top-rated journal or because the authors are already famous or from 'elite' institutions. In such cases, the paper will get much more publicity and exposure than comparable work conducted by less well-known writers from less prestigious universities. Readers of these publications will take the author or journal's 'brand value' as a proxy for the quality. Researchers also tend to cite easily accessible papers, and they tend to mention the same work that other researchers in the area are referencing. This referencing pattern results in the distribution of citations being heavily skewed towards a few mega-hits while many academic studies receive almost no citations at all.

An interesting illustration of this is the so-called 'GARCH'-model which became extremely popular in the 1990s for capturing and forecasting volatility in finance. Two researchers independently developed and published ostensibly the same model in 1986: Stephen Taylor, who presented the model in his book, *Modelling Financial Time Series* (Wiley, New York, NY); and Tim Bollerslev, who published it in the *Journal of Econometrics*, a leading outlet. At the time of writing this book, Bollerslev's paper has 28,521 citations according to Google Scholar, while Taylor's equivalent work in his book has just a seventh of that number, 3,821.

From time to time, papers become widely cited not because they are the first to present a new idea but rather because they popularise an existing one, for example, by making it more accessible to a particular audience. Perhaps the previous study in the area that did not gain widespread acclaim arrived too early when the research community was not ready to consider it seriously, or it was initially published in an obscure outlet that most scholars do not look at. In such cases, both the famous

Table 8.1: *Journals of Distinction* in the Academic Journal Guide

Accounting	Finance
Accounting Review	Journal of Finance
Accounting, Organizations and Society	Journal of Financial Economics
Journal of Accounting and Economics	Review of Financial Studies
Journal of Accounting Research	

paper and the original study should be mentioned in your review.

8.3.3 Should your literature review focus only on the 'best' journals?

Whether your review should only incorporate materials from the highest rated journals is a relevant question, and if you decided to restrict your reading in that way, how could you identify them? The numbers of journals in accounting and finance are vast, but, as for all fields of study, there is a handful of journals considered to be the most prestigious of all. These outlets are highly competitive for authors to get into, and as a result, they usually reject the overwhelming majority of articles submitted there for possible publication. Many of the papers that become the most widely cited in accounting and finance are published in these journals, and they tend to have very high standards of refereeing and a requirement that, to be accepted, work must make a significant contribution to knowledge.

The Chartered Association of Business Schools (CABS) is a professional body representing business schools in the UK. Among other activities, they produce the Academic Journal Guide (AJG), formerly known as the 'ABS List', which provides a rating of many journals across 22 business and management areas, including accounting and finance (which are considered as two separate fields). The journals included in the list are rated on a four-point scale, with the very highest-rated few of these in the top category further designated as 'Journals of Distinction' (JoDs). In the most recent version of the AJG at the time of writing (refined in 2018), in accounting and finance, the JoDs are given in Table 8.1.

The entire AJG can be accessed freely, but to do so you would need to register first.[1] The Guide contains around 90 journals in accounting and 110 in finance, each rated on the scale described above.

However, while many academics might consider the work published in JoDs to be leading the field, it is frequently not the most accessible material for students new to research, and these journals often contain a large proportion of theoretical or conceptual pieces. More straightforward applications of models that can be employed as a template for a PhD can usually be found in lower-ranked journals. Therefore, it would not be appropriate to limit a literature search to only work published in these top-rated journals, which would likely miss a considerable amount of relevant and

---

[1] https://charteredabs.org/academic-journal-guide-2018/

readable material. While less esteemed than those in the short table above, many other journals publish original and high-quality articles across a much broader range of topics.

Should papers from very low-ranking or unknown (even unrefereed) outlets, poorly written or methodologically inferior studies, and so on be incorporated into the review? You might suggest that the obvious answer is 'no', but this is a tricky choice in reality. In general, you probably would not want to include them for the reason discussed above because their findings could be unreliable and the conclusions misleading.

You will need to seek out and examine working papers, however, as discussed in a sub-section below. Also, as you become more experienced in reading papers and evaluating research quality, you will be able to make up your own mind whether a flawed paper in an unrefereed journal is nonetheless worth citing.

Journals where the articles are not peer-reviewed (refereed) or where the authors pay to place their work in the outlets (so-called 'vanity publishing') are sometimes best avoided as the quality of the articles contained within them may be weak in many senses – poorly written, biased, shoddy empirical work, inappropriate conclusions, etc. You can generally tell if journals are refereed by looking at their webpages. Usually, journals organised by the major publishers, with prestigious editorial boards, having available impact factors (a measure of how much the work in the journal is cited that is compared to other outlets, which allows them to be ranked) or that are in the AJG, are likely to be refereed.

It would, however, be worth incorporating even weak studies if they are directly relevant to your topic (especially if they are more relevant than better quality studies). But be sure to highlight the weaknesses of such studies and warn the reader that, while you are citing the work because of its applicability to your research, it should not be taken at face value due to its flaws.

You should also try to ensure that your outlook is sufficiently broad that you are able to capture research on your topic that is published in journals outside of its discipline. For instance, I have published finance research in management, economics and accounting journals. If you do not do so, there is a danger that you could miss relevant studies, and those published in outside-of-field outlets are more likely to take an interdisciplinary perspective or to use a different methodological approach compared with papers published in the core journals. This feature often makes the work refreshingly different and inspiring, and therefore definitely worth seeking out and reading.

8.3.4   Review papers

Writing a literature review is simplified by the existence of a survey paper (which is sometimes known as a review paper) on approximately the same topic. Review papers are (usually) high quality and detailed reports on a particular area of research. Survey papers were traditionally written by 'heavyweight' academics in the field, and journals would only accept them if the authors were exceptionally renowned and well established in the area, but that is probably no longer the case.

Finding one or more of these articles will make your job much more manageable and will provide you with a rapid and handy overview of the state of knowledge on a particular topic at the point in time that the review was written. They can be an excellent place to start before you delve deeper into the literature since they will usually provide a broad-based but possibly shallow introduction to that topic, which will enable you to identify the order in which you should read the other studies. Review papers will also provide you with a ready-made bibliography of further research to read.

There are particular journals in each field that publish numerous survey papers, and indeed, it might be all that they publish, such as *International Journal of Management Reviews*; *Journal of Economic Surveys*; *Transport Reviews*. The *Journal of Economic Literature* provides excellent survey articles in economics (occasionally also covering finance topics), and likewise, the *Journal of Accounting Literature* publishes reviews in its field, although there is currently no directly comparable journal specialised in finance.

A quick word of warning, though – just because a journal has the word 'review' in the title does not necessarily imply that it specialises in, or even accepts, review articles. For instance, the 'Review' in the titles of the *American Economic Review* and the *Financial Review* are misnomers in that they are both generalist journals rather than publishing literature reviews. Survey papers are found alongside regular articles in (most) other journals, so you have to search for them. Editors increasingly like review papers because they tend to become more widely cited than new investigative work, therefore increasing the impact factor and hence the stature of the journal.

If you are fortunate enough to find a survey paper on your dissertation topic, it might be tempting simply to copy (or paraphrase from) it, but there are several reasons why this would be highly inadvisable:

- Your topic may not map precisely onto the review, in which case the latter will not provide a complete treatment of all of the sources you need to examine
- Unless it was written within the past year or so, there could be some recent studies that, because of their timing, are excluded from the survey paper, and your literature summary may appear dated if you do not incorporate the latest thinking on the topic
- The emphasis in your study could be slightly different, or you might want a more or less comprehensive perspective than the review. For instance, the review may focus only on arguments in favour of something while you wish to provide a more balanced discussion
- The review might plausibly be 10,000 words long, whereas you perhaps might want to write much less on that particular aspect of your study and therefore you will have to be briefer

8.3.5   PhD Theses

Ethos, part of the British Library website, has electronic access to more than half a million PhDs produced by students at UK universities.[2] You need to register to access the full text of the theses directly from Ethos, although there is frequently an option to download it without registration from the university repository where the PhD student studied. This repository is an incredible resource with a vast amount of free and almost instantly accessible information. For example, I typed tax + accounting and obtained 252 hits; asset pricing yielded 808 hits; even fintech returned three theses.

PhDs are usually also more penetrable than journal articles, providing detailed literature reviews and a thorough discussion of any empirical procedures and data handling details. Doctoral theses are typically 60,000–90,000 words long and do not struggle with the word limits applied to journal articles. Hence it is worth logging onto the Ethos site and using the keyword search facility to see whether there are any theses available covering your topic.

Only final versions of 'accepted' theses will be posted on the website, and so whilst this does not guarantee that the work will be free of inconsistencies or even errors, it will have, at least, been subject to an examinations process and reached the standard required at that university to award a PhD degree.

8.3.6   Blogsites, websites and newspaper or magazine articles

While blogs or unsubstantiated opinion pieces do not fit well in a scholarly literature review, they may nonetheless provide useful ideas for writing the introduction to the thesis. In the introductory chapter, writers would usually step back from the specifics of the academic research to motivate the ideas and models discussed by explaining them in general terms or showing that they are relevant in a broader context.

It is straightforward to obtain information from the internet, including on blogsites, personal webpages and elsewhere, but how can you be assured that a particular piece you are reading is of sufficient quality that you can rely on the information it contains? Experienced scholars will be able to identify quickly whether a piece of work looks solid but evaluating the worth of an article or book is much more challenging for novice researchers.

Blogsites and magazine-type articles will not be 'refereed', so the validity of the claims made usually cannot be verified, and the pieces are typically short, lacking in depth or findings backed by data with analysis. Just when the author of such an article starts to get into the core of the arguments, the study is finished. A discussion of some of the issues that this raises is given in the next section.

8.3.7   Working papers

Should you read and cite all relevant work or impose a limit to only studies that have been published? In my view, it is essential to seek out not only published work but

---

[2]https://ethos.bl.uk/Home.do

also working papers, which represent the latest research that has more recently been completed. The scholarly publication process is slow, and it might typically be a year and possibly even two or more years from when an author completes the first draft of a new piece of work until the point where it is published. Usually, on-line versions of work accepted for publication become available well before the print versions come out. Sometimes working papers are, alongside other unpublished reports by companies or government bodies, conference proceedings, etc., known as the 'grey literature'.

However, the danger of examining unpublished work, such as a working paper, is that it has not been subject to any peer-review. For unpublished papers, you have to make a leap of faith that the researchers who conducted the study and wrote it up have been competent and honest in all aspects. An experienced scholar ought to be able to read a piece of unpublished research and evaluate its quality, but being able to make such a judgement requires a skill that can only be learned with experience (and ideally some training). The best approach is always to be sceptical, and if in doubt, be tentative in the way that you write about a specific author's claims, particularly if the study has not been peer-reviewed.

8.4 Checking the validity of your reading material

Ensuring the validity of what you read and cite is vital for several reasons. First, and at the most basic level, poorly written articles or books will waste a considerable amount of your precious time trying to decipher and understand what the author means. Second, even if the authors of the work had no idea what they were writing about, your supervisor and examiners will, and so if you quote in your thesis studies that contain errors, it is plausible that these will be spotted by the people evaluating it. Third, if you follow a method that an existing author inappropriately or incorrectly applied, you will inadvertently make the same error as they did.

With time, you will develop the skills needed to make your own judgements about the quality and integrity of the material you are reading, but in the meantime, there are several proxies that you can use – these are 'gold seals' that can usually be taken as implying that the work is at least of reasonable quality:

- Use the author's credentials as a proxy for quality assurance. If the author is well established, has written on the topic before and is affiliated with a reputable university, that usually implies that the work should be of at least an acceptable standard. Naturally, even the world's leading scholars make errors, but their output should nonetheless be more reliable than something posted by an unknown individual on a website
- Use the publisher as a proxy for quality assurance – for books, publishers usually put proposals and draft manuscripts through an extensive review process before accepting them for print, and hopefully, any that were not of a sufficient standard would have been rejected
- Use the journal's prestige as a proxy for quality assurance – as for books,

the majority of journals have rigorous refereeing processes where articles are 'peer-reviewed' by acknowledged experts in the field

- Use the style and presentation as a proxy for quality assurance. If the work is poorly organised, poorly written, or the presentation is very unprofessional, that can be a sign that it is not a solid piece and should be read with caution. Poorly written work with grammatical or spelling errors, or where the structure is bad, should probably be discarded as it is highly likely that there are also more substantive errors in the investigative parts

- On the other hand, a shiny pamphlet report is a sign of a high marketing budget and not necessarily good underpinning research. Therefore, don't be duped by a glitzy presentation either; instead, focus on what has been written

- If an author uses numerous citations from relevant and acknowledged sources, that is a good sign regarding the likely standard of their work, albeit not a guarantee; equally, a small number of poor-quality sources is indicative of inferior research

- Check a range of sources: if many authors are independently making the same point or find the same result, it is more likely to be valid. It is, unfortunately, the case that sometimes an entire research area goes down the wrong track when one researcher makes an error that other scholars then repeat following the original erroneous approach. In that case, the subsequent studies cannot be considered independent from the first one. Eventually, other researchers will come to realise the issue, and they will write about it and correct it, but this may take a considerable time to occur

- Use the age of the work as a proxy for its validity. Following on from the previous point, although not always the case, we expect the literature to progress towards 'the truth' so that newer findings build upon older research and hence the former should supersede the latter. The progress of a research literature over time does not imply that older work is necessarily flawed, but instead that newer studies are likely to be more reliable. There has also been a greater emphasis on rigour and robustness in published academic work over the past decade or so than there was previously

Peer review

For most journals, the publication process involves an in-built quality seal known as peer-review. What happens is that each academic author selects a journal to which to submit a paper that they have been working on, and once submitted, the journal editor will usually send the work out to a reviewer (also sometimes known as a referee). This is the peer-review process, where the work is evaluated by the peers of the submitting author (i.e., other, established academics who have published previously on the same topic). Here, one or more scholars independent of the author(s) of the work (i.e., the referee(s)) evaluate it and make comments for improvement before recommending whether the journal accepts the paper for publication or rejects it. Such a process ought to imply that, once the work has jumped over this hurdle, the research is sufficiently reliable that the contents can be taken at face value and the findings and conclusions assumed to be justified.

The peer-review system for journals is better than nothing but far from a perfect way to ensure that all published work is free from errors, inaccuracies or biases. In particular, the refereeing quality will depend upon the skills, experience, and knowledge of the reviewers. Many leading journals use only one referee for each submitted paper, meaning that there could easily be flaws in the work that the reviewer misses. Referees are usually unpaid, and therefore the incentives for being very thorough are limited to professional pride and a belief in scholarship.

What this means for readers of articles is that, ideally, you should always be sceptical of everything written, never taking what a book or article says at face value, even if published in the most respected journals. If the same argument is made or the same result emerges in several independent studies, it can probably be accepted as a genuine finding. Nonetheless, I will end this point by stating that while there can be flaws in the articles published in peer-reviewed journals, these are nevertheless far more reliable than non-refereed outlets such as blogs, webpages, newspaper articles and pieces in popular magazines.

8.5 How do we define 'research quality'?

Evaluating the quality of research presents challenges and is controversial because people with different perspectives and backgrounds will form varying opinions of a given piece. Comparing quantitative versus qualitative research is particularly hard because they are so very different, and of course, it is not the case that more technical work is necessarily better, whereas making a comparative evaluation of two articles in the same field would be much more straightforward.

Given these difficulties in objectively evaluating research, the quality of studies has increasingly come to be assessed according to the status of the journal in which they are published, although equating article quality with journal quality is unfortunate for many reasons, as papers by Willmott (2011a and 2011b) among numerous others have argued. Therefore, PhD students undergoing their research training and socialisation into the profession should learn how to make their own quality judgements. This book has already stated that good research should advance knowledge, providing a novel contribution to the field. But is it enough to just develop something new if it is of no use? Are new ideas that cannot be used either within the academy or by practitioners or governments still valuable? On the other hand, some research has a very high practical value, but is research important if it uses standard techniques on slightly different data? In other words, is research of high quality if it is instrumental but has very little novelty? Finally, suppose that a particular study contains some new and exciting ideas that have potentially important implications for policymakers but is sloppily executed with insufficient data and inappropriate methods. Would that still be a valuable study?

These three ideas motivate the definitions of research quality used in the UK's national evaluations of research, which happen around once every seven years. In 2002 and 2008, these were known as the Research Assessment Exercise (RAE) but it was renamed the Research Excellence Framework (REF) for the 2014 and 2021 iterations. These evaluations all began with the principle that good research should embody three characteristics: it should be original, significant and rigorous,, which links with the discussions above. UK university departments submit their publications to the REF panel, which assesses them alongside so-called impact case studies demonstrating how the department's research is used in policy or practice and a document that describes its research environment.

The REF panel scores each *output* (e.g., a journal article, a book chapter or a research monograph) in terms of its originality, significance and rigour on a 0-4 scale, where four is the highest and zero would imply that the work did not meet the basic definition of scholarly work.

The AJG also uses a scale aligned to that used by REF panels, although aggregate-level comparisons indicate that more work appears in 4-rated journals than is awarded four by the REF panels. A considerable amount of effort goes into trying to ensure that the output scores provided by REF panels are 'fair', but no individual scores are made public. The REF2014 panel in Business and Management (which evaluated work in the accounting and finance fields) stated categorically that they would not use journal rating lists or impact factors to assess submissions. Instead, they confirmed that they would read each output to provide an individual evaluation.

The RAE and REF are taken very seriously by UK universities since a considerable amount of reputational capital is generated for those schools that perform well, and the results also feed into government research funding allocations.

Rather than using a journal rating as a proxy for the worth of a particular article published in that outlet, I would encourage you to read it and make up your own mind. While no academics can be experts in all sub-fields (and even if they were, they would not have the time to read everything), being able to evaluate studies, noting their strengths and weaknesses, is a valuable skill that all scholars should possess.

8.5.1   What determines how many citations a paper will receive?

Citations are the studies that are referred to in other work, and one method of evaluating the influence that a particular piece has on other academic researchers is to count the number of citations it receives over a period of time. Thus, citations are sometimes considered to be another measure of 'research quality'. Scopus, owned by Elsevier, and Google Scholar, produce a wide range of measurements of the numbers of citations for each paper and aggregated to the level of an academic's whole catalogue of publications or the level of entire departments or universities.

However, citation indices require careful interpretation since there are significant variations across subject areas. In some fields, it is the convention to include very long reference lists, which tend to result in large numbers of citations for work in such areas (e.g., corporate social responsibility), whereas in others where there are relatively few studies being written (such as accounting history), citation counts are generally low. Even within specific areas, populist topics (e.g., cryptocurrencies now) generate many citations while they are hot, but they can rapidly diminish with the topic's fashionableness. Rather worryingly, around a third of papers in social sciences are never cited, according to a blog on the LSE website.[3]

Citations are important, not just to authors but to editors as well, since they determine the journal's impact factor, which is in turn used as a measure of the journal's prestige. But what factors determine how much an article is cited? What you might expect is that the best quality work, perhaps evaluated in terms of its originality, significance and rigour, as outlined above, would garner the most citations. Yet, a study by Judge et al. (2007) looked at this issue in the context of management journals. They found that citation counts are based not just on the quality of the work but also on the 'academic distinction' of the individual(s) writing it. The key factors in determining the number of citations an article receives were the:

- Number of references in the article
- Novelty of the research
- Quality of the writing
- Stature of the author
- Prestige of the author's institution
- Prestige of the journal (which was actually the most important factor)

Perhaps it is not surprising that prestigious authors' work at elite institutions is cited the most, but is that bad? A clever paper by Macdonald and Kam (2007) suggests that it is. They argue that the publication outlet has become more important than the publication itself, and there is a cyclicality about the whole exercise: 'top authors' publish in the 'top journals', but the top journals are top because they publish the work of top authors. Top authors get hired by 'top institutions' because they publish in the top journals, etc. This circularity generates parallel hierarchies of authors, institutions and journals that become ossified, which encourages scholars to lose sight of the subject matter and quality of the work being produced.

The rejection rates at the top journals are usually more than 90% (so less than one paper in 10 submitted for possible publication is eventually accepted). But since rejection rates themselves are often considered a badge of honour and prestige, the higher this figure, the more authors are encouraged to submit their papers there, further depressing the acceptance rate. Perhaps this would be reasonable if the journals acted as a filter so that indeed the best work was published in the highest-rated journals. However, Macdonald and Kam (op cit.) argue that the reliability of screening plummets when rejection rates increase too far so that it becomes more like a lottery.

According to Macdonald and Kam, there are several reasons why the assessment

---

[3] https://blogs.lse.ac.uk/impactofsocialsciences/2014/04/23/academic-papers-citation-rates-remler/

process becomes unreliable if rejection rates are too high:

- The journal becomes a victim of its own success, with the editorial board being swamped with submissions to the extent that they cannot cope with the volume. This overload means that they are unable to send even half the papers out for review. Therefore, they are forced to revert to simple heuristics to evaluate each submission's quality and identify, often tenuous, reasons to quickly desk reject a large percentage of the papers that they don't have time to even skim through. As a result, they may use the author's prestige or affiliation as a crude proxy for the work's quality

- Editors have large amounts of latitude to smooth the process for their preferred authors or pet topics. For instance, they can solicit submissions from specific authors and fast-track papers they like the look of

- Editors will be aware of which referees are 'tough' and reject everything, so they can choose the referees to elicit the outcome they desire, possibly even providing the referee with an informal 'steer' of the result they are expecting. Since the referee is likely conducting the review for free, they will be only too happy to do as the editor suggests so that the latter owes them a favour that can be called in when they submit a paper to the journal, even if their independent reading of the paper would have led them to a different conclusion

- Editors require authors to cite other work in that journal, which distorts citation patterns further towards papers already published in the top journals that new authors are trying to aim at

- Editors select articles that they believe will be widely cited because a key performance indicator for their tenure in that role is the journal's impact factor

- The upshot is that authors are forced to cite weak or irrelevant work in the top journals rather than higher quality and more relevant work in lower-rated journals in the hope of obtaining their own publication in a leading journal. Over time, the publications process becomes inward-looking and stagnates. Particular types of research and on certain topics are favoured by the top journals, while studies on other issues are squeezed out and hard to publish. Many lower-rated journals have an emulation strategy rather than aiming to do something different because the editors want their journals to be like the top journals. This copying results in the narrowness of top journals trickling down through the hierarchy so that the lower-rated journals end up publishing work on similar topics as those at the top but by less well-known authors. Out-of-favour topics become virtually unpublishable anywhere, and it would be career suicide for junior academics who want successful careers to work on them.

The top journals in a field rarely change, even over decades, while new journals find it hard to establish themselves and are discouraged because they initially have no impact factor or AJG rating, making scholars reluctant to submit their work there. Unfortunately, the advent of open access journals where authors are charged an article processing fee to publish their work, but readers can view it freely, has made no difference to the top journals' hegemony.

Agreement between referees is often very low, with correlations of as little as 0.12 reported (Clark and Wright, 2007). Reviewers are often too harsh in their refereeing and are trying to find faults so that the paper can be rejected to increase their own self-esteem. They then become 'uninvited ghost writers', going well beyond their intended remit and effectively telling authors what to say.

One of the principal reasons why papers are rejected from journals is because it is argued that their novel contribution is insufficient, but evaluating the size of a contribution is often challenging. At the same time, the most substantial contributions that are radical, using new approaches lying outside of the established paradigm and having the potential to open up a new field, may be seen as too radical – crazy, even – and so are rejected. This narrow definition of acceptable research means that while the top journals might publish good studies, often the very most innovative work is only publishable in second and third-tier journals. We might therefore conclude that in order to have any non-negligible chance of publication in a top journal, new studies have to be different from those that are already published but not too distant.

What does all this mean for PhD students?

There will be some implications for these 'rules of the game' that come into play when doctoral students come to submit their work to journals as discussed in chapter 14. But there are also some lessons for those who are currently at the stage of deciding what material to read and review:

1. You can be assured that almost all of the work in reputable journals is of at least reasonable quality. There could be flaws of course, and no research is perfect, but it should have been through a rigorous refereeing process to have gained acceptance in that outlet
2. The most innovative and inspiring studies are frequently published outside the top journals
3. As a result of the previous point, it is limiting and potentially dangerous to narrow your perspective to examining only the leading journals as you would run the risk of missing out on some of the most worthwhile papers

8.5.2 Is good quality research 'interesting'?

There is a considerable focus in the academic literature on measuring research quality, with some such discussion presented in this textbook. A related way to evaluate a particular research study would be to ask whether the work it contains is 'interesting'. This is a somewhat slippery concept but could perhaps be thought of as embodying whether going through the piece excites the reader, holds their attention and inspires them to study more on the topic. In a fascinating study, Bartunek *et al.* (2006) examine precisely this question. Interest is arguably an under-valued attribute of academic studies, but one that they argue is important because:

- More interesting research is more likely to be read, understood and remembered
- As a result of the previous point, such a study is more likely to be acted upon
- Interesting work will garner coverage from the media, and the additional publicity will again increase the likelihood that it makes an impact on policy or practice and further encourages other scholars to read and cite it
- Interesting work provides useful discussion points, attracting and motivating new students and colleagues.

According to Bartunek *et al.* (*op cit.*), interesting work could have several features, including:

- Being counterintuitive, so providing unexpected findings
- Going against conventional thinking or previous research on this topic
- Despite not being the primary consideration of the research, it should still nonetheless be of good quality, using a rigorous methodology including theory where relevant and providing an excellent fit to the data
- The work has practical implications, addressing real-world problems, and is not just a study aimed at other academics
- The work also has an academic impact so that it takes our understanding of a phenomenon forward and becomes widely cited, opening up new avenues for research
- The article is well written and has an engaging style
- It includes good examples, so it is not a purely abstract or theoretical piece.

However, according to Bartunek *et al.* (*op cit.*), the work's validity and importance are seen as more crucial aspects than its interest value. They suggest that generating interesting research is not about investigating 'hot topics', so don't scour the newspapers looking for ideas as this brings the danger of producing faddy research that will have a very short shelf-life. Instead, they propose aiming high at producing really novel research that answers big questions rather than looking for narrow gaps and working very hard on the writing style.

Determining the scope of your literature search

When determining what to read, you need to think about the scope of your search – both geographically in terms of which countries and markets you will cover, and also over what time period. A common presumption is that older work has been subsumed in what is written more recently so that there is less requirement to read the former, although you should nonetheless cite the classic studies in the area that formed the foundations of subsequent thinking on the topic.

On the other hand, try to ensure that you examine the most current sources, not just focusing on the classical references on a particular subject. As a rough measure, skim through your reference list as it develops, and if it is up-to-date enough, it ought to contain a sufficient sprinkling of work published in the last few years, particularly if you are working in an active research area. If you are unable to locate much work over this time period despite having conducted an extensive search, it might be an indication that the topic is not currently fashionable in the academy. That is not necessarily a problem or a reason to choose something else to study, and it means that you are less likely to discover part-way through that someone has already done what you wanted to do. But it does mean that you might find less interest in your work than would have been the case if you had chosen something more contemporary.

In terms of the sequence in which to read a large volume of papers, when I start working in a new area, I sometimes find it useful to order the research studies I have gathered chronologically and begin by reading the oldest. This ordering can be helpful because each new study on a particular theme usually builds on previous research, skimming only very briefly over this, and assuming that the reader is familiar with much of it. If you read papers out of chronological order, it can be confusing when the authors have assumed that you are familiar with prior studies. Reading papers in date order allows you to chart the development of the literature over time to see how (or if) it has progressed and whether the trends in the subject matter of this line of research have changed.

8.6   How to focus if there is too much to read

Suppose that you're working on a topic where there is already a large body of research. In that case, you will need to be selective in what you read and what you write about as there will be simply too much existing literature for you to be able to cover all of it in the available time and words. For example, if your topic is empirical tests of the capital asset pricing model (CAPM), economic value added versus cash value added (EVA versus CVA), or fair value accounting, there will be thousands of potentially relevant studies. In this situation, how do you decide what to read and what to include in your review? I would suggest focusing on three sets of studies:

1. The 'seminal' papers in the area – these will be the few core studies that everyone else cites in their work and are likely to represent the major breakthroughs in the subject area.
2. The most relevant work in the area, narrowly defined. So, more precisely, your topic might be 'Testing the four-moment CAPM in emerging markets.' Then you would probably want to look at as many studies as you can get hold of on higher-moment models and tests of the CAPM while ignoring any work broader types of tests of other variants of the CAPM. If that still yields an unmanageable volume of existing literature, then the search could be further narrowed, for example, to 'higher-moment CAPM models and tests applied in the context of emerging markets,' and so on.
3. The latest research on the topic so that your review is fully up to date.

In this sort of situation, the most important aspect is that you have covered the topic's key elements, not that you have covered every paper. When you are swamped with potentially relevant material, there are some types of studies that might be best avoided. Given that your time is limited, don't waste it reading:

- Work that is of low quality – poorly written, unreliable findings, insufficient or inadequate data, weak methodology, etc. If a paper is highly relevant and contains exciting or new ideas but has some flaws in the execution, then cite it and point out the problems – this is all part and parcel of drafting a critical literature review
- Work that merely replicates the findings of existing studies or applies them identically to a new data set (unless your work involves using precisely that data set)
- Purely mathematical work (unless your topic involves developing a mathematical model)

As well as knowing where to seek out the relevant literature, another essential aspect is being aware of when to stop looking. There will come the point when you have uncovered (almost) all of the most pertinent studies – the ones that everyone else is citing and some more specialist pieces on precisely your topic. As discussed above, it is also crucial to examine the working paper repositories to become aware of the most recent additions to the literature, but once you have done that, it is time to stop looking and start consolidating what you have found. If you continue to search in ever more opaque locations that are hard to reach (for example, seeking papers written in other languages), they will almost certainly be much less relevant and not worth your time to find or examine. Incorporating obscure studies will also make your review document longer and less focused than it needs to be, which can unbalance the thesis document as a whole.

8.7   Where to find the literature

Once you are aware of the various outlets, as presented in the previous section, where research – both published and unpublished – can be found, the next stage is to begin the process of searching for the material. Some authors suggest that a literature review search should be 'systematic', and in some fields such as health studies, this seems to be an absolute requirement for an acceptable dissertation. But my view is that there is no such thing, for it could only be systematic if you knew exactly what you were looking for, in which order, and where you were going to find it. Your search can be extensive and perhaps even almost exhaustive so that you have searched as hard for relevant existing work as could reasonably be expected of a student, and in virtually all cases that will be sufficient.

Fortunately, there are several key (virtual) locations to identify and obtain the material you need to read for your review, making the process of searching comprehensively relatively straightforward. Although in the past I spent many productive (and enjoyable!) hours in university libraries 'browsing the stacks', nowadays it is improbable that you will have to set foot in the building when gathering the literature for your study unless you are doing work that requires specific historical documents or old books that are not available electronically. Everything you need will almost certainly be available through the internet.

If you are totally unsure where to start looking for relevant literature, even after following the suggestions below, your university library is bound to run courses – either on-line or in-person – that will start right from the beginning and will explain in detail all of the resources that are available to you.

Gathering the reading material required for your review is a two-stage process. The first step involves getting together a list of bibliometric data pertaining to the items you need. This means you need to identify the author(s), article or book title, date, and journal information (the title, volume number, issue number and page number) if the piece is a journal article or publisher and place of publication if it is a book. The second step comprises using the data you obtained at the first step to find and download the articles or books.

For the first stage, you will probably use a search engine, a database, or the reference list from your course material or articles you are already aware of. I will now discuss each of these sources.

8.7.1   Using search engines

These are the obvious places to start when gathering the information to do a literature review. Hence, the initial phase to collecting the research articles will be to think about and note down a set of keywords that encapsulate the essence of the mass of work you are interested in tapping into. Examining the first few search results will probably suggest further, or more refined, keywords.

Usually, a search engine linked with a database of journals or working papers will only look for matches in the title, abstract and author-selected keywords, and not the main body of the article. This limitation is unfortunate since it might be that a particular methodological detail you are interested in is only discussed in that section of the paper and not in the abstract. Other search engines such as Google that look inside pdf files will examine the entire document, not differentiating between sections, which might be more useful in that sense.

If the search terms you enter into the engine are too vague, you will obtain too many hits, making it a tiresome job to trawl through them all, a lot of which will be irrelevant. On the other hand, if your terms are too specific, you will get few hits, and there is a danger that you will miss some useful material.

In order to ensure that your searches include the most relevant material possible (and exclude irrelevant hits), use 'and', which in this context is known as a Boolean (logic) operator, with your search terms in quotation marks. For example, typing 'four-moment capm emerging markets' will lead to over 500,000 hits on Google, although the most relevant matches appearing at the top are right on topic. By default, engines will list results containing any of the search terms (in essence, implicitly using 'or' between the search words). However, it will probably list the web pages containing the highest number of matching words, which will be the most useful hits, at the top. On the other hand, a search by typing four-moment 'capm' and 'emerging markets' yields a little over 800 hits, all of which look highly relevant. Note that, in

Figure 8.1: Screenshot from Google Scholar

Corporate social performance and stock returns: UK evidence from disaggregate   [PDF] reading.ac.uk
measures
<u>S Brammer</u>, C **Brooks**, <u>S Pavelin</u> - Financial management, 2006 - Wiley Online Library
This study examines the relation between corporate social performance and stock returns in
the UK. We closely evaluate the interactions between social and financial performance with
a set of disaggregated social performance indicators for environment, employment, and …
☆ ⁇ Cited by 1039   Related articles   All 19 versions

general, search engines are not case sensitive, so there is no need to use any capitals.

8.7.2 Google Scholar

It is also worth using Google Scholar rather than Google since the former is focused purely on scholarly output and will yield a list of relevant material focused predominantly on academic articles rather than newspapers or blogsites.[4] For example, Figure 8.1 shows one such output from Google Scholar, which provides information on the title, authors, journal or other publication outlet, abstract, and how many times it has been cited. It also shows, on the right-hand side, a clickable link to a place where the paper can be downloaded. In this case, the paper is one that I co-authored, which appeared in the journal *Financial Management*. A pre-publication version of the paper is available free of charge without registration from the University of Reading repository.

If you are specifically interested in books rather than working papers or journal articles, then search using Google Books. Another benefit of using Google Scholar is that it is possible to download a citation by clicking on the quotation mark. When you do, the screen will appear as in Figure 8.2. It is also possible to download this information in several different formats to be dropped straight into reference management software such as EndNote, ProCite or BibTeX. This consistency not only saves time but will also ensure a standard of consistency and accuracy that would be hard to achieve when typing the references manually.

8.7.3 Your university library catalogue

An essential source of material will be your university library's electronic catalogue. Several searchable databases can probably be accessed from the library's webpages. The web links below provide general information about the databases but obtaining articles can only go through your institution:

- Ingenta (formerly BIDS) is a repository for journal articles[5]
- Web of Science (which was formerly known as the Web of Knowledge) provides access to large numbers of journals, particularly in the natural and physical sciences[6]

---

[4]https://scholar.google.com
[5]https://www.ingentaconnect.com
[6]https://www.webofknowledge.com

Figure 8.2: Citation downloads from Google Scholar

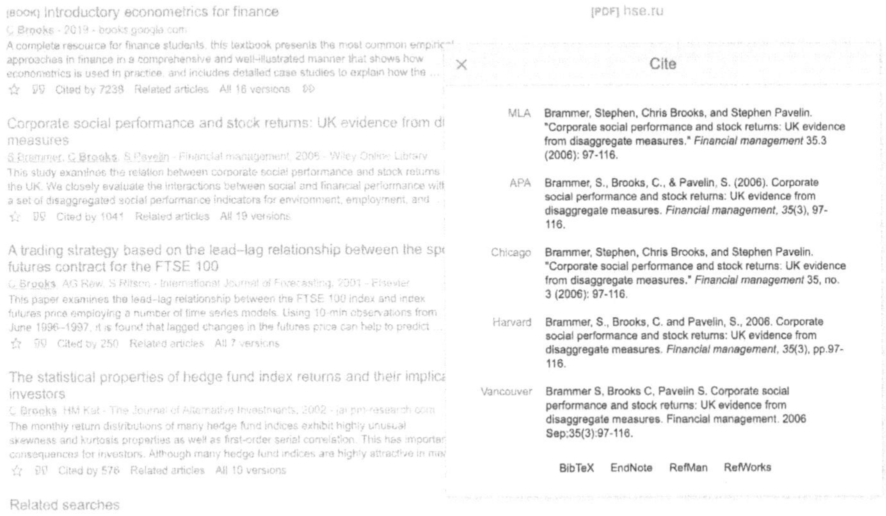

- JStor is an on-line repository for over 2,000 journals and 90,000 e-books and other media[7]
- Ebsco (Business Source Ulitmate) is a repository containing the full text of over 2,500 journals spanning much of business and management, including accounting, economics and finance[8]
- Sciences Direct is the publisher Elsevier's portal and repository for its extensive collection of journals across the sciences, arts and humanities, and social sciences[9]
- ProQuest Central is a database and archive containing large numbers of journals, books, theses, and newspapers[10]

Most universities subscribe to bundles of journals from all of the leading scholarly publishers (Cambridge University Press, Elsevier, Oxford University Press, Palgrave, Wiley, etc.), and so you should have access to a broad range of titles. But in general, the library catalogue can only be used to search for journal and book titles and not for individual articles within each title. So you need to know precisely which items (and the names and volume/issue/page numbers or books) you need before you start.

How to find a known journal article using a university library catalogue

Each library will have a slightly different system, but the approach in each case will be broadly the same:

1. Go to your university's main website, and from there, find the library pages

---

[7] https://www.jstor.com
[8] https://www.ebsco.com/products/research-databases/business-source-ultimate
[9] https://www.sciencedirect.com/browse/journals-and-books?subject=business-management-and-accounting
[10] https://www.proquest.com

Figure 8.3: Screenshot from ejournal search

Showing results 1 to 1 of 1
for the search: Title begins with "British Accounting Review"

Note Alternative titles may have matched your search terms. Remove alternate titles

Limit by: Peer Reviewed | Open Access

The British accounting review   Terms of Use
Alternate Title: *British accounting review*
ISSN: 0890-8389
Look up Article
Peer Reviewed
1988 to 1994 in Elsevier Business, Management and Accounting Archive inc. supplement For off-campus access, select "Sign In" in
                 the top right of the screen, then click the 'sign in via your institution' option. Search for the University of Reading. Click
                 'Sign In via your Institution' again and then log in as normal.
01.03.1995 to Present in Elsevier:Jisc Collections:ScienceDirect Freedom Collection:2017-2021 For off-campus access, select "Sign
                 In" in the top right of the screen, then select "Other Institution" and search for University of Reading. Click
                 this and then log in as normal.
1996 to 1999 in IngentaConnect

   (possibly via the student portal)

2. Find the link to 'e-resources' or 'e-journals'

3. Type the title of the journal or book (or part of it) in the search bar and hit
   enter. For example, I typed 'British Accounting Review' and got the output in
   Figure 8.3

4. Click on the link to the date range that the paper you want to download falls
   within. You will probably now be asked to enter your university IT system
   login details. You might have to go through 'OpenAthens', a system for
   managing journal access used by most universities. Even if this is the case,
   you would still use your usual university login username and password, which
   will automatically link with your university's server to verify the details

5. Find the journal volume and issue number in which the paper is located, then
   click on and download a pdf of the article.

As the screenshot shows, all articles going right back to 1988 are available to
University of Reading researchers for this journal. All of the major publishers have
similar bundle deals with universities to make their content available electronically,
so if the article you need is published in a reputable journal, it will probably be
available through your university's library catalogue. When you click through to a
journal article, you will usually be given access options, and it is often possible to
enter your university's name, followed by your IT Services username and password.
If your institution subscribes to the journal, access will be free and should lead you

straight through to access a pdf of the article.

Other places to find specific journal articles

But what if the article you need is located in a journal that is not part of a bundle (e.g., a journal published by a learned society that your university does not subscribe to)? If the material is peripheral to your core research topic or you were investigating it primarily out of curiosity, you might elect to ignore that piece and concentrate on more easily accessible sources. However, if it was an essential reference, there are several other places you could look for the paper:

1. See whether the work is available through Google Scholar, as discussed above
2. Most universities have repositories where they store all of their staff members' published articles. These are made available free of charge to everyone without registration once a publisher-determined embargo period after initial publication (usually 1–3 years) has passed. Try to find the authors' university repositories and see if the work is in there
3. Many authors put all of their work on the Social Sciences Research Network (SSRN) when it is completed in working paper form prior to publication and then leave it there indefinitely where it can be downloaded freely and without registration unless a journal publisher removes it[11]
4. Similar to 3, many authors use Research Gate as a repository for their work, although you may have to register to access the papers stored there[12]
5. If all else fails, you could e-mail the author of a particular paper directly, tell them how interested you are to read their work, and politely request that they send you an electronic copy of the document. In almost all cases, they will oblige.

If an essential reference is a book rather than a journal, it is often trickier to obtain it electronically. It is still worth going through your university library catalogue to see if you can get an e-book version as they often have copies that they can loan out electronically. As for journals, some publishers now have bundle deals allowing unlimited access to a wide range of books from their collections. Be aware, though, that unlike journal articles that can be downloaded as pdf files and printed, e-books usually have tight digital rights management (DRM) protection, which means that they cannot be printed, and it might not even be possible to download them, so they have to be read directly on-line.

Google Books, Amazon Kindle Books and Apple iBooks also have a comprehensive coverage of recent books. Although most of them must be purchased or rented for a fee, the electronic versions tend to be significantly cheaper than their print equivalents.

---

[11] https://www.ssrn.com/index.cfm/en/
[12] https://www.researchgate.net

8.7.4   Working papers and literature on the internet

Unfortunately, the lag between a paper being written and published in a journal is often two years (and increasing fast), so that research in even the most recent issues of the printed journals will be somewhat dated. Additionally, many securities firms, banks and central banks worldwide produce high-quality research output in report form, which they often do not bother to try to publish in journals. Much of this is now available on the internet, so it is worth conducting searches with keywords using readily available web search engines. A few suggestions for places to start are given below.

Searchable sources of unpublished articles and working papers

Besides general search engines, including Google Scholar, there are other, more specialist databases that can be used for keyword searches. These include:

- SSRN is an incredibly vast repository of close to a million working papers across a range of relevant fields in the social sciences, including accounting, economics, and finance. It is keyword searchable, and the documents can be downloaded freely and without registration[13]
- ResearchGate is, like SSRN, a large, searchable repository of working papers but not limited to the social sciences[14]
- IDEAS is a vast database and repository of articles and working papers in economics[15]
- The National Bureau of Economic Research (NBER) holds a vast database of discussion papers and links including data sources[16]

Universities

Almost all universities around the world now make copies of their discussion papers available electronically. Two examples from leading accounting and finance departments, although of course there are many more, are:

- Department of Finance, Stern School, New York University[17]
- Wharton Financial Institutions Center, University of Pennsylvania[18]

Central banks

The US Federal Reserve Banks and the Bank of England also have sets of working papers and other resources:

- Bank of England, containing their working papers, news and discussion[19]

---

[13]https://www.ssrn.com/index.cfm/en/

[14]https://www.researchgate.net

[15]https://ideas.repec.org

[16]https://www.nber.org

[17]https://www.stern.nyu.edu/experience-stern/about/departments-centers-initiatives/academic-departments/finance/research/working-papers

[18]https://fic.wharton.upenn.edu/working-papers/

[19]https://www.bankofengland.co.uk/research

- Federal Reserve Bank of Atlanta, including information on economic and research data and publications[20]
- Federal Reserve Board of Governors International Finance Discussion Papers[21]
- Federal Reserve Bank of New York discussion papers[22]

International bodies

- International Accounting Standards Board (IASB) discussion papers[23]
- International Monetary Fund (IMF) World Economic Outlook Report, Global Financial Stability Report, Fiscal Monitor Report and their discussion papers[24]
- World Bank working papers in finance[25]
- Organisation for Economic Cooperation and Development (OECD) working papers[26]

Professional associations and learned societies in accounting and finance

Professional associations represent the industry and its participants and employees, while learned societies represent academic staff. Professional associations are usually responsible for setting professional standards in that sector, and they provide training, education and examinations that lead to industry qualifications. The education aspect means that they can often be a valuable source of materials for dissertation research. Professional Association websites sometimes host blogs or opinion pieces regarding new field issues, which can help generate ideas and drive awareness of the current problems of particular interest in the industry. The relevant bodies, which can easily be searched, are:

Professional Associations

- Association of Chartered Certified Accountants (ACCA)
- Chartered Institute of Management Accountants (CIMA)
- UK Finance (including what was formerly the British Bankers Association)
- Chartered Institute of Public Finance and Accountancy (CIPFA)
- Chartered Institute of Taxation
- Institute of Chartered Accountants in England and Wales (ICAEW)
- Institute of Chartered Accountants in Scotland (ICAS)

The learned societies include

- American Accounting Association (AAA)
- American Finance Association (AFA)
- British Accounting and Finance Association (BAFA)

---

[20] https://www.frbatlanta.org

[21] https://www.federalreserve.gov/econres.htm

[22] https://www.newyorkfed.org/research

[23] https://www.iasplus.com/en/resources/ifrsf/due-process/iasb-discussion-papers

[24] https://www.imf.org/en/Research

[25] https://www.worldbank.org/en/research

[26] https://www.oecd-ilibrary.org

- European Accounting Association (EAA)
- European Finance Association (EFA)

The learned societies are usually responsible for organising and editing one or more of the leading field journals. For example, BAFA is responsible for the *British Accounting Review,* published by Elsevier.

What to do if you can't find any relevant literature

The obvious first response to this issue would be to suggest looking harder and in different places. Have you checked for published sources, working papers, theses and books using all of the resources identified in this book? If that is the case, and you have still not found anything, then it might be that you have construed your topic too narrowly and excluded studies that would have been within the scope if you defined your search more widely. It is better to write a review including a range of marginally relevant material than to have nothing to write about at all.

A final possibility is that there genuinely is very little scholarly literature on the topic that you chose either because it is a very new idea that you are among the first to work on, or that it is perhaps not an amenable topic for academic-type research which is why no scholars have written about it before. This is an unlikely scenario, but if you think this might be the case, it is worth checking your supervisor's view on whether they consider it an appropriate subject for a thesis. If the topic has received supervisory approval, then you would need to redouble your efforts to find some underpinning literature as in the first two paragraphs in response to this question. Your supervisor might also have suggestions for other places you could search for material.

8.8 How to read an academic paper

Knowing how to read a research article is another skill that takes some time and practice to develop. In particular, you need to know:
- What to look for in the work
- How to determine where the paper fits into the broader literature and how it is related to previous studies
- How to summarise the key points in a few lines
- How to identify any weaknesses or omissions (as well as the strengths of the piece), and, more generally, how to evaluate the study critically.

Clearly, when you decide to read a particular piece, you will start with the presumption that the work has some relevance for your PhD. Sometimes, upon reading the abstract, doubts might already begin to creep in that perhaps the paper is not so useful after all. That being the case, it is still worth very briefly skimming the rest of the article to check that, indeed, the apparently irrelevant contents of the summary did not hide a gem. Try to look for keywords or phrases that link with your topic.

When the work is not relevant, discard it; if it is only peripherally relevant, it is worth just making some brief notes, and you could always return to it subsequently if necessary. If, upon a quick skim, it is evident that the paper is related to your PhD, you would continue to read it in depth.

If you are very short of time, you might need to focus your reading, and in such eventualities, you might consider examining only the abstract, introduction and conclusions in cases where the work has some relevance, but you would not consider it a primary reference for what you are doing. In some ways, these are the most important sections – the introduction will explain the motivation for the work and will probably provide a more detailed summary than the abstract, while the conclusions will again discuss what was found and how it fits into the wider literature. For some studies, you will need to review the core methodology employed carefully and the results obtained, especially if the conceptual approach is similar to the one that you will use.

Particularly when you first begin the detailed reading for your review, there will surely be large numbers of specialist or technical words and acronyms that are unfamiliar, and this will impede your understanding. But if you persevere, using search engines or an on-line glossary to establish their meaning where necessary, it will become much more straightforward with experience, and you will be able to go through each paper faster and increasingly effectively. When you come across unfamiliar technical terms, there are several useful, specialist on-line glossaries available that can be used to find the meaning of specialist words, including:

In accounting
- The Accounting Dictionary at My Accounting Course[27]
- The Accounting Tools Dictionary of Accounting Topics (which has very detailed information)[28]
- The Accounting Coach Dictionary of Accounting Terms[29]

In finance
- The Dictionary by Farlex[30]
- Investopedia[31]

Making and organising notes

Make notes on each paper as you go along – try to record the gist of the information in the study. It is common for students to gather an extensive collection of research articles – either photocopies or pdf files – and then to feel somehow that a significant part of their work is done. But just having possession of an article does not mean

---

[27]https://www.myaccountingcourse.com/accounting-dictionary

[28]https://www.accountingtools.com/dictionary

[29]https://www.accountingcoach.com/terms

[30]https://financial-dictionary.thefreedictionary.com

[31]https://www.investopedia.com/financial-term-dictionary-4769738

that you have absorbed the contents, let alone understood them. Only by reading the articles and, crucially, making notes will you be able to say that you have reviewed the literature. Unfortunately, reading the papers and then organising your notes and ideas into the review chapter are the time-consuming steps. Identifying and gathering the material is usually the relatively quick and easy part.

Going through the pile of papers and making brief notes on each one is not in itself sufficient: you need to have some understanding of the work and be able to remember and articulate the key points from each study. Later, you will also need to be able to classify and compare them, drawing out the similarities and differences, but this is discussed in the next chapter. Be careful to use your own words from the outset and make it clear in your notes if you are quoting directly, which will avoid inadvertent plagiarism. Although some people prefer to make hand-written notes and only type things up at the end, it will save a lot of time if you keep everything electronically from the outset.

While different research articles will vary substantially in their length, structure and writing style, several key aspects will be common that you should be able to identify and make a mental note of:

- The research questions
- The key investigative methods used
- The nature of the data – sources, coverage, timespan, etc.
- The main findings
- Is there anything particularly new, inspiring or different about this study compared with others on this theme?

Sometimes you will need to read a particular passage or whole section several times before it begins to make sense. Don't be concerned as this is entirely normal. It might be that you are new to this subject, and so you have less background knowledge about it than the author had assumed. It is also true that some authors are better communicators than others, and your lack of understanding might be a result of a poorly drafted article and a confusing writing style.

If you think this might be the case, put that paper to one side and have a go at reading a different study on the same topic. If this piece makes greater sense, the previous one was indeed poorly written; if you still don't follow it, you probably need to move back a step to a more straightforward treatment such as that in a textbook before returning to the research literature.

Also, try to identify which aspect of the writing you don't understand – is it the language, because the proportion of unfamiliar words is too great, so the meaning is obscured? Or do you know the terms but not how they are being used so that you cannot see what the author is trying to say? In that case, perhaps it is the methods or models that are not clear, or maybe you understand how the author is using the techniques, but you cannot see why or to what end?

If the terminology is the source of confusion, a dictionary (or a glossary of technical terms) might be useful – see above for relevant dictionaries in accounting and finance. Or you could try a different piece by another writer who uses a more accessible language; in the latter situation where you cannot grasp why the steps in the paper are being taken, move back down the chain to an article published earlier where perhaps more will be explained.

When reading an article, it is possible to make notes concurrently, but it is usually better to read a whole piece of text first, then to summarise it from memory, which will give you a better overview, enabling you to better extract the essence of the work rather than just paraphrasing directly from what is written. But equally, don't leave it too long after reading a piece before you write a summary of it; otherwise, there is a danger that the details will become fuzzy and you would have to reread it, or worse, that several studies merge in your mind, leading you to mix up the elements from one paper with another.

Make it clear in your notes which parts you have paraphrased into your own words and which you are quoting directly. Making careful notes in this way is essential for several reasons. First, it will help you remember the most important aspects of the work to ensure that you don't waste time rereading it. Second, it should help to avoid errors later where you inadvertently plagiarise from a source because you thought you had written it into your own words as you were going along, but you had not. If you identify particular sentences that you might want to quote directly in your thesis, copy them down accurately with full bibliometric details. Also, remember to update your reference list at this stage, including all of the details of the source – this will make it much easier at the end than trying to create the list from scratch.

A particular difficulty when you initially begin the reading is that you will be unsure of which parts of each paper are the most relevant to make notes on. Sometimes it will just be the core findings or interpretation that is relevant to you, but for other studies it might be the detailed data and methods that are of interest. Ideally, you would read several studies first, get a feel for the subject area as a whole, and then go back to the first studies you read and re-examine them, although this process would be repetitive and therefore time-consuming.

Remember that since you will be working on that piece of research for months or even years, your notes will need to be clear and detailed. The summaries still need to make sense to you later when, for example, you come to write your conclusions, and you had forgotten the details of the papers you had read when you were drafting your literature review.

You should retain all of your notes, whether they are in electronic or paper form, until after you submit the thesis document and have the viva examination as you might need to refer to them later or require them as evidence that you had done this groundwork in case you are accused of any malpractice (see chapter 7).

As well as just making notes, you will need to decide at an early stage about how you will organise them. Without doing so, you will have two enormous tasks: one identifying the relevant literature and reading it, and the other to make sense of your mass of summaries and try to work out how to get them into any kind of continuous narrative. The better quality, more accurate and organised are the notes you make as you are reading now, the quicker you will be able to pull the literature review document together later.

It is worth pointing out that different people remember and interpret information in varying ways, and this will determine the best way for them to develop their notes. I prefer a linear summary written in words in a single colour since, in my case, it is the words and phrases that stick out rather than the way that they look on the page. But many people find that it helps them visualise the threads between the studies better and extract the key messages by using different colours, spider diagrams, or concept maps. You could also arrange the summaries chronologically if you are working on a topic where the literature developed steadily over time.

Keeping all your notes electronically will make them much easier to work with, move around, and incorporate directly than if you write them on paper. It will also make them much easier to back up. If you haven't already, experiment with different approaches to note-taking and organisation until you find a style that works well for you.

Be a sceptical reader and a persuasive writer

Always be on the lookout for a 'sales job' and in such cases be sceptical of the veracity of the arguments being made. You need to be able to distinguish between three things:

1. Widely accepted fact
2. Supported perspective based on evidence
3. Unsubstantiated opinion

The first type will be entirely objective and the last entirely subjective, while the middle one may contain elements of both objectivity and subjectivity (for instance, if the evidence is weak or the researcher applies their own interpretation to ambiguous results). It is fine to quote and discuss all three writing types in your dissertation, but you need to make it clear to your readers which category a particular piece falls within.

Also, employ a degree of scepticism when looking at the statistical output in a study: don't assume that because there is quantitative work, it is necessarily correct. The author may have made errors in conducting the analysis, and even if the work has been carried out competently, they might have deliberately misrepresented the findings to emphasise the stronger aspects and hide any anomalous results. In general, the more sophisticated the techniques used, the harder it is for readers to understand and challenge the results, but the more likely it is that something will have gone wrong.

In a large number of situations, the writing style used has to be persuasive. Although you are not selling a product, you are nonetheless trying to sell your ideas – why your topic is interesting, why the methods you chose are the most appropriate, why your data are relevant, why your results are robust, and why your findings might be useful to a wider audience. To persuade people that your arguments are valid, you need to make them in a logical structure and using language that is precise and will resonate with your audience. You need to use evidence, either from your own empirical work or by citing a paper from the existing literature, for every point you make that would not be considered 'common knowledge'.

Equally, you should be aware that other authors will be using their writing intending to persuade their readers (including you) that their methods, data and analysis are not only correct but better in some senses than those employed in previous studies. The use of persuasive language makes critical thinking and always being on the lookout for flaws in empirical design and implementation all the more important. Each time you read a study, there are several questions that it helps to hold in the back of your mind:

- Does the paper present new findings or new insights that make it worth reading and citing? Or is it merely recycling old ideas?
- Does the work have implications for end users, such as practitioners or regulators? Or does it contribute to scholars' understanding of a particular problem or phenomenon?
- What information has the writer omitted from their argument or description of what they did?
- On which aspects of the results in the tables or figures did the writer not comment?
- Is the sample used sufficiently large and representative to justify the writer's conclusions?
- Were there other methods or models that could have been more appropriate to achieve the writer's empirical aims? For example, did the author select a quantitative study when a series of interviews would have addressed the research questions more effectively?
- Is the dataset employed appropriate and of a sufficient size? How was it chosen: because of its relevance or for convenience (possibly resulting in a so-called easy data bias)?
- Has all of the relevant work that was available at the time of writing been cited? Or is the literature review in the paper deficient?
- Is there a disconnect between the theory presented and the empirical implementation of it?
- Is there a lack of theory leading to the potential for spurious findings?
- Are the author's analyses and the findings stated the only plausible interpretations, or are there other, equally valid inferences?
- Are all of the conclusions justified by the evidence that the author (or previous authors) has (had) presented, or are some speculative?

It is vital that you read and include in the review studies that take a different position in their arguments to yours; if nothing else, it demonstrates that you are aware of such studies and citing them will enable you to demolish their lines of reasoning.

For example, if you are arguing that 'the CAPM beta is dead', you should also refer to other studies suggesting that it is still valid and useful.

8.9 Reading rapidly

Learning how to read effectively but rapidly is a useful skill to master. You need to be willing to put in many hours of reading to become knowledgeable enough about the subject to produce a solid literature review. But if you learn to be selective and identify what is likely to be worth delving deeper into, and you can develop the skill to go through the papers quickly, you can save a lot of time.

For instance, speed readers can group blocks of several words together rather than reading each word individually, meaning that their eyes can scan over the page far more quickly. Another aspect of reading quickly is scanning for relevant keywords, which means that the sentences involving them are reviewed more thoroughly, and sentences omitting them can be skipped over. You might also be able to recognise groups of words that tend to go together so that you know how a sentence will finish without reading it closely, in the same way as autocomplete functions in e-mail and text message software work.

Of course, there are dangers with this approach if you go into autopilot and sacrifice understanding for rapidity. Reading a paragraph twice quickly might take longer than if you had gone through it more slowly and thoroughly in the first instance, but if you can effectively scan over documents, you could save a significant amount of time.

Reading quickly can also be supported by good eyesight, good lighting, clear printing or a good screen, appropriate font size, a lack of distractions, and not being drowsy. Therefore, to make the quickest possible progress with your literature mountain climb:

- Use reading glasses if you need them, and have an eye test if you think your short distance vision is less than perfect
- Invest in a desk lamp and position yourself near a window where possible
- Ensure that the printer has enough ink and that the font size is sufficiently large; don't be tempted to save paper to the extent that the output is hard to read. Some of my colleagues shrink two A4 pages to fit onto one, which I find almost impossible to examine
- Minimise or remove distractions (see section 6.1)
- Get a good night's sleep before working, and plan your reading to take place at times when you are at your most alert
- Never read for more than an hour without taking a break, otherwise your concentration level will slip, and your mind will drift even if you don't initially realise it

Skimming has the same objective as speed reading, but in the latter case, you would aim to read every word in an article, just faster than usual, getting through the material much quicker but still obtaining a good understanding of the material.

Scan reading for a literature review is hard because you don't know precisely what you are looking for, you only have a general idea. Using a handful of keywords and entirely excluding everything else would likely lead to missing many relevant, perhaps even vital, pieces of information. Skimming successfully is a skill that takes time to cultivate but one that is nonetheless worth acquiring. There are some interesting resources on how to speed read that might be fun to follow up and try:

- An extended article on the BBC website that is a useful place to start[32]
- Several articles with links to other pieces on Speedreadingtechniques.org[33]
- The SpeedReadGuide channel on YouTube[34]

As with learning to touch-type, becoming an effective speed reader would be worthwhile, but it will take a lot of time and practice to develop. Initially, while learning to touch-type, it would take longer to key in a block of text than doing it the more conventional way. Similarly, you might decide that you do not have the time to invest in learning to speed read, but if you do, it will be a skill that you would be able to draw on throughout life.

8.9.1 What you should read in detail and what to skim

Do not merely rely on article or book titles to decide what to read in detail, what to skim read, and what to ignore. Titles can be extremely misleading as authors often select idioms or well-known catchphrases to grab attention; titles also contain so few words that it is hard to cover all aspects of the study.

There are broadly two approaches to skim reading: covering virtually the entire article or reading only some individual sections but more thoroughly. Either way, the abstract is, of course, the place to start and should provide a strong indication of whether the paper is likely to be worth reading further or not. But, like the title, the number of words in the abstract is strictly constrained and consequently, unless the author is exceptionally skilled in maximising the amount of information provided in a tiny space, there will be numerous details that will not come across from reading the abstract alone.

If you choose to skim read the whole piece, you will scan through, paragraph-by-paragraph, looking for keywords or specific phrases relevant to your topic, skipping over the rest of the text. At the same time, you would be aiming to get the essence of what is being written so that, if you were asked to, you could provide someone with a brief summary of the main point of the article.

A further suggestion is to link the speed and detail of your reading with the material you are covering. Background and peripheral material can be gone through reasonably quickly, while articles that are core to your objectives or where you are trying to understand the methods so that you can replicate them need a thorough examination.

---

[32]https://www.bbc.com/future/article/20191129-how-to-learn-to-speed-read

[33]https://www.speedreadingtechniques.org/how-to-speed-read

[34]https://www.youtube.com/user/SpeedReadGuide

Skimming books

If some of the material you are reviewing constitutes entire books (as opposed to book chapters, where the same approach as for journal articles can be adopted), you will need to focus your reading on small parts of them, at least initially, as it will be infeasible to read several books in detail in the time available. You can start by using the book's synopsis in place of an article's abstract and the table of contents to identify the most relevant parts.

Skim reading books can be quite challenging, not just because of their sheer length but also because they are usually written so that each chapter builds upon previous chapters, with the author taking for granted that the reader will subsequently recall any definitions and notation already introduced. Hence the chapters are not self-contained, and it might be that if you find chapter Z to be particularly relevant, you need to go back to chapters Z-1, Z-2, etc., to be able to understand it fully.

Books have the additional benefit of an index, which can be used to perform a keyword search. However, frequently, index entries relate to pages in the book where that word gets a mere brief mention with no useful detail and hence an index is usually much less helpful than a table of contents for guiding skim reading.

Ensure that a book is really going to be useful before ordering it from the library or buying it. I have wasted a considerable amount of time and money over the years on books that their blurb appeared to suggest would be just what I needed but caused significant disappointment when they arrived.

To be useful, books need to be pitched at the right level, given your knowledge and understanding at the time you read them, and they need to contain an appropriate amount of detail. Books that are too easy, telling you again what you already knew, or too hard so that you understand nothing, are of little use to you. On balance, it is usually preferable to go for books that challenge you, though, since your level of knowledge will multiply as you read more and get deeper into the investigative work.

8.10 Reflecting on a research area

Once you are in the position of having read and made notes on a reasonable amount of material, you will begin to be able to identify the common threads between the studies and make tentative steps to see the direction the literature on your chosen topic is going and how it is evolving. At that stage, some questions to reflect on are:

1. What are the primary themes that have emerged in this area?
2. Does this topic have a solid theoretical underpinning (if so, from which types of theories), or are the bulk of the studies purely empirical in nature?
3. Are there specific individuals or particular universities leading this research effort, or is it geographically well spread? Have practitioners, research agencies or central banks produced any of this body of work, or is it only of interest to academics?
4. Are there any pivotal studies that changed the research direction on the topic and that nearly every other study since then has cited?

5. Are the majority of studies using the same methods and data, or is a range of techniques employed?
6. How has this topic developed chronologically? Was there a burst of activity at a specific point in time, or did the research efforts span many years? Is it still being investigated, or has the volume of material waned?
7. Are studies on this topic published mainly in journals (and are they the leading journals), books, or working papers?
8. Is there evidence of a disagreement between authors regarding their findings, or is there a consensus that has emerged?
9. Is there any interdisciplinary work in this area, or is it all within the discipline?
10. Are there any apparent gaps in this body of work where queries that arise to you have not been answered? This question is perhaps the most challenging yet the most important of all: if you can come up with a good response here, you have the basis for your investigative work.

As I will discuss in detail in the following chapter, a literature review needs to be critical of the studies it is discussing. Therefore, when analysing a paper, try to identify flaws in the arguments being made, which can then form the basis of your critique. For instance:

- Does the study's empirical work lack a theoretical foundation? A common criticism of accounting and finance research is that the investigator throws together a set of variables and writes about any statistically significant relationships without thinking why these items were in the model until after it was estimated
- Are dubious assumptions being made? These might be implausible, but have they been justified and has the findings' sensitivity to them been examined?
- Are the arguments made in the paper based on false logic?
- Have competing ideas or explanations of the findings been ignored entirely rather than considered and then dismissed based on evidence? In other words, have the authors selected one interpretation of the results which is consistent with the explanation that they wanted to put forward, but where there are also other possible explanations that they have ignored or not discussed? This one-sided perspective is surprisingly common in research studies.

Chapter takeaways – top tips for success

- ⊛ Be aware of the reasons why researchers conduct literature reviews and the pitfalls that lie in wait if the review is ineffective or incomplete
- ⊛ It might be advisable to begin your review with basic sources such as lecture materials or textbooks, but the core of the review will likely be drawn from academic journal articles
- ⊛ Know how to evaluate the quality of your reading material and ensure its validity

Chapter takeaways – continued

⊛ Ensure that you also examine unpublished studies, especially recently produced working papers

⊛ Know where to find relevant literature using search engines, Google Scholar, library-based databases such as JStor, Ebsco and Web of Science, as well as repositories such as SSRN and ResearchGate

⊛ Ensure that you are aware of what you should be looking for in academic studies and how to identify flaws and limitations of the work

⊛ Reflect on where each article you read fits within its wider genre

9. WRITING THE LITERATURE REVIEW

Learning outcomes: this chapter covers

✓ How to write a literature review
✓ How to make your writing critical
✓ How to structure and format the review
✓ How to incorporate direct quotations
✓ How to correctly reference existing studies

9.1 Writing the review: some preliminary considerations

This section presents some initial questions that will likely arise in your mind as you begin to think about organising your notes and writing the review. Each of those threads is then expanded throughout subsequent sections in this chapter.

9.1.1 How long should the review be?

Determining the length of the review and how many chapters it should span within the thesis is not as straightforward a matter to resolve as it might appear. There is no definitive response to this issue, and the most appropriate length will vary depending on the subject matter and the volume of existing output on the topic, as well as the total number of words available for the thesis and whether there is any danger that you might come close to this limit.

In general, the more discursive (less technical) and the greater the extant body of work, the longer your review is likely to be. The convention, which also seems the optimal choice in most cases, is to make the review exactly one chapter long. A review that spans more than a single chapter is likely to be unwieldy and excessive. It would be possible to combine the introduction and literature review into a single chapter, but this would only be sensible if both chapters were too short or too interconnected to stand alone. This situation might suggest that the review was not sufficiently long or detailed and ought to be expanded.

Another issue to consider is whether the literature review will be gathered together into a single chapter or separated and the relevant parts placed within each investigative chapter. This question is discussed in subsection 11.5.1, but it is worth noting here that even if the final thesis includes several mini-reviews, students will usually be required to produce a single substantive literature review initially prior to commencing their investigative work.

Inevitably, when you begin writing your literature review, you will have a substantial amount of material in the form of notes, ideas, summaries and articles marked with a highlighter pen. Deciding how to organise the subject matter is an essential step to going from a mess to a coherent draft. But it is often hard to know where to start.

Drafting the literature review to say what you want it to is a skill that usually takes time to perfect. Ideally, the review will set the scene for your investigative work and put your research into a proper context. Just as many research proposals are review-heavy, so too are the dissertations themselves. Although the length of the review will depend on how much material there is to review (for example, as already mentioned, if you are writing on accounting standards or the capital asset pricing model, it is not feasible to examine everything), in general, it should not comprise more than about a fifth of the whole thesis.

You need to quickly develop a system to classify the literature that you have gathered. This classification will also help you to organise the review. For example, you could arrange it by the methodology used (e.g., descriptive, interviews, quantitative analysis, or by a theoretical vs. empirical approach), by sub-topic covered, chronologically, etc. Organising the review logically is often one of the trickiest parts as you are likely to have a mass of studies and be unsure where to place them, initially having no way to order the material. If you have used a two-dimensional approach to classifying the studies, such as a spider diagram, at some stage, this will need to be transformed into a single-dimensional collation of the material with a storyline that creates a sensible ordering.

You will need to structure the information and relate it to the research questions you are developing. Try to identify the common threads that link research studies together thematically – this could be through their methods, the perspective they take (e.g., for or against a particular viewpoint), data coverage, country or market focus, findings, or when they were written. The work can then be organised in several ways

– for instance, by topic, method (the technique used), country or market covered, findings (researchers A, B and C all found evidence in favour of the theory while X, Y and Z found evidence against it), and so on.

A good way to start is by categorising the material according to the class of models or theories. The classes can then be ordered chronologically (where the earliest developed model class appears first in the draft), or by importance (with the models currently considered most important ordered first), or by the level of sophistication of the model class (beginning with the most straightforward types and gradually increasing in complexity). Then, within each of these categories, you can describe when and how the model or idea was derived, what are its key features and benefits, what were the results of empirical research on it, whether the model or theory has been criticised (and if so, why and how), and what are the alternatives.

Merely summarising the literature is relatively easy but writing an effective literature review takes considerable skill and organisation. The appropriate style of the review will vary slightly depending on the subject matter. For example, if you are covering a highly technical subject such as mathematical finance, you would need to include numerous equations, compared with more discursive material on a topic such as how to account for corporate environmental damage.

The literature review should follow the style of a comprehensive appraisal published in a scholarly journal and should always be critical in nature. It should comment on the relevance, value, advantages and shortcomings of the cited articles. The review should be written in continuous prose and not in note form. It is important to demonstrate an understanding of the work and provide a critical assessment – i.e., to point out key weaknesses in existing studies. Being critical is not always easy and is a delicate balance; the critique's tone should remain polite, as further discussed in subsection 11.1.5.

Accounting has an extensive and well-established critical stream, with a range of journals publishing critical research, including, most notably: *Critical Perspectives on Accounting*,[1] and the *International Journal of Critical Accounting*,[2] although many other accounting journals also publish some studies of a critical nature such as the *Accounting, Auditing & Accountability Journal*.[3] But this tradition never really established itself in finance where there is only one such journal (the *Critical Finance Review*,[4] which, according to the journal's home page, will 'take more risks to try to attract more controversial and provocative papers'). It should be noted that studies in critical accounting are not just concerned with pointing out the weaknesses in individual studies, which is what all good literature reviews will be doing. Rather, studies in critical accounting (or finance) will be aiming to highlight at a high level the limitations of entire approaches to theory and practice.

---

[1] https://www.journals.elsevier.com/critical-perspectives-on-accounting/
[2] https://www.inderscience.com/jhome.php?jcode=ijca
[3] https://www.emeraldgrouppublishing.com/journal/aaaj#aims-and-scope
[4] https://www.nowpublishers.com/CFR

9.2   The beginning, middle and end of the review

Just as for a novel or a thesis document as a whole, a good literature review will have a beginning, a middle, and an end. It will also have a narrative – a flowing story that links together as if there is a single thread running through it from beginning to end.

The opening part of the review should provide a gentle introduction to the problem. It should put the issues you will investigate into a wider context, and it should also explain why the problem or area is interesting and for whom. In the introduction to the literature review, provide some insight into the relationship between the central topic of your review and other related areas. Where does your topic fit into the wider context? The introduction should then provide a brief outline of the rest of the review. The review's main body would then follow, separated into sections as described in section 9.6 below.

The final section of the review should provide a summary of the literature that you have reviewed that leads naturally onto the 'gap' in the body of knowledge that your investigative work helps to fill. When writing the concluding section to the literature review, maintain the focus established in the introduction so that the precis is directed towards your study's topic. The summary should be reasonably short and straightforward – perhaps a couple of paragraphs or so – even if the volume of work you are reviewing is vast and technical.

A good review should lead naturally onto your theoretical or empirical work and should complement it. When you are considering which existing studies to include in your review, think about whether they will add to or detract from what you are trying to achieve overall in your thesis. You need to incorporate all of the key sources in the area but avoid padding with irrelevant or marginally relevant material that will take up valuable words and make the core material harder for the reader to locate. While you are writing the review, look out for gaps ('lacunae' as they are sometimes called) in the body of work and think about aspects of the subject area that have not been explored. Identifying lacunae will help you to refine your research ideas or to replace them with new suggestions that have more relevance or are more feasible.

Synthesise the results into a summary of what is and is not known. This synthesis will allow you to identify:

- Trends (e.g., 'most researchers used to believe X but now the majority of studies seem to suggest that Y is the reason')
- Gaps (e.g., 'as far as I am aware, nobody has as yet examined . . .')
- Controversies (i.e., topics upon which researchers cannot agree and where there are mixed findings)

All of these will help you to develop or refine your research questions.

Don't just include a list of authors and their papers but explain what each study is doing, what is different about it compared with other studies in the area and why it is relevant for your work. When time is limited, it is often better to have a modest number of sources explained in detail, with their relevance and shortcomings shining through, than to have a long list of references with each study given merely a cursory treatment. Your draft needs to include the issues raised by the following questions:

1. What are the main topics of interest in this research area? How do they fit together?
2. How has the research area developed over time?
3. What is the theory or conceptual framework underpinning this area of study?
4. What methods are usually used to tackle the research questions? Is there a good spread of approaches, or are all the papers using the same techniques? Have any interdisciplinary investigations been applied to this topic?
5. What sorts of data are being used? Is the evidence pervasive or confined to certain countries, especially the US?
6. Is there consensus across the literature in the answers to the research questions, or are the conclusions disputed?

In terms of style, it is better to vary the way you describe papers rather than starting each sentence with, the authors' names, such as: 'Brooks (2008) examines X . . . and finds this. Smith (2013) studies Y . . . and finds that. Jones (2017) develops Smith's ideas to include Z. . . ' This almost reads like a set of notes for each paper that has been unimaginatively spliced together, which is an amateurish approach and is dull for the reader.

9.3 Making your review 'critical'

One of the essential aspects of an effective review is that it should be critical of the studies it cites, which means identifying and pointing out the weaknesses in existing research and the points where it could be improved. Don't merely provide a list of authors and their research or use a style that involves no depth, such as 'X argued this while Y suggested that', which would be a superficial treatment of their work. Instead, you should demonstrate understanding by providing some detail and a critical assessment. Being critical is not always easy to do appropriately – it is a delicate balance to achieve, and the tone should always remain delicate and slightly understated.

Sometimes, students find it surprising that they are expected to criticise existing studies. After all, these were produced by established, accredited and sometimes well-known scholars – how can you, as someone near the beginning of their academic journey, find problems with top researchers' work? However, you should feel empowered to challenge findings or statements that you disagree with, and your confidence in doing this will grow as you read, learn and understand more about the subject. This is all part of being able to produce a critical literature review.

Most of the time, being critical does not mean identifying fatal errors in the studies; instead, it is about seeking out the limitations or aspects of the research that could be improved. It is rather like those who conduct research on car engines intending to release updated versions. They are not trying to develop a totally new type of engine design, and they are not suggesting that the previous versions were dangerous or likely to break down. Instead, they hope to develop new designs that are more fuel-efficient, faster or quieter, etc.

But the critique is essential to incorporate – after all, if the current work is beyond criticism, then that particular research problem has been solved, and no further study of it is needed. Critical comments should be backed up with evidence from the work being criticised or from other sources as far as possible so that they do not appear as unfair or unsubstantiated accusations.

Finally, note that while your review should have elements of critique, it is not necessary to be critical about every study you cite, and many can be presented as statements about what previous researchers have written using neutral language. Of course, all research has some flaws, even ground-breaking studies published in the leading journals, so when writing a critique, try to focus on the most substantive issues. Don't bother to point out trivial matters such as typos, grammatical mistakes or minor errors in the analysis; focus on sufficiently grave problems that could influence the findings or call them into question.

9.4   The importance of presenting a balanced argument

It is imperative when writing the review that you consider studies taking a different perspective from your own. For example, it is sometimes the case that there are two entirely opposing ways to tackle a particular problem. This might be two different classes of model, or more fundamentally, two methodological paradigms.

To give one illustration of a situation where this may occur, in many sub-fields within business and management, the 'big data' approach based on quantitative analysis and formal mathematical models has become predominant while the alternative way of obtaining findings from qualitative analysis of interviews and non-participant observation is eschewed.

It might be that your review would be richer if it sought out and acknowledged that there is another approach to the one that you are using, although yours will naturally make up the bulk of your review. Of course, it might be a much lower-level difference across studies, such as estimating the efficiency of a particular banking market using nonparametric (data envelopment analysis) or parametric (the stochastic frontier approach) techniques. In that case, your review ought to discuss both parametric and non-parametric approaches, together with their relative strengths and weaknesses, even if you intend to focus on only one of these techniques in your investigation.

Providing another example, in economics, the 'Chicago school' (so-called because it was initially developed by faculty at the University of Chicago) holds a strong philosophical belief in the superiority of free markets for making economic decisions and in the efficiency of financial markets, associated with Eugene Fama amongst many others. An opposing view is held by Robert Shiller, a behavioural economist at Yale University, that markets frequently depart from efficiency and experience speculative bubbles. Sometimes journals will only publish research taking a specific viewpoint, so there are, for example, journals that take an efficient markets perspective and those taking a behavioural view. If you limit your literature search to one set of journals in such circumstances, the work will lack balance. It will not reflect the diversity of opinions and approaches that exist, and you would be implicitly suggesting that there is consensus where, in fact, there is none.

If you are working on a controversial topic – for instance, one with a political dimension or where there is more than one strand to an argument, you also need to be careful of misleading or one-sided statements. This situation is subtly different to the one above – here, it might be the case that the author is an expert on the topic and knows precisely what they are doing, but they deliberately use their writing to try to persuade the reader to accept a particular viewpoint when the truth might be more subtle. Government propaganda fits into this category – while there might be some elements of truth in what is being said, the strength of the evidence is exaggerated to push the individual to act (or not act) in a particular way.

In your thesis, you will likely need to provide a balanced treatment rather than a biased one, which is more in the spirit of a scholarly investigation. You should also present the information you find that runs against the central perspective you are making or the results you obtain. But put this into context, and say that, on balance, you favour explanation X rather than Y because the weight of evidence supports the former. You can then dismiss the counterevidence or counterargument as being weaker for some specific reasons that you have identified.

If different studies reach conflicting conclusions, this implies that the current state of knowledge cannot solve the puzzle, and your write-up should reflect that, in which case further research is needed to determine which, if any, of the perspectives is correct. It is also an interesting situation when one study seems to yield different findings than all the others on that topic. One possibility is that the outlying piece contains methodological errors that make its conclusions invalid. But it is also plausible that this study simply used a different yet equally acceptable approach, and therefore the consensus in the rest of the literature on that issue is shaky.

9.5 Should the review include quotations?

Including brief quotations from existing studies can be highly valuable in getting a point across. Often, an acknowledged expert would have phrased an argument in a particular way that is profound and encapsulates what you want to say better than you could do so yourself. If that is the case, it is valuable to include the quote. Quotations can also be used as evidence to demonstrate particular points that you want to make.

But in general, avoid quotes longer than, perhaps, three or four lines since incorporating so many of someone else's words diminishes the worth of your review. For something longer than this, you should put it into your own words and there will always be numerous different ways to do that. Regarding the appropriate presentational style to adopt for quotations, those which are short should be incorporated directly into the sentence that discusses them. More extensive quotes (e.g., three or four lines or more) should be placed on a separate line in your document and indented from the left-hand margin. An example of this is given in subsection 11.5.8.

It is also best to explain what you are quoting and why, rather than just dropping it in, which might confuse the reader as to its relevance or purpose and disrupt the flow. Relatedly, in terms of the volume of quotes to incorporate, a small number sprinkled into a review can add interest and a strong connection with existing studies. But including too many is detrimental since the whole point of the review is to demonstrate that you have assimilated what you have read and that you can paraphrase it rather than copying it verbatim from an existing source.

Although including quotations (when appropriately cited to make it clear that they are taken from an existing source) is not plagiarism, if you incorporate too many of them, it might be considered that your work is excessively derivative. This means that it is too closely related to what is already published so that you are adding nothing new, even in terms of your writing, let alone the ideas. If your examiners conclude that some aspects of your dissertation are excessively derivative, you would likely be asked to rewrite those parts and it would create a terrible impression of your work. Therefore, there is a delicate balance in the inclusion of quotations in a review: a few short ones enhance and enrich it; quotes that are too long or too numerous damage it.

9.6   Should your literature review include sub-headings?

Sub-headings can help organise a piece of work and will usually make it easier to read, so they are recommended. However, it is also advisable to avoid using too many, which would disrupt the flow and make the document appear amateurish. Each sub-section needs to be substantial, for example comprising roughly between half a page and a few pages; if a sub-section is just four or five lines long, merge it with the one before or after.

It is of less concern whether the sub-sections are numbered, which is a matter of personal preference. It could be that only the main section headings (so-called A-headings) are numbered, for instance, while those of a lower level are not numbered but are simply underlined:

> Chapter 2: Introduction and Motivation
> > Section 2.1 The development of asset pricing models
> > > The CAPM
> > > Arbitrage pricing
> > > Atheoretical factor models
> > Section 2.2 Empirical tests of asset pricing models
> > > . . .
> > Section 2.3 Intended contribution of the dissertation
> > Section 2.4 Outline of the remainder of the document

It would also be possible to move to even lower hierarchical levels (e.g., Section 2.2.1.4), whether numbered or not, but this always seems like overkill and is not necessary or helpful in a PhD thesis. So, in the example above, in my view it is preferable for the sub-headings relating to the CAPM, arbitrage pricing, and so on to remain unnumbered.

9.7 Referencing

Citations have two purposes. First, they show your readers the sources of some of your research ideas, which gives due credit to existing authors. Second, they allow readers to follow up those references if they want more detail on what had been done. The latter purpose implies a requirement that the references are complete and accurate; it is annoying and a waste of time trying to track down a piece of work that somebody else had cited only to find that some of the referencing details are wrong.

There are two general approaches to referencing – putting the details in footnotes on each page with no list at the end of the document and gathering all the references together into a list without full information in footnotes. The former style is typical in the humanities, such as history, but is rare in accounting and finance and so it is safest to have a list. Within this category, there are various referencing styles concerning how the information is displayed, but this is a second-order consideration – the most important aspect is that the details are all there and correct.

In some journals in the natural and physical sciences, the convention is to use a numeric system for references. Here, each reference in the list is given a number, and that number is used as the in-text citation rather than the author surname and year. For instance:

'Finance has been argued to lack the critical stream that has been crucial in the development of accounting research' [7]

where the number refers to the seventh numbered citation in the list at the end of the document. This convention is rarely used in the social sciences, however, and I suggest avoiding it.

Try to keep full and accurate bibliographic records for all the papers you read – if you do this carefully from the outset, it will save much time and hassle later. Pay attention to names and journal titles since your supervisor will likely be familiar with these, and so any typographical errors here will be spotted and could undermine confidence in more substantive aspects of your work.

If you are in any doubt about how the reference list should look in your dissertation, simply examine the list at the end of almost any published academic paper or a completed PhD. Most schools are not overly concerned about the formatting of the references so long as the list is accurate, in a consistent style, and alphabetically ordered by the first author's surname. If no more specific stipulations are made, the 'Harvard style' is standard and works well. Although it has a large number of minor variations, it is broadly the approach that has been used throughout this text.

9.7.1   Latin terms in referencing

Some good Latin terms to know for when referencing (or understanding the referencing style used by others) are:

- *op. cit.* (short for *opere citato*), which is used to refer to a piece that has already been cited, but, perhaps, a few sentences or paragraphs ago. For example, 'Brooks and Oikonomou (2018) survey the literature on the link between environmental, social and governance disclosures and firm value. Much of this work builds on stakeholder theory (Freeman, 1983; Jones, 1995) that discusses how firms establish and prioritise relationships with their constituents. Firms may have well-intentioned or cynical reasons for trying to enhance their social performance (Brooks and Oikonomou, *op. cit.*).'
- *et al.* (short for *et alia*), which means 'and other authors.' *et al.* is the most common such abbreviation and is very useful when there are several authors to an article that you are referring to more than once. For example, Brooks, Hoepner, McMillan, Vivian, and Wese Simen (2019) can be shortened to the much more manageable Brooks *et al.* (2019). A standard convention uses the entire list of author names the first time it is referred to in the document before switching to *et al.* in all subsequent citations of the same piece.
- *Ibid.* (short for *ibidem*), which means 'in the same study'. You would use this when the study you have just referred to makes another valid point but perhaps on a different page. So, for example, you might write 'Finance has been argued to lack the critical stream that has been crucial in the development of accounting research (Brooks and Schopohl, 2018, p.615), and it also lacks diversity in the methodological approaches it uses (*ibid.*, p.632).'

Note that Latin terms are usually written in italics, and a full stop should follow any abbreviated words in each case.

9.7.2   Direct and indirect referencing

There are two broad styles of working references into a passage of text, and these are sometimes known as direct and indirect referencing. Examples of each are as follows:

Direct referencing

'Brooks *et al.* (2019) argue that finance scholars have devoted insufficient attention to the study of ethics.'

Indirect referencing

'Insufficient attention has been devoted by finance scholars to the study of ethics (Brooks *et al.*, 2019).'

Notice that in the second case, the parentheses surround the entire reference, and there is no second set of parentheses around the publication year. Either approach is equally acceptable, and using both within the document will vary the style and make it more entertaining to read. References can also be stacked up (usually in alphabetical order by author name or chronologically with the earliest listed first) if more than one study makes a similar point (e.g., Brooks *et al.*, 2019; Persand, 2014).

9.7.3 Secondary references

Ideally, you would read every piece of existing research that you cite. However, this might be too time-consuming in reality, and there might be articles that you feel compelled to mention due to their relevance and importance but which you cannot get hold of (for example, due to their age or limitations in your library's journal subscription bundle). In such cases, there are two options. One is to cite the unread work as if you had read it based on paraphrasing what the study you have examined writes about it. The other possibility is to write it as a 'secondary reference', where you explicitly recognise that you are reporting an idea 'second-hand'. For example, you might write: 'the careers of women in academia have been held back by a lack of senior female role models (Sealy and Singh, 2010, cited in Brooks *et al.*, 2014).'

It is clear here that you have read the paper by Brooks *et al.* but not the one by Sealy and Singh, although it is the latter whose point you are including in your argument.

Neither approach is ideal: if you cite a paper without reading it, you rely on the author whose work you did read having reported accurately the findings of the piece you didn't. On the other hand, while one or two secondary references are acceptable, more than that will make you appear lazy and unprofessional. In that case, your supervisor will question why you didn't make more effort to track down and read the original work yourself. On balance, my preference is to refrain from using any secondary referencing.

9.7.4 Making a list of references

At some point, you will need to construct a reference list. It is much easier to do this as you go along rather than trying to pull it together at the end when you have forgotten the details of where some of your materials came from, and you need to look for them again.

The reference list in the thesis will just be a list of papers and books. But still, when you are working on the literature review, you might find it helpful to use some software to classify each item using topics, dates, a short summary of the methods and main findings, etc. If you keep a systematic record of what you have read and what are the key papers, this will save you a lot of time constructing the reference list at the end. It will also help ensure that you do not miss anything and avoid inadvertently reading the same work more than once, which I am embarrassed to admit that I have done on several occasions. The most straightforward way to do this is to use a word processor or spreadsheet package with which you are already familiar.

Alternatively, you could use specific software such as EndNote, ProCite or

BibTeX (the latter is for those who use LaTeX to typeset their documents, which was used for this book, rather than Microsoft Word or Apple Pages). The advantage of this automated referencing software is that once you have inputted all of the information into the database, it is possible to search and extract it in various styles, already formatted to drop straight into your dissertation. Using a specialist referencing package is valuable if you will have a large number of references or will be using them for more than one piece of work. But it might not be worth the effort to learn how to use the software if you have a limited number of references to be used in only in this research.

9.7.5   How many references should be on your list?

The primary focus will be on the reference list for the thesis as a whole rather than for the literature review part alone, and at a later stage, you will need to combine the reference list from your literature review with those from citations across the rest of the document (the introduction, methods, conclusions, etc.).

In general, and as stated in several places in this text, the number of references will depend to a considerable extent on the material being covered. The more discursive and the more mature a subject area, the longer the reference list would be expected to be. Therefore, while it is hard to give a precise figure, if your literature review has fewer than about 20 references, it is likely to appear as if the link with existing work is insufficient. You will probably want to include citations in the methods and data sections to other studies that have used a similar approach and compare your findings with those in existing papers or books. Adding such citations will increase the overall reference count, and thus I would typically expect that there would be at least 20-30 citations in the list for the literature review alone and perhaps 40-50 in the thesis as a whole.

9.8   Problems with a literature review and fixing them

The first and most fundamental reason why a literature review can turn out badly is when the author did not come up with any (or many) relevant studies to write about, so the review has no core and is full of peripheral material from websites on irrelevant topics.

In general, if you can find almost no existing research whatsoever related to your topic, it is probably not an ideal one for you to focus on either as you will have no prior studies to guide you or to help establish a framework. The lack of previous research also indicates that, for some reason, established scholars have not found it to be a topic worthy of investigation and publishing. It might be because the phenomenon is entirely new or due to a lack of data since the main variables of interest are almost impossible to measure. Alternatively, it could be because the subject matter is very practical and populist, so not amenable to academic study.

Aside from being unable to find sufficient relevant research to survey, literature reviews can fail to live up to their potential for several reasons:

1. Important studies have been omitted
2. Recent studies have been omitted so that the review is dated and reads as if it had been written years ago
3. The number of sources is too low
4. The sources are focused primarily on basic internet material
5. The writing lacks a good structure so that it drifts and is hard to follow
6. The style is repetitive or not engaging
7. The review is descriptive and not critical
8. Too many marginally relevant or unimportant studies are cited, so it is hard to identify what the purpose of the review is
9. The review jumps in too quickly at the beginning, so it takes a long time for the reader to discover what material is going to be covered and why
10. The review 'falls off a cliff' at the end without summarising what has been covered
11. Overall, the review is either too short or too long
12. The referencing style is poor or inaccurate

Any of the above faults will diminish the quality of the work, but none is fatal. They can all be remedied, mostly fairly straightforwardly. The numbers in the list below correspond to those in the list immediately above, and provide some suggestions to fix common problems with the literature review:

1. Ensure from the outset that you identify the pivotal studies on each particular topic. These should become evident fairly quickly since they will be the studies that many other researchers are citing. Make certain that your literature search is as comprehensive as possible, looking at a wide range of the sources described above. Also, use the full range of years during which relevant research was published rather than a narrow time window
2. This issue follows from the previous one. The most recent work on a particular topic might not yet be published since the lag between papers being written by scholars and published in journals can be as much as two or three years. Consequently, it is vital to examine both published and unpublished sources. Students who rely on paraphrasing from a small number of existing studies with excessive secondary reading and referencing rather than reading widely and drawing information from the individual studies run a higher risk of their reviews being outdated. A thesis that omits recent studies also has a higher chance of repeating investigations that have already been conducted and of failing to use cutting-edge techniques
3. A sound literature review needs to cover a sufficient number of sources. While the appropriate number varies depending upon the material and the amount of existing work on the topic, it is clear that eight or ten sources would be insufficient, and perhaps 20 would be a minimum acceptable number
4. Not only the number of references but also their origin requires some consideration. The list should not only comprise popular pieces (e.g., blogs

or newspaper articles) or basic internet-based sources such as Wikipedia, notwithstanding its value as a starting point. While it is acceptable to include some such sources, at its core, the review needs to delve deep into the academic literature, which means looking at papers published in journals, working papers not yet published, and possibly scholarly books

5. The structure is almost as important for readability as the writing style. For example, using sub-headings (but not too many and not too many sub-levels) will help the reader avoid getting lost in the flow of the document and mapping out the sections before commencing writing should also help ensure that the structure is clear and works

6. Developing a fluid writing style is something that takes practice and clear, detailed feedback. But some steps can be taken at an early stage, and which will help enormously. First, a good structure and planning should limit repetition. Second, try to link paragraphs and sections together so that the writing flows naturally rather than being 'bitty' or disjointed. Third, and as discussed above, try to avoid starting too many sentences with 'Bloggs (2009) argued X and then Jones (2012) stated Y'

7. Again, as discussed above, literature reviews should be critical, not just presenting existing work but also pointing out the limitations, flaws, and what the authors did not do

8. Literature reviews should be organised around the most important studies on the topic. Dependent on how extensive the body of work is, they should not cover research that is not really at the core of the subject and should not cover work that is of low quality or excessively derivative of prior studies. Such research should only be included at all if the number of studies on your precise topic is minimal and expanding the choice set to include this work is necessary to generate a review of a reasonable length. Also, try to avoid undergoing a sojourn along a blind alley where a self-contained but barely marginally relevant body of work is presented in great detail. Including such material would use up valuable words and detract from the focus of the piece

9. An effective review should have a beginning and an end, as well as a middle. This means that the start of the review chapter should explain what strand of the literature you will be discussing and why. Perhaps, if space allows, you could provide a mini-roadmap of the structure of the chapter. Ideally, it will be apparent to the reader how the work you are reviewing ties in with your thesis' overall aims and objectives

10. At the end, the review should not just stop with a discussion of the final existing study that you wish to mention; instead, it should summarise what is known and what is not, providing a lead-in to your investigative work that will begin in the following chapter

11. The literature review's total length is very much a 'Goldilocks and the Three Bears' situation – it needs to be just right. If the review is too short, it will give

the impression that you did not spend long on it, and it could omit key studies or cover them superficially. On the other hand, if the review is too long, it will swamp the thesis document, using up valuable words and possibly pushing you up to the word limit or making the work less enjoyable to read

12. Accurate referencing is one of the easiest aspects to get right, and so there are no excuses. Always make sure that you take precise notes about which study said what and when. Also, make sure that there is a 1:1 correspondence between the citations made in the text and the list at the end of the thesis. Ensure that all of the references are complete, including full titles, journal names, volume and page numbers, etc., and listed in alphabetical order by (first) author surname. Pay particular attention to author names, which might be from an unfamiliar language or be written in different ways (e.g., Brooks versus Brookes). It is hard to spot and correct such errors once they have been made, so it is better to get them right the first time

9.8.1 Final literature review checks

Before submitting the review for comments from your supervisor or putting it on the shelf and starting on the investigative parts of your PhD, when you complete the first draft of your review, run through the following checklist. You should be able to answer the following questions effortlessly, so if you have any doubts, then reflect on how the work can be improved before you move on. These are all issues that your examiners will be considering, so if you are unsure about any of the points, think about how you might be able to modify the review to address them.

- Does my literature review cover a mathematical or discursive topic? This will significantly affect the style required.
- What should be the scope of my literature review?
- How good are my literature searching abilities? Will I have uncovered relevant material published in non-core journals and working papers?
- Have I set the perspective appropriately so that I will find all the relevant material but excluding any irrelevant material?
- Does my review include the latest thinking on the topic, or is it dated?
- Does the literature that I am reviewing link with my research aims? In other words, is the material I have reviewed relevant to my research questions?
- Have I critically analysed the literature I write about, identifying and pinpointing weaknesses?
- Do I just summarise the articles, or do I reflect on and draw the links between them?
- Is the review balanced, and have I cited and discussed papers that take an opposing view compared with my perspective?
- Is the review well-structured and pleasant to read?
- Have I set the scene appropriately in the introductory section of the review and summarised the body of work in the conclusions?

- Have I identified any gaps in the field's knowledge about the subject?

Further reading

There are numerous, detailed books on how to survey the literature and write the review. Some popular texts include Booth *et al.* (2016), Ridley (2012), and the very detailed text by Greetham (2020).

Chapter takeaways – top tips for success

⊛ You need to develop a system to organise and classify the literature you have reviewed

⊛ The review should have a beginning, middle and end. It needs to set the scene with context and motivation first before moving onto the main body and then finishing with a summary of what you have covered and what is known and not known on the subject

⊛ Your review should be balanced and include alternative approaches or viewpoints that contradict yours

⊛ Small numbers of judiciously chosen quotes can enliven the review, but don't make them too long or numerous

⊛ Your review should include an appropriate number of sources, which will depend on the nature of the subject matter and the extent of existing research on the topic

⊛ Ensure that your referencing is consistent and precise

10. RESEARCH METHODS

Learning outcomes: this chapter covers

- ✓ The difference between methodology and methods
- ✓ How to select your research methods
- ✓ How theory is used in research
- ✓ The kinds of theories that are relevant for accounting and finance
- ✓ The differences between primary and secondary data
- ✓ What a sample is and different sampling techniques
- ✓ How to choose the software for quantitative data analysis

10.1 Preparing for the investigative part of your PhD

This part of your thesis is at the core, and it is the aspect on which the decision on whether it is acceptable or not will primarily be based. It is beyond the scope of this book to teach either quantitative or qualitative approaches from scratch, and although many doctoral research textbooks try to do just that, it is usually a disaster with their treatment not having sufficient space to explain the techniques in any detail. Most students will undoubtedly have covered this material in other modules on using quantitative or qualitative methods in much more detail than covered in those books, while readers who have not sat such courses are left confused by the sparse, lighting-speed coverage.

That being the case, at this stage, I will not cover either quantitative or qualitative approaches in detail. For readers of this book, the task will be to select the appropriate methodology for your chosen topic and apply it effectively. Consequently, this chapter is partly focused on achieving that objective, with additional information sources provided throughout the chapter.

Both accounting and finance are usually considered social sciences – that is, the 'unit of analysis' is usually people and the outcomes that we observe and measure in both fields are the results of decisions and actions by people. However, unlike sociology, for example, finance in particular but increasingly accounting too, draw methods from the natural and physical sciences. This plurality of approaches provides researchers with an enormous array of possible strategies to tackle their research aims.

As well as examining the existing research on your chosen topic as covered in the previous two chapters of this book, the other area where you are likely to have to do some additional reading is on the methods. Whether you are using an econometric analysis of secondary data, questionnaires or interviews, unfortunately, it is unlikely that you will have covered the approaches in sufficient detail to be able to proceed without further groundwork.

Therefore, even if you have completed the literature review, there is still additional reading to do, albeit more specialised and less in volume. As you begin to pin down the details of the investigative methods to use, you would probably not need to read each article in detail, and it would make sense to skip straight to the methodology section of the paper to see if it employs an approach that you are considering. If so, you might also focus on the results section to see how it worked when that author used those techniques.

Once you have read enough of the subject-specific material to be aware of how researchers usually address their research questions in your topic area, you will need to become more of an expert in that technique yourself. At that point, where do you start? There are essentially three stages in the process. First, you need to identify the most appropriate methods to tackle your research problem. This is covered in the following section of this book.

Second, learn about and implement the chosen method. This is the research design step, which is about establishing a framework to apply the techniques you have chosen and determining how you will use them to answer your questions. It is an essential part of the process that must be nailed down before the investigative work begins. Having a weak or ill-conceived design will lead to problems later down the line and has been likened to building a house without any plans to guide the construction. If you determine how you will go about the investigation on the hoof, it will show through in the final draft, so map out how you will gather the data and how you will analyse them before you start.

The third stage is to interpret and analyse the results. Whatever means you use to collect the data (download, survey or interview), don't get so carried away with it that there is insufficient time remaining to conduct the analysis and writing. These latter aspects are at least as important, and to do a good job might take longer than you expected. Getting the results into tables and graphs, describing them, explaining what they mean, how they relate to your research aims or hypotheses, and comparing them to other studies' findings all require time. So aim to stick to the schedule that you established at the beginning and spread your time accordingly.

10.1.1 Are 'methodology' and 'method' the same?

Strictly, no, the two are different, although they are frequently used interchangeably in accounting and finance. The two terms will now be defined and contrasted.

Method

'Method' is a somewhat lower level and straightforward concept that refers to the systematic, concrete process used to obtain and analyse investigative data. The method is the tool you use on a practical level: an interview, survey, regression analysis of secondary data, and so on.

Methodology

'Methodology', on the other hand, is the high-level strategy for generating knowledge and the rationale for the approach taken to research – in some ways, it is an analysis of methods and, for example, why one method is chosen over another.

In essence, given how the term is usually used loosely in accounting and finance, the methodology involves determining the best approach to answer your research questions or hypotheses, comparing the advantages and disadvantages of one technique compared with another. For instance, you might have a reason to believe that firms with more diversity in their management boards will perform better on environmental issues than those with less variety or that younger investors are more risk-tolerant than those who are older. How will you assess each of these suggestions? The testing approach you use can be thought of as the methodological choice.

10.2 Choosing your research methods

Selecting the exact subject for PhD research and the methods to study it is a long process, and you should not rush it. Your proposal will have been of sufficient interest and quality to get you through the door and to allocate supervisor(s), but it will likely bear little resemblance to the finished thesis. In the first year, most of your time will be taken up attending courses and learning new skills, and at that stage, you might feel that the research itself – what you had come to the programme to do – is taking a backseat. Do not be overly concerned if progress seems disappointing in the first few months of registration – this is normal, and you will pick considerable momentum at a later stage when the preliminaries and foundation-building are out of the way.

As you read, learn and discuss more, the depth of your knowledge about the subject will grow immeasurably. Doing a PhD and writing it up is not a process involving writing a research agenda first and then following it. Instead, the plan will be under continual modification and refinement right until the point where all of the investigative work is completed. You only need a good idea for the first piece of investigative research to get you started, and ideas for the following chapters will emerge as you are working on the first one. This section covers a key milestone in progressing the research, namely determining the appropriate methods to use for for the investigation.

10.2.1 The research design and strategy

It might be worth beginning by stating that sometimes researchers begin with a particular method that they have become familiar with and they then try to identify an appropriate context in which to apply it. However, this is far from ideal as an approach to generating new knowledge; rather, the research questions should be at the heart of the investigation and should drive the methods chosen, not the other way around.

Therefore, the starting point for selecting the investigative methods should be your research strategy, which is the overall approach that you will use based on the objectives you have set for the research. The strategy relates to the highest-level decisions that you need to make when determining how to do your research, including the scale and scope of the investigation and what you intend to achieve. It will also involve the choice between the use of quantitative or qualitative techniques. The strategy will then lead to a research design, which is the methodological framework that you will use to address your research aims, including selecting the investigative approach and methods, the types of data you will collect, and how you will analyse them.

You might need to justify your research strategy, particularly if the method you use is not the most commonly applied to that topic. For example, suppose you are examining the link between the characteristics of chief executive officers (CEOs) and the operational performance of the companies they run using a panel regression. In that case, you probably do not need to take time to explain why that is the best approach to use since, after all, this is what almost all existing studies will have done. But if instead, you decided that you would try to address the question by in-depth interviews of a small group of CEOs, that would benefit from a justification and explanation about how you would achieve your aims. Some discussion would be valuable since your methods are different to those used by existing studies, which might initially cause concern among your examiners if they doubt the appropriateness of the technique.

It is worth spending some time considering your research design carefully before you fix on the methods to use and launch into data collection since these aspects are related and need to tie in with your research objectives. If the design is not thought through, you could waste time obtaining the wrong data or selecting an approach that will not allow you to test what you had wanted to.

In more detail, your research design will involve several interlinked aspects. It incorporates the research questions or hypotheses; the sources, types and extent of the data; the methods you will use to gather and analyse the data; the ordering and timescale over which each aspect of the investigative work in your research will take place. Before beginning their investigative work, some students find it useful to sketch out in writing all of these components of their research design, as doing so helps them identify any potential inconsistencies or other issues before they waste a significant amount of time going up a blind alley.

10.2.2   How to choose the methods

A risk-return trade-off applies with the choice of methods. If you stick with the same approach that has been widely used in the established literature, the risks are low, but the work is less likely to be ground-breaking. On the other hand, attempting to apply an entirely different technique (such as using surveys to address a particular research question when every existing study has used market data from Bloomberg) could lead to exciting new findings that are vastly different from anything already out there. But there is also much more scope for the study to be criticised or for the method not to work as anticipated. Hence, most students take the safe route for their chosen topic and use the established methods used previously in the literature.

The challenge of working in an area that is new to you and using methods that you are not familiar with will develop your skills and knowledge. But do you want to be challenged in this way, and do you have the time and energy to devote to the additional reading and learning required?

Note that this does not mean it is wrong to try different methods than those used in existing studies. In fact, quite the reverse – using an alternative approach is an excellent way to provide new and exciting evidence on the topic. But it is riskier since you would be breaking new ground rather than treading a well-worn path with an established framework to follow. Consequently, you need to provide additional confirmation that you have reflected on the appropriateness of the alternative methods and that you are aware of the difficulties that you might encounter. Your supervisor will also help you ensure that you have the requisite skills and possibly recommend specialist training or additional resources if these are needed. Moving out of your comfort zone is risky – you are more likely to face problems along the way and possibly even make mistakes – but if you overcome these issues, your learning development will be significantly enhanced.

Alongside the choice of topic, thinking about your strengths and weaknesses and what you enjoy doing will help you select a methodological approach that could be applied. You will learn new skills if you move slightly out of your comfort zone and try something somewhat different from what you have done before. But there are evident dangers if you try to move too far and stray deep into an approach that you have never been taught and have limited time to learn during your PhD registration period. For instance, it ought to be well within most students' capabilities to learn how to implement a new econometric model if they have already attended a module on econometrics as part of their programme. On the other hand, using a qualitative approach such as interviews or detailed case study analysis would be highly challenging if your programme has taught only quantitative techniques, and you had also not covered qualitative methods previously.

The following checklist might help you to think about the kinds of approaches you could use. Do you know how to do the following, and do you enjoy using such techniques? In each case the method is presented alongside an example of the types of problem that is commonly tackled using it:

1. Deriving formulae using algebra – an economic theory-type study or sophisticated empirical approach would suit this

2. Analysing data using statistical models – an empirical approach would suit this

3. Writing code in languages such as Python or C++ – again, an empirical study but where new models are being constructed would suit this; similarly the conducting textual analysis or pricing derivatives contracts will require the use of a programming language rather than an econometrics package

4. Understanding and writing arguments for or against a particular viewpoint – this might suggest the use of a case-study or archival approach or perhaps using interviews or surveys to seek people's opinions

5. Working with conceptual or theoretical models – this would be done where the purpose is to develop a framework to understand a particular phenomenon (although probably without testing it)

6. Talking with people and understanding how they make decisions – the use of interviews or surveys would fit this type of interest best

7. Setting up and running computer-based experiments in a lab – this requires some prior background in psychology or other experimental settings since there is unlikely to be sufficient time available to learn from scratch the technical skills needed to conduct them validly

8. Working with historical documents in archives – this would be appropriate if using case studies or gathering historical data for analysis

9. Understanding practical problems faced by firms or individuals and identifying resolutions – again, the use of surveys or interviews would work well here

Each of the research methods in the above list will imbue the user with various competencies and knowledge, but among these, data handling, statistical and programming skills are particularly valued nowadays by potential employers. You may wish to bear in mind the possible positive impact on your CV of having experience with particular techniques as one factor to consider when selecting a topic and the methods you will employ to study it.

10.2.3   The methods available for research in accounting or finance

Accounting and finance are often considered both as sciences and as social sciences, and the methods used to tackle research problems reflect this variety of possible techniques. Case studies, surveys, interviews, conceptual models, and the empirical analysis of existing data are all used in various ways. Each of these techniques will now be discussed, but first, it is helpful to categorise each approach as being either quantitative or qualitative in nature.

Qualitative versus quantitative research – what's the difference?

Qualitative research is scarce in finance and less frequently used in accounting than other social sciences such as politics, philosophy or sociology, where the approach originated. In many ways, that it is so little used is a considerable loss to scholarship in our subject since it can generate richer insights and answer numerous important questions that could not be addressed with a quantitative study.

In general, qualitative studies can be preferable where the researcher wishes to investigate why particular outcomes occurred related to people's behaviour, opinions or feelings. Such an approach is also useful where the study focuses on the interactions between people (e.g., are there leaders and followers on a trading floor, and what factors determine the group to which each person belongs?) Qualitative research can also be expedient to see how a process works in action (as opposed to how it should work in principle), particularly in a stressed environment. For instance, how does a firm react when it discovers an accounting fraud by its Chief Financial Officer?

All of the above situations have in common that the data and information needed to draw conclusions about the issues cannot be observed or recorded without explicitly asking the people involved what they think or observing them in the situation. Qualitative research also has the added benefit of flexibility as its relatively unstructured nature is amenable to modification on the go as the findings begin to emerge.

Objectivity is crucial to build into such investigations but challenging to achieve because of the researcher's perspective and preconceptions, and the scope that they have to design the methodological framework, establish the sample and set the questions in many different ways with little or no capacity for later replication.

Since it can be more time-consuming to gather the data for qualitative studies, which must usually be done manually, sample sizes tend to be small. Consequently, in some ways, the choice of qualitative versus quantitative research is one of depth versus breadth, i.e., between looking in detail at a small number of subjects versus examining a larger number but much less closely.

Perusing a cross-section of the research in contemporary accounting or finance, it is clear that most studies adopt a quantitative design involving either the empirical analysis of data or the construction of artificial data (simulation). In accounting research, there is more balance, but still, quantitative work dominates. Even if this will also be your chosen method, it is useful to be aware of the numerous other types of research available under the qualitative umbrella, such as case studies and interviews.

Both quantitative and qualitative methods each have their advantages and disadvantages, and these will now be discussed in turn, which should support readers in making an informed choice about the approach that is most appropriate for them to employ given their background, interests, and research objectives.

The disadvantages of quantitative research

Qualitative research is sometimes chosen over more technical approaches because the researcher is concerned about the limitations of the statistical analysis of data, which include:

- Quantitative research can confuse correlation and causality – just because two variables change together does not mean that one causes the other since, in reality, it could be that a third variable causes changes in both. This is a hard issue to address
- Quantitative research neglects the context in which data are measured and assumes that all measurements of a given variable are equal
- Empirical work is usually conducted in the context of real data, and thus the investigator will have little control over the quantity or quality of information available or the scope of the variables
- Some concepts are very hard to measure objectively at arm's length (such as expectations, beliefs, or emotions). Yet these variables are crucial in underpinning many theories in accounting and finance
- Long lists of assumptions may be required – either implicit or explicit – and these could be pivotal. The assumptions are essential to conduct the analysis but slight changes in them may lead to big variations in the results
- Quantitative research is not genuinely value-free as is sometimes claimed because the research is conducted by investigators who will have their own preconceptions and biases that will influence their research design, methods, data and interpretations of the results
- The quantitative approach encourages researchers to focus on the details at the expense of a bigger picture, meaning that it may give precise answers to trivial questions but maybe unable to provide resolutions to the most fundamental issues
- The research design is rather fixed, and this can diminish the opportunities for a bigger intellectual contribution and a fundamental shift in the way people think about a particular phenomenon. It is too easy for quantitative researchers to switch into autopilot mode and follow down a well trodden path to produce incremental research that makes at best a small contribution

The advantages of quantitative research

Quantitative research usually involves developing an empirical model that links a dependent or explained variable with one or more independent or explanatory variables. This approach embodies several advantages compared with qualitative research:

- The data can be analysed formally with statistics, and the results are usually more generalisable since they are not context-specific
- Related to the previous point, the findings can be compared more readily across countries or over time
- It is possible to produce precise, numerical descriptions of the relationships between variables and also accurate forecasts about plausible future values of a variable
- It should be relatively straightforward for other researchers to replicate what a given study has done, thus validating the results
- The findings are less likely to be affected by the views or approach of the investigator than qualitative studies, and thus there is less scope for biases to creep in

If you are using a quantitative method, it is probably just a question of pushing your knowledge boundaries further in implementing a model or technique that you have not used before. It is then a matter of understanding how the model works at a conceptual level, how to implement the model using software, and how to interpret and check the output's validity.

The range of possible quantitative techniques is vast, but fortunately, there are many resources available, including numerous excellent textbooks. Still, as you would expect, I recommend my own, Introductory Econometrics for Finance (IEfF), Brooks (2019), available from the publisher and in e-book format from Amazon and Apple.[1] I also co-authored software guides to accompany the textbook for Python, R, Stata and EViews – these can be downloaded in pdf format from my page at SSRN, or in Mobi or Epub formats from Amazon and Apple Books, respectively – the software guides can be downloaded free of charge on all platforms.

Although IEfF was written primarily with finance students in mind, most of the material presented is also relevant for the statistical analysis of accounting-related data. In addition to the software guides, a substantial volume of other free resources is available to accompany IEfF from the publisher's website, including answers to end of chapter questions, an electronic glossary, a self-study multiple choice question bank and video lectures.

Quantitative work is usually associated with 'the scientific method' for conceptualising and understanding a problem. It involves establishing a theory or a set of testable hypotheses that are then transformed into an empirical model that can be estimated using statistical software. Next, a relevant dataset is collected and analysed using quantitative models, and the hypotheses are either supported or refuted by the data and appropriate conclusions drawn. The process operates according to the flowchart in Figure 10.1, taken from Brooks (2019).

---

[1] https://www.cambridge.org/gb/academic/subjects/economics/finance/introductory-econometrics-finance-4th-edition?format=PB

1a. Economic or financial theory (previous studies)

1b. Formulation of an estimable theoretical model

2. Collection of data

3. Model estimation

4. Is the model statistically adequate?

No   Yes

Reformulate model   5. Interpret model

6. Use for analysis

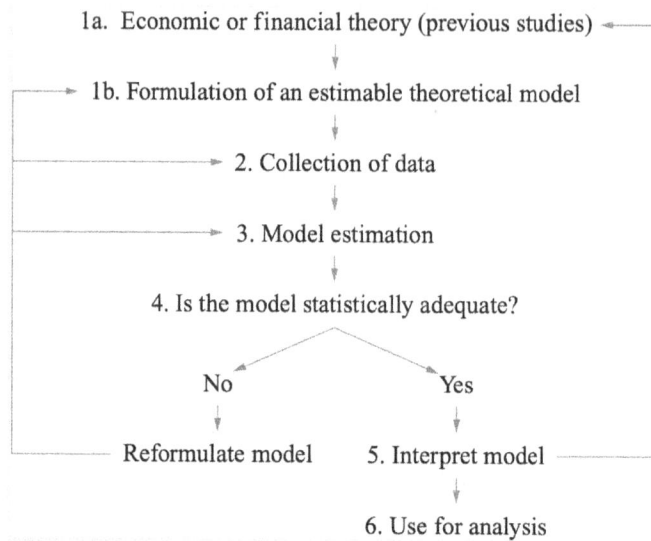

Figure 10.1: Steps in the quantitative approach to research

10.2.4 The role of hypotheses in research

A hypothesis is a statement specified and then test using data. In essence, it is simply a well-informed guess (based on theory or prior knowledge) about what will happen in a particular situation and why. Note that the part in parentheses is essential – the hypothesis has to be grounded within the knowledge base and not just a randomly generated suggestion.

More formally, a hypothesis could be defined as a proposition that arises from your theoretical or conceptual model, but it may or may not be correct. By definition, if you knew that the hypothesis was correct before you tested it, there would be no point in proceeding, and it would instead be a law or generally accepted principle, not a hypothesis. Hence a hypothesis should not be so broad or obviously correct (or incorrect) that it is not interesting to test, and knowing the result of the hypothesis test should be relevant and useful to other people for it to be worthwhile.

Like good research questions, effective hypotheses should be sufficiently involved that they cannot be answered by looking at figures that could be obtained from the internet, which is why incorporating causality into hypotheses based on specific, pre-defined variables can be worthwhile. For instance, the hypothesis:

'H1: people in the public sector save more for their pensions than those in the private sector'

would not be very interesting because a quick use of a search engine would reveal the answer. But if this was specified with some possible reasoning as:

'H2: people in the public sector save more for their pensions because their schemes are more generous, they can take the benefits sooner, and they are on average older than those in the private sector' then it would be more exciting. This would probably best be split into three separate sub-hypotheses, none of which has an immediately obvious answer. It would be hard to tackle this without conducting a survey or interviews as the information would not already be available, and the information you would obtain could be examined using several different techniques, including, if you wished, a formal statistical analysis.

Falsifying hypotheses

The Austrian philosopher Karl Popper (1959) argued that hypotheses should also be falsifiable. In other words, if the hypothesis is wrong, the testing method should be designed to be able to reject it. If a researcher is unable to refute the hypothesis, then it is supported by the data. Even if a scientific statement passes every attempt to refute it, it can still never be proved correct or definitively accepted as true.

But only one piece of evidence against a hypothesis or theory is sufficient for it to be rejected. Popper gave the example of the hypothesis, 'all swans are white': even if there are vast numbers of only white swans on a particular lake, this does not prove the hypothesis correct. But a sighting of only one black swan is required to prove it false. Consequently, hypotheses are either rejected or not rejected by the data, and just as in classical statistics, they are never accepted. If a hypothesis or theory is falsified (i.e., proved to be wrong), it could be modified and retested or rejected entirely.

However, we also need to remember that, unfortunately, because no testing framework is entirely accurate, is it even possible to reject a correct theory, which is analogous to a Type I error in statistics. Therefore, just because we find evidence against a theory, it could still be right, and if we find evidence in favour of a theory, it could still be wrong! While researchers always try to set up the testing framework to minimise the chances of both types of error as much as possible, there is a trade-off: making the rule for rejecting a hypothesis more strict means that the probability of incorrectly rejecting a correct null is reduced but the probability of incorrectly not rejecting a wrong null is increased. The way to reduce the probabilities of both types of error is to improve the size and quality of the sample. This is why repeated investigations of a given research problem using different techniques and in various settings are so valuable.

Popper argued that it is the possibility that an assertion can be falsified that sets science apart from non-science, and any hypothesis or theory that is not open to being refuted is not scientific. A hypothesis must be sufficiently explicit (i.e., not vague) that it is testable – i.e., it needs to be set up in such a fashion that it can be demonstrated to be wrong if it is so. In other words, hypotheses should be as tightly defined as possible, which makes them more testable.

In this vein, we could perhaps argue, for instance, that the efficient markets hypothesis is a scientific theory since it is possible to test and refute it (which it has been in a vast number of studies), but many concepts in behavioural finance are not. To illustrate, if we find that investors update their beliefs too quickly in the light of new information, we might argue that they suffer from recency bias; if they are too slow to update their beliefs, then they suffer from anchoring bias. Hence, either way, we could argue that they suffer from behavioural biases when they form their beliefs about future price movements with no way to demonstrate that they do not. Therefore, when considered in this way, the behavioural finance explanation is not falsifiable unless the hypothesis is set up to specify precisely which bias is being tested.

How to establish meaningful hypotheses

Hypotheses need to be precisely written to be testable, and they need to convey something beyond what is already known. For example, consider the hypothesis:

'H1: Men and women have different degrees of risk tolerance'.

This hypothesis would not be useful since it is too vague. In particular, it does not state whether men's or women's tolerances are expected to be higher, and it does not specify the domain (finances, driving, job choices, sports, etc.). Replacing the hypothesis above with:

'H2: Men are more financially risk-tolerant than women'

would resolve the domain vagueness, but it would still not be a strong statement since this issue has been investigated very many times before, and so the findings are already widely available in the literature. A hypothesis:

'H3: Men are more financially risk-tolerant because they are more confident than women'

would tick all the boxes. This hypothesis is not only written in a precise and testable language, but also the added clause would relate to a new and exciting question where there is some existing work, but it is still an open area.

Hypotheses, research aims and research questions

Returning to the point made above about different means to express the research problem, it is worth noting that H3 could alternatively be written in other ways. The general research problem could be written as:

'it has been observed in numerous studies that men tend to be more financially risk- tolerant than women. A range of explanations for this phenomenon has been proposed, with one idea focusing on differences in their average levels of confidence.'

This statement then leads to two alternative ways to write this problem as an aim or as a question:

- As a research aim – e.g., 'I aim to investigate whether men are more financially risk-tolerant because they are more confident than women;'
- Or as a research question – e.g., 'Are men more financially risk-tolerant because they are more confident than women?'

These three approaches (research hypotheses, research aims, and research questions) are equivalent, but some researchers prefer not to state hypotheses explicitly, and the style varies somewhat from one field to another. Most fields within management seem to like the use of hypotheses, but in accounting and finance, the convention is mostly to write research problems in the form of aims or questions. This style is more useful if your research is somewhat exploratory, and it is not possible to express your ideas as formally as a hypothesis, although the advantage of hypotheses is that they limit the scope for excessively vague ideas to be included. Questions including 'why' can be too vague to be testable, but conveniently they cannot usually be formulated into a hypothesis. Returning to the previous example to illustrate this, we might have asked:

'why are women less risk-tolerant than men?'

This would take us back to H2, which was rejected on the grounds that it is not sufficiently precise.

The hypothesis, stated aim or research question needs to cover all contexts rather than being specific to the sample you are investigating. For instance, it might be that you are exploring the final hypothesis, H3, listed above using a selection of undergraduate students at your university. But even though your data are limited to that group, your hypothesis would relate to all men and women, not just students. However, you might need to justify why you believe that the results are generalisable from your specific sample.

Notice a distinction in style between the hypotheses as they are constructed here compared with those specified in statistics and econometrics. In the latter cases, there is a formal approach where there are null and alternative hypotheses, specified using an equality and an inequality, respectively. In accounting and finance research studies and other branches of business and management, these statements would generally be set up somewhat less formally as individual hypotheses rather than pairs, with no null or alternative, but instead, a single statement expressed in words.

10.3   The role of theory in research

The word 'theory' is used in various contexts and to capture something at different levels of abstraction and also dependent upon the researcher's ontological perspective. As a basic working definition, we could think of a theory as a statement or set of statements that embody several ideas about how something operates or what causes a particular phenomenon. Theories are usually intangible ideas that link concepts together, embodying one or more hypotheses. For positivists, theory is the key to explaining causal relationships and making predictions. On the other hand, for interpretivists, theories are not tested using data; rather, they are constructed after fieldwork.

In finance, the term theory is confusingly used on many different levels, so it is crucial to explain precisely which theories you are referring to. The word is employed both loosely to talk about a general set of ideas before empirical implementation and formally to define precise notions of why specific groups of individuals behave in a certain way in a given situation. For instance, signalling theory (where one party in a transaction or negotiation has better information than the other, and so provides a signal to convey that information) is one aspect of capital structure theory (which refers to the way that firms select combinations of equity, bonds and loans in their project financing mix).

Theories can also be classified as being either positive or normative: positive theories dispassionately relate to the facts of what is happening without passing judgement, whereas normative theories embody a set of values or moral judgements about what is right or wrong (in other words, how things should be).

Unlike a 'law', which is a statement that scholars generally accept to be true, 'theories', 'models', and 'hypotheses' may or may not be true, which is why they must be subject to testing and then tentatively rejected or supported by the data. If the data refute the theory, it needs to be modified or replaced and then subjected to further testing, although this sort of iterative process does not strictly follow the positivist tradition that the theory must come first. In practice, however, many (perhaps the majority of) researchers engage in what might be termed 'post hoc rationalisations of their empirical findings' where they estimate an empirical model, see what the data are telling them, and then try to identify an 'off-the-shelf' theory that is consistent with what they observe from that data. But when they write up the theory and methods, they do so as if they had proposed the theory first, which then miraculously works when they test it empirically.

Perhaps an advantage of the grounded theory approach discussed in subsection 2.3.7 is that it explicitly acknowledges that theory can be developed after observing the data. However, a further problem with the scientific method is that rigid, pre-conceived ideas from an existing theory about the relationship between variables can narrow the research agenda's scope from the outset.

Why theory is needed

It is, of course, possible to conduct research without having a theory, but arguably such research is purely exploratory, it would lack a framework or structure, and some scholars might argue that any findings emerging from such research are not rigorous and could be statistical flukes that are specific to that sample and context. In essence, they might state, the conclusions are the result of data mining.

While the empirical analysis of secondary data is by far the most common type of method employed in our field, good research is rarely purely data-driven. The empirical model should arise from an accounting, economic or financial theory, and this theory should be presented and discussed before the investigative work begins. Theory shows what features in the data and what relationships would be expected based on some underlying principles. Theory can give order to empirical results and ensure that the findings are not the result of a data-mining exercise.

While theory strengthens and adds depth to empirical work, it is important to note that it should only be used when useful and relevant. If an inappropriate theory is 'bolted on' to investigative work, the theory would detract from it. The theory and empirics need to complement each other, else it will cause confusion as the theory should allow the investigator to step back and put the findings into a wider context. If theory is not a useful tool, it should not be included.

Characteristics of a good theory

Ideally, good theories should embody the following characteristics:

- Theories are usually deliberately broad and high-level, abstracting from most of the specific details, and hence they are often called 'theoretical frameworks' or 'underpinning theory'
- Following from the previous point, a theory should not attempt to explain everything and should be capable of being specified in at most a few short statements. In other words, it should embody the concept of parsimony, explaining as much as possible while remaining compact
- A useful theory will be generalisable and predictive, so it should enable the researcher to determine what is likely to happen in a given set of circumstances. It should also be capable of being used in different contexts to the one where it was developed
- Following from the previous point, a theory needs to be abstract enough to generalise the research findings, but not so abstract that it has no practical applicability

Theory relates to what a researcher expects to find *ex ante*, rather than what they actually do find *ex post*, and theories should be independent of the data they are designed to model, not developed after looking at the outcomes (except for grounded theories – see subsection 2.3.7). The theory should lead naturally to the methods and data selection, and it has no value if it does not link with the empirical aspects of the work.

Some researchers have argued that theory is not useful since it is implausible that people making decisions will be aware of it, let alone understand it. Therefore, such a perspective would argue, how could decision-makers follow theory? However, the economist Milton Friedman (1953) argued that it does not matter whether agents are aware of the relevant theory, the only relevant question is whether they behave as if they followed the model, and if they do, then the theory is worthwhile. Friedman provided the analogy of billiards players who perform as if they have employed mathematical models to work out the correct trajectory and force to apply for a shot even though they might have had no training in physics. Consequently, so long as people end up behaving in the same way as a theory describes, then it is useful even if they get to that behaviour through a different path. Moreover, according to Friedman, 'descriptively inaccurate' theories are perfectly adequate so long as they are 'analytically relevant' (i.e., they still work in predicting outcomes).

10.3.1   Where do theories come from?

Researchers usually develop theories from first principles based on a consideration of why and how relevant individuals (sometimes known as 'agents' in this context) make choices, given the information and knowledge that those decision-makers have and what they aim to achieve. Theories can also arise from the expected outcomes from interactions between groups of agents – for example, different groups of stakeholders within a firm (shareholders, customers, employees, the government or regulators, etc.).

Often, to operationalise a theory and to predict or mathematically model the outcome will require a set of assumptions to be made since, without them, the model is intractable and therefore of no use. In other words, the model could not be solved, either mathematically or in a more informal sense, so that it would not be possible to determine the expected outcome. Many such models in accounting and finance are based on economic principles. Therefore, the assumptions usually revolve around matters such as rational agents (always preferring more to less, and only taking risks if there is sufficient reward) or markets being frictionless (no taxes, freedom to buy and sell in any quantity, and so on).

It is also clear that theories will often incorporate concepts from psychology or sociology since people rather than machines ultimately make the decisions. Hence, the role of personality, emotions, biased expectations or inaccurate forecasts of risks or payoffs for individuals are built into theories of how people behave. Also relevant are the interactions between them when they operate in groups (such as the effects of herding or information cascades), which affect their decisions and, therefore, the outcomes.

Numerous studies in finance, in particular, develop their theoretical frameworks into a set of mathematical equations that are then solved to determine the outcome. So we can think of a model being that aspect of a theory that is expressed mathematically. The model's solution can be obtained either by algebraic substitution and rearrangement of the equations (a so-called 'analytical solution') or, if the problem is too complex to disentangle algebraically, by simulating the model with artificially generated data to determine the expected outcome conditional on the assumptions made.

However, theoretical models don't need to be set up formally as equations, and they can remain at a more intangible level, with the outcomes determined using logical arguments in words rather than numbers. This approach is more likely to be used in accounting and most other branches of management – for example, in marketing or strategy. In such cases, authors sometimes refer to their collection of interlinked ideas as a 'conceptual model' or 'conceptual framework'. The concepts can be based on variables that can be observed or measured (such as risk aversion, wealth, auditor independence, etc.) or they can be abstract notions such as utility.

The difference between a concept and a theory

Although the terms theory and concept are related, they are often used as if they are interchangeable, but in reality, there is a subtle distinction between them. A concept is more of an abstract idea and is not necessarily testable, whereas a theory is usually thought of as more formal, testable and scientific. Theories are built up from concepts, but both should only be employed if they are useful, and they are tentative, so they might be incorrect.

A conceptual framework arises when several concepts are brought together and linked in some way. For example, there could be a causal relationship between several variables (e.g., 'if X1 and X2 both happen, it will cause Y to occur'). The causality could be in one direction, or there could be feedback so that changes in Y then lead subsequently to shifts in X1 or X2. A theoretical framework will be more formal than a conceptual framework and based on a model of how and why specific variables interact arising from first principles of decision-making. Both conceptual and theoretical models abstract from reality with the aim to simplify rather than explain everything.

As should be clear from the discussion above, the term theory can mean very diverse things to different groups of researchers. Here are two examples of recent research that I co-authored, and that used very different kinds of theories from sociology and psychology to underpin empirical studies in finance.

1. The paper by Brooks *et al.* (2019) mentioned in chapter 7 sought to explain why academic finance had grown and remained so strong despite being so little used to influence policy or practice in the financial services sector. A conceptual framework due to the French sociologist Pierre Bourdieu was employed to argue that scholars of finance obtain their sense of worth and the capital that they possess from metrics generated within universities including the recognition of their peers through publication in top journals. Therefore, conducting research with practical value is, in most cases, not something that matters to them

2. In an entirely different recent study, Hillenbrand *et al.* (2021), we were interested in examining the impact of retail investor characteristics, their emotional states and their attitudes towards finance on the kind of investment products they were most attracted to. Specifically, we aimed to determine the factors that affected whether they were more likely to select short- or long-term investments and those that focused on protecting the value of the capital versus a type having more growth potential.

   To develop the hypotheses in Hillenbrand et al. (*op. cit.*), we relied upon the theory of construal level from psychology, which explains how investors will determine their inter-temporal discount rates when they compare an object to be received soon with the same one to be obtained further into the future. We also used regulatory focus theory, which relates to how people make decisions to attain their goals. Applying these two sets of established theoretical frameworks and their interaction allowed us to develop our hypotheses.

   We found that adverts for short-term products with growth potential attracted sensation-seeking investors who were highly risk-tolerant, and people with positive emotions towards finance were drawn to products that were focused on the preservation of capital rather than growth, while those with negative emotions were more prone to short-termism.

Developing a new theory involves an in-depth examination of a particular phenomenon, market, type of firm, or behaviour with a view to establishing a causal framework that could explain how or why specific outcomes occurred. The theoretical model developed could be testable or untestable. A testable model would be one where the necessary information can be observed or collected, and a statistical framework used to show whether the theoretical model is supported or refuted by the data. The development of a solid, well-reasoned theoretical framework is a substantial undertaking, especially if it is highly novel, and so it would probably not be necessary to empirically test the model in the same research study, although it would add strength if the work did both.

A model might be untestable because its concepts are too high-level and so are not observable. However, this sort of model might still help researchers organise their thoughts into a framework and conduct a counterfactual analysis ('if X were to happen, what would be the impact on Y'?)

Although most PhD dissertations will not propose or develop new theories since to do so would require specialist skills that take longer to develop than the tools to undertake empirical work, they will use theory to underpin any empirical work and make sense of the findings. The careful use of theory will considerably strengthen a research study and should be utilised to underpin the research hypotheses or questions. When the data are analysed, you can then return to the theory and explain whether it is supported by your findings or refuted. Could the theory be modified to make it fit your data better, and if so, how?

If you have a conceptual or theoretical framework, it makes the process of data collection and analysis more straightforward because the framework will inform which variables you need to measure, how, and why. Theory is the backbone of empirical investigations, and its absence can leave a study looking weak. It allows the researcher to make predictions about what the relationships between variables will or will not be. If there is no theory, a researcher can simply experiment with large numbers of candidate variables until several statistically significant coefficient estimates are found. Any relationships found this way without recourse to theory could be entirely spurious and the result of data mining, which is sometimes termed a 'fishing exercise' where you would dip your finishing rod (large empirical model) into the river with no idea what kind of fish (significant parameter estimates) you might pull out.

10.3.2 Examples of relevant theories

Many established theoretical frameworks underpinning recent empirical investigations have been around for a long time. Each field (including finance, accounting, sociology, psychology, and economics) has its own theories, with differences in how they are specified and tested. But there is also a considerable degree of cross-fertilisation, with some fields borrowing theories from others. In particular, since accounting and finance are social sciences where decisions are ultimately made by people, theories that originated in psychology and sociology are widely adopted to account for how individuals make choices either individually (psychology) or within the context of group interactions and dynamics incorporating the influences of others (sociology).

It is worth noting that which field's researchers developed a particular theory might be contested – for instance, when psychologists lay claim to having developed an idea that is also employed (perhaps under a different name) by sociologists. Accounting, in particular, is short on theories developed within the field and has adopted many from other disciplines. Researchers sometimes appeal to more than one theory, or they combine theories to explain a particular phenomenon.

The lists below provide a few examples of some fundamental theories that have been developed and widely implemented in each field (accounting, economics, finance, management, psychology, sociology and politics), alongside brief definitions or explanations in each case. However, merely a handful of illustrations are presented to give some ideas and the lists are by no means exhaustive as for all of these fields there are very many other examples that could have been provided. These are, in some cases, the 'highest level' grand theories that cover many situations and aspects of behaviour and hence are harder to isolate and test than narrower theories. The theories presented from the fields of psychology, sociology and politics focus on the ideas of most relevance to accounting and finance.

I have not provided any references or suggested further reading in this section as there are simply too many for that to be useful, and each researcher needs to select a relevant theory given the nature of the problem they are investigating.

Accounting

- Residual theory of dividends – argues that firms should continue to invest in any projects with positive net present value and only distribute funds as dividends once such project possibilities have been exhausted.
- Behavioural accounting theory – considers the impact of psychological factors, including personality and emotions, on the interpretation of accounting information and accounting decisions.
- Positive accounting theory – a very high level, all-embracing set of principles that has been variously interpreted as corresponding to the use of positivist, scientific principles to study accounting issues by some authors and interpreted by other writers as relating to how corporate accountants determine their firm's accounting policies and how they respond to changes in externally imposed standards.
- Structuration theory – originated in sociology but is now widely applied in management accounting to analyse accounting frameworks, recognising the importance of social systems and social structures, also considering the impact that accounting systems can have on organisational development.
- Legitimacy theory – relates to the notion that a firm has a 'social contract' with its stakeholders, is expected to act in certain ways that conform with ethical norms and principles, and that fulfilling this wider role provides the company with the credibility to conduct its core business.

Economics

- Expected utility theory – where people make the choices that will maximise the expected utility of the decision (by weighting the outcomes by the probabilities that each will occur).
- Theory of optimal taxation – the notion that taxes should be set (in terms of their level and coverage) to maximise societal welfare, causing the least possible distortion in economic activity.
- Theory of information asymmetry – this relates to how people behave when one party in a transaction has much more information about the situation than the other. For example, in the 'market for lemons', George Akerlof explained how markets could fail in the context where a car seller has much more information about its condition than the buyer so that only poor-quality cars ('lemons') will have a market.
- Theory of comparative advantage – countries specialise in producing goods and services where their production costs (measured in terms of opportunity cost) are lower.
- New growth theory – argues that by the process of consumption and investment to fulfil their wants and needs, individual actions will lead to economic growth over time. It emphasises the importance of knowledge and information in driving rises in gross domestic product.
- The classical theory of central bank lending – central banks should act as lender of the last resort and always provide liquidity to the banking system in times of stress but at high rates of interest where appropriate, and insolvent banks ought to be left to fail rather than bailed out.

Finance

- Greater fool theory – linked with speculative bubbles, this idea explains why people buy assets even when they know the prices are too high (i.e., the securities are over-valued) because they believe that a 'greater fool' will purchase the asset from them at an even higher price in the future.
- The theory of capital structure irrelevance – the idea that corporate financing (i.e., how firms finance expansion via retained cash, bond or stock issue) and dividend decisions do not affect firm value since investors could generate the same impacts themselves through the combinations of assets they buy and sell.
- Efficient market theory – that securities' prices will fully and immediately encompass the effects of all available and relevant information.
- Short interest theory – the counter-intuitive notion that the prices of stocks having a large volume of short sales are expected to rise since, at some point, these short positions will have to be covered by purchasing the shares, which will cause net buying pressure.

Management

- Stakeholder theory – a perspective on how firms will operate based on the notion that they will make decisions that benefit all of the agents whom the firm interacts with, including customers, workers, and the government, rather than just maximising profits for shareholders.
- Agency theory – describes the interactions between the principal in a firm (i.e., its owners or shareholders) and the agents (managers), who will act in a self-interested way that can lead to conflicts of interest and may not maximise value for owners.
- Stewardship theory – the idea that corporate managers will primarily aim to serve the best interests of the organisation for which they work rather than acting for their own personal gain since they feel a sense of responsibility and professional pride. The predictions from this theory go against those from agency theory.
- Resource dependency theory – suggests that a firm will have dependencies on others due to its requirement for raw materials and further inputs, and equally, there may also exist firms that depend on it. Therefore, having control over its resources gives a firm power.

Psychology

- Cognitive theory – argues that decisions are based on the way people process information and form their beliefs, which is in turn related to memory, attention and perceptions.
- Prospect theory – when making financial decisions, people do not maximise expected utility but instead exhibit loss aversion due to asymmetries in their utility functions. These arise because people feel the pain of a given monetary loss more than they feel the pleasure from an equal amount of gain.
- The ripple effect theory – moods are contagious within groups, so spending a great deal of time among people in a negative mind state will encourage an individual to develop such negative feelings.
- The theory of offsetting behaviour – embodies people's tendency to take greater risks when in a safer environment. For instance, drivers tend to be more aggressive when wearing a seatbelt, and children take more risks when playing near a river if they can swim. Hence their modified behaviour offsets the risk reductions in other aspects of their environments.
- The theory of multiple intelligences – the notion that people have several different 'intelligences' so individuals are good at particular tasks depending on which intelligence they are stronger in, including linguistic, musical, spatial, and mathematical.
- The theory of planned behaviour – suggests that a person's behaviour depends on three aspects: their attitude to this action, the view of others regarding it, and the extent to which the individual believes they can control it. According to the first of these, the person is more likely to go ahead and do something

if they view it positively, i.e., they believe it will benefit them. Second, the person is more likely to take this action if the people in their social circle view it positively. Third, if the person believes they have the skills and ability to do something, they are more likely to do it.

Sociology and politics

- Symbolic interaction theory – people use labels (i.e., language) to make sense of the social world, which exists only through those individuals' actions and perceptions. The experiences that people have with particular entities (both people and objects) will modify what the words attached to the entities mean to them.
- Conflict theory – argues that the world is permanently in a state of conflict because resources are limited. Those with wealth develop the means to hold onto it through the exercise of domination and power over others.
- Labelling theory – people act according to the way that they have been labelled. For instance, if someone is branded a criminal, they are more likely to behave in that way. Deviance from social norms occurs not as a result of an individual's behaviour but rather as a result of the label that is attached to their behaviour by others defining it as a deviant action.
- Social learning theory – people learn via observing others in action, identifying their behaviour and imitating it, and seeing whether these behaviours yield good or bad consequences and are either reinforced or frowned upon by others.
- Public choice theory – covers many ideas relating to how those in the public sector make decisions on behalf of the general population, often in a self-interested manner that focuses on the former's utility rather than the latter's.

10.4   Data collection and analysis

10.4.1   Approaches to investigative work

An array of methods is available to students when conducting the investigative parts of their PhD in accounting and finance in order to collect and analyse the data. Whatever method you choose, it is essential to clearly explain the methods you are using to inspire confidence in readers that the techniques are appropriate and that you know what you are doing - if not, the results could be considered worthless. In particular, since the vast majority of PhDs in our fields are empirical, involving gathering and analysing data, you will probably need to think about the following questions if you have not already had to do so when you wrote the proposal:

- What data will you collect?
- From where will the data be obtained?
- Why is this the relevant data to address your research aims?
- How will you analyse the data, and what do you expect the analysis to show?

Wherever your data arise from – surveys, archives, or databases, and even if your aims involve estimating complex econometric models, ensure that you begin with rudimentary analysis. Always plot the data (where feasible) and present summary statistics and simple correlations between the variables. This will help you build the more complex models effectively and allow a sense check of the data's quality. It will also enable you to sharpen your research questions or hypotheses and gently lead the reader into the more in-depth analysis that follows. Qualitative studies, however, will usually have few tables or charts, if any, which will be limited to basic summary measures and hence the presentation of the findings will be all about the narrative.

A large amount of useful information can always be gleaned from simple means, variances, plots over time, and so on. However, while including summary information is vital, equally, try to avoid swamping the reader with endless tables, and unless the sample is tiny, do not paste the raw data into the dissertation, even in an appendix. It will take a vast amount of space, yet it is unlikely that anyone will look at it.

10.4.2 Primary versus secondary data

The difference between primary and secondary data

It is surprisingly tricky to define primary and secondary data precisely, but we can think of the former as applying anywhere that new information is created for the first time – for example, through interviews or surveys, while the latter occurs when existing information is reused or re-interpreted.

Collecting primary data is an essential component of conducting a research study in some disciplines such as many of the sciences and some social sciences, including psychology. Still, in accounting and finance, it is usually optional and rare given the widespread availability of extensive off-the-shelf databases and the speed with which they can be put to use. Therefore, rather than using surveys, interviews or experiments, most students will download their data from an established source.

The pros and cons of primary versus secondary data

Primary data collection has several advantages:
- A range of techniques is available, including web-based surveys, which could allow you to gather a sample of comparable size to secondary sources but on a unique and more diverse range of topics
- It allows you complete flexibility over what you study since you are in control and creating the data rather than relying on the choices that someone else has previously made
- Secondary data sources will not have been set up with your research aims in mind, and so it might be the case that you cannot obtain the information you need unless you create your own data
- Secondary databases can be used freely if your school subscribes to them, but if not, the access fee could be prohibitively expensive.

There are, of course, also downsides to using primary, rather than secondary, data:
- Market-type finance and accounting questions can realistically only be addressed using an established secondary database. For example, anything to

do with the prices, yields, volumes or volatilities of assets, unless you wanted to conduct a study in the context of an experimental or simulated market

- Collecting and organising primary data is likely to be much more time-consuming than using an off-the-shelf solution. Many students conclude that they simply don't have the scope to obtain primary data within the time available, and if they do, there is a danger that collection will take the time that could have been used in analysing the data
- Opting for primary data use runs more risk that something will go wrong, and the sample will be inadequate in some way; on the other hand, there is less scope for problems with secondary data
- Collecting primary data is usually only feasible in your own country, where you have contacts and expertise. Therefore, if you intend to study another country (either on its own or as part of an international sample), there is probably no chance to use primary data

10.4.3 Choosing your sample

Whether you are engaged in primary or secondary data collection, it is worth defining your population at the outset and reflecting on the size and coverage of the sample you hope to obtain. Once you have identified the population, you need to establish the sampling frame, which defines how you will select the entities from within the population. If the data are secondary, the first choice, which should be made based on data availability and the requirements to answer your research questions, will be between time-series, cross-sectional or panel datasets. The secondary choice then concerns the coverage (geographical coverage, spanning which assets or markets, or time period, etc.)

Although, as stated above, the larger the sample, the better, there will no doubt be constraints that might either be in terms of the scope of the information covered in the database or the volume of data that you could process during the time you have available to complete the thesis. While it makes sense to download time-series going back as far as they are present on the system, you may not want to conduct the same analysis repeatedly for many countries as it would be repetitive unless that is an integral part of your research design.

Types of sampling

Random sampling is usually considered the best approach since, provided that the number of data points is sufficiently large, its properties will converge upon those of the underlying population, and hence the former can be used to make valid inferences about the latter. Sampling in a non-random fashion could lead to biases favouring one sub-group rather than another, thus breaking the link with the population characteristics. Random sampling is sometimes known as probability sampling because each entity within the population has an equal probability of being selected. To illustrate, suppose that we wanted to examine the impact of news wire announcements for a random sample of ten FTSE100 companies. It might not be possible to examine all 100 companies due to time constraints, but the ten selected would imply that each company has a 10% chance of being chosen.

A related possibility would be to use a stratified sampling technique, where the population would be separated into strata (layers) and random sampling takes place within each stratum. For instance, we could split the FTSE100 firms by size (say, small and large) and by sector (into five broad sectors), which would yield $2 \times 5 = 10$ categories, with one firm chosen from each. This process of stratified sampling would ensure that, despite the small number of data points, it would be more representative of the population of interest and would include an appropriate spread along the size and industrial classification dimensions.

However, in some instances, the bias from non-random sampling may be desirable and even necessary, in which case non-random or non-probability sampling would be implemented. Here, the sample would be selected to achieve a higher proportion of (or contain exclusively) individuals with particular features. For example, we might be interested in investigating whether people who get into extreme difficulties with their debts are more likely to have particular personality types compared to the rest of the population. But the proportion of the overall population that has got into severe debt management problems might be so low that a random sample would pick up just a tiny number of them, in which case it would not be possible to conduct any valid quantitative analysis. In that case, we might prefer to systematically over-sample from that specific group.

In the case of qualitative research, there is often no interest in generalising the findings, but rather the purpose is simply to demonstrate how one particular instance works. Returning to a previous example, a researcher might be interested in writing a case study of a trader they know who was convicted of having illegally manipulated market prices for personal gain. In this instance, the focus could be on the individual's motivations, how they felt at the time, whether they feared being caught or losing money, how they hid their activities, and so on. There would probably be no attempt to suggest that the insights gained would apply to others engaged in market price distortion, let alone other types of traders. Therefore, the concepts of sampling, inference and populations usually have little relevance for qualitative research.

10.4.4 Sources of secondary data

It is worth planning your analysis and carefully considering what you will do with your data before beginning the collection process. Sometimes your data will need to be downloaded from a system where you have restricted access (e.g., you have to book a slot in advance). If that is the case, make sure that you take everything that you might need as your opportunities for another dip later may be limited.

You will hopefully have access to a range of commercial databases through your university department (such as Reuters/Eikon/Datastream, Bloomberg, FAME, CRSP and Compustat, OptionMetrics, etc.), and if so, these will provide a rich resource amenable to a wide range of topics and approaches. These databases are so vast, each with a distinct user-interface, that it might require formal training or at least some time getting used to the interface before you can download the information you want. No further details are presented of these sources since, if your institution subscribes to them, full information will be available from there, and possibly free training on how to use the databases.

Many internet-based sources offer free data without registration, which might be your only option if your university does not subscribe to (often eye-wateringly expensive) commercial databases. Some useful links to free data on the internet include:

Financial Data
- Yahoo! Finance – an incredible range of free financial data, information, research and commentary[2]
- Ken French's data library – this contains the Fama-French factor data, mainly US-focused but also international factors[3]
- Robert Shiller's stock market confidence and cyclically adjusted price-earnings ratio data[4]
- An archive of US stock data from 2009-2017[5] and on the VIX volatility index from 2004-2018[6]
- US and German annual company accounting data (income statements, cashflow, share prices, etc.)[7]

US-based data sources (mainly macroeconomics)
- Federal Reserve Bank of Chicago – including interest data and useful links[8]
- Federal Reserve Bank of Dallas – including macroeconomic, interest rate, monetary and bank data[9]
- US Bureau of Labor Statistics – US macroeconomic series[10]
- US Federal Reserve Board – US macroeconomic series, exchange rates, interest rates, household finance series[11]
- FRED, the St. Louis Fed – a vast array of (three-quarters of a million) US and international macroeconomic series, even including cryptocurrency prices, available daily, weekly or monthly[12]
- All US Treasury – a wide range of US interest rate series[13]

---

[2]https://finance.yahoo.com
[3]http://mba.tuck.dartmouth.edu/pages/faculty/ken.french/data_library.html
[4]http://www.econ.yale.edu/ shiller/data.htm
[5]https://github.com/eliangcs/pystock-data
[6]https://github.com/datasets/finance-vix/blob/master/data/vix-daily.csv
[7]https://simfin.com
[8]https://www.chicagofed.org/research/data/index
[9]https://www.dallasfed.org/research.aspx
[10]https://www.bls.gov
[11]https://www.federalreserve.gov/econres.htm
[12]https://fred.stlouisfed.org
[13]https://www.treasury.gov/resource-center/data-chart-center/interest-

UK and other European macroeconomic data

- The UK Treasury – a range of UK macroeconomic and other series[14]
- The Bank of England has several series, including exchange rates and yield curves[15]
- European macroeconomic data are available from the EU Open Data portal[16]
- UK house price series[17]

Global macroeconomic data

- The International Montary Fund (IMF)[18]
- The World Bank[19]
- The Bank for International Settlements (BIS), which provides a range of macro-financial series sourced from the world's central banks, including data on exchange rates, debt securities, property prices, liquidity, and payment systems. [20]

If you have no choice but to use these, the range of topics you will be able to tackle will be severely constrained compared to the commercial databases, but nonetheless, it is possible to use them for good quality research, and they are sufficiently credible that the reliability of your findings will not be called into question. There are other, more dubious internet-based sources where, for example, illegal copies of commercial data have been uploaded, or the source of the information is unclear. But for precisely these reasons (legality, credibility and reliability), these are best avoided.

Many of the URLs listed above include extensive databases, and furthermore, many markets and exchanges have their own web pages detailing data availability. However, one needs to be slightly careful to ensure the accuracy of freely available data; 'free' data also sometimes turn out not to be.

Do not be afraid to send established researchers an e-mail if they have used specialist data or they have written some code that would be of value to your work. If the information has a commercial origin (e.g., the researcher's university has purchased it), then it is unlikely that the terms of their licence would enable the data to be sent to you. Academics are also keen to hold on for some time to information that they have collected if they intend to continue to publish from it, to avoid other researchers being able to free-ride from their initial efforts to get research on the same topic out quicker.

---

rates/Pages/TextView.aspx?data=longtermrate

[14] https://www.gov.uk/search/research-and-statistics

[15] https://www.bankofengland.co.uk/statistics

[16] https://data.europa.eu/euodp/en/data/dataset?sort=views_total+desc&vocab_theme= http%3A%2F%2Fpublications.europa.eu%2Fresource%2Fauthority%2Fdata-theme%2FECON

[17] https://www.gov.uk/government/collections/uk-house-price-index-reports

[18] https://www.imf.org/en/

[19] https://data.worldbank.org

[20] https://www.bis.org/statistics/index.htm

Table 10.1: Software choices for quantitative analysis

Package	Commercial or Freeware	Advantages	Disadvantages
Microsoft Excel	Commercial	Straightforward to use, you almost certainly already know how to use it, and your data will probably already be in the correct format. Very easy to configure the output to an attractive layout to drop straight into a document.	Only very basic analyses are possible without a lot of function writing. It is also inefficient if you have a large amount of data or need to run the same models repeatedly. Since the data, models or functions and results are kept together, it is easier than other packages to damage the raw data or make errors without realising it.
EViews	Commercial	Straightforward to use and quite powerful with numerous built-in models and a programming language available within the software as well as a menu-driven system.	The programming language is less intuitive than others, and some built-in functions have limited options.
Gretl	Freeware	Menu-driven but freely available. Most of the main classes of models are available. Fairly straightforward to use.	Only available on the Windows platform and not for Mac. Limited range of built-in functions, although since it is open-source, a programmer could extend the available routines.
R	Freeware	The extensive and rapidly growing range of functions is available make it very powerful, and it is becoming the standard package for sophisticated analysis	Requires some programming skills and will take longer to get up to speed than some other packages.
Stata	Commercial	Wide range of built-in functions and guides on how to use it. More straightforward to use than programming languages.	Requires some limited programming skills. Expensive to purchase if your institution does not have a site licence.
Python	Freeware	Particularly useful for textual analysis, extraordinarily flexible and increasingly in demand in the corporate world.	It is a programming language, not a statistical package and takes much longer to get up to speed than the latter. The toolboxes for econometrics are currently less well developed than the specialist packages.
RATS	Commercial	Straightforward to use and quite powerful with numerous built-in models and a programming language available but with most routines accessible through simple one-line commands.	Less widely used than some other packages, and so your institution is less likely to hold a licence.
SPSS	Commercial	Very straightforward to use with an Excel-like interface and sometimes considered the standard tool for student project data analysis. There is also a similar-looking cutdown freeware package available, PSPP.	Considerably less flexible and less powerful than some other packages, particularly for econometrics, including time-series analysis.

But aside from these situations, scholars are often happy to share their data and code for others to use, especially research students and early career researchers – after all, that is an important aspect of why they chose a university career.

10.4.5   Choosing the software for quantitative analysis

If you are conducting quantitative analysis using secondary data, you will need to use a package to do the computations. Selecting the appropriate software to analyse the data is a significant decision since it will affect how you are able to conduct the investigation and how long it will take. If you intend to conduct only straightforward analyses of your data, such as constructing summary statistics (means, standard deviations), cross-tabulations, correlations, etc., or standard linear regressions, you may find it easier just to use a spreadsheet such as Microsoft Excel.

However, for more sophisticated analysis, including specialist econometric models, it will be preferable to use a statistical software package. Although a wide range of such packages exists, the quickest way to make progress will be to stick with the package you have been taught on your previous or current programme(s). If you have not received any such training before, identify the packages that are available to you free of charge as a result of your university's site licences. If you have to purchase a commercial package licence, it will likely cost several hundred pounds (although some suppliers offer student versions at a substantial discount).

Clearly, the choice of computer software will depend on the tasks at hand. Studies that seek to offer opinions, synthesise the literature, and provide a review may not require any specialist software. However, even for those conducting highly technical research, PhD students might not have the time to learn an entirely new programming language from scratch while conducting the research. Therefore, it might be advisable, if possible, to use a standard software package.

It is also worth stating that no implicit credit will be given for students who 'reinvent the wheel', as this would not be making a contribution to knowledge. Therefore, learning to program a multivariate extreme value model estimation routine in C++ may be a valuable exercise for career development for those who wish to be quantitative researchers but is unlikely to impress examiners as part of a PhD thesis unless there is some other value added. The best approach is usually to conduct the estimation as quickly and accurately as possible to leave time free for other parts of the work. Table 10.1 provides details of some of the packages on offer and their advantages and disadvantages.

Further reading

- Many books have been written on research methods in general, and one of the most relevant is by Creswell and Creswell (2018)
- There are also two good books explicitly aimed at research methods in accounting or finance: Paterson *et al.* (2016) and Smith (2020)

- There was not sufficient space in this book to cover either qualitative or quantitative methods at great length, and therefore readers might wish to consult more detailed treatments. For books that cover a range of qualitative techniques, I suggest Hinnink *et al.* (2020) or Ritchie *et al.* (2013). My own textbook, Brooks (2019), covers a wide range of quantitative techniques.
- Each of the major categories of research methods also has several specialist texts that are worth considering once you have selected the approach you will use, including Yin (2018) on case study methods, Fink (2016) or Fowler (2013) on surveys, and Cassell (2015) on interviews.

Chapter takeaways – top tips for success

- ⊛ Be aware of the wide range of research methods available, noting their strengths and weaknesses, and in particular how much time each would take to implement
- ⊛ Your thesis should state clear research aims, hypotheses or questions and you should address each of them in your analysis
- ⊛ The research methods must match your aims and objectives
- ⊛ If you opt to use an approach that is unfamiliar to you, seek appropriate training through courses or self-study
- ⊛ Ensure that your thesis integrates a conceptual framework or an appropriate theory to underpin your investigative research. The theory could come from economics, psychology or sociology as well as from accounting or finance themselves
- ⊛ Check data availability at the earliest possible stage
- ⊛ Think about your data sample and whether it is sufficiently large and representative of the underlying population

Finishing, viva & after

11. WRITING UP THE THESIS

Learning outcomes: this chapter covers

✓ The academic style of writing
✓ How to structure your thesis
✓ What to include in each chapter
✓ How to write in an entertaining way

This is the big moment when it all starts to come together, and your thesis document begins to take shape. It's an exciting stage, but one that many students dread. How will you organise so much material, and how will it fit together? This chapter will cover all aspects of the process of writing up the document from the cover page to the appendices and aims to make the task as painless and effective as possible.

It is advisable always to start writing at the earliest possible stage and to continue progressively with it rather than leaving all the writing until the final stage because:

- Writing can help to pin ideas down and make them more concrete
- It can help you identify problems with the research design before you waste a lot of time and improve the quality of the investigative work
- Intermingling the writing, data collection and analysis may reduce the boredom related to spending all your current research time on one type of activity
- Writing is something you can always continue to ensure that time is not wasted when you hit blocks with the investigative work – for example, waiting for e-mail replies about data or waiting for surveys to be completed or trying to fix bugs in non-functioning code

- You will be able to get early feedback on sample chapters or sections from classmates or your supervisor that can be taken on board to improve the style of the final draft

11.1   Preparing to write and laying the foundations

11.1.1   Getting support to improve your writing

Having great research ideas or producing high-quality empirical work is not sufficient to generate an excellent PhD thesis, since examiners will be looking for a well-written draft that makes strong arguments as well. Therefore, it is essential that your writing is as polished as possible. If you are sufficiently early in the registration process, your university will probably run writing courses as part of their study skills development offerings, and you could enrol on one of those. This will provide generic advice about how to improve your writing skills, particularly if English is not your first language, and is likely to provide resources and exercises.

Alternatively, there are naturally a range of resources available on-line including useful documents at the University of Essex,[1] and at Kibin,[2] among many others. Also, try to adopt the style used in academic articles in the field and don't be afraid to get as much feedback as possible from your supervisor, other academics and fellow students. Finally, it is perfectly reasonable to pay a professional proof-reader to help polish your final draft prior to submission. That person will be able to fix up your grammar and ensure that the spelling is spot-on.

11.1.2   When and how to write

Writing is hard work and draining yet requires creativity, so it is hard to do it well if you are tired, stressed or distracted; always try to schedule your best time for writing. It is also evident that different people need varying environments to motivate them to get the job done. Some need deadlines to discipline them, but others find it hard to work under pressure. Set yourself realistic targets (or agree on these with your supervisor) and try to stick to them even if they are artificial and not formal submission points. Some researchers need to 'crank up', which means that they start slowly but build up momentum, writing very little initially but then progressing much faster once they get into it. If you are such a person, don't be concerned if you find you are making slow progress with your drafting initially.

The most important aspect is to set aside regular quality time for writing – indeed, it is worth noting that almost all professional writers treat it as they would a job, working consistent hours each day rather than in fits and starts. Frequent, short blocks of one to two hours will probably be best, alongside realistic targets of how many words or which sub-sections to write in each sitting.

---

[1]https://www1.essex.ac.uk/outreach/documents/how-to-improve-academic-writing.pdf
[2]https://www.kibin.com/essay-writing-blog/academic-writing/

Many people find writing difficult, and they sit for hours and write very little. One reason they are slow is that in their own mind, they have convinced themselves that it should be possible to write something brilliant, and so they agonise over every word and end up writing almost nothing. Their own self-criticism prevents them from making any progress. Others insist on having a detailed structure for the draft worked out and penned before they can begin write a single word of the actual piece. However, this is not necessary since, often, the chapter or section will assume both structure and shape at the same time as the process of thinking about what to write clarifies the appropriate ordering and flow of the material.

For those who prefer to have a structure to work towards, a good way to start can be to develop a roadmap for the chapter, where they explain to the reader what will be covered there. This will satisfy two objectives: it will be a valuable guide for the reader in the final version but more importantly it will satisfy the person's desire to work from a pre-existing outline.

Writing something reasonably good is better than aiming to write an outstanding piece and not getting past the first sentence. Remind yourself that you are starting, not finishing, and the redraft will be easier than the first draft. There is a saying that 'you cannot edit a blank page'. Writing the first draft is by far the hardest aspect, while improving what you have already written is relatively straightforward. Once you begin constructing the chapters, the 'writer's block' will quickly clear, and the words will start to flow more easily.

Most researchers for whom writing does not come naturally find it hardest to get started than to continue or finish. Such individuals are best just to write something relevant to get 'in the zone', and in that case, it is likely to be more effective to write the most straightforward part first, then do the hard parts and fill in the gaps later.

Related to this, you should not feel obliged to write a piece in the correct order. In reality, almost no academics or professional writers do that. A common approach for each investigative chapter would be to write an initial draft of the literature review first, followed by the methodology, data and results next, and then finally create a story around them that builds into a coherent picture. This strategy implies that you would probably write most of the introduction and conclusion to the chapter last.

Concerning the order in which to draft the thesis as a whole, the most common approach would be to follow the same approach as for the empirical chapters: again starting with the literature review chapter, followed by the investigative parts, then the introduction and conclusion to the whole thesis. Then finally, the abstract, other front matter and references would be put together last.

Some researchers, albeit a declining number, also find that hand-writing early drafts helps them, especially for those who can write more quickly than they can type. They might also note down a skeleton plan or structure first before writing the actual piece, which helps them organise their thoughts. But you should use the approach that seems the most natural and works best for you. Hand-writing initial drafts will of course take longer overall than moving straight to a word-processor but is worthwhile if it helps you to be more creative.

11.1.3   At what are you aiming?

There will likely be stipulations regarding the form of the thesis – for example, as well as the maximum length, these regulations will specify the paper size (usually A4 in the UK), margin size (generally at least one inch, but possibly more on the left-hand margin), minimum font size (usually 11-point), line spacing (usually one and a half or double-line), and whether the pages should be single- or double-sided. Ensure that you find these rules and apply them to your thesis.

As well as learning the formal requirements for the thesis structure and layout, it is worth reading carefully through some completed theses in the subject area to know precisely what you are aiming at and to avoid wasting much time doing unnecessary work while skimping on essential aspects. Even if you have already taken a look through these at the ideas and proposal-writing stage, it is worth doing so again since now you will be focusing on different aspects of the work. Specifically, you will be examining the presentation – the structure, length, chapter headings, layout, font and margin sizes, and so on. Completed thesis documents will provide a useful guide as to what you are aiming to produce. You can also assess the strengths and weaknesses of the sample PhDs so that yours is even better.

Before you dig deep into the writing phase, it is worth stepping back and considering the structure – what will be the main chapters in the thesis, how long will they be, and in what order? Thinking about this at an early stage will be worthwhile because it will allow you to write according to a formula to some extent – if the skeleton outline is already there, it is just a matter of filling in the gaps. You will then also have a reasonable idea if you have perhaps written too much on some aspects and not enough on others.

11.1.4   Some tips for successful writing

The importance of clear, persuasive drafting should never be underestimated. As a leading academic economist, John Cochrane, argues, 'Many economists falsely think of themselves as scientists who just "write up" research. We are not; we are primarily writers. Economics and finance papers are essays. Most good economists spend at least 50% of the time they put into any project on writing.' The same principle applies equally in accounting and finance as economics.

Even if your core idea was not very good or the results didn't go in your favour, you can make up for a lot of that and improve your thesis substantially with a good layout and precise, polished writing. Learning to write with clarity, reasonable structure, accurate grammar and in an engaging way is also a useful life skill that many employers value. You can save time by thinking in advance about what you want to write, thus avoiding the need for endless redrafting.

Your writing needs to be succinct – i.e., using as few words as possible to get the point across. Your supervisor (and examiners when the thesis is submitted) will have many other calls on their time, and so writing that is too wordy and doesn't get to the point will frustrate them. Their minds will drift, they will begin to skim read, and their impression of the overall quality of your work will suffer.

Whenever you write, whether it is for the PhD dissertation or anything else, it is essential to consider your audience:

1. For whom are you writing?
2. What do they want to read?
3. What is their prior level of knowledge and understanding, both about the general subject area and also about your topic more specifically?

Your supervisor and examiners are your primary audience here, and you can think of them as being knowledgeable about accounting or finance in general, but they may or may not be experts on your precise subject. You need to bear that in mind, in particular, when drafting the literature review and methods chapters. Write for intelligent people familiar with the area, broadly described, so you do not need to cover elementary material ('accounting and finance 101').

Try to be clear, succinct and use language that is neither stilted (i.e., old fashioned, e.g., never write, 'one needs to write formally') nor too informal (like a text message that you might send to friends). Writing is like many other crafts, with some people being naturally talented and being able to express themselves quickly and effortlessly, turning out polished, final drafts in just one hit; others will never be powerful writers, but everyone can improve with practice.

Writing is probably best thought of as an art rather than a science – in other words, there are numerous different ways to get the same message across to your readers, so there is no magic formula and no single right answer. Writing is an exercise in explaining yourself clearly, trying to place yourself in the position of the reader who has probably read less of the literature than you (or at least, read it a while ago and now remembers less of it) and thinking carefully about ways to make them understand it better. The ordering of the material is important, so make sure that you introduce new concepts first and then discuss and make use of them; it is very easy to get this the wrong way around, especially when you write the thesis out of page order.

11.1.5 The 'scholarly style' of writing

Although each academic writes differently, with some being more successful than others at communicating their message, a certain literary style pervades academic work. Focusing predominantly on accounting and finance as disciplines, we could characterise it in the following way:

- Academics tend to write at length and with depth, and so most studies written by scholars tend to be longer and more exhaustive than pieces written on the same topic by non-academics.
- The presentation should be clear and straightforward, visually appealing but not glitzy, focusing on the writing quality and the underpinning investigative

work

- The style is formal. For example, even though I have used contractions in this book because I think the informality makes it easier to read given its length, I would not use 'don't', 'can't', etc., in an academic paper. Similarly, loose, overly friendly, informal, and slang language should be avoided. For instance, don't use words such as 'gutted', 'ballpark', or 'dodgy'
- Try to avoid writing sentences that are too long or contain too many clauses as it makes the draft dense and hard to follow. In general, if a sentence is more than a couple of lines long, see if it can be broken into two sentences
- The thesis structure can be varied slightly, but the key ingredients and order are almost always the same. This is what is expected in an academic piece, and to depart substantially in the dissertation from the usual formula would be highly risky and could give the examiners cause for concern
- Technical terminology is frequently used, but the specialist language is always carefully defined the first time that it is used in a document with an appropriate level of knowledge assumed of the reader
- The arguments are always somewhat understated. There is no boasting, and there should be no exaggerating the strength of the findings. Precision and accuracy in descriptions are expected. It is common to see wording such as 'the results are suggestive of...' or 'the parameter estimates point to...' rather than 'the results prove ...'. Remember, your results are tentative, not definitive, so avoid giving the impression that you believe them to be indisputable. Perhaps another researcher with slightly different data or models would have come up with dissimilar findings
- Related to the previous point, your arguments' tone should be balanced and not in any way emotional, whether you were particularly impressed or unimpressed by a study. It is fine to say that one author's approach is more robust than another or that the findings are more plausible, but don't suggest that one paper is excellent while another is weak
- There is an emphasis on ensuring the robustness of results, and so it is common to repeatedly vary the methods and data slightly to determine whether the main results remain unaltered. The proliferation of similar results tables and discussion can be somewhat dull for the reader, so a careful balance is required to avoid excessive repetition. A common approach is to put the robustness checks in a clearly named, separate section so that they can be skimmed over unless the reader wants to focus specifically on these additional details
- As discussed in chapter 9, critique is an essential part of academic writing, but it is always subtle and polite
- Viewpoints should be balanced, and even if you end up following one line of reasoning, the alternatives should always be presented and discussed, with explanations as to why these approaches are not appropriate or optimal
- The writing is heavily referenced with citations to existing studies. This is a

key difference compared with formal non-academic writing, such as reports written by management consultants or regulatory bodies, which might share many of the other characteristics described in this list
- The number of citations per page of text needs to be just right, which is a delicate balance to achieve. Too few citations implies an under-referenced document that is not sufficiently well embedded in the existing literature while too many will disrupt the flow of text and make the work appear excessively derivative of prior studies so that the present piece is adding little that is new
- Even more important than adopting a good style is to adopt a consistent one, so ensure that all your chapters are written in the same fashion and to the same standard
- Always substantiate any claims you make with evidence – this can be drawn from your own research findings or from the previous literature, where you would then include a citation in parentheses to the existing study which identified it. In general, unsubstantiated opinions are best avoided, except perhaps in the concluding chapter of your dissertation, which could, for instance, be somewhat speculative about future research or the implications of your findings. But if you are making a value judgement, you should state that rather than giving the impression that the statement being presented is a fact.

While slang should be avoided entirely, it is acceptable to write in the first person ('I evaluated X and then I also examined Y') or use the passive voice ('X was evaluated and then Y was also examined...'). Whether the active or passive style should be used is the subject of much disagreement between authors. Automated grammar checkers usually frown upon the use of the passive voice and recommend that it is changed to an active style. But the passive approach is the standard way that scientific studies are described to give an impression of independence between the research and the researcher. Not having personal pronouns (I or we) allows the focus to be on the research rather than the researcher(s). On this point, we might conclude that academic writing is different from that for other purposes, and thus both active and passive styles are suitable.

11.1.6   Are you an informer or an entertainer?

When you write, your primary task is to explain what you are doing, how and why, with as much clarity as possible. After all, writing is first and foremost an exercise in communication: you know what you think about your research topic and what you have done, and now the task is to get that across as effectively as possible to your supervisor, examiners and other readers of your dissertation document.

But your secondary role is as an entertainer. Just as some individuals give lectures that send the listener to sleep, so too do some writers bore the reader. Make your writing as lively as possible so that the reader is keen to keep turning the page rather than finding it a chore with their mind wandering to putting the dishwasher on or what to feed the cat. Entertaining doesn't mean filling the pages with jokes or funny pictures; it means writing in a lively and engaging way. There are many webpages on improving academic writing but be careful with these, as many are simply a front to advertise an essay mill. I found the oxford-royale.com site to have some useful tips.[3]

Here are some further suggestions to make your writing more entertaining:

- Your writing needs to be reasonably formal, and so this makes it challenging to introduce humour or use the style you might see in a blog piece. For example, although it is acceptable to include funny images in a slideshow presentation to illustrate a point, it would seem out of place to do so in a thesis. But you can make the material pleasant to read by being clear, not repeating yourself, and varying both the phraseology and the presentation. This means not using the same phrases repeatedly – try to think of different ways to explain things

- Use some bullet points or numbered lists rather than just long paragraphs – this helps to make the material more digestible and breaks up the sections of text

- Spend plenty of time on your abstract and introduction – these are the first parts the reader sees, and they set the scene for the rest of the project. These are also the aspects where you can use some imagination in what and how you write. By contrast, the methods, data and results are much more factual and harder to draft appealingly (although they should still be clear and succinct)

- Including pictures, tables, or quotes (where relevant) helps break up the sections and make them visually more interesting. Anecdotes, examples, or short case studies help bring a narrative to life even if the project's core focus is a quantitative big data study

- It is common for working paper versions of academic studies to gather all of the tables and figures at the end of the document after the references. But when the document is typeset into its published form once accepted by a journal, the tables are shifted into the relevant places within the text where they are first mentioned. I think the latter is also a much better style for a thesis than putting them all at the end where they probably won't even be seen. Intermingling the tables and figures with the writing makes the project more fun to read

11.2 Getting the document structure right

The more 'scientific' fields tend to favour a larger quantity of numbered sub-headings. In contrast, more discursive work (such as that in historical accounting, behavioural finance, or critical accounting) makes less use of them, typically using only main headings, with sub-headings limited in frequency of use and unnumbered. Write the project around the contributions that you are making. Your investigative work should be the star of the show, with everything before building up to it and everything after explaining what you have done, what it means, and why it is important and for

---

[3]https://www.oxford-royale.com/articles/make-writing-interesting/

whom.

Try to avoid repetition since this will waste valuable words and take the place of more original content you could have included. Having said that, you will still need to summarise the key findings several times: in the introduction and conclusions of that particular investigative chapter, then in the abstract, introduction and conclusions of the thesis as a whole. Hence a valuable skill is learning to write ostensibly the same thing using different language. Never just copy and paste the same blocks of phrases from one part of the document to another – the reader will probably spot this, it makes the work tiresome to read, and you will appear lazy.

If you look carefully at the best-written journal papers, you will notice a subtle change in style through the article. The introductory section, while being more general in terms of the subject matter covered, also tends to be written in a somewhat less formal style, perhaps referring to articles in the popular press or blogs as motivational tools. This slightly journalistic style might also apply in the final paragraphs of the conclusions, where the author aims to make some long-lasting impressions about the relevance and gravity of the findings. The parts in the middle, though – the data, methods, and results sections – will probably be written formally in a style as dry as unbuttered toast.

Try to avoid using too many footnotes – they disrupt the flow of the document so that the reader has to keep moving between the body text and the bottom of each page unless they entirely ignore the footnotes, which would defeat the object of including them. Endnotes, where the notes are gathered together in a single list at the end of the document rather than in the footers of each page, are even worse from this perspective. If the footnoted (or 'endnoted') material is essential, include it in the main body instead; if it is not vital, drop it altogether.

Also, aim to link each section or sub-section together so that the narrative flows seamlessly through the document. This can be achieved in various ways, including linking sentences at the end of a section or the beginning of the following one. For example, 'the previous sub-section described how accounting standards developed in the UK over the past half-century. This section now proceeds to discuss the Financial Reporting Council's contemporary role in setting standards since 2004 and how it is funded and governed.'

11.3 How to structure the thesis

Different theses will, of course, require somewhat varying structures dependent upon the type of material being covered, but it is worth outlining the form that a good dissertation will take. As stated previously, unless there are good reasons for doing otherwise (for example, because of the nature of the subject), it is advisable for each investigative chapter to follow the format and structure of a full-length article in a scholarly journal. Each thesis chapter will be approximately the same length as a journal article. A suggested outline for an empirical thesis in accounting or finance is presented below, with each component then examined in turn.

A basic structure for a typical PhD dissertation

Title page

Declaration

Acknowledgements

Abstract

Table of Contents

List of Tables

List of Figures

Glossary

Chapter 1 - General introduction

Chapter 2 – Literature review

Chapter 3 – Data description

Chapter 4 – First investigative project

Chapter 5 – Second investigative project

Chapter 6 – Third investigative project

Chapter 7 – Conclusions

References

Appendices

The declaration will be a statement that you will be required to include in the thesis to the effect that you confirm that all the work contained within it is yours and that any existing material has been appropriately referenced. In other words, your thesis is free from plagiarism. It might be that a scanned signature is required beneath the statement.

11.4   Two models for organising a thesis

There are broadly two approaches to conducting the work required for a PhD in accounting or finance. The first is where the thesis chapters combine into a cohesive whole rather like a research monograph so that the investigative chapters are closely related to one another. For instance, the thesis might be on using text mining to interpret accounting narratives and linking them with market reactions to their publication, containing three empirical chapters, each using different models to assess the price impacts of accounting information. Alternatively, but still under the first approach, would be where the investigative method is the star of the show. For example, the thesis might develop a new econometric model for forecasting financial time-series applied in three different contexts. In both cases, there would be a clear, common thread running through the investigative parts of the work – in the first example, this thread was the data, while in the second it was the model. When this structure for the thesis is used, the document should flow a bit like a book, and there would probably be a separate literature review chapter. This structure is the traditional UK and European approach to drafting a PhD.

A structure that has been common in the US and that has become more widely adopted in Europe including the UK in recent years is the 'three essays in accounting' or 'three essays in finance' model, where there might be very little connecting the investigative chapters and possibly no attempt to do so. These chapters might employ different models and different datasets so that the only aspect that binds them in any way is that they are in the same very broad field. In that case, the thesis will still need to include introductory and concluding chapters, but even these will be somewhat disjointed, each discussing the three investigative chapters in a reasonably separate fashion. The literature review in the thesis will be spread between these three chapters rather than being combined. The idea behind this approach to thesis construction is that it is based around distinct, publishable papers that are slotted into the document.

Initially, in the UK, the first of the two models above was almost exclusively employed, and although the second has become more acceptable in recent years, not all scholars find it equally appealing, and some still prefer the traditional structure. Many theses nowadays are a sort of hybrid of the two, where there are some connections between the empirical works in the document, but they are somewhat loose.

Under the first approach, the thesis is written as a book, and then publishable individual papers may be extracted and drafted from it. But under the second style, the candidate writes the investigative chapters as individual papers first and then combines them. The latter makes submitting articles to journals faster and easier since they originate in the correct format for that purpose. Given that PhD students are nowadays frequently focused on publishing as quickly as possible to support their job applications, this structure is becoming increasingly popular.

Note that while the number of investigative chapters in a thesis has tended to be three by a convention that has emerged in UK universities over the past few years, this is not a specific requirement but rather a standard number that constitutes sufficient work to be commensurate with three years of full-time study. It might be the case that a thesis contains four or even five separate empirical chapters, each of which is perhaps a little less extensive than would have been the case for a thesis containing only three such chapters. Thus it is the total volume and strength of the investigative work that counts, not the number of separate pieces.

11.5   Thesis formatting

11.5.1   The positioning of the literature review within the thesis

There are broadly two ways in which the review can be incorporated into the thesis. The first is that there is no specific literature chapter, but instead, each investigative chapter includes a comprehensive literature review section. This approach would be optimal if the investigative chapters each drew on a separate body of work so that combining the reviews would not make sense because there are few common threads to bind them.

A second style is to combine all of the literature review material into a single chapter with that heading. This style works well if the thesis material is cohesive and largely on the same topic so that the core of underpinning work is identical for each chapter. In that case, separating it would be artificial and may lead to repetition.

Similarly, if each empirical chapter is employing the same data but perhaps utilising it differently or applying varying models to it, it would make sense to present the data within a single chapter to avoid repeating the description several times in separate empirical chapters. Finally, likewise with any theoretical or methodological details: if they are used repeatedly across chapters, combine them, whereas if not, place the material in the specific chapter where it belongs.

Note that the ordering of the investigative chapters should be whatever is most intuitive when you have finished writing them, and that might not be the order in which you completed the work. If there is no natural ordering of these chapters, you might wish to note that when reading a document, people usually remember most of the parts that they read first and last, recalling less about the bits in the middle. That being the case, it might make sense to put your strongest empirical chapters at the beginning and end with what you consider your weakest work in between.

11.5.2 Glossary

It can be helpful to include a glossary in a PhD thesis, which defines any technical terms or acronyms used in the document, particularly if the material is esoteric or uses numerous abbreviations. For instance, in the volatility forecasting literature, there are many variants of the GARCH (Generalised Autoregressive Conditionally Heteroscedastic) model: ARCH, EGARCH, GJR, PARCH, APARCH, EGARCH, MGARCH, IGARCH, BEKK, DCC, etc. A clear and detailed glossary would help readers unfamiliar with these acronyms to remember each model and its main features.

11.5.3 The title page

The title page will usually contain the following information:
- Title of the thesis
- Candidate's name
- Degree for which thesis is submitted (i.e., PhD or MPhil)
- Name of the school or department in which the candidate is registered
- Date of submission of the thesis

Try to make the cover page neat and tidy with appropriate font size and spacing. The title should be succinct but contain sufficient detail to explain what the work is about rather than trying to be too smart with only a pun or idiom. 'Back to the Future' would be a bad choice of title as it essentially gives the reader almost no idea of what the thesis will be about. But 'Back to the Future: Revisiting Out of Favour Models for Forecasting Earnings Revisions' would be much better. The first part of the title could generate interest, linking with a series of films from the 1980s, while the second part explains clearly what the thesis is actually about.

Similarly, a recent paper that I co-authored was entitled: 'Tomorrow's fish and chip paper? Slowly incorporated news and the cross-section of stock returns.' The first part links with an idiom or old saying that 'today's news is tomorrow's fish and chip paper,' referring to the traditional practice that fish and chip takeaways were wrapped in old newspapers. The saying suggests that news is only relevant for a single day, and then it no longer has any information value.

In both cases, of course, dropping the first part altogether would also be acceptable but be less striking and with less entertainment value.

For another illustration of the sorts of titles that work and that don't, look at the following suggested titles for the same study. Which do you think is most appropriate?

1. Asset Pricing Tests
2. Tests of the CAPM
3. Empirical Tests of the Four-moment CAPM
4. Empirical Tests of the Four-moment CAPM in Frontier Markets
5. Empirical Tests of the CAPM in Frontier Markets using Daily Data from 3 January 2007 - 31 October 2020

Clearly, the first title is far too broad and gives the reader little idea of what the thesis might be about as there are so many tests that could be conducted in numerous different ways. The second title is an improvement since it narrows down the scope to a single model, but it could still be more explicit, and there will undoubtedly be vast numbers of existing theses and academic studies with precisely this title.

Title 3 is again an improvement as the number of applications of the four-moment CAPM is smaller still compared with those of the CAPM more broadly defined. Within this list, however, title 4 probably nails it: the addition of the clause stating the markets that the model will be tested on makes the title quite unique, and it clearly explains what the document will be about while remaining succinct. The final title pushes in the wrong direction compared with title 4 by adding excessive and unnecessary detail; the reader doesn't need to know the sample data period and frequency at this stage, so it works less well.

It is also possible and sometimes effective to generate intrigue within the reader by phrasing the title as a question, encouraging them to delve inside the document's covers to see the answer. Continuing the theme of the examples given above, a title containing a question might be, 'The Four-moment CAPM: Do Empirical Tests in Frontier Markets Show More Promise than those in Developed Countries?'

If you are stuck as to what title to select for your thesis, one way to decide is to write down a set of keywords that describes your research:

- What is the topic?
- What main investigative method are you using?
- What data, covering which markets or countries, and over what period?

Remember, though, that there should not be too much specific detail
Once you have listed perhaps six keywords or short phrases that describe the PhD, try to write a sentence that includes them all. Then delete any non-essential or recurring parts, and you should have a working title.

The title needs some careful thought because that, and the abstract, are by far the most important parts of the whole thesis because these are always the aspects that will be read first. The title, abstract and the first couple of paragraphs of the introductory chapter represent your opportunity to draw the reader into your dissertation, so you need your writing to entice and excite them. If these pique the reader's interest and generate a good impression of the likely quality of the work as a whole, it will mean the overall assessment that is beginning to form in your examiners' minds will be a good one. On the other hand, if the title is vague and the abstract is noticeably rushed, the supervisor and examiners will have the idea that the work is not of high quality, and the rest of the document would have to be truly impressive to win them back over.

11.5.4   The other front matter

Your thesis definitely needs a table of contents but also adding lists of tables and figures will give the document a professional feel; you do not need an index, however. As suggested above, you might consider incorporating in the front matter a glossary of technical terms used if your topic is esoteric and includes a lot of acronyms or specialist terminology.

11.5.5   The abstract

The abstract is a short summary of the problem being addressed and of the research's main results and conclusions. The maximum permissible length of the abstract will vary, but as a general guide, it should not be more than 300 words in total, and the maximum can even be as few as 100 words for some journals. Perhaps 200-300 words is an ideal number to aim for in a PhD thesis. A conventional (and usually good) style is for the entire abstract to be contained in a single paragraph or two.

Unlike the introductory chapter, the abstract will simply state what is done in the thesis without referring to specific parts of the document. For instance, it is not considered necessary to incorporate phrases as follows, 'This dissertation presents and compares several approaches to measuring financial literacy. I review the literature in chapter 2; then, using a large survey of UK-based investors of varying ages, in chapter 3, I demonstrate...' There is no need to mention the literature review in the abstract as it can be taken for granted in this part that you conducted one. There is also no need to refer to 'chapter 3' and so on here either, so that phrase should be dropped as this sort of material belongs in the introduction where there is more space.

The abstract should usually not contain any quotations, and it should not be unduly technical even if the subject matter of the thesis is. It should not include any references – these should be left for the main body of the work and the abstract written in general terms without citing any specific studies. It should summarise the research problem and main aims of the work, the broad methodology used, and the main findings and conclusions. In other words, the abstract needs to summarise the entire dissertation, not just the results. Academic papers are not like murder-mysteries, where you don't find out 'whodunit' right until the end. You should put the punchline right at the front in the abstract and the introduction – this will cement the importance of the work in the reader's mind from the outset.

An abstract is always the most crucial aspect of a research paper. It will be the first thing that is read, and if it is dull or hard to follow, the most likely outcome is that the reader will stop going through the whole paper. The abstract is often used as a sort of advertising blurb for the full article, where it is included on websites and is searchable and viewable without restriction or payment in a way that the whole paper is not. Abstracts are frequently listed on websites without the rest of the article, and so they should always stand-alone – in other words, they need to make sense if, together with the title, that is all the reader sees. This is the primary reason why they should not refer to other sections in the dissertation and should use as little technical terminology as possible given the subject matter.

Likewise, in a thesis the abstract is arguably the single most important aspect of the entire document. Once you had gone through a few journal articles, no doubt that you started using the abstract as a filter: if what was written in it did not grab your attention, you probably put the paper on the 'read later if time permits' pile. Your supervisor and examiners won't have the luxury of discarding your thesis if the abstract is uninspiring, but it will set their expectations for the remainder of the work at a low level. Consequently, this aspect must be as strong as possible, yet unfortunately, it is often rushed and significantly less well written than the rest of the document. A further common pitfall is to write the abstract as if it were the opening paragraph of the introductory chapter - in other words, it is all or mostly background information and allocates insufficient space to discussing the work in the dissertation.

It is often best to write the abstract at the very last stage since then it can most accurately reflect the contents of the whole document as it stands at the end, rather than representing what you initially thought you would be writing the thesis about. But every word in the abstract should be carefully considered for the first impressions reason outlined above.

It is surprising how many times the abstract does not hit the target and is not as strong as it could be. Indeed, sometimes the abstract is the very worst part of a thesis because a student writes it last but by then has run out of time or enthusiasm and so just rushes it through. I have also seen situations where the main body of a thesis is relatively well written because the author paid a proof-reader to go through the grammar, but they did not do so for the abstract, which they wrote after the proof-reader had already finished. Yet since it is arguably the most crucial part of the whole dissertation, it should be the best; it's only a couple of hundred words, so put in the effort.

11.5.6 The acknowledgements

The acknowledgements section is a brief list of people whose help you would like to note. For example, it is courteous to begin by thanking your PhD supervisor (even if they were useless and didn't help at all). Remember, this person is also likely to be writing your references and nominating your examiners so them in a good mood by flattering their ego. Thank any agency that gave you the data, other PhD students who helped to debug your code, a librarian who showed you how to use a database, anyone you interviewed, friends who read and checked or commented upon the work, and so on.

It is traditional 'academic etiquette' to put a disclaimer after the acknowledgements in research papers, worded something like 'Responsibility for any remaining errors lies with the author(s) alone.' In some ways, this also seems appropriate for a dissertation, for it symbolises that the student is entirely responsible for the topic chosen and for the contents and the structure of the thesis. It is your project, so you cannot blame anyone else, either deliberately or inadvertently, for anything wrong with it. The disclaimer also reminds PhD thesis authors that it is not valid to take others' work and pass it off as their own. Any ideas taken from other papers should be adequately referenced as such, and any sentences lifted directly from other research should be placed in quotations and attributed to their original author(s) as discussed in chapter 7. You will probably have seen this quoted line written in many papers, although its use is declining as it is increasingly seen as somewhat old-fashioned, and therefore it is up to you whether you include such a statement.

11.5.7 The table of contents

The table of contents should list the chapters and sections (and possibly also the sub-sections) contained in the report. The chapter and section headings should reflect accurately and concisely the subject matter that is contained within them. It should also list the number of each chapter's first page or section, including the references and any appendices.

The abstract, acknowledgements and table of contents pages are usually numbered with lower case Roman numerals (e.g., i, ii, iii, iv, etc.), and the introduction then starts on page 1 (reverting to Arabic numbers), with page numbering being consecutive thereafter for the whole document, including references and any appendices.

You should never number the title page, and it will appear sloppy if the first page of the introduction is numbered 5, for example. Also, do not let the page numbering restart from 1 on a differently formatted page (e.g., when moving from portrait to landscape layout), which Microsoft Word has a habit of doing sometimes by default.

11.5.8 The introduction

The introduction should give some very general background information on the problem considered and why it is a vital area for research. An excellent introductory section will also describe what is original in the study – in other words, how does this study help to advance the literature on this topic, or how does it address a new problem or an old problem in a new way? What are the aims and objectives of the research? If these can be clearly and concisely expressed, it usually demonstrates that the thesis topic is well defined. The introduction should be sufficiently non-technical that the intelligent non-specialist can understand what the study is about, even if the investigative work is narrow or arcane.

Setting the context in the introductory chapter is vital. This part explains to readers where the current state of thinking is and how it got there. Hence, this aspect needs to include some of the historical background (but not too much), laying the foundations for you to explain precisely what you are working on. Without this context, it is difficult for readers to see where your material fits.

The first paragraph is the most crucial to get right since the evidence suggests that markers will make up their minds about the quality of a piece of work quickly after reading just a few sentences. It is, of course, possible to win the reader back over and to recover after a poor-quality introduction followed by much better investigative work, but it will then be an unnecessary uphill struggle.

The introduction also needs to present the 'motivation' for the study. This aspect explains why the research you are doing is useful in the context of what is already known and what is not known. This part of the introductory section is your chance to sell your ideas and approach to the reader, hooking them in with statements about why the work is important and for whom.

Some authors choose to begin the introductory section with their contribution, and then they broaden it back out, using a similar writing approach as a journalist writing in a newspaper. Other researchers give a gentle build-up first, trying to motivate why the general area is important – in essence, they are identifying a knowledge gap (the whole world's knowledge gap, not just theirs) which the research conducted through the dissertation can then fill. I prefer the latter ordering, but it is really just a matter of style.

An example of the gentle build-up style is presented below from a paper by Rendall, Brooks and Hillenbrand (2021), displayed a few paragraphs below. The alternative approach of jumping in with the contribution after providing some preliminary definitions before moving back to discuss the wider literature is given in Brooks, Chen and Zeng (2018), now reported:

> 'Previous studies suggest that institutional ownership keeps growing in US stock markets and has an important role in both corporate strategy and equity pricing [references removed from here]. Institutional investors manage portfolios that are not only much greater in financial terms than those of most retail investors but also contain much larger numbers of

stocks. Compared to retail investors, there is a much higher probability that institutional investors will become owners of the stocks on both sides of a proposed merger deal — i.e., they hold shares in both the acquirer and the target. In the context of mergers and acquisitions (M&As), this is termed an "institutional cross-holding."

In this paper, we investigate the externality of institutional cross-holdings for corporate strategies through an important corporate event: M&As. Unlike non-cross-owners, who only hold the stock on one side of a merger deal, cross-holders tend to make decisions from a broader perspective that nets off any potential losses from one side (usually the acquirer) with gains made on the other (usually the target) and will consider how the newly formed joint entity would sit within their portfolios compared with the two existing separate stocks.'

(Brooks *et al.*, 2018, p.187).

While it is good to put the problem that you are investigating into a wider context and to initially avoid being esoteric or using highly technical jargon, equally, try to avoid starting with a well-used philosophical cliché such as, 'financial economists have long been fascinated by the question of whether markets are efficient...' It is often useful to include some simple summary statistics or a quote from the popular press when you are starting a piece to get the reader excited about the work and emphasise that it is a topic with practical, as well as scholarly, interest.

For example, I recently co-authored a paper that sought to investigate the effects of borrowers' emotions and personality traits on their abilities to undertake appropriate courses of action when they unexpectedly got into difficulties in repaying their debts. Although the paper involved setting up hypotheses, conducting an on-line survey and running econometric models on the data, the introduction started gently by including some summary statistics from popular websites as follows (I have removed the footnote references here to save space):

'In recent decades, the UK has seen a rapid rise in consumer indebtedness, which has more than quadrupled since 1990. According to personal debt statistics from The Money Charity, total UK household debt had risen by 381% to £1669bn in 2019 from £347bn in 1990, with the average debt per adult at £31,643. As of March 2019, average total household debt was around £64,000, comprising of credit card balances, student loans, personal loans and mortgage debt – an increase of 17% in just five years.'
(Rendall, Brooks and Hillenbrand, 2021).

You need to elucidate the value that your work will add in a confident, but not arrogant, manner. What is the significance of your study? This is sometimes called the 'so what question'. Is your research timely because of something that is happening now? For instance, you might be studying real estate market bubbles at a time when house prices have risen by a third in five years, and many people are suggesting that housing might be overvalued. Are you using an empirical approach that is new in that research area or applying established models to a different set of data compared with existing studies? Are any of the variables you include different from those of existing studies in an interesting way?

Returning to the debt problems paper by Rendall *et al.* mentioned above, here is how we defined our contribution and arising from a lack of previous research investigating how borrowers cope with unforeseen financial problems:

> 'While there is a reasonable body of research on individual personality and psychological attributes associated with consumer indebtedness, the vast majority of extant studies focus on modelling the original decision to take on debts. Hence, to the best of our knowledge, research focusing on the factors associated with whether individuals make risky or sensible financial decisions when already in debt and experiencing financial difficulties is lacking. We argue that this latter issue is the one that is most pertinent for exploration and analysis: being in debt is not particularly problematic if one is able to manage the debt and repayment is within one's means. Rather, the problem arises when an individual finds themselves in a situation of financial difficulty, which could be due to several factors, including unanticipated unemployment or poor health affecting the ability to earn a full income. In such situations, how individuals cope with their existing debt repayments and the choices they make to manage their debts and ensure that they remain on track could mean the difference between a temporary bump in the road or a worsening spiral into indebtedness, leading ultimately to county court judgements or even, in the most extreme circumstances, the loss of their home. Therefore, it is this all too frequent but under-researched situation – unforeseen circumstances leading to a diminished ability to make debt repayments – which is the focus of the present study'
>
> (Rendall *et al.*, *op. cit.*).

It is fine to include some references in the introduction to demonstrate early on that you are aware of where your work fits into the wider picture. But don't fill the introduction with literature review to the extent that the reasons for doing the research and the intended contribution become lost. If you need the review part to be more than a few pages, put it in a separate section or literature review chapter that can appear right after the introduction.

Your investigative work is the centrepiece of your thesis, and so it makes sense to build the document around it so that everything coming before (i.e., the introduction and literature review) leads up to it, and everything coming after (principally the conclusions) emphasises how good it was. To support this, researchers often include a brief summary of their results in the introductory section of their papers to give a flavour of the main findings to whet the reader's appetite. If you do this, be careful not to overdo it by including too much information here since you will also be discussing the results in more or less detail in the abstract, investigative and concluding chapters.

Avoid repetition where possible and always paraphrase, never copying and pasting directly from one chapter to another. For information, in the debt paper (Rendall *et al.*) discussed above, we elected not to summarise the results in the introductory section since we felt that the section was already lengthy and there was an adequate synopsis in the abstract.

It is good to finish the introduction with an outline of the remainder of the report. Sometimes this is called the 'roadmap' because it shows the reader where they will be going from here. This roadmap in the introduction should discuss what is each of the subsequent chapters in the thesis, and it might be in its own section entitled something like 'outline of the remainder of the thesis'. It will be, perhaps, a page or two long in total so it will contain a single extensive paragraph or two on each chapter. Unlike the abstract, it will usually not mention the findings, only what is contained in each chapter. Then each of the investigative chapters will probably have their own mini-roadmaps.

When writing the introduction, the roadmap can help prepare the reader for what they should expect you to cover in the rest of that chapter (or the whole thesis). In the introduction, you can also explain the study's span – in other words, what you will focus on and what is out of scope and so will not be covered. This will help to avoid any subsequent misunderstandings where the reader had expected you to include some aspects or to cover a topic in a particular way, and you did not. Naturally, if you have plenty of space available, each stage of the roadmap can be further broken down into a whole paragraph with a heading (e.g., 'In the data section of Chapter 3, I...'), instead of one sentence, so that more detail is presented.

The roadmap is just one aspect of the signposting that should be present throughout your dissertation. The reader should always be aware of where they are currently in the document, where they have been and where they are going. Using page numbers, headings, and a table of contents are all aspects of this, but the signposting should also be hard-coded into the writing. Use phrases such as, 'in the previous section, I did A and B; now, I will proceed to discuss C before deriving the theoretical model in section X'.

11.5.9   The literature review

Reviewing the literature and writing the review has been the subject of the whole of chapter 9 of this book so that no further details will be given here. What you have already written should be capable of being slotted directly into the dissertation draft (possibly with some minor amendments to make it fit with the rest of the material and to remove any repetition).

11.5.10   The data

Depending on whether the entire thesis employs the same dataset or each empirical piece uses its own data, the thesis might or might not include a separate chapter that describes the data. If it does, and if you have used secondary data in the PhD, it is worth beginning this chapter by stepping back and explaining why you selected this particular dataset from the source that you used. Are there features of this information that are not present in alternatives? Are the data you selected more comprehensive or more reliable than others?

The core of this section (if contained in each investigative chapter) or chapter (if gathered together) should then describe the data in detail – the source, the format, the features of the data, and any limitations relevant for later analysis. For example, are there missing observations? Is the sample period short? Does the sample include large potential structural breaks, e.g., caused by a stock market crash? Suppose that your research uses small numbers of series which are being primarily investigated. In that case, it would make sense to plot them in this section, noting any interesting features, and to supply summary statistics – such as the mean, variance, skewness, kurtosis, minimum and maximum values of each series. If the data are time-series, you should also tests for non-stationarity and measures of autocorrelation, and do on. The main results will appear later in the investigative chapters in their own section following the methodology part but data summary statistics belong here.

11.5.11 The methodology

As for the data, the methods can be separated across several chapters or gathered into a single, focused chapter that exclusively covers it. If all of the empirical chapters use the same methods, it makes sense to have a single chapter on this to avoid repetition. If not, each investigative chapter will contain its own methods section. The methodology chapter or section should describe the estimation technique(s) used to compute estimates of the models' parameters. Why did you choose the approaches you did rather than others that could have been used? The models should be outlined and explained, using equations where appropriate. Again, this description should be written critically, noting any potential weaknesses in the approach and, if relevant, why more robust or up-to-date techniques were not employed.

The methods and data taken together should be described in sufficient detail that somebody else could follow what you had done as a recipe. Although researchers sometimes provide brief derivations of the steps that led to a particular mathematical model that they use, in general, it is not helpful to spend time writing in detail about other methods that you did not use. Presenting extensive information about excluded models would likely cause confusion, as well as taking up valuable space. Instead, simply explain why you chose the approach that you did and describe that in detail. Similarly, it is unnecessary to run through a derivation of the final equations you used if the steps are already available in an existing study. Instead, refer the reader to that unless the algebra is required to explain how the model works or the derivation itself is new.

Whatever methods you use to collect and analyse data, your empirical work should be replicable, which means that someone else should be able to read what you have written about how you have conducted the study and understand it. That person should then be able to repeat the steps and obtain the same results as you did, so you need to explain what you did clearly and in order.

Rather than re-defining terms or variables repeatedly, refer the reader back to the part of your document where those definitions were first presented. Also, make sure that your notation is consistent across chapters. I have seen PhDs where the same symbol was used to refer to different variables in different places in the thesis, which can be very confusing.

If you are briefly mentioning something, you can tell the reader that you will be discussing it in greater detail subsequently in chapter Z. As often is the case, though, there is a balance: too much linking backwards or forwards will make the text confusing as you will be writing this several times.

Equations and numbering

If your document includes equations, there are two conventions regarding whether these should be numbered or not:

1. The first approach is to number every equation sequentially in the order that they appear. The equation numbers are usually placed against the right-hand margin. I prefer this approach, as it is more straightforward to implement and avoids misunderstandings.

2. A second approach is to number only equations explicitly referred to in the document's main body text. Again, the equations should be numbered sequentially in the order that they appear, but some equations will have no numbers.

All letters (Greek or Roman) should in *italics* when used in equations, but numbers and operators ($+$, $-$, $\times$, etc.) should not. When letters in the main body text refer to the same terms as in the equations, they too should be italicised.

11.5.12   The results

Every thesis that includes empirical work (that is, every type excluding purely theoretical PhDs) will include a section in each empirical chapter that presents the findings. The style of this part will probably be different from the introduction, literature, and conclusions since it needs to be precise and will involve some description, including the presentation of numerical data. Nonetheless, each results section should begin with one or two introductory paragraphs that outline what it is about and what you will cover.

It would help if you then referred back to the research objectives or hypotheses you had presented in a previous section in the order you had shown them. You should also, in just a line or two, restate the main methods that you are using to analyse the data. A thesis does not need to include any details that describe how you came to the findings you did (i.e., the personal 'journey' that you experienced), but it is good to give brief details of all of the models you also tried that you don't report.

Even if your thesis is predominantly a quantitative study using an extensive database, it is still of value to plot the numbers, identifying some examples to illustrate the data's nature and bring the analysis to life, making it more tangible and enjoyable to read. For instance, if you were using automated text-mining software to determine the sentiment in company statements, display one such message and highlight the words contributing to the sentiment counts. Examples of both typical and extreme cases are of interest to present as illustrations. Don't just go into autopilot and jump straight into highly complex analysis – start simply and work up from there.

Your examiners will be looking for evidence that you have analysed the data systematically, in-depth and using the appropriate techniques. A common mistake is to include large numbers of tables of results but only offer a couple of lines of discussion on each. Once you have taken the time to collect the data and run the models, it is a tragic waste not to extract the maximum amount of information that you can from them.

Also, every table presented in the document should be numbered and explicitly referenced in the main text. Do not include any tables that you do not discuss since no discussion means that the table is not useful and so not needed. While tables and figures are an important aspect of almost every thesis, you should not infer that the reader will spot information that is only contained in the tables or figures. It is still your job to identify the essential features of the tables, charts and diagrams and to point these out to the reader in your text. On the other hand, don't provide a transcript of every feature of every table and chart, which would bore the reader senseless and take up too many words.

If your approach involves the estimation of statistical models such as regressions, don't just discuss the key variables of interest to your study but also analyse the parameter estimates on the control variables – are these plausible and in line with those in existing studies? Remember to discuss the sizes, signs and statistical significances of the parameter estimates. Do they support any hypotheses that you developed in a previous section or refute them?

You are trying to build up a story gradually. As well as beginning with simple summary statistics and plots, next, run the models including only the variable(s) of interest on their own before finally adding control variables (covariates) and possibly include a set of results where only the controls are used and not the main variables. That way, you will have several groups of model estimates, which avoids the problem of putting in a large amount of effort to get the results for a particular chapter only to find that you have just one table. Merely including a single table would give the incorrect impression that there was not much work involved, making the thesis appear thin and weak.

A good results section will refer back to the literature discussed previously and explain how and why the present research findings differ from those of existing studies. This is a synthesis of what you have found from your data in the context of what was already known. Any limitations of the techniques you used for data analysis are probably best discussed in the concluding section of the chapter (or the overall conclusions to the whole thesis) rather than here. Don't just present the results, but also try to explain what they mean, put them into context, and compare them with the findings that emerged in previous studies.

Your discussion of the results should note any interesting features – whether expected or unexpected – and, in particular, inferences should relate to the original aims and objectives of the research you outlined previously. You should devote the most space in the write-up to the results that focus the most closely on your research aims. The findings should be discussed and analysed in-depth, not merely presented blandly. Comparisons should also be drawn with the results of similar existing studies if relevant – do your results confirm or contradict those of previous research? And can you reconcile any differences in your findings compared with the others – for example, because you have used a different data source or model? Each table or figure should be mentioned explicitly in the text (e.g., 'Results from the estimation of equation (11) are presented in Table 4').

Try to avoid over-claiming the strength or importance of your work or findings. For instance, it is acceptable to write, 'my results demonstrate' or 'show' or 'indicate' but don't write, 'my results prove', or 'it is indisputable that'. At best, the latter phrases appear arrogant, but at worst, these statements would be incorrect since you have not proved a result, only shown that it applies with your model and sample data.

How to deal with negative results

If you are conducting primarily empirical research and applying an established model to new data, but the results are not as you had hoped, should you abandon the work and do something else? Probably not. If the results are plausible but just weak, then this matters only a little for a PhD, although it is often hard to publish such results in a well rated academic journal.

If, on the other hand, the results don't make any sense at all and are implausible – for example, the parameter estimates are way too big or too small, or they are statistically significant but with the wrong sign (e.g., a positive relationship is expected but the coefficient is negative and significant) then you should investigate and try to identify the source of the problem. Is there an issue with the data or your implementation of the model? If possible, try to re-estimate the model using a different statistical package or different code. Or perhaps your interpretation of the results is incorrect (e.g., check the data's scaling or the way you created or transformed the variables, which is perhaps different from other studies)? Or maybe the results are plausible after all, but your expectations were wrong? Do your best to fix any problems, but if they still persist, even after you have asked others, including your supervisor, for advice, then you have no choice but to write up the findings as you see them and try your best to explain them in the drafting.

Therefore, don't be excessively concerned if you obtain some 'negative findings', which we define as unexpected or implausible results that are challenging to explain.

Negative results are disappointing and require some careful explanation. But they are nonetheless a vital part of the development of knowledge so that other researchers become aware of what you tried. Such findings are much more challenging for academics to publish in highly rated journals. But provided that you have followed appropriate methods and there was a strong theoretical or intuitive rationale behind the approach you used, in a dissertation setting, negative results will be viewed on an almost equal footing with positive results. Your supervisor and examiners will want to see evidence that you know how to do research and write it up, and the fact that you were a bit unlucky this time will not overly worry them. They will no doubt have faced the same situation numerous times with their own research.

Negative findings can not only occur when your results seem bizarre, but more commonly also when the parameter attached to the key variable in your model is statistically insignificant, or you find no difference between treatment and control groups in an experiment, or you find that all of your hypotheses are rejected. You might obtain more favourable results by modifying the methods or data, which would be worth a try. The thesis is likely to contain a large volume of results, and in this context it is expectable that some will be negative but these will not detract from the positive findings, which can be emphasised in the write-up.

If your results are 'mixed' in the sense that either the parameter estimates on your main explanatory variables are insignificant, or when you examine the data in different ways, you get different conclusions, then don't be afraid to state that. It is much better to be up-front and honest about such results than to try to pretend that you have robust findings that support your hypothesis when they don't.

Try to tackle any odd-looking or unexpected results head-on. Some researchers try to bury them, fearful that such findings will damage the credibility of the work and hoping that the reader won't notice. But if you have such results, and you can explain them, they could lead to particularly valuable and exciting new knowledge useful to other researchers. Present the unexpected results, state what you had been expecting and why, and then explain how and why, in your case, the findings are different. Remember, it is the anomalous results that lead to scientific revolutions, so consider them an opportunity and a source of intrigue rather than necessarily a problem.

Tips on the presentation of results

It is a common stylistic flaw to include too many decimal places of accuracy in tables of results, which is unhelpful for two reasons. First, the excess accuracy is probably spurious since it is unlikely that your data would have been measured precisely enough for you to have that level of confidence in the findings. Second, it makes the numbers in the tables much harder for the reader to interpret. For instance, 0.63489271 could be reported much more succinctly as 0.635 or even 0.64. I usually find that three decimal places or three significant figures are sufficient. To save you from having to make the adjustments manually, if your statistical software provides excess precision in the output, you can use a spreadsheet to round the figures displayed before pasting the table into the document.

Furthermore, don't use 'engineering notation' in your results tables (e.g., 3.4E-

2), even if the output appears in that format from your statistical software package. Instead, convert it to a decimal figure (0.034) unless it is infeasible because the number is too small or too large (e.g., 3.4E-8 or 3.4E6). Also, don't just use the default options for presenting tables or figures from a spreadsheet; instead, make an active choice based on the information you are trying to get across to the reader and how you want it to look.

Number every table and graph you incorporate in the document, and they should appear in the order to which they are referred in the text. I have seen theses where Table 2 appears before Table 1, which does not make sense, and the numbers should have been simply swapped around.

A long book with very many tables and figures is likely to recommence the numbering in each chapter – for instance, Table 3.2 would be the second table in Chapter 3, and so on. But for a typical PhD thesis, there is unlikely to be a sufficient number of tables to make doing that worthwhile, so it is more straightforward to number them sequentially as Table 1, Table 2, etc., in whatever chapter they appear. Also, ensure that every table and figure has a number and a title, and any graphs have axis labels, axis scales, and a key that explains what each line or bar is showing.

If the rules permit, and they likely will, using colour in your dissertation will make it more pleasant and entertaining to read – for example, headers can be in colour, as can figures and tables. But don't overdo it – keep the colours subtle and consistent. It is probably also best to avoid overly flamboyant table designs; instead, stick to the clean and simple formats most commonly used in academic journal articles and books. When displaying tables in the document, try to make these appear professional, clear, and of appropriate size, as they would in a published paper – try to avoid using a tiny typeface (which will be hard to read) or one that is too big (which will look silly).

Remember in your descriptions of the results, tables and figures that 'data' and 'axes' are both plurals, not singular forms, so, for instance, you would write, 'the axes are labelled...', 'the data are presented...', etc. Writing axes and data as singulars are widespread grammatical errors.

Include all relevant details in your results tables. For example, if they are the estimation outputs from regression models, include standard errors or t-ratios in parentheses, and have the number of data points and the R^2 values in separate rows after the coefficients. It is also good practice, and now standard in many journals in accounting and finance, for tables to include comprehensive notes in a header or footer that explain where the information presented came from – for example, what were the data and model, and also defining any symbols or acronyms that are not obvious. Incorporating detailed notes ensures that the tables are as self-contained as possible and avoids the reader having to flip back and forth between a table and the main text (which might well be on an entirely different page) to understand what the former contains. It is also useful to number the columns in a table so that these labels can be referred to in the text to avoid confusion when discussing the results.

Virtually every empirical paper will include tables of results, but here as Table 11.1, I present one example, which is Table 4 from a pre-print version of the paper by Brooks *et al.* (2018) mentioned above and available in the University of Reading repository.[4] This table is a typical one from the finance literature, and is formatted as it would be in a working paper and perhaps a thesis rather than typeset by a publisher. It has a number of characteristic features:

- It includes extensive notes explaining the variables in a header
- Each column is headed with a number so that it can be easily identified in the body text
- Statistically significant parameters are denoted by asterisks, with $*$, $**$ and $***$ conventionally used to denote statistical significance at the 10%, 5% and 1% levels, respectively
- It is common to place standard errors in parentheses or sometimes *t*-ratios, but in this case it is *p*-values
- The parameter estimates appear first and then other information, such as the numbers of data points or the R^2 values, appear in later rows

Try to discuss your results methodically rather than in a haphazard, seemingly random fashion. Think carefully about the ordering of not only the tables as a whole but also the columns within each table of results. For instance, it makes sense to start the discussion of the findings with the first column before moving onto the second (the next one to the right of it), and so on, in which case you may need to modify the column order accordingly. You could start with the most basic form of the model on the left-hand side before moving to incrementally more sophisticated specifications, with the full model including all the variables in the far-most right-hand column.

Also, aim to use a variety of presentational styles for the results. If you are conducting quantitative data analysis, most of the information will likely be displayed in a tabular format, but having many such tables one after another can be boring for the reader. Interspersing them with graphs (e.g., line graphs, pie charts, bar charts, etc.) will be more visually appealing. Since 'a picture says a thousand words', it might also help make the most critical points that you are trying to get across more salient, whereas they would be buried in a table and therefore unnoticed. When readers (and markers) are short of time, they might skip over a table but nonetheless glance at a picture, which would consequently make more impact.

Although, as discussed above, their inclusion is essential, don't use too much space on summary statistics and preliminaries when presenting the results, otherwise you can quickly run up to the word limit. Prioritise the inclusion of the main findings that are the focus of the research and add additional details if you have sufficient words remaining. Give the key results first and then others that are more peripheral in a robustness checks sub-section or an appendix at the end of the document. Write up the main results succinctly at first and then add further details when you know

---

[4]http://centaur.reading.ac.uk/73681/

Table 11.1: Sample table: probability of firms being acquirers

This table reports the coefficient estimates from conditional logit models for the probability of firms being acquirers. The dependent variable is equal to one for the sample acquirer and zero for the matched acquirers in the control group. The matched acquirers are firms in the sample acquirer's industry (Fama–French 10 industries), of similar size (within a 20% band of market capitalization) and of similar B/M ratio (within a 20% band of B/M). The relative size between the sample target and matched acquirers is above 5%. Detailed definitions of acquirer control variables can be found in Appendix A. Deal fixed effects are controlled for in all regressions. Robust standard errors are clustered at the deal level. p-values are reported in parentheses. Significance at the 0.01, 0.05, and 0.10 levels is indicated by $***$, $**$, and $*$, respectively.

	1	2	3	4	5	6
Ac_CrossIO	3.565***					
	(0.000)					
Ac_CrossIO_1%		8.912***				
		(0.000)				
Mvweighted_CrossIO			6.867***			
			(0.000)			
Top5Count				0.583***		
				(0.000)		
Top10Count					0.403***	
					(0.000)	
Top20Count						0.283***
						(0.000)
IO	0.683***	1.663***	1.111***	0.334***	0.305***	0.229**
	(0.000)	(0.000)	(0.000)	(0.002)	(0.007)	(0.047)
Size	1.925***	1.825***	1.995***	1.940***	1.982***	1.967***
	(0.000)	(0.000)	(0.000)	(0.000)	(0.000)	(0.000)
B/M	1.008***	0.930***	1.022***	1.023***	1.042***	1.053***
	(0.000)	(0.000)	(0.000)	(0.000)	(0.000)	(0.000)
Leverage	0.005***	0.007***	0.005***	0.005***	0.004***	0.004***
	(0.001)	(0.000)	(0.000)	(0.001)	(0.002)	(0.003)
ROA	-0.682***	-0.767***	-0.631**	-0.656**	-0.601**	-0.538**
	(0.009)	(0.005)	(0.016)	(0.015)	(0.027)	(0.046)
Cashholding	-0.119	0.013	-0.086	-0.047	-0.034	-0.046
	(0.541)	(0.945)	(0.657)	(0.808)	(0.863)	(0.814)
Sales_Growth	0.000	-0.008*	0.001	-0.004	-0.002	-0.001
	(0.931)	(0.079)	(0.785)	(0.345)	(0.548)	(0.733)
Runup	0.284***	0.299***	0.266***	0.281***	0.286***	0.295***
	(0.000)	(0.000)	(0.000)	(0.000)	(0.000)	(0.000)
Sigma	-25.615***	-26.664***	-24.916***	-25.671***	-25.351***	-25.013***
	(0.000)	(0.000)	(0.000)	(0.000)	(0.000)	(0.000)
Deal fixed effects	Yes	Yes	Yes	Yes	Yes	Yes
Observations	36,944	36,944	36,944	36,944	36,944	36,944
Actual acquirer No.	2,177	2,177	2,177	2,177	2,177	2,177
Control acquirer No.	34,767	34,767	34,767	34,767	34,767	34,767
Pseudo R-squared	0.045	0.080	0.067	0.058	0.065	0.074

that you have spare words still available within the limit.

Many econometric and statistical software packages can output results into an attractive tabular format that can be pasted directly into a word processor, which is preferable to retyping the numbers into a table that you have created yourself. Not only will this save you from a laborious and tedious task, but it will also minimise 'transcription errors' where you make typographical mistakes. Similarly, it is always best to use a straight-through data input method when you move from one package to another (e.g., from a data provider through to a spreadsheet then the statistical software to finally getting the results into your thesis document).

In some areas within business and management, it is common to have a 'discussion' section in addition to the results. In that case, the latter would be reserved for the more straightforward presentation and description of the findings, with in-depth analysis, links with the existing literature and reflection on what it all means being left to the discussion part. This style is less common in accounting and finance and could lead to you having two very short pieces. Therefore, unless your results section feels unwieldy (even when broken into sub-sections), a separate Discussion section is probably unnecessary.

11.5.13 The conclusions

As for the results aspects, you will have two levels of conclusions: a concluding section at the end of each investigative chapter and an entire chapter of conclusions for the whole thesis at the end but before the references. The concluding sections within each investigative chapter will usually comprise brief summaries of that empirical work, pointing out the main data and methods used as well as the findings. These sections will also ideally include a couple of lines that link in with the following chapter.

The remainder of this section focuses on the concluding chapter, which will be a considerably more substantive undertaking than the concluding sections, both in terms of its length and scope of coverage. The concluding chapter is your foremost opportunity to reflect on what you have done, why you did it and how, why you chose particular methods and not others, what aspects worked well, and areas that could be improved if the topic were to be tackled by you or someone else in the future. Being reflective and critical in this chapter is essential to demonstrate that you have developed evaluatory skills, and you can take a high-level view of your work's strengths and weaknesses.

Like the abstract, the concluding chapter should be able to stand alone so that it could be read by someone who had not seen the rest of the document, and it would still make sense to them. The conclusions should finish the thesis in the same general, high-level style that the introductory chapter began it.

The concluding chapter should comprise several elements, each of which will usually have its own section, and each is discussed further below:

1. First and foremost, a not-too-technical summary of the key findings of your

thesis
2. Next, the limitations of the work as a whole should be noted.
3. Third, some suggestions for further research in the area should be presented
4. Finally, some theses finish off by introducing recommendations for policy or practice if these are relevant given the subject matter

The concluding summary

This section needs to cover all aspects of the investigative process, including the motivation you identified from the existing literature and where the gap is; a restatement of your hypotheses or research aims; the methods used; and the main results. It should be written in such a way as to emphasise the contribution, so tell the reader (again) what you have done that is exciting and new and why it makes a useful contribution to knowledge and for whom. Avoid copying and pasting the wording you used in previous chapters, even though you will be covering much the same ground, albeit in less detail.

It is unnecessary to repeat details of all of the specific results discussed in the previous chapters, only the headline findings. Although the conclusions need to restate the main results, this part needs to be brief and probably not including any numerical values at all unless one or two are very notable.

It is also not necessary, and probably not helpful, to discuss the issues that you faced along the road to completion – especially if these reflected a lack of knowledge or experience on your part so that it was a steep learning curve. However, it is sensible to highlight any issues that you could not resolve where they are material to the outcome and where explaining the situation will reassure the reader that you were aware of the problems and knew what you were doing.

The conclusions are not the place to introduce any entirely new ideas; instead, they should be a logical extension of what you have already found and stated in previous chapters. The concluding summary section should usually be reasonably short as a proportion of the total thesis length since there is no need to repeat all of the methods or results. The chapter's very final paragraph is the one that will stick in the reader's mind, so try to say something memorable and perhaps even profound. For instance, in a paper that I co-authored that examined gender differences in research evaluations in business and management (Brooks, Fenton, Schopohl and Walker, 2014), we ended the conclusions with, 'Taken together these findings suggest that a shift towards the "objective assessment" of research using journal lists or other crude quantitative measures may tend to reduce diversity and in some cases may blunt women's career prospects while impeding intellectual discovery and the development of knowledge-based economies' (p. 1000).

Limitations of the study

It is good practice in a thesis (although far from universally done) to include a sub-section in the conclusions entitled 'Limitations of the study', which does precisely what the heading suggests. Evidently, no research study is flawless, and your dissertation will not be an exception. Identifying the limitations and explaining why they apply and how they could be remedied is worthwhile since it helps to demonstrate that you are capable of being a 'reflective practitioner', able to understand and learn from problems to self-improve in the future.

The wording in this part requires careful consideration, however, since it is crucial not to undermine your research by highlighting to the reader any fatal flaws. Also, try not to give the impression that you had been lazy or thoughtless in the investigative work you have conducted. For example, the truth might be that 'I was so slow in getting my survey out that I could only leave it open for a few days and hence I got a modest number of responses.' This explanation could instead be written as 'Since I was unable to provide a monetary incentive for participants to complete the survey, it was challenging to get them to engage with it, which resulted in the sample being quite small.' The second way of wording the problem does not cast you in an unfavourable light and instead lays the blame on an unavoidable difficulty, albeit it is a slight distortion of the truth.

Therefore, try to list only relatively minor issues that would not damage the credibility of the main findings, and in particular, aspects that you could not reasonably have been expected to have dealt with in the time available. Points around the scope of the data used are an obvious choice as data availability is frequently a challenge that many researchers face and one which is not easily overcome. If you conducted a survey, was the number of participants as great as you would have liked, and was it somewhat skewed towards particular groups? If you used interviews, were there other relevant stakeholders that you would love to have had a discussion with but to whom you could not gain access, and so those you spoke to were not the real decision-makers? If you were using secondary data, was the coverage of countries or companies or the timespan as extensive as you would have liked? Don't just make a bullet list of concerns, but explain each point and why it is relevant.

You could also discuss whether your findings could be generalised to other contexts (other companies, assets or countries, for example) or whether they are specific to the focus that you adopted. Generalisable results are in some ways more valuable, and hence if your findings are context-specific, that should be noted as a limitation in the concluding section, along with a short discussion of why that is the case.

Suggestions for further research

The 'limitations' sub-section can then lead naturally to a 'suggestions for further research' sub-section. This aspect could be used to discuss all the ideas that you might have developed relating to the thesis if you had another year to work on it. A few indications of the sort of material you could incorporate here are:

- Are there additional datasets that you would have collected? Other markets, regions or countries, for example?
- If your research involved quantitative analysis, are there additional variables that could have been incorporated into the models or different ways to measure

the variables?

- Were there other methods you would have used had you more time available?
- Are there emerging techniques or models that you would have tried for analysis?
- Would you have additionally used different approaches – for instance, following up quantitative analysis with detailed case studies or interviews to get a deeper insight into specific aspects of the findings or using an experiment where you are able to control the conditions?

Recommendations

A final sub-section to consider including in the Conclusions chapter is for recommendations. This aspect would step away from the results themselves towards thinking about who the end-users of your findings might be, how they might use the results, and what they should do. In other words, what are the implications of your research output for policy or practice? These could be recommendations for government policymakers, regulators, financial market practitioners, or the general public. For example:

- Your findings might identify a need for a tighter regulatory environment in a particular market
- You might have suggestions for how environmental risks could be better incorporated into accounts
- You could have identified issues with private finance initiatives
- You might have concluded that information is spreading too slowly in certain markets and approaches need to be developed to speed up dissemination
- Your research might have been able to identify which models are most effective for accurately determining value at risk so that banks could improve their approaches

In each case, explain your recommendations, what the organisation or individuals should do, how the suggestions relate to your findings, and why and how they will improve outcomes for the organisation(s) or people affected by them.

While it is good practice to include some recommendations for non-academic users of the findings if these arise from your research, whether it is worthwhile to have a specific sub-section for them or the suggestions could be rolled into the rest of the concluding chapter will depend on how much you have to write here.

If you were engaged in research that is purely scholarly with no direct external users, this part would not be relevant. But if your original list of aims stated that you would draw recommendations for policymakers or whoever, you need to ensure that you do so.

More generally, it is essential at this stage in the process to ensure that you have addressed all of the research aims that you set yourself in the introductory chapter. If you find that you set up aims or research questions that you did not address once you came to conduct the investigative work, delete them.

11.5.14 Back matter

You have now covered all of the core aspects of the writing, and all that is left is the parts at the end, which are sometimes known as the back matter. This part includes the references and appendices (if used). While these will probably be read with less scrutiny than the front matter and main body of the document, they nonetheless need to be present and accurate.

11.5.15 The references

A list of references should be provided in alphabetical order by the first author surname. Note that a list of references (a list of all the papers, books or webpages referred to in the study, irrespective of whether you read them or found them cited in other studies), rather than a bibliography (a list of items that you read, regardless of whether you referred to them in the study), is usually needed here. If you wish, you can include both a reference list and an extended bibliography to highlight the additional material that you read but which you have not cited.

All works cited should be listed in the references section using the style discussed in the literature review material of chapter 9, where an extensive treatment of referencing is given. Equally, do not list in the reference section any item that you did not cite in the thesis. There is no excuse for sloppy referencing. Although it is tedious to check through to make sure that none are missing and that all the information is present and in the same format for every citation, it is worth it as not doing so is to throw away an easy opportunity to improve the thesis.

11.5.16 Appendices

Finally, an appendix or appendices can be used to improve the study's structure as a whole when placing a specific item in the text would interrupt the flow of the document. For example, if you want to outline how a particular variable was constructed, or you had to write some computer code to estimate the models, and you think this could be interesting to readers, then it can be placed in an appendix.

The appendices should not be used as a dumping ground for irrelevant material or padding and should not be filled with printouts of raw output from computer packages. Always format any information that you include in your thesis to improve its presentation and make the style of appendix material the same as the rest of the document. Remove any redundant aspects (such as parts of the statistical results that repeat information given elsewhere) unless they are included as pictures that cannot be edited (e.g., screenshots).

What should go in an appendix?

Appendices can be useful for incorporating further evidence of what you have done when including it in the main body would disrupt the text's flow or would use up too many words. It makes sense to have more than one appendix where you want to include several types of material and where bundling it all into a single

appendix would look odd. The following types of material can usefully be included
in appendices:

- A full list of the survey or interview questions you used
- A list of variable definitions and sources
- A mathematical derivation of a core model you employed in the empirical work
- A list of all the entities used in a data sample (e.g., a list of companies or countries, if the number is too great to include in a table in the document's main body)
- Additional (non-core) tables or graphs of results such as 'robustness checks' where you estimated several different models

Any material included in appendices should still be referenced explicitly in the main
document, although, unlike the evidence presented in the latter (i.e., the tables and
figures in the main body, which should be described in detail), appendix matter can
be given only a one- or two-line overview (e.g., 'Tables A1 to A6 include additional
results on the cross-country panel models including random effects. These are
qualitatively identical to the findings presented in the main tables.')

Although appendices can add considerable value by allowing you to include
additional material, they can be overdone, so try to ensure that they remain
manageable in terms of both their number and their length. It would not, for instance,
be appropriate to include appendices that extend to almost as many pages as the rest
of the document, although I have seen this happen numerous times.

11.6   How long is a typical PhD thesis?

A thesis is typically around 150–200 pages long, but this will be dependent on many
factors, most notably how technical the material is and the presentation (font size,
margins and line spacing). If you have numerous appendices of additional results or
robustness checks, it could be very much longer. There will be word limits, typically
set at 90,000 for a PhD and possibly 60,000 for an MPhil, although in accounting
and finance the vast majority of theses will be considerably smaller than these limits.

Each investigative chapter will probably be roughly similar in terms of both
the layout and the overall length to those of a published paper in the PhD's subject
area. Note, though, that published articles often look much shorter than they are
because the small font and tight spacing turns a 50-page working paper into a 20-page
published paper.

Although every thesis will be different and there is not just one format that
will work, in general, there needs to be a sensible balance between the amount of
space devoted to each of the major parts of the document. As a very rough guide,
I propose the following for an example of a thesis where the main body is 150
pages of 400 words each (total, 60,000 words), with the front matter, references, and
any appendices considered separately, as suggested in Table 11.2. Therefore, the
total thesis length will probably be around 180 pages when the acknowledgements,

Table 11.2: Suggested thesis chapter lengths, model 1

Chapter	Expected length	Expected number of words	Expected percentage of entire document
Introduction	10 pages	4,000 words	7%
Literature review	25 pages	10,000 words	17%
Investigation 1	35 pages	14,000 words	23%
Investigation 2	35 pages	14,000 words	23%
Investigation 3	35 pages	14,000 words	23%
Conclusions	10 pages	4,000 words	7%
Overall length	150 pages	60,000 words	100%

Table 11.3: Suggested thesis chapter lengths, model 2

Chapter	Expected length	Expected number of words	Expected percentage of entire document
Introduction	10 pages	4,000 words	7%
Investigation 1	43 pages	17,300 words	29%
Investigation 2	43 pages	17,300 words	29%
Investigation 3	43 pages	17,300 words	29%
Conclusions	10 pages	4,000 words	7%
Overall length	149 pages	59,900 words	101%

Note: percentages do not sum to 100 due to rounding errors.

abstract, table of contents, references and some appendices are added. The first example highlights the case where the literature review is located in a separate chapter to the investigative work.

A second possibility is where the literature review is embedded within each investigative chapter rather than being hived off into its own chapter. This structure might make more sense where the investigative chapters are distinct from one another and do not share a common underpinning literature. This would require the structure and word lengths of the remaining chapters to be modified to accommodate this as in Table 11.3.

Note that the above are just rough suggestions rather than a fixed rules, but there should be a sensible balance between the thesis' main components to avoid giving the reader the impression that some parts are overwhelming the others. For instance, as discussed in chapter 4, it is common for research proposals to be review-heavy, and the same is true of the thesis document as a whole, which is undesirable since it is primarily your ideas and new work that the reader is interested in. On the other hand, a thesis where half of the pages are taken up with detailed tables of results would also be unbalanced.

The suggested proportions for each component indicate that the description and discussion of your investigative work will be at the heart of the PhD, constituting a bit over half of the overall space available. The total word limits are not a concern for the majority of PhD students as their theses naturally arrive at comfortably below that number, but what to do in such circumstances is discussed in the following chapter. In any case, counting the number of words or pages accurately is surprisingly tricky and probably a fruitless endeavour as there are several plausible ways to do so that could lead to quite different numbers. For instance, do tables count towards the word total? How about footnotes? If you reduce the margins or reduce the font size, have you reduced the word count? (of course not, but it can make the document length look substantially different).

It is often the case that students put disappointingly little effort into the introductory and concluding chapters, leaving these aspects too brief and not sufficiently imaginative. I have seen numerous theses where the concluding chapters are not even two pages long, which fail to do justice to the excellent empirical work that has come before them.

Finally, pay attention to the readability of the document as a whole. Each chapter in the thesis should flow seamlessly from the previous one so that they fit together like a book. Consequently, the chapters do not have to be self-contained, and you can assume that readers will read the document in page order from the front to the back cover and will therefore be familiar with any material that you had discussed previously (although reminding them of the meaning of unfamiliar acronyms or esoteric words might still be helpful).

Further reading

There are several valuable books that you could consult if you want more detail on to improve your academic writing, such as those by Bailey (2017), Coleman (2019) or Day (2018), although there are many others.

Chapter takeaways – top tips for success

- ⊛ Begin the 'writing up phase' as soon as possible and avoid leaving it all until the last stage
- ⊛ Avoid being excessively pedantic when working on the initial draft. The critical aspect is to get a first attempt written that can be improved subsequently
- ⊛ Write at an appropriate level and with a suitable amount of detail. You could consider your readers to be generalists in accounting and finance but not experts in the minutiae of dissertation topic
- ⊛ Before you start drafting, try to get hold of successfully completed theses and reflect on their style and structure

Chapter takeaways – continued

- ⊛ Ensure that each aspect of your thesis covers a roughly appropriate proportion of the words or space available
- ⊛ Adopt a scholarly, formal approach to writing but endeavour to maintain reader interest nonetheless
- ⊛ Use appendices where appropriate to maintain the flow in the main text, but don't make them too extensive

12. POLISHING AND SUBMISSION

Learning outcomes: this chapter covers

✓ How to improve the quality of your writing
✓ Hot to deal with feedback and criticism
✓ What to do if your thesis is too short or too long
✓ What to look out for in pre-submission checks

12.1 Why further editing is needed

You might have thought that chapter 11 ought to be the end of this book because your job is done. Unfortunately, just when you thought you had finished, you will now come to realise that there is an essential task remaining, namely editing and polishing the document. While the completion of a first draft of the whole dissertation – if that is what you have achieved by the time you reach this chapter of the book – is a huge step forward, there is still a lot to do if you are going to maximise the quality of your thesis.

Even though the remaining aspects will be less challenging and less time-consuming, it is still nonetheless worthwhile going the extra mile to make sure that the dissertation document is as polished and refined as possible, both in terms of the writing and the structure, ordering and presentation. It is definitely worth reserving as much time as you can towards the end of your PhD registration period to read the draft thesis carefully at least twice. Hence the purpose of the present chapter is to provide a range of additional guidance and tips to achieve this aim.

In order for this crucial editing phase to be as productive as possible, it is valuable to find some way to distance yourself from your work because repeatedly re-reading the same material in the same format encourages the brain to become lazy, skimming over aspects of the document and making it hard to spot errors or inconsistencies. There are several approaches to achieve this distance, including:

- time – wait at least a few days, or if the schedule to submission allows, a couple of weeks. In that time, the document will become less familiar and without noticing you will read it more carefully.
- medium – changing the medium could involve printing the draft if you usually read it on screen, or vice versa. The difference in the way the document looks on a screen versus on paper will make it appear less familiar
- font – changing the font size and style so that the pagination alters will also make the document seem different as the layout and positioning of the text on the page will be different
- location – even something as straightforward as working in a different place with different lighting will mix things up slightly

It is best to read the material in page order, however, even though this might be the same as you have done previously. This will enable you match the experience of the reader so that you can see if anything is out of sequence – for instance, if you had referred to some ideas or models assuming you had already presented them although they don't actually appear until a later chapter.

When you get to the editing stage, prioritise the most important aspects and don't waste time on trivial issues that will have little effect on the quality of the work as a whole, such as fiddling with presentational aspects of the references and table formatting. Make both references and tables clear and consistent, including all the relevant information. Then stop and work on more substantial aspects of the thesis.

Examiners are likely to consider how the document is presented, not just the content, even if they only do so subconsciously. Therefore, a poor presentation, including grammatical or spelling errors, will diminish the reader's perception of the work. If the examiners view these aspects of your thesis as inadequate, improving them is likely to be a requirement at the corrections stage after the viva exam. Thus, students are better to tidy up their theses prior to initial submission, and should ensure that their report's structure is orderly and logical, that equations are correctly specified, and that there are no spelling or other typographical mistakes or grammatical errors.

It is also expedient to remember that your examiners will be reading and evaluating your thesis alongside many other commitments, so the better you can make the structure and presentation of the document, the easier and more pleasurable their job will be. On the other hand, bad structure and a poor standard of English are frustrating for the reader and make the task of reviewing the thesis harder than it needs to be. These problems will likely be reflected in the reception you receive in the viva and the number of corrections you are asked to complete. It is best to approach this as a two-stage process: fixing up the presentation and structure first before then editing the text itself, although you might have to go back to the presentation again if the editing caused you to make significant changes to the layout, such as moving substantive amounts of material around.

12.2   Polishing your thesis and improving its structure

The main issues to consider first are the layout of the text and its legibility. The document should be both highly readable and professional-looking. The following sub-sections provide further tips for presenting and organising your material optimally.

12.2.1   Perfect paragraphs

Don't use an elaborate, curly font. *Gyre Chorus*, for example, might look nice on a birthday card or party invitation but not an academic research paper. It is best to stick with something standard such as Times, or Helvetica. Usually, 11 or 12-point font is best, with 10-point for footnotes. Headers can either be in the same size but in bold or a couple of points larger than the main body text.

There is an optimum range of lengths for paragraphs. On the one hand, if they are too short, it makes the writing appear 'bitty' and makes it harder for the story to flow. On the other hand, paragraphs that are too long make the text dense and impenetrable, which is exhausting for the reader. Most blogs and newspaper articles tend to use shorter paragraphs (as little one or two sentences for each), but they are writing for an audience of predominantly non-specialists who want to read quickly. For academic writing, however, paragraphs tend to be longer, say four to ten lines is ideal. But again, this tends to depend somewhat on the nature of the material: the more technical the subject matter, the shorter the paragraphs tend to be.

There might be a rule concerning thesis line-spacing in your department, but in general single-line spacing looks slightly more professional but is harder to read; double-line spacing is easy to read but takes up too much space on the page; 1.5-line spacing is often a good compromise. Use clear and consistent paragraph spacing – either with a line between each paragraph or a tab indent at the start of each new paragraph. Both the indented paragraph style and block paragraphs are usually acceptable but pick one of the two and don't mix them. Separating the paragraphs in one of these ways is essential since it considerably eases readability as it makes it evident when you are moving onto a slightly different thread of the argument or a new topic.

Although it is challenging to do so with subject-specific or technical words, try to maintain interest and avoid repetition by varying the words and phrases you use. Connectives such as 'however', 'but', 'additionally', and so on, are helpful to improve the flow, but even these can be overused, and the same word should not be included more than once within a paragraph or two. Avoid using vague and wordy phrases that do not really say anything, such as 'it could be stated that'. This string is ambiguous: it could be stated, but what sentiment about the matter are you expressing, and what did other researchers say?

Suppose you include the tables in the main body text rather than all gathered at the end. In that case, you will have to fiddle a bit to 'float them' around the page to avoid having large amounts of space ('white space' as it is known in publishing spheres), or a table splitting across two pages (which is best avoided unless a table is too large to fit onto a single page, and if that is the case, consider splitting it into two or more smaller tables).

Relatedly, adequate spacing throughout will aid the readability of the document. Don't be tempted to squash the components together to save a couple of pages. Start each chapter on a new page, leave space around tables and figures and leave an extra line of space between the end of one section and the start of the next.

12.2.2 Is there an optimal length for thesis chapters?

When a thesis is being assessed, the primary consideration is the overall amount of material within it rather than its distribution across the chapters. Therefore, there are many acceptable models for how a good PhD might look rather than a single style requirement. A typical thesis chapter might be around 15,000 words long – roughly the same length as a comprehensive journal article – but this will depend on how many chapters there are. A small number of really 'meaty' chapters or a larger number of shorter chapters could both work, and so it is preferable to select a combination of these that best suits the material and feels most natural.

12.2.3 Perfect prose: check, check and check again

Editing and polishing the document is a crucial stage in the writing process. It is an exciting aspect since you can see all of the hard work you have put in so far coming together, and the point where you can say that the thesis is ready to submit is getting close. While the amount of time that this stage will take should not be underestimated, it is also important not to begin too soon. In particular, if possible, it is better to complete all of the investigative work and produce a complete first draft of the entire thesis before commencing the editing. If you edit part of the document thoroughly and then make further changes, especially if they are substantive, there is a danger that you could fail to spot presentational or drafting issues with the newly added material. Or there might be abrupt jumps between the new and existing parts.

Even published books contain typographical errors, despite that in most cases, they have been drafted by experienced writers, copy-edited and proof-read (usually twice) by professionals. No doubt there are errors in the one you are reading too. However, the lesson is that small numbers of minor grammatical or spelling mistakes, while best if not present of course, are almost unavoidable in reality and are not of too much concern. But a manuscript that is riddled with apparent errors gives the impression that the writer was careless. The reader will then worry that if the writer was sloppy with the drafting, were they similarly haphazard with the investigative work? So large numbers of typographical mistakes will not only be treated as a weak aspect of the presentation, but it might also cause the examiners to be particularly fastidious in reviewing other parts of the work, looking even harder for errors than they otherwise would have done.

The first stage in the editing process is to make sure that you read your work a few times, ideally with several days in between as discussed in the previous section. Reciting the work aloud can help you judge whether sentences are easy or hard to read. Make sure that you read it in page order at least once from the very first page to the last. Since you likely wrote the dissertation 'out-of-order', it is easy for issues to arise with the flow of material that you otherwise might overlook. For example, you discuss a model in chapter 2 that you don't define or explain until chapter 3, but you initially did not realise because you wrote chapter 3 first. On the other hand, your examiners will read the document in page sequence from beginning to end and be frustrated if they are left scratching their heads for five pages until you eventually define what a particular acronym stands for.

The automated spelling and grammar checkers in word processors have made the task of polishing documents quicker and more straightforward, and the Grammarly add-in for Word is even better at spotting a range of issues. But while these packages play a vital role in improving your writing, there is also a danger of complacency since there are numerous errors that such automated software cannot identify. This means that it is still essential that you (and ideally, someone else too) go through your work carefully by hand.

An important point to consider when reading through your draft is how well the text flows both within and across sections. A pleasant experience for the reader will be like a smooth car journey where both the movement on each road and the transitions between them have no bumps or jumps. Sometimes writing can be disjointed, with the paragraphs not linking together, making it harder for the reader to follow. If that is the case, go through and add connections and linking sentences that smooth the transition from one paragraph or section to the next.

If your first language is not English, then writing an extended piece of work such as a thesis can be particularly challenging. By reading extensively from the literature and getting tips from this book, you will have a good idea of how academics tend to write in our subject area. Don't be excessively concerned with bad grammar or punctuation, and, as stated numerous times, don't be tempted to copy someone else's work. If you can get your ideas drafted into some text, even if it is not smoothly written in perfect English initially, so long as it is understandable, it can be polished into a solid piece of prose. Your supervisor and examiners will be well accustomed to reading work written by non-native English speakers and will be sympathetic to their cause, tending to ignore minor errors.

It is perfectly acceptable to get a proof-reader to go through your work and suggest edits to improve the spelling, grammar and other aspects of the writing style. However, you should mention their help and what they did in the acknowledgements section of your thesis. A proof-reader will merely be improving the explanation of your ideas, not generating those ideas, and hence employing a third party to enhance the writing style will not diminish your contribution. Specialists such as these can be found relatively easily on the internet, and most will only charge a modest amount (perhaps £200 for a typical thesis, although this sum will vary significantly between one and another). Poor grammar, spelling and drafting are probably the easiest aspects of a bad thesis to fix, so long as you allow sufficient time to engage the proof-reader's services and implement their suggestions.

Editing the thesis

You will need to edit your work on several levels, and this will probably be more successful if you address each level in a separate reading rather than attempting to fix everything in one go. It might be helpful to think of editing as requiring micro-level and macro-level work.

The macro-level should be done first, and this involves reflecting on whether your document covers all of the required aspects and that they are in the correct order. You will probably have to move material around – both within and across chapters – as the thesis draft takes shape. You also need to check for consistency of typeface, font, margin size, heading style and size, etc. Also, check that the equation, table and figure numbering is consistent and starts at 1. Are the paragraphs of an appropriate length, or do they need to be split or merged?

One way to ensure that the formatting of the document is consistent throughout is to use a template. Whatever word processor you use (e.g., Microsoft Word, Apple Pages, or TeX), you can apply a template that will control all these issues without you needing to worry. All you need to do is choose the template then implement it throughout rather than choosing formats (e.g., chapter heading sizes, fonts, justification, etc.) manually.

At the micro-level, this means reading the draft very carefully, in page order, line-by-line, checking for grammatical or spelling errors, inconsistencies in spelling where both are correct (e.g., heteroscedasticity and heteroskedasticity) or hyphenation (e.g., built in or built-in; on-line or online). Are all arguments fluid and well-made? Do the paragraphs link together, or are there any abrupt movements in the writing? Are the citations correct and matching the reference list at the end? Have any controversial statements been substantiated with evidence or references?

When you start to remove material from your dissertation draft, don't just delete the words but create a new file that you can call 'spare stuff' or something similar, and paste it there. It might be that this material will come in handy later if you find that you have pruned more heavily than you needed to or you have removed the wrong parts. Regret at having deleted some content that the author later realises to be useful is surprisingly common.

The final polishing stage at the end will involve several elements. As well as the above points, there are numerous minor stylistic issues to consider:

1. Read through carefully, looking for any typos or grammatical errors, which should be removed. Look especially for incorrect words that a spell-checker would miss (e.g., 'there' versus 'their' and 'every month' versus 'very month').

2. Ensure that the document is as readable as possible, which includes confirming that there are no excessively long sentences or containing too many clauses. It also means having paragraphs of a reasonable length – neither just two lines nor an entire page.

3. Ensure that the style is consistent throughout. Consistency is quite challenging for a novice who is unsure of what to look for, but for instance, check that:

   - You have included the title, your name and the date on the front cover (plus any other information required by the department)
   - You have numbered the pages with Roman numerals for the front matter and Arabic numbers for the main body, with the first page of the introduction being numbered 1.
   - Section heading styles are consistent (e.g., are the first letters of all words in headers capitalised? Do the headings have a larger font or bold or underlined typeface?) As a suggestion, use *italics* (or <u>underline</u>) for emphasis on particular words that you want to highlight or for terms in Latin (or abbreviated from Latin such as *et al.*). Use **bold** (or larger font, or **both**) for headings and titles
   - Equation numbering is consistent if present
   - The font and line spacing are the same throughout the document
   - Your use of either a justified or 'ragged' right-hand margin is consistent throughout
   - Your use of quotation marks ('single' or "double", 'smart' or 'straight') and hyphens (e.g., line-break or line break) is consistent
   - Appropriate country spellings have been used throughout (i.e., UK spellings for students studying in the UK, US spellings in the US, etc.). If you are studying in the UK, it is best to stick to UK spelling throughout, but the worst style is to mix UK and US versions within the same dissertation. Most word processors can be configured to check for any particular country's spelling conventions, so ensure that you use the built-in function correctly
   - Tenses have been used consistently throughout. It is fine to use the past, present and future tenses in the appropriate places but be constant in their usage. For example, in the literature review, when describing the work of other scholars, you could use the present ('Brooks and Persand (2000) estimate a model with time-varying volatility and find that ...') or the past tense ('Brooks and Persand (2000) estimated a model with time-varying volatility and found that...') but do not mix the two. When writing the introductory chapter, you will need to describe what you are

going to do in subsequent chapters, and this could be written as ('In chapter 2, I will review the existing literature') or in the present as ('In chapter 2, I review the existing literature') Similarly, it is more natural to use the past tense in the concluding chapter when discussing what you have already done ('In chapter 4, I evaluated the extent to which multinationals are able to reduce their corporation tax bills by operating in low tax jurisdictions')

- There are no 'widows or orphans' – where you have a section heading at the end of a page with no body text after it

In many instances, the precise style is unimportant, but consistency is imperative. If in doubt about what to do regarding any aspect, just make a sensible judgement call, and it will usually be acceptable.

As stated previously, even when the investigative work has been carefully conducted, the introductions, conclusions and abstracts of PhDs are often relatively weak. This poor quality arises because these aspects are typically written last when the candidate has run out of time or energy or both and just wants to get the job done as quickly as possible. In contrast, the empirical work went through a lengthy process of iterating between student and supervisor with extensive polishing and revisions in between. This situation is unfortunate because it means that the thesis as a whole is not as strong as it could have been, and such a thesis has skimped on the parts that might be at the forefront of the examiners' minds when evaluating the work, even though the investigative aspects could be considered more important in assessing whether the thesis should pass. So make sure that you give these important aspects of the thesis as much attention as the empirical chapters.

As a final consistency check, if the thesis is submitted in both electronic and hard-copy formats, ensure that the two match precisely page-for-page to avoid any confusion or misunderstandings when going through the document in the oral exam.

12.3   Dealing with feedback

Your supervisor will be expected to read through the draft and offer comments upon it before final submission. By the time that you get to having a first draft of the entire thesis, you should already have received detailed feedback on the investigative chapters, possibly with several rounds of review, feedback, changes and refinement followed by further review and so on.

It is also worth asking as many other relevant people for feedback as possible, including academic staff other than your supervisor, PhD student colleagues and post docs. Any comments are useful since, after all, those that you do not like or agree with can be ignored. If your supervisor offers tips, though, they should be taken very seriously – not only because it is likely that they are highly experienced researchers who are knowledgeable about the topic, but also because the supervisor will select the examiners and will have some understanding of what they are likely to be looking for in a thesis.

Actively encouraging feedback, reflecting on the comments and implementing improvements is another key skill learned as part of successful dissertation completion. Your supervisor has probably read through numerous theses as well as countless research papers and student projects over the years, and so their comments will be well informed and almost undoubtedly valuable.

Learning to cope with criticism is an essential skill for any aspiring scholar because critique – both giving and receiving it – is a major part of academic life. Try not to take offence at negative comments made by your supervisor or others when they are providing feedback, although this is not always easy. It can be hurtful even for senior and highly experienced staff when work they spent many months or years producing and were proud of is denigrated, particularly if the author feels that the comments are unfounded. Occasionally, there is the opportunity for academics to respond to the criticism, but most of the time, there is not. Therefore, the trick is to view any negative comments constructively and learn from them without becoming disheartened.

Don't be discouraged if your first draft is returned covered with comments and suggestions for improvement; in fact, that is a good sign that you have piqued your supervisor's interest sufficiently that they want to spend the time to help you make the work even better. If your supervisor is not engaged with what you have written, you will receive only a handful of 'high-level' comments, which are those of a very general nature that could be made by someone who had only skimmed through the draft and not read it closely.

While it can be disheartening to receive back a piece of work that you were proud of covered in red ink with tens of comments, this does not imply that the work is of bad quality or will run into trouble at the viva stage. Some supervisors will do a very thorough job of providing feedback and even if the tone of their comments appears to be predominantly negative, that might just be their style of providing suggestions and not reflective of their view of the standard of the thesis.

Take any feedback in good spirit and use it as an opportunity to further improve your work. If you are still worried that the comments are suggestive that your thesis is not up to scratch, get back to your supervisor or whoever made the suggestions and explain your concerns. It might be worthwhile to explore whether your supervisor is willing to engage in a further round of feedback to see whether your revisions to the work after the first set of comments are going on the right track, or to ask for further opinions from others before you submit the final version for formal examination.

When receiving a report or your supervisor's feedback on your work, avoid the temptation to respond immediately. The first reaction is invariably a more emotional one than how you will feel about it after a day or two. So read the comments carefully, then do something else – watch TV, go for a run, etc., and forget about it for at least 24 hours. You can then begin to concoct a response (if needed) or address the issues in your next draft. Even if you are unhappy with the comments or don't feel that they are useful, send a polite thank-you note to the person who wrote them.

Usually, you will only have the opportunity of one round of supervisory comment and written feedback on a version of the whole thesis, so try to submit a solid draft. The completer and more polished is the version you give in for advice, the more useful will be the suggestions you receive.

But if you are fortunate to be permitted a second turn of supervisory review, ensure that you incorporated all of the feedback from the first round of comments before asking for another set. There is nothing worse for a marker than to have taken the time to read a draft carefully and provide feedback only to find that the same issues are apparent in the next iteration, and the suggestions have been ignored. If you did not feel that your supervisor's comments were valuable in the first round, it is probably best not to ask them for feedback again.

If you have the opportunity to meet with your supervisor to discuss their comments after they have sent you their feedback, make sure you read and reflect on it first. You can then seek clarification for any points you don't understand.

Receiving and acting upon feedback provided on drafts of your work can lead to significant improvements in its quality. Suggestions from non-specialists can also be useful, particularly if you have a friend or family member with a good eye for spotting typos or inconsistencies in the presentation, as they are likely to be much cheaper than a professional proof-reader. People with dissimilar backgrounds will focus on different aspects of the thesis, and their varying perspectives can be instrumental in helping you to refine the work before submission.

Feel free to ask as many people for feedback as possible, but you have to want their comments and if you really don't intend to make any further changes, don't feel obliged to ask people to read the work. I have been asked numerous times to comment on a colleague's grant application or promotion documentation but later realised my suggestions had been largely ignored. Often, when people say they want feedback, they don't: they are really asking for a reassuring response that what they have already written is brilliant. Comments that would require additional work, even if well-informed and well-intentioned, are not welcome. If you don't want someone to point out the weak points in what you have done so far, then it would not be a worthwhile use of that person's time to read your draft, so don't ask them.

Be aware of the enormity of the task you are asking people to undertake. To read and provide detailed feedback on a document that is 150 or more pages long will be at least a day, and possibly quite a bit more, of full-time work to do thoroughly. Therefore, it would be entirely inappropriate to ask someone to invest that amount of time free of charge to help you out if you are not intending to reflect carefully on any comments they make and incorporate their suggestions.

12.4 Counting your words

All universities will have a formal word limit for MPhil and PhD theses. These limits are likely to be large – perhaps of the order of 80,000 to 100,000 words, which will be more than sufficient for the vast majority of students in accounting or finance.

Therefore, in most cases, students can happily ignore the limit and write whatever they wish. However, what happens if you have written in an extensive style on a discursive topic so that you are in danger of exceeding the limit? This section discusses the issues around this figure and what to do if the draft of your thesis is significantly above the boundary.

Even if you have one eye on the word limit as you are drafting, don't merely cease writing when you reach it – you still need to devote a reasonable amount of space to the other aspects, and you need to include all of the ingredients within each chapter. Getting this balance right means that you might need subsequently to cut out some of the material that you had written. Although it can feel painful to throw away precious words that you spent time writing, it is all part of honing and refining the draft to make it as clear and sharp as it can be.

In general, the word count only involves what is written in the main body of the text – so the front matter (title page, acknowledgements, table of contents, lists of tables and figures), plus the abstract, references, tables and any diagrams, would not contribute towards the number of words. However, be careful as your school might have a policy that one or more of these aspects counts.

It is good for the discussions and analysis in your thesis document to be detailed and including depth and richness, which will enhance the perceived quality of the writing. But it is a delicate balance. In general, try to write concisely and avoid excess verbiage, repetition or the inclusion of irrelevant or marginally relevant material, all of which will make the reader weary and irritated. Rather than enhancing your examiners' impression of the thesis, unnecessary wordage will probably diminish it. When, I am asked to examine a PhD and the hard copy that arrives in the post is three inches thick, it fills me with dread. No PhD needs to be that long, and remember once you pass a certain point, less is more.

12.4.1   If you write too much, will you be penalised?

Being able to produce a thesis document within a specific word limit is one of the parameters on which you are being assessed, and so if you cannot adhere to this constraint, you have failed one of the criteria. Producing a document of the right length is a skill in itself that is needed in many jobs where you need to create a report, a blog or an application with strict word constraints.

Besides, your supervisor and examiners will be involved in a wide range of roles with numerous responsibilities, and your thesis document is unnecessarily wordy, it will make their job even harder, putting them in a bad frame of mind and giving the impression that you don't care enough to write succinctly. There is little sense in making the final document longer than it needs to be. Even if you are not in danger of exceeding the word limit, superfluous material will generate no additional benefits and may be a detractor.

Despite the above advice, it is implausible that your PhD examiners will count the number of words you write in your thesis, and especially if you submit it in hard copy or as a pdf, that would be quite challenging and time-consuming for them to do. So it is likely that they will use some discretion in determining whether you have exceeded the word limit, leaving you with a margin of error to play with. Therefore, if you slightly exceed the word limit, you probably have little to worry about.

But if you vastly exceed the limit, or your writing is repetitive or boring, including material that is not relevant to the topic, then there is a high chance that you will be asked to reduce the length in your corrections. For the most extreme breaches, it could be fatal, where the examiners refuse to read the document, in which case, you would be asked to revise it and resubmit a shorter version. Therefore, it is essential that you do not exceed the word limit by more than a trivial amount.

12.4.2 What to do if you are over the word limit

If you have written too much, try to edit the draft down by removing the least important parts, moving material to an appendix or presenting it in a tabular or graphical form if these do not count towards the number of words. Even if you are not over the word limit, it is still worth making sure that the draft does not include any redundant material. It is mentally hard to do this – throwing away words that you might have spent a long time writing is painful. I share your pain, but you need to employ the economic concept of a sunk cost: you cannot get back the time you already spent on superfluous writing, so just focus on the way to make your thesis the best it can be, and this might well imply making it shorter. Many people feel similarly despondent at cutting away material that they worked hard to write, but it is better to consider pruning your document as an opportunity to make the writing sharper, more concise, of greater relevance, and therefore more pleasant to read. If that means cutting words out and deleting them, then do it because your examiners will be more impressed if your work is succinct and readable. The time spent writing the original material was not wasted since it helped you get to the version you have now.

Whenever you remove parts from the draft, ensure that what remains still makes sense and that the argument flows. Ideally, you would read again in their entireties all sections where you have made edits.

What you should do about an excess of words depends on how far over the boundary you are and how much time you have to work on the edits. I suggest the following courses of action:

- If you only need to trim a small number of words and have sufficient time available, you could read through the entire draft (again) line-by-line, adjusting sentences to make them more concise and remove any redundancy. Delete any sentences or blocks of text that are not needed or repeat something you already wrote in a previous section

- If you need to take away many words, or you only have a relatively short time available to do it, it is unlikely that you will be able to make sufficient changes line-by-line in the time available, so you need to be more aggressive in taking away whole paragraphs or, possibly, entire sections or sub-sections

- An obvious first place to look is the literature review since this chapter often tends to be longer than necessary in proportion to the rest of the document. Are there any parts of the review that could be removed altogether without significantly diminishing the chapter's quality? Are there models, theories or concepts that are only marginally relevant and could therefore be eliminated?
- Are there any significant repetitions across sections or chapters that could be stripped out or trimmed? For example, if you summarise the results in the introductory and concluding chapters, consider shortening these just to cover the core points
- Consider whether any material could be moved to appendices (assuming that these do not count towards the word limit, which they usually do not, but check the guidelines). For example, if you have derived a model or described your survey or your data in detail, these sorts of purely descriptive materials can fit well in appendices. Similarly, tables of variable definitions can be placed in an appendix as discussed above.

12.4.3 What to do if you believe that your thesis is short

Bear in mind that the word limit is usually precisely that – it is an upper constraint and not a target. If you have written somewhat less than this figure, your thesis is probably of about the right length. For example, if the limit is 80,000 words and you have written 60,000 or more, you will likely be within the range that your supervisor and examiners will expect. Provided that the thesis also includes all of the required elements, and each chapter is an appropriate proportion of the complete document, there is no need for undue concern about the overall length.

However, it might make your work look thin and feeble if your thesis is very much shorter than this figure. Remember that a thesis should be commensurate with the work of three years' full-time study and a document that is excessively brief might fail to give the impression that it meets this criterion.

So, if the word limit is, say, 80,000 words again, then a draft of 30,000 words might be considered inadequate, and you could think of it as an opportunity to add depth to your arguments and analysis if you have the time remaining. In such a situation, some remedial action is needed:

- A first step is to ensure that you have included all of the required elements listed in section 11.3 of this book. If any key aspect is missing, this will provide a relatively fast way to increase the word count
- Ideally, you would go back through the whole draft to identify chapters or sections that are insufficiently detailed or where your treatment has been cursory and then expand these parts. Your writing should be detailed throughout with a depth of argument rather than skimming over the surface. For example, when you analyse the results or provide suggestions for further research, don't just offer short bullet points but thoroughly explain your

reasoning

- When PhD dissertations are brief, it is usually because the critical or evaluative parts are limited all over the document rather than a specific individual section being missing
- If your supervisor will be reading a draft, you could highlight to them that your work is currently on the short side, and they might have suggestions for which aspects should be expanded upon or further developed
- If you have placed any material in appendices, consider moving it into the main body to bulk up the latter
- As a final strategy, if you have gone through the list above and been unable to increase the word count sufficiently, or there is no time left to write a significant amount of new detail, you might consider whether it is possible to adapt the presentation of the document to give the impression of it being more substantive than it actually is. Such a step is really a last resort, but you could:
  - Use block paragraphs with line spaces between rather than tab indents
  - Ensure that each chapter starts on a fresh page
  - Slightly increase the margin sizes
  - Slightly increase the font size
  - Spread the pages out so that, for example, each table or figure is on a separate page with large section and chapter headings
  - Spread the references so that there is a line space between each one
  - Add a table of contents, list of tables and list of figures, each on their own page

In each case, take care not to make it evident that you are spreading the work out to make it look bigger than it actually is since this is slightly deceitful. So do not, for example, increase the font size to 14, which will make your deliberate repackaging job too visible.

12.5   Pre-submission checklist

There now follows a list of points that you can tick off to ensure that you have covered all of the main features that need to be in the thesis. If there are any elements of the inventory below that you are unsure about whether you have incorporated or not, then check back through that chapter or section and add to it or redraft as necessary.

Front matter
- Is your title clear, relevant and succinct?
- Have you included an acknowledgements section that recognises the role of everyone who contributed to the PhD, including your supervisor?
- Have you included a table of contents?
- Is your abstract of the right length, comprising a summary of all aspects of the thesis, including the topic, main aims, methods used, key findings and

conclusions?

- Is the thesis divided into suitable chapters and sections, with the appropriate material in each area?

Introduction

- Does your introductory chapter motivate your work and put it into context?
- Have you explained why your study is needed, and what is interesting and original about it?
- Have you briefly stated the aims?
- Have you provided an outline of the rest of the thesis?

Literature review

- Have you conducted a literature review summarising relevant studies from the existing body of work?
- Have you critically evaluated the work rather than just presenting it descriptively?
- Have you directed the writing of the review towards your aims and what you want to achieve in your thesis?
- Have you used a wide range of sources, including published and unpublished academic studies as well as popular or blog pieces?
- Have you summarised what is known, and have you identified gaps in the existing literature?

Methods and data

In each investigative chapter:

- How you stated your research aims and justified an appropriate methodology to achieve them?
- Have you explained the data collection approach and thoroughly described the data before embarking on a more detailed analysis?
- Are the methods and data explained with sufficient detail and clarity that another researcher could replicate the results?
- Have you explained any notation, equations or technical terms that you have included?

Results

In each investigative chapter:

- Do your results conform with the research aims that you established in a previous section?
- Have you used a varied presentation style for the results as far as possible, including both tables and charts or graphs?
- Have you discussed all of your tables of results thoroughly, explaining how they relate to your aims and objectives?
- Have you related your findings to the existing literature?
- Are your tables and figures tidy and self-explanatory with titles and notes?

- Is the volume of investigative work in your thesis commensurate with three years' full-time study?

Conclusions

- Have you written a concluding chapter that restates your aims and summarises your findings?
- Have you presented some ideas for future research?
- Have you reflected on the limitations of your chosen methods and data?
- Have you outlined any implications from your findings for non-academic user groups?

References and appendices

- Have you cited every piece of existing work upon which you have relied?
- Is there a 1:1 mapping between the work cited in the body text and listed in the references section?
- Are the references listed in alphabetical order by author surname with all details entered for every reference (including volume and page numbers for journals and place of publication for books)?
- If appendices are included, are they relevant and referred to in the main body of the document?

12.5.1   What to do if you find a study similar to yours

Suppose that you are just about to submit your thesis, and you find an existing article or thesis that has done precisely the same thing. Do you need to start again? This is an unfortunate situation. Some students worry a lot about this possibility, throughout their registration period, but it is a surprisingly rare occurrence. Before panicking, look again. It is unlikely that the existing research is identical to your own. Perhaps the models, geographical coverage, sample period, or the interpretations of the results are different. You should acknowledge in your thesis any research that was in the public domain before you finished yours. It might be tempting, but it would be dangerous, to just ignore this research and pretend that you had not spotted it. To do so would be dishonest; if your supervisor or examiners became aware of the existing study, it would highlight that your literature search had been deficient. Worse, it could even lead to an accusation of plagiarism if it was argued that you used ideas in the other study without giving its author(s) due credit.

But when drafting your write-up, look for and emphasise the differences between the two pieces of work, not the similarities. Try to differentiate your research from that study as much as possible. In the unlikely event that there really is little distinction between the two pieces, ask your supervisor for urgent advice. Rather than abandoning it entirely straight away, try to see if it could be re-worked or modified and improved slightly to build on the existing study, which would be much simpler and less time consuming than starting over.

12.6   Thesis submission

Just as some students struggle to start their research, others struggle to stop. Some people find it hard to know when to stop the investigative part of their work and get to the tidying up stage. Others agonise excessively over the writing, forever shifting the text around and redrafting. While it is always possible to make a piece of work better by working longer on it, there comes the point when further work on the thesis seems unnecessary – either because it is almost as good as it can be without starting again, or because time has run out and the end of registration or submission deadline looms. Therefore, you will need to learn to judge when you are at this point and resist any temptation to tinker further with the draft. It will probably not be the final report you ever write, and for that reason, nor is it likely to be the best, so spend a proportionate amount of time polishing the draft and no more.

It is OK to submit your PhD dissertation well before the deadline if it is finished. But once that is done, you will have no opportunities for any changes, so you need to be confident that you could not spend any of the remaining time doing further checks or obtaining and incorporating additional feedback. Remember: finance teaches us that options have value, and if you submit your thesis considerably before the deadline, you are freely surrendering an option to do more work on it.

12.6.1   How do you know when your PhD is ready to submit?

By the time you have produced a complete draft of your thesis and have received comments on all aspects of it from your supervisor and others, you should have a pretty good idea of the standard of exposition and presentation that is incorporated in other theses produced by former students in the department who have already completed their doctorates and passed.

Your supervisor's guidance that the thesis is in a sufficiently completed and polished form that it can be presented for the examination should provide you with confidence that you are ready as their experiences with other students (and, for junior staff, their own PhD) will place them in a solid position to judge your work.

If your supervisor suggests that the thesis is not yet ready for submission, then it is usually best to heed their advice and develop a plan with them for further work on the document with a timetable to completion. However, technically, it is usually permissible within an institution's rules for students to submit their thesis for examination without their supervisor's support. As indicated, this would be a risky course of action and not recommended unless there was no other choice – such as when the maximum registration period has been reached with no opportunity for (further) extension.

If the clock has run down and you are pushing close to the maximum registration period, you might have no choice but to stop any additional investigative work and write up what you have done, preparing as quickly as possible for submission. If you get into that position, it would be better to produce a slightly rough but complete draft rather than omitting key sections entirely or failing to meet the deadline and running the risk of deregistration and having to leave the university with nothing.

It might be possible to obtain an extension of registration to buy you more time to finish the thesis, and universities are usually sympathetic to students who have used their best endeavours and worked consistently but for some legitimate reason have not quite been able to complete within the standard timeframe. After all, forcing out a student who has been at the university for four years and is very close to completion is not in anyone's best interest.

If you need more time, do complete the necessary forms to request it, explaining any extenuating circumstances, but ensure that you do so well before the deadline rather than leaving it until the last minute. For instance, if you had particular challenges in gathering data or obtaining software, or illness or bereavement had affected your progress for a period during your registration, these can all be listed (with evidence) as mitigations. As always, your supervisor or the Director of the PhD programme will be able to provide further guidance, so discuss any request for an extension with them before formally requesting it.

Further reading

- Despite the title, the book by Ide (2013) is actually more a book about good grammar and writing style than proof-reading *per se*, although it could nonetheless be handy
- The book by Hampton (2019) provides many useful exercises to train you to identify common typographical errors in writing
- Similarly, Evans (2013) is a good general guide on how to proof-read, including examples and exercises

Chapter takeaways – top tips for success

- ⊛ Save plenty of time for final refinement and polishing at the end, which invariably takes longer than expected
- ⊛ Pay particular attention to the title, abstract, the start of the introduction, and the conclusions since these will remain at the forefront of the reader's mind yet are often the weakest aspects of a thesis
- ⊛ Make sure that the document is typo-, grammatical error- and spelling error-free: pay a proof-reader to do the checking if necessary
- ⊛ Try to include an appropriate number of tables and figures: too few makes the thesis look thin, while too many may become repetitive
- ⊛ Ensure that you remain within, or only just over, the word or page limit
- ⊛ Check that your thesis contains all of the required elements
- ⊛ Ask for feedback from as many people as possible. Reflect on their comments, incorporate any suggestions for improvements but don't take criticism to heart

13. YOUR VIVA VOCE EXAMINATION

Learning outcomes: this chapter covers

✓ How to prepare for your viva voce exam
✓ What will happen during the viva
✓ How to act in the viva
✓ Possible outcomes from the exam

13.1 Pre-submission: choice of examiners

In the UK system, all students must undergo a viva voce (oral exam) after submitting their thesis to the university. There will be two examiners, one from within the university at which the candidate is studying (the internal examiner) and another from a different university (the external examiner). Both the examiners have an equal role in determining the outcome.

The external examiner will usually be a senior academic (a Senior Lecturer, Associate Professor or Full Professor) who is an acknowledged expert in the candidate's research field, broadly defined. They will be experienced in both supervising and examining doctoral candidates and will have published in respected journals, although possibly not on the precise thesis topic. The internal examiner might have conducted fewer vivas, and it could be their first time in that role, although equally, they might be a highly experienced full professor. Both examiners will likely be familiar with the high-level methodological approach taken in the thesis – for example, in terms of the use of qualitative versus quantitative techniques, surveys, interviews or empirical analysis of secondary data.

The candidate's supervisor(s) will usually select appropriate examiners after discussing the possibilities with the candidate. Sometimes students worry excessively about the choice of examiners, but it is usually best to have some faith in your supervisor's judgement. As a supervisor, I have always selected examiners that I knew personally, and I respected on both professional and personal levels for my students, and I am sure the overwhelming majority of others would do the same. The supervisor would then approach the selected examiners to ensure that they are willing to serve in that role.

Next, there will be a process to formally nominate and appoint the examiners who have been chosen. This procedure usually involves the supervisor completing a form well before the thesis is submitted, detailing the examiners' backgrounds and experiences and explaining why they are appropriate to examine the work. A committee will then review the form, which can either approve or reject the examining team. Usually, an experienced supervisor would not select examiners that were not appropriate for the job, and therefore approval is by far the most likely decision.

Candidates are ordinarily free to submit their thesis at any point between the minimum and maximum registration periods, which are usually three and four years, respectively, for full-time students. Special permission will be required to submit before the minimum or to extend registration beyond the maximum. Typically, students only need to submit their thesis within the maximum registration period, and therefore it is not necessary to have undertaken the viva exam within that period. The university registry will only send the thesis out to the examiners after the latter have been approved by the relevant committee, and the nomination and approval process might take some time (possibly several weeks) to complete. Therefore, to ensure that there are no delays between submission and distribution of the thesis, it is worth completing this procedure well before the intended submission date.

One final point to make in passing is that when you know who your examiners will be, go to their web pages and determine whether they have written any studies relevant to your thesis. If they have, ensure that you cite these studies: a bit of flattery by noting the relevance of your examiners' work will put them in a good mood when reflecting on your document and will also suggest to them that you have searched carefully for relevant literature. However, when citing in your thesis work conducted by your examiners, considerable care is required not to be excessively critical. To ensure that this does not happen, re-read the thesis before it is finalised and cast in a neutral or positive light any relevant work they have authored.

13.2 After submission

This is it. You have finally submitted your thesis, and the viva has been scheduled. It's an exciting milestone, and now you are getting closer to your goal of obtaining the qualification. The viva is a fantastic opportunity to discuss your research with two specially selected experts on the subject who will have read the document carefully and want to know more about the thesis. It is truly a once-in-a-lifetime opportunity. Yet it is an experience that many, perhaps even most, candidates absolutely dread. Preparing well and knowing what to expect will help to build your confidence, and the rest of this chapter is devoted to precisely that objective.

The viva is typically held around two to three months after submission of the thesis, although it could be within a month while other less fortunate candidates have to wait longer – perhaps even four months. The timing will depend mainly on the examiners' availability as the exam must be scheduled around their other commitments while allowing adequate time for them to read the document and draft their preliminary reports.

Viva voce exams were invariably held face-to-face until the advent of the covid-19 pandemic when they moved on-line. At the time of writing, it is not clear whether on-line vivas will be permitted to continue once the pandemic has subsided and restrictions on movement have been removed.

Following the viva, the examiners will draft a joint, final report that outlines their views on the thesis, how the candidate performed in the oral exam, and their recommendation regarding whether the degree should be awarded. In their report form, the examiners will typically be asked to confirm that the:

- Work submitted is commensurate with three years of full-time study for a PhD or two years for an MPhil
- Abstract of the thesis is acceptable
- Candidate is aware of how their work fits into the wider body of literature
- Candidate has made an original contribution to knowledge through their research
- Candidate has selected, designed and conducted a programme of independent research
- Thesis contains material that is suitable for publication, possibly following modifications

Usually, the internal examiner will discuss any modifications required of the thesis directly with the candidate, who will then usually communicate with the examiner(s) once these changes to the work have been made. If the candidate does not submit the revised version of the thesis to the examiners within the required timescale, the former would not be awarded the degree.

There can only be a single outcome following the viva, and therefore the examiners must reach an agreement and make a joint decision. Such a consensus has always been possible in every case I have been involved with, both as an examiner and supervisor. Still, if this could not happen, the university would appoint an independent adjudicator (in effect, a second external examiner) to read the thesis and the original examiners' reports and make their own recommendation of the result. Also, unlike many other European countries, PhDs in the UK are not graded, they either pass (possibly after some required modifications) or fail.

13.2.1   The purpose of a viva

The viva voce exam is compulsory, and every PhD student must undertake one before they can be awarded the doctorate. The only situation where a viva would not take place is where the examiners were certain that the thesis would fail and therefore undergoing the oral exam would be pointless.

The viva is an essential part of the process, and therefore you should try to make the most of the experience and get as much as you can from it. The exam has two primary purposes:

1. To check that the work is your own. If you had purchased either the whole thesis of large parts of it from someone else rather than undertaking the work yourself, you would not be able to answer unseen, detailed and specialist questions about the material. Therefore, a viva is a quick way to identify a severe form of plagiarism

2. The viva is sometimes called the 'oral defence' for a good reason since its other core motivation is to enable the examiners to seek clarification points. When the examiners read the work, some parts may puzzle them regarding the approaches you used and the methodological choices you made. It might be that your techniques were appropriate but, perhaps, you had not explained them as well in the thesis as you could have done, or possibly the examiners' knowledge of these specifics is patchy. Questioning you on these aspects will help the examiners determine whether the thesis has reached the required standard, whether further work is needed first, or whether it is a lost cause so that it could not be made to reach that standard even with considerable additional effort.

13.2.2   Who will be present in the oral exam?

In the UK system, viva voce exams are conducted in private. Therefore, the attendees will be the candidate, the internal examiner, and the external examiner only. Some institutions also require a chair to be present, whose role is to ensure that the university's processes are adhered to. This individual would also advise on rules if something is unclear, and they would complete the paperwork at the end and submit it to the university.

Both the internal and external examiners will usually have research interests fairly closely matching the subject matter of the thesis, but the chair might be from another department within the university and is typically a senior and experienced member of staff. They need not be knowledgeable about the subject, will not have read the thesis document, and will not participate in the questioning.

If there is no requirement at a particular institution for there to be a chair (sometimes known as a convenor) at the viva, these responsibilities would be taken up by the internal examiner. The latter would then have a dual role: to act as an examiner of the thesis and ensure that due process is followed and that the examination stays on track, treating the candidate fairly. The external examiner will usually adopt the primary interrogator role, asking the bulk of the questions, and driving the process.

It is the convention at some universities for a candidate's supervisor to be present at the viva. If that is the case, they are there as non-participant observers only, and they will not be permitted to do or say anything, for instance, by helping the candidate answer challenging questions. The supervisor is not routinely invited to the viva at most institutions but may be permitted to attend at the candidate's request and if the examiners allow it. If a candidate has two supervisors, it would be excessive for both to be there.

My view is that having a supervisor present at a viva is neither necessary nor helpful. The fact that they are present but unable to participate can be frustrating for all parties and may make the candidate feel even more nervous rather than at ease. The viva is the candidate's big chance to shine as an independent researcher and to represent their work. This is the time for PhD students to emerge from their supervisor's shadow and stand on their own two feet.

13.2.3 How to prepare for the oral exam

Find out whether the examiners require you to make a presentation, either with a slide deck or just speaking with a few notes. Alternatively, they may wish to jump straight into the questions. The examiners are in charge, so allow them to choose themselves rather than making an assumption and running the risk of getting off to a bad start.

Take a paper copy of the thesis to the viva with identical pagination to the version the examiners have (so that if they say, 'can you explain the first paragraph on page 39,' your p.39 will be the same as theirs). It would help if you also took a pen and a pad to note any points you need to remember about what is discussed.

If you are not feeling confident about the viva or are unsure what to expect, ask your supervisor whether it is possible to arrange a 'mock viva'. This practice could be set up like the real thing, where two people from the department (who could be your supervisor, other staff members or even PhD students) would ask you questions to simulate the kind of experience you will have in the real thing.

Try to find out about your examiners (both internal and external) regarding their backgrounds and research areas. I always tell my students to look particularly carefully for papers relevant to the thesis that either of the examiners has written, which can then be cited in the PhD. The examiners will be pleased (and flattered) that you have found their work to be sufficiently germane to reference in your document. Knowing a bit about the examiners might give you a general idea about the areas of the thesis or the kinds of questions they will focus on, and it will also help you make polite conversation before or after the viva.

The most effective way of preparing is to ensure that you know your thesis very well. Given that the work has been completed over several years, and then the viva often takes place two or three months after the document is submitted, candidates have sometimes forgotten the details of what they did and why, especially the parts they completed earlier during their registration period. Hence you might need to re-familiarise yourself with the details of the techniques and models you used, how you implemented them, and their advantages and disadvantages. It is very awkward if an examiner asks the candidate about a part of the work, and the latter cannot remember doing or writing that.

Re-read the thesis from cover to cover, at least a couple of times close to the viva date. As you are doing so, think about how and why you made the choices you did in terms of the data and methods you used and how you implemented them. Also, reflect on what you consider to be the thesis' strengths and weaknesses and what you might have done differently. It seems likely that the examiners will ask you these sorts of high-level questions, and so it is worth preparing possible responses to them.

However, I would suggest not bothering to re-read much of the underlying literature unless there are one or two core studies that underpin everything you are doing. The amount of background research is simply too vast for that to be feasible, and in any case, the examiners will want to ask you about your work and your ideas, not somebody else's.

I would also suggest that it is pointless to try to predict what questions the examiners will ask you about the detail of the work. If, before the viva, you made a list of the questions you expect to be asked, and after the viva, you made another list of the questions that you were asked, the two sets would have almost nothing in common. The examiners will be at a different stage of their academic career, with dissimilar backgrounds and expertise than you, so they will not approach the material in the same way.

Ultimately, the viva is a bit like a job interview in the sense that you will need to be able to 'think on your feet' to some extent, providing informative and insightful answers to questions that you had not had the opportunity to prepare in advance. This is a skill that you can improve with practice, and that also benefits from being confident and knowledgeable about the thesis.

Some candidates identify, note, and print a list of typos and other errors they spotted after submitting the thesis, which they then hand to the examiners at the beginning of the viva. I think this is a terrible idea. Not only would it make you appear sloppy (why didn't you read it more carefully before submission?), but you will be deliberately identifying mistakes that the examiners might not have spotted. By all means, make such a list but keep it to yourself and quietly fix any errors before submitting the final version after the viva.

What to wear

It may be safest to err on the side of formality, but smart-casual dress is fine. It is vital that you feel comfortable as this will help you to be at ease. I stopped wearing a suit and tie years ago unless I really have to. Even for formal meetings and interviews, I wear a shirt and jacket (with jeans if I can get away with it) but no tie. In my opinion, it is fine for candidates to do similarly, but jeans and a T-shirt might shock the examiners and create the impression that you didn't care enough about the viva to make a minimal effort.

13.2.4 What happens during the viva?

The lengths of viva voce exams vary enormously, but most are between an hour and a half and three hours in total. A longer exam generally occurs if the examiners have read the document exceptionally carefully and have numerous questions; it does not necessarily mean that they have identified many problems that will require further work from the PhD student.

If the candidate is making a presentation, they will usually do that first. If you are giving a presentation, it is vital that you stick within any time limit you have been told – if you go over, it might put the examiners in a lousy frame of mind from the outset, which would be counterproductive. The presentation need not be extensive or detailed: remember, your examiners will (usually) have read the thesis in considerable detail, so there is no need to tell them again what they already know.

The presentation needs to summarise your entire thesis but emphasising your original contributions, which is the most vital aspect to get across. If your thesis involves three investigative chapters, you could have a slide or two that motivate the general subject matter followed by, perhaps, two or three slides on each of the empirical or theoretical chapters, and then two for conclusions and recommendations. So maybe 12 slides in total for a 20-minute talk.

The examiners might ask questions during the presentation or come back to specific points afterwards for follow-up queries. If a presentation was not required, the first question is likely to be along the lines of, 'can you please start by spending around five minutes summarising your thesis and explaining your original contribution.' The examiners will probably let you get through that talk uninterrupted, and again there could be follow-up questions on what you just said. Being able to articulate what you wrote your thesis on and what was novel about it is probably the very most important thing to do during the viva.

Next, they are likely to ask a few general questions relating to the subject matter or thesis as a whole. For example:

- What motivated you to work on this subject?
- What do you consider to be the strengths and weaknesses of the thesis?
- Which aspect do you believe constitutes your best work, and why?
- If you were starting to work on the thesis all over again, what would you have done differently?
- What software or code did you use to estimate the models in the thesis, and did you write it yourself?
- Have you attempted to publish any aspects of the work, and what kinds of journals have you targeted, or will you target?

After that, the bulk of the time in the viva will be spent going through each chapter with the examiners alternating in firing questions at you. These questions will relate to:

- Why you made certain choices rather than others in terms of the models and data you used
- Where some aspects are unclear, and they do not understand what you mean
- Where something looks amiss, and they think you might have made an error
- Where your findings are at odds with those of existing studies that they are aware of

Finally, at the end of the viva, there might be further broad questions that relate to your concluding chapter:

- Overall, what are the most important things you found?
- If you had another year to work on the thesis, what would you do?
- How could users outside of the academy employ your findings?
- What are the consequences of your work for what scholars know about the subject?
- Are there implications for other academic research on this topic?

How to act in the viva

Try to remain calm and polite. Remember that even if the examiners are eminent and highly experienced, you are still the premier expert on your thesis: you know more about it than the examiners, even if they know more about the subject defined more widely.

Good examiners will never be disparaging, but they will push the questioning to the limits of your knowledge so expect a harsh interrogation that challenges you. Even if you cannot answer every question confidently and fluently, this is entirely expectable and means that the examiners are doing their job thoroughly, not that you are doing yours badly.

When answering questions, avoid one word or one sentence responses and add as much relevant detail as possible. But pick up on the cues to know when you have said enough, and the examiners want to move onto their next question. Saying too little or too much in response to each question are both undesirable. If you don't know the answer to a particular problem, then don't be afraid to say that, and if you are hazarding a guess, explain that too. It is also acceptable to pause for a short while after a question before responding.

Try to have a structure for your answers. For example, if there are several possible explanations of a result you found, go through them logically one-by-one rather than in a haphazard fashion, and start each point with an overview before going into the details.

Most of the time, examiners put considerable effort into reading a thesis and writing their reports: I usually expect to spend two to three entire days doing this. Given their care and attention, you owe it to your examiners not to be summarily dismissive of their points. Occasionally, they will make ill-founded and possibly even nonsensical suggestions; in such instances, let them down gently. Politely explain, with evidence if possible, why your understanding of the issue is different from theirs. If you aggressively contest every point the examiners make, they will wonder why they bothered to read the thesis. Your work will not improve – either now or in the future – if you ignore informed feedback from subject experts who have read it very carefully. They could also take offence and become more aggressive too in their lines of questioning, being less sympathetic to any flaws in your work.

On the other hand, I have experienced vivas where the candidate has smiled and nodded at every point the examiners made. Being so passive is also a mistake: it is important to challenge them when they make a point with which you disagree. Contesting such issues might limit the number of changes you are asked to make to the thesis after the viva. For instance, if the examiners suggest, 'you used model X, but actually model Y would have been more appropriate for the type of data you have, wouldn't it?' and your response is, 'well, I suppose so.' But if actually, you are confident that your approach has been vindicated in another study that the examiners might not be aware of and you missed an opportunity to put them straight politely, they might ask you to have a try at model Y as part of the 'corrections' to the thesis before it is finally approved. This outcome would imply you would be required to undertake unnecessary work that you might have been able to avoid, which would be a waste of your time.

Towards the end of the viva, the examiners are likely to ask whether you have any questions for them. It is fine to ask them for advice about making your work better, and whether they have any useful tips on what needs to be done to get it up to the standard for publication in a good journal and where they would suggest you send it. They might well be providing the answers to such questions as the viva proceeds anyway. They might ask you about your career ambitions and whether you plan to remain in the academy or seek a position in the commercial sector or a central bank, etc., if you have not already secured a post.

13.2.5 Possible outcomes

Once the questions have drawn to a close, the examiners will ask you to leave the room while they discuss the thesis, your performance in the viva, and what the outcome should be. Stay reasonably close by rather than retreating to the other side of the building. Mostly, the examiners will agree and can reach a decision within a few minutes. Occasionally, it may take longer if one of them has a more negative view of the work than the other and believes that a different outcome would be appropriate. Even in such circumstances, they can usually find some common ground and settle on a particular result. At that point, they will call you back into the room and inform you of their joint decision. Technically, the examiners only make a recommendation to the University Senate, but in reality, this recommendation will virtually never be overturned.

The possible outcomes are:

1. Pass – the thesis is acceptable as it is, and no changes are required. You can

print the final, hard-bound copies immediately.

2. Minor amendments – the thesis requires minor modifications to be undertaken by the candidate, and the internal examiner only will usually check the revised thesis. The changes might include small redrafting, adding further explanations, fixing typos or minor errors. Three months will usually be given to complete the additional work.

3. Major amendments – the thesis requires more significant revisions before it is reconsidered. This will be the case if, for instance, there are substantial errors in some of the empirical work that require re-estimation, the volume of investigative work is deemed insufficient so that an additional chapter is needed, or the thesis requires a substantial rewriting as the current drafting is weak. For this outcome, the candidate will usually be given at least six months and possibly an additional year to complete it. Both examiners will likely need to sign off on the revised version. The examiners might also have the option to request that the candidate undergoes a further viva voce examination.

4. MPhil – the thesis work is not of a sufficient standard to award a PhD and could not be brought up to the requirement with even an additional year of full-time study, and therefore an MPhil, which is a lesser award, is recommended. Usually, this would be the case where the volume of investigative work fell well short of what would be commensurate with three years of full-time study, or the original contribution is deemed insufficient.

5. Fail – the quality of the work in the thesis is not worthy of even an MPhil award. The thesis could be excessively brief, there might be little novelty, or the work contains fatal errors. It could not be redeemed with even a further year of full-time study.

The second outcome in the above list is by far the most common. As a very rough guess, I would suggest that perhaps 70% of students get this outcome, with 15% receiving a straight pass and the remaining 15% getting one of the final three results.

Failure is (almost) not an option

As for a presentation or job interview, feeling somewhat nervous about the viva is both natural and useful to focus your mind and energy on the task. It is normal for students to be apprehensive about their oral exam since, after all, a lot is riding on the outcome of this one discussion. Candidates might fear that three or more years of work will have been wasted if they blow it.

However, the odds of a successful outcome are very heavily stacked in your favour. Your supervisor will likely have chosen someone they respect, and they know to make reasonable and fair judgements as the external examiner. Although the external examiner is usually paid specifically to undertake the task, the sum is a trivial, token amount, and the internal examiner won't be paid anything in addition to their normal salary. Therefore, examiners typically act in that capacity as a favour to the supervisor and as a service to the profession. Often, professor X will be the examiner of a student for whom professor Y is the supervisor, and then at some point in the future the two academics will swap roles when Y examines X's student.

If the viva result is that the candidate fails or is given an unduly difficult time, no goodwill is built between the examiners and the supervisor. In that case, the examiners will have done a job that turned out to be unpleasant, very poorly paid, and made them a potential enemy. The internal examiner will usually be a member of the same department as the supervisor and will find it awkward to work with the supervisor again if the former fails a student of the latter. So why would the examiners bother to examine a thesis and then fail it? Usually, if a prospective examiner thought that a thesis might not be strong enough to pass, they would decline to examine it.

By the same token, it is extremely rare for examiners to require the candidate to undergo another viva exam. Unless they had very strong reservations about the quality of the work or concerns that the candidate had not written it themselves that had not been allayed during the first viva, they would be reluctant to go through the process again, which would constitute significant additional work with no benefit for them.

Candidates do fail occasionally, but it is extremely rare and usually the result of a perfect storm where several things go wrong simultaneously, including:

- The thesis being on the weak side
- The candidate being aggressive or unwilling to answer the examiners' questions in detail during the viva
- One or both of the examiners is particularly unsympathetic due to some serious external, personal factors unrelated to the candidate, the supervisor or thesis (e.g., amid a messy divorce – this explanation might have raised your eyebrows but I have seen this situation a couple of times).

Even in the implausible scenario when a candidate 'fails' and the examiners recommend no award, usually the former will have the opportunity to work on the thesis for a further year and to resubmit it then to be reconsidered by a new set of examiners. If we add to this that a supervisor will only support the submission of a thesis when they believe it is ready and overwhelmingly likely to pass, there are many reasons why PhD candidates almost never fail at the viva stage. I hope that this section has inspired confidence that you too will pass when you reach this stage, although you might have a little more work to do.

Handling your corrections

As discussed above, the most likely outcome from the viva is that you will 'pass with corrections' – hopefully, these will be minor rather than major, but either way, the approach to dealing with them would be the same. Usually, your internal examiner would e-mail you a single, consolidated list that details the work that both examiners require and you might also receive this formally from the university along with a letter explaining the viva outcome and telling you how long you have to complete the additional tasks. Pay close attention to the deadline for resubmitting the thesis as there is a danger that your registration could be terminated with no degree awarded if you exceed it without approval.

It is best to treat the required modifications as you would the referee report from a journal: go through each point individually, and as you make the corrections, also prepare a document that re-iterates each point and provides your response to it, explaining what changes or additions you have made to the thesis document. For example, the comment might be, 'the literature review in chapter 3 is dated. The candidate should cite some of the recent work on environmental accounting such as X (2019), Y (2020) and Z (2021)...' Then your response could be, 'I would like to thank the examiners for pointing this out. I have thoroughly reviewed the latest developments in this area, and have added a whole page of additional review on p.73 of the revised version of the thesis.' You could also copy and paste the new material into your responses document.

You would repeat this for every point that the examiners make. If there are some comments that you do not agree with – for instance, if you believe the examiners have misunderstood a particular point and therefore their suggestion is not necessary, then your response can state and explain this. But tread carefully, since you don't want to cause offence or run the risk of having to do a further round of corrections because the examiner(s) was(were) not happy with your efforts after the first round. If a particular point requires only a minimal amount of effort on your part, it is often easier just to do what is asked rather than argue why it is not necessary. If, however, you are intending to contest any of the points, it would be worthwhile to obtain advice from your supervisor about how to handle the situation before making a final decision on not doing some of the work that has been requested. It would also be good practice to ask them to read through the revised parts of the thesis and your responses to the examiners' comments before you send these on.

Once you have completed the corrections and prepared a response document as well as updating the thesis, and obtained supervisory approval of them, the two documents can be e-mailed to the internal examiner with a polite thank you for their time in reviewing the thesis. The usual outcome would be that they will reply within a few days (although it could be much longer if they are very busy and wish to go through the revised thesis meticulously) and hopefully they will be satisfied with what you have done, in which case they will write to the university to state that. You will then be able to submit the revised, final version of the thesis and graduate.

Chapter takeaways – top tips for success

⊛ Identify and read any papers by your examiners related to the topic of your thesis
⊛ Find out whether a presentation will be required at the start of the viva and if so, how long you will have. Keep it short and focused on your contributions
⊛ Ensure that you are very familiar with all the contents in your thesis but there is no need to re-review the literature

Chapter takeaways – continued

- ⊛ Answer questions with an appropriate amount of detail
- ⊛ Don't be dismissive of the examiners' questions, but equally, point out any instances where they appear to have a misunderstanding
- ⊛ Prepare of the viva but don't worry or panic – you are very much more likely to pass than fail!

14. PRESENTING AND PUBLISHING

Learning outcomes: this chapter covers

✓ How to prepare and deliver excellent research presentations
✓ Why, where, and how to publish your work
✓ Preparing thesis chapters for publication
✓ Writing for practitioner magazines and newspapers
✓ Refereeing journal submissions

14.1 Why give research presentations?

Presenting at a conference is a fantastic experience. Although you will probably be nervous, particularly before you start, if you are well prepared and practised, the anxieties will soon give way to confidence. If you attend a conference without giving a presentation, it is hard to meet people – coffee breaks, lunch, and dinners are your only opportunity. Even then, it is an uphill struggle because nobody will know you. But if you give a talk, you will be a centre of attention for the rest of the event, and people will want to come over and chat with you about your work. Enjoy the fame while it lasts, for it will be fleeting, but it is much easier to build a lasting network of contacts if people see you talking at the front of the room than if you were an anonymous figure in the audience. Use the opportunity to maximally engage with others, get their details, send them follow-up e-mails, try to stay in touch and reintroduce yourself if you see them at a subsequent event.

14.1.1 Selecting conferences

In addition to getting feedback on your research, attending conferences is a valuable experience for junior researchers to learn more about the latest developments and connect with others working in the same research area. As well as the material, when you attend a conference, reflect on how the presenter has delivered their talk. When you have seen a few of these, you will get to know which styles seem to work, and you can emulate their best practices when preparing and delivering your own talks:

- What sort of talk works well?
- What slide designs come across clearly?
- How did the speaker deal with tricky or irrelevant questions?
- How did they cope when something unexpectedly went wrong?

The number of academic conferences in accounting and finance is vast, leading to a need to think strategically about which conferences to attend as the costs can be considerable (submission fee, travel – both long-distance and local transfers, accommodation, and food). Therefore, you are unlikely to be able to fund more than one international conference per year if you are lucky enough to have any financial support at all. How will you choose which conferences to target?

The most prestigious conferences are usually ultra-competitive and are also often the largest, most formal, and costliest Smaller, localised workshops are worth considering as you will really get to know the participants even if the speakers are less eminent. If you pursue an academic career, the network you need will comprise predominantly other academics at nearby universities since these will be the people examining your PhD students, commenting on your work and writing supporting statements for your grant applications. You might feel excited to meet a world-leading researcher or Nobel prize-winner, but you will likely never have any contact with them again, and they will be less useful to you than Associate Professor Bloggs from the university in the neighbouring city.

Your research budget will stretch much further if you stay close to home. Suppose that you are based at a UK institution, and you have a £1000 conference budget. You will be fortunate if it stretches to one conference outside the EU, but you might just about squeeze one in Europe and one in the UK, or up to three if they are all in the UK. Do you want a free vacation or a learning and networking experience to further your PhD and job chances? Maybe the one closer to home could be a better choice than the Caribbean.

If you are fortunate to be able to attend a major conference, it is worth making the most of the opportunities it presents. Try to attend all the keynote and plenary sessions. Go carefully through the speaker list, plan the sessions you will attend and stick to the schedule. These talks can centre on your thesis topic, but it will broaden your horizons and knowledge to participate in unrelated sessions as well.

Also, attend as many coffee breaks, lunches and conference dinners as possible. These are the opportunities to meet people and network, and many scholars would argue that these personal interactions are the most beneficial parts of conferences rather than the presentations. Try to chat with a wide range of delegates, not only the uber-famous or keynote speakers – they are the hardest to get time with and the most likely to forget your name. On the other hand, junior academics can be much more amenable to a discussion and valuable contacts. People tend not to have business cards anymore but at the end of each day, write down the names and affiliations of all the people that you have spoken to before you forget the details.

Where to find conferences

The sub-section above discussed some of the advantages of local versus overseas and large versus specialist conferences, but where can you identify the opportunities available? Unfortunately, there is not a list of them all, but there are several places to look:

1. Your supervisor, as always, is an obvious starting point. They will be familiar with all of the possibilities and will be aware of which are the most competitive or the most worthwhile meetings

2. Other PhD students in further ahead cohorts will likely have already attended conferences in previous years and be able to provide suggestions based on their experiences

3. The learned societies, as discussed in section 8.7.4, usually each have their own conferences. These are large annual events that present fairly good value for money and span all areas in accounting or finance. They will also organise more frequent special interest group meetings that focus on particular themes (e.g., financial accounting; corporate finance).

There are also practitioner conferences, where the topics of interest, presenters and delegates are predominantly drawn from the industry. These are mainly highly expensive and unlikely to be sufficiently closely related to most PhD students' research areas to be worthwhile seriously considering.

14.1.2   Poster sessions

In the natural and physical sciences, it is prevalent for PhD students to present their work in the form of large (A2 or A1) posters displayed on boards in a specially set out room at the conference. Each coffee break, lunchtime and at certain other specific points throughout the schedule, delegates will be invited to look at the posters. The author of the poster is expected to stand next to it for at least some of the time and be available to answer questions about the work.

Poster sessions are less common in accounting and finance but are increasingly used at more significant events to increase the number of junior participants without placing additional pressure on the schedule and room availability. Presenting a poster can be a useful introduction to conferences since you can gain some feedback on your work, and your department might fund your attendance (which they probably would not if you were not presenting at all). The experience is also likely to be less stressful than giving a full oral presentation, but posters are less prestigious, and you will probably receive less helpful feedback and less exposure than from a talk.

Except for absolute beginners and unless the conference is the most competitive in the field, if your paper is only accepted for a poster and not the main sessions, you might be better to save your conference budget for another opportunity.

If you decide to present a poster, some careful thought and planning is required to ensure that it is as effective as possible. The purpose of a poster is to get the essence of the research across within a limited space using a visually appealing design that is easy for the eye to follow. Find out what size of board you have available and plan accordingly. A4 is approximately 20cm by 30cm; A3 is double this, while an A2 sheet is equivalent to two A3 or four A4 pages. If you have an A2 board but no access to a printer beyond A4 size, then you can print onto eight individual A4 pages and pin them close together. Some people get their posters professionally printed, although this might be excessively time-consuming and expensive; you could see whether your school has access to such a print shop and will pay for it.

If you are producing a poster, there are several aspects to making it as good as possible:

- It needs to be a hybrid between a piece of scholarly output and a product advertisement. There needs to be an element that will attract people passing by, so use colours, large fonts, and charts or pictures.
- Keep charts and tables simple and include only essential information.
- Make the font big enough to be seen from two or three feet away and use bullet points rather than full paragraphs where possible.
- The poster should cover all sections of your research paper (but perhaps with minimal review or references, if any), including motivation, contribution, methods, data, results and findings.
- It is best to focus on one or two headline findings and build the story around those. You don't have the space to explain everything you have done, and it will lose the reader if you try to.
- Don't forget to include your name (plus those of co-authors), your affiliation and an e-mail address in case someone sees your poster while you are not there and wants to contact you about it. Also include brief acknowledgements if you received significant funding or other support from a person or organisation.
- Make the poster easy for the eye to move around – for example, by using columns and with reasonable spaces between each part.

There are some excellent on-line resources available for poster design, including:

- Colin Purrington (including downloadable PowerPoint templates)[1]
- The LSE[2]
- NYU Libraries[3]
- University of Central Lancashire[4]

---

[1] https://colinpurrington.com/2019/06/templates-for-better-posters/
[2] https://blogs.lse.ac.uk/impactofsocialsciences/2018/05/11/how-to-design-an-award-winning-conference-poster/
[3] https://guides.nyu.edu/posters
[4] https://www.uclan.ac.uk/students/assets/QRG-MS-PPT-Creating-Academic-Posters.pdf

- University of Liverpool[5]

14.2 How to give research presentations

Students usually have to make presentations annually as part of an assessment process to ensure that they are on track to complete on time, which provides scope to develop this performance skill. There is also the opportunity to give presentations if work is accepted at a conference, and there might be a requirement to provide one as part of the viva voce exam or at an academic job interview. Therefore, it is an important skill to develop and hone so that your delivery comes naturally, is always effective and hits the targets in terms of level and timing.

When you know that you are going to be giving a talk, the first stage is to determine the parameters, which will provide guidance on how to set up the address:

- How long will you have, and does that include time for introductions and questions?
- Can you use slides?
- What is the audience's level of knowledge and background on the topic?
- Will there be a formal discussant? See subsection 14.2.3 for a definition of these and what they do

14.2.1 Timing and slides

It is essential to be consistently well prepared, with an appropriate number of polished and clear slides. Regarding the number of slides, the vast majority of student presentations include too many. For instance, I attended an on-line PhD talk recently where the candidate was asked to speak for five to ten minutes before questions and had prepared 48 slides!

As a rule of thumb, I reckon on one slide for every two minutes of talking time (excluding the title and those with only pictures). A typical conference presentation will be twenty minutes for the talk plus five minutes for a discussant and five minutes for general questions, in which case it would make sense to have around 12 slides, including the cover and end. But the amount of time allocated for your presentation could be as little as five to ten minutes or as much as an hour. The keynote speaker at a conference might even get an hour and a half (including questions and general debate afterwards). Therefore, you need to find out precisely how long you will have for the talk and plan accordingly.

Ensure that you can use slides before preparing your presentation. Evidently, you would be able to if you were giving a presentation at a conference or workshop, but there might be some situations where there are no such facilities or where the time available is so limited that the organisers feel that a formal presentation would be excessive, such as an interview or appraisal talk.

---

[5]https://www.liverpool.ac.uk/media/livacuk/computingservices/printing/making-an-impact-with-your-poster.pdf

14.2.2 The level of the talk

Before preparing your presentation, ensure that you identify the audience's likely level of knowledge about the subject. Will they be experts in the field, narrowly defined (as you could assume at a specialist conference, for example), or will they be 'intelligent non-specialists' (e.g., a university-wide graduate school workshop)? You will need to tailor the amount of detail accordingly and define any esoteric terms you use if the audience comprises non-specialists predominantly.

14.2.3 A discussant?

A discussant is a person who is given your slides (and ideally, if there is one, the full research paper that underpins them) to read and review before your talk. They will then provide a short critical discussion of it which includes two aspects, a bit like an orally delivered referee report following a journal submission:

- A brief summary of their interpretation of what your research is about (one slide)
- A set of comments and suggestions for enhancement (one to three slides).

Therefore, it is essential to find out whether you will have a discussant and, if so, to ensure that they have a copy of your materials well in advance of the presentation to allow them plenty of time for review. If you are accepted to present at a conference where every paper has a discussant, it is likely that you will be asked to act in that capacity too.

Note that slides are optional for discussants but usually recommended as they make the talk easier to follow. As with writing a referee report, keep the tone polite and constructive, and try to focus on the most substantive points rather than trivial issues. It is also common to include a question or two for the presenter as well as comments.

It is even more essential for discussants to remain within their time allocation than for presenters. Most commonly, the former will have just five to ten minutes, so it is essential to focus right from the start. Usually, once the discussant has completed their part, the session chair will open up to general questions from the floor. But if no such questions are forthcoming, the discussant might step in to make additional points rather than leaving the speaker to face an embarrassing silence.

14.2.4 Structuring your talk

Here is a suggested ordering for your talk:

1. The first slide – the cover slide – should introduce you, your affiliation and co-authors (or supervisors if it is a PhD workshop presentation). It should also provide a title for the talk and the date.
2. For longer talks with a lot of time, the next slide might be a roadmap that explains what the address will be about and describes the sections that follow. For a 20-minute talk, skip this.

3. The following slide will usually provide the background and motivation for the study. It can be valuable to make this slide entertaining, including pictures or quotations from the media or other papers to draw in the audience.

4. After that, there could be a slide that outlines the work's main contribution and a very short (three-line) summary of the main results.

5. Next comes the presentation's main body spanning several slides: some literature review, methods, data, and results.

6. A final slide would then summarise the findings again, presenting suggestions for future work (possibly your research agenda for the next year) and perhaps a couple of implications or recommendations for policy or practice if these are relevant to your work.

So, in summary, a sample contents list for a 20-minute slide could be as follows:

1. Cover slide (slide 1)
2. Motivation (slide 2)
3. Contribution and summary (slides 3-4)
4. Review of existing work (slides 5-6)
5. Methods (slides 7-8)
6. Data (slide 9)
7. Results (slides 10-12)
8. Conclusions (slide 13)

Some further tips for delivering a successful presentation are given now.

Preparing your slides and yourself

- Ensure that the font size is optimal: 20-24 point is usually good; smaller might be hard to read while larger will look silly and excessively limit the information you can include on each page. Never paste written material directly from your paper or chapter; always use lists or bullet points

- Number the slides – this will help you and viewers to keep track of where you are in the presentation

- Don't try to make the slides very fancy with an elaborate design – for example, white writing on a dark background can be hard to see. But include relevant images where you can – for example, using graphs rather than tables if possible as this will make the slides more exciting

- Like PhD theses themselves, talks are often 'review heavy'. Only include enough discussion of the prior literature to motivate your work and demonstrate that you know how your research contributes to it. The audience is attending to hear about your ideas and findings, not those already published

- Make any tables clear and not too small. If necessary, reconstruct them to include only the critical information and don't just paste them from your paper if they take up whole pages and are full of tiny numbers

- Practice your talk in front of the mirror or, even better, get together with a group of fellow PhD students, watch each other's performances and offer constructive feedback. This interaction will help you ensure that your timing is spot on and diminish your nerves on the day as you will know that you can do it because you have already

- Unless you have a lot of time to spare, there is probably no scope to involve the audience with some interactive games or discussion. Save these forms of entertainment for undergraduate teaching
- It's fine to start or finish with a humorous line or two, which certainly makes the talk memorable. But don't deflect from the quality of the work by filling the material with jokes
- Prepare well, but don't let a forthcoming presentation take over your life. Do the best you can, but the outcome will seldom be pivotal for your PhD or career

On the day of the talk

- Have two copies of the presentation with you – perhaps one on your laptop and another on a backup pen drive or cloud storage. Even better, also send the organiser the presentation before the talk and ask them to load it onto the computer system in the room so that you don't have any delays (stressful for you and annoying for the audience).
- Keep some water with you during the presentation. Nerves can lead to a dry mouth or an unstoppable tickly cough.
- It is quite common for presenters (even those with experience who should know better) to begin with an apology (for not having done more work or for any typos or bad grammar in the slides). Starting with 'sorry' is an avoidable disaster and will diminish the confidence that your viewers will have in everything you say thereafter. Even if your self-critique is valid, the audience would probably not have noticed had you refrained from pointing the issues out.
- During the talk, timing is crucial. My timing is terrible and seems to be getting worse. Take a watch or timer with you if there is not a clock in the room. Keep an eye on this as you are going through and be prepared to skip or skim one or two of the least important slides if you are behind. The person running the session should support you with this, providing a warning if you are getting close to the end of the allocated time, but some people are more effective in this chair's role than others.
- Deliver the material at an appropriate speed. It is common for people who are nervous to end up speaking too quickly. Rather than preparing an appropriate amount of material for the time available, some presenters produce twice as much and talk twice as quickly!
- Look at the audience frequently during the presentation and try to pan your eyes around the room, so those attending catch your view at regular intervals. Looking at the audience will not only help them feel connected with you and the talk, but it will also enable you to gauge how well the material is getting across to them. Do they look inspired? Bored? Confused? If the viewers look

bored, consider speeding up or trying to make the talk livelier. If people look confused, pause and provide more detailed explanations, possibly even asking them if they follow your arguments. However, don't merely focus your gaze on one area of the room or one person, which would be creepy.

- Feel free to wander across the room a bit, but not excessively and try to avoid moving right to the back as those at the front will no longer be able to see you unless they twist their necks around.
- Use an appropriate volume of voice. If the room or audience numbers are large, see whether you can use a microphone. It not, make sure that you are nonetheless loud enough that everyone can hear clearly at the back.
- Some presenters print out copies of the slides for the audience. My view is that this is an unnecessary waste of paper as, sadly, the majority of your printouts will never be looked at and will remain on the corner table in the lecture room. Instead, give your e-mail address on the first and last slides of the talk and encourage the audience to contact you afterwards if they would like a soft copy of the slides or have any further comments.

You also need to consider how to deal with people who ask questions or otherwise interrupt during your talk. If you have made an error and they are pointing it out for the sake of clarity, that is probably fine. If you have a lot of time (e.g., you have a whole hour or more for the presentation), then you can either elect to take questions whenever the audience wants to ask them or request that as far as possible, they hold their points until you are done with your slides. But if you have very limited time, you might have to politely but forcefully ask the audience to keep their questions until the end.

Don't just read out the slides, which is a terribly bad style and dull for the audience. As a rough rule, I believe that the slides should contain about half the material, while the rest is what you deliver orally. If there is too much information on the slides, not only will they 'look busy', but more importantly, it will make you largely irrelevant. Your audience can read, so if you provide nothing in addition to the slides, you may as well set up your presentation to switch slides automatically every minute and stay at home.

On the other hand, some presenters just put a few words or a title on each slide. But if there is too little on the screen, it makes it harder for listeners to take everything in, and if they 'zone out' for just a few seconds, they won't be able to get back into the presentation. If the audience loses track, they will also lose interest.

Some presenters, especially those with little experience, might be worried that they will forget what they intended to say at each point during the talk. Obviously, the slides can act as a series of prompts, and you are less likely to suffer from forgetful nerves if you have thoroughly practised the talk beforehand. In the past, it was common for presenters to keep small flashcards or other notes with them to refer to at various points during their talks. If you feel you cannot do without these, then go ahead, but you will come across as much more professional if you have no prompts and just *ad lib* from what is on the slides.

Try to feel comfortable and be yourself. If you can engage with the audience and give each person the impression that your presentation is just for them, you will hold their attention. You will be aware from the lectures that you have attended that some speakers are just dull, and the time in their sessions seems to drag even if the material is inherently interesting. But other presenters can make the work appealing, even if the topic is 'formulae for approximating the gamma function.'

You can make the presentation more appealing if you, as the person delivering the talk, are excited by the topic, it will be contagious, and this enthusiasm will come across to the audience. You can't expect listeners to be enthusiastic about your research if you sound bored by it.

Dealing with the questions

There is likely to be time for freestyle questions from the floor at the end of the talk. This aspect can be stressful as it is quite hard to predict the kinds of issues that might come up, and the rest of the audience will hear the questions you are asked and look to you with eager anticipation for answers. If you have no idea how to respond, it can be a very public humiliation, which is why many presenters fear the questions at the end more than the talk itself. However, there are approaches you can use to make this part less painful:

- As you face the questions, remain confident by remembering that you are the expert on your talk, and hence you know more about it than anyone in the audience. If you are asked a question that you did not understand, feel free to ask them to repeat it or expand on it. If you still don't understand, or you do, but you do not know the answer, be willing to admit that rather than trying to bluff your way through with a vacuous response
- You could tell the person you will think about it and get back to them or ask them to come and meet you after the talk to discuss it further in person. That will then be a signal to move onto the next question
- The most challenging questions to deal with are totally 'left of field' – in other words, entirely off-topic and bizarre. Always aim to remain polite and offer a sensible response to even a silly question. If you try to do that, the other audience members will probably appreciate the absurdity of the person's line of questioning and be impressed with you for dealing with it
- If people offer advice or suggestions, always receive them graciously, offer your thanks and write the ideas down. It is not a battle to defend your work against attack, and summarily batting back any ideas that audience members give in good faith might offend. Remember that the whole point of giving a presentation is to get feedback on your work to make it better. If you get a lot of questions and comments, rather than implying that your research has major flaws, this is a great sign that you have engaged the audience and inspired them.

14.3   A guide to publishing

14.3.1   Why aim to publish your work?

The sad fact is that most PhD theses will only be read by four people: the author, the supervisor and the two examiners. Given the amount of effort that goes into conducting the research and writing the document spread over several years, that seems like a tragic waste. If you want your work to be read by others and influence how future researchers conduct their investigations, you need to get it out to a wider audience.

There are several routes to doing this, including presenting at conferences or workshops, writing blog pieces or practitioner magazine articles. But all of these outlets for your work have a short shelf-life: you might get five minutes of fame, but whatever you wrote will be forgotten within weeks or even days afterwards. As the saying goes, 'today's newspaper is tomorrow's fish and chip paper.' By contrast, journal and book publications leave a permanent record that people can refer to for many years afterwards. Moreover, while popular outlets such as newspapers and magazines probably have a wider readership than journals, the latter are the primary vehicles for disseminating knowledge among academics, and it is these that will be cited in future research.

Seeing your work published will bring a new sense of satisfaction and achievement beyond what you will obtain from completing and passing your doctorate. Publication, particularly in prestigious journals or with prestigious publishing houses, will bring honour and recognition that will allow you to gain entry to a virtuous circle with many other benefits. Published authors are more likely to be accepted to speak at international conferences, be invited to serve on interesting external committees, become involved in lucrative consultancy work and make grant applications more credible. In turn, all of these factors will enhance the author's reputation and make the path to future publication smoother.

Having publications, or at least work under review, is now a standard requirement to be a serious candidate for a lectureship (assistant professorship) position in a teaching and research role. Many applicants will already have one or more publications, and so if you don't, it will be tough to compete with them for posts. Academics who are consistently successful in publishing might be rewarded with reduced teaching loads and a greater chance of promotion. Indeed, while research-active academics are increasingly expected to succeed across a range of performance measures, including grant income capture, having an impact on policy or practice, and successful PhD supervision, it is still the case that publication in leading journals is considered the most important.

14.3.2   When to publish

As for the thesis document as a whole, you should get a sense, formed after discussion with your supervisor or other experienced academics, of when you have a paper ready for submission. Some students prefer to wait until after they have submitted their thesis before aiming to carve it up into publishable pieces. While I can understand their preference for focusing on one thing at a time, in my view, there is no need to wait until after getting your PhD, and it can be good to submit papers as soon as they are ready. As discussed in several places in this book, the lags in the refereeing and publication process are so long that, on average, it will be at least six months from submission to acceptance and possibly much longer. Therefore, to have a reasonable chance of having a forthcoming paper (accepted, but not yet in print) when going on the job market, you would need to start early.

If you aim for an academic career, in a role that involves doing research, an acceptance, or at least something under review, will enormously improve your chances of securing a post. You will also get feedback from editors and referees that might help you refine your thesis further and prepare for the viva.

Equally, don't send a paper out to a journal until it is thoroughly polished. Before submission, show the article to colleagues or others in the field for their comments. If possible, also present it at seminars and conferences to gain additional feedback.

14.3.3 How to choose an appropriate outlet

In accounting and finance, the vast majority of authors focus on journal publication rather than books or book chapters as the primary outlets for their work, unlike the arts and humanities, where having a monograph (single-authored research book) is considered vital for career progression. Writing a book could make sense if your thesis fits together as a cohesive whole (i.e., all the investigative chapters are on the same topic), especially if it is a subject with a broad current appeal (e.g., on cryptocurrencies or currency trading).

However, drafting books is very time-consuming owing to their length, and the more prestigious publishers might have reviewing processes that are just as onerous as those of journals. Books are often less well-read and cited than journal articles simply because they are harder or more expensive for researchers to get hold of. In contrast, journal articles are usually available at the click of a mouse and for free through the researcher's university library journal bundle or the author's institutional repository. Even if there is a royalty deal on the book, research monographs sell so few copies that the money earned would barely cover the cost of the coffee you had to drink to stay awake long enough to write it. Writing textbooks can be highly lucrative, but theses usually cannot be transformed into this medium. Another issue is that by turning an entire thesis into a book, the most you can hope for is a single publication, whereas a good PhD might potentially contain three distinct journal articles. Evidently, three publications will be much better for your career progression than one.

A final possibility would be to consider publishing individual parts from the thesis as book chapters if you know someone editing a book where it would be relevant. Although book chapters are generally considered to be less prestigious than journal publications, they typically have less stringent novelty and refereeing requirements, and it might be that the editor having a quick skim through your work would suffice. This implies that the process will be quicker, less stressful and less risky for junior researchers who want to get a guaranteed publication quickly, although most academics would be reulcant to publish their best work in the form of book chapters. Drafting books or book chapters is more common in the arts and humanities than accounting and finance, although it is worth considering.

The rest of this chapter focuses on journals since this is the most common choice for publishing research in accounting and finance. Selecting the most appropriate journal to which to submit your work for possible publication is a crucial choice. To maximise the utility of the outcome, you need to think strategically, remain realistic about the work's contribution, and select a journal accordingly. There is a clear trade-off here between prestige and ease of publication:

- If the journal you select is lowly ranked, you will have a higher chance that the journal will accept the work, but if it does, it will have less prestige and will have less of a positive impact in helping you to secure an academic post. Also, almost by definition, lesser-ranked journals tend to have lower impact factors, meaning that libraries are less likely to subscribe to them, and other researchers are less likely to read and cite the work published in such journals. Therefore, publishing in a lower-ranked journal will likely mean that your paper will have less visibility than if it had been placed in one with a higher impact factor. Over time, papers in journals in lower impact factor journals garner lower citations

- On the other hand, if you aim for an unrealistically highly rated journal, it is incredibly likely to be rejected. This rejection would mean that the time until that point (and possibly a submission fee paid to the journal to consider your paper) will have been wasted, and you will be back to square one. As well as constituting a rather dispiriting experience, the lack of any publications could make it harder for you to get a job in the academy

In summary, don't let your ego get in the way, but equally, don't sell your work short. Think critically about where your work fits in the continuum of research from seminal to trivial.

Evidently, the journal you select must be relevant for your paper and publish that kind of work. For example, if yours is a purely empirical paper, and you have chosen a journal that publishes technical pieces containing much theory, you may have made a poor choice. Equally, if the journal that you selected publishes mainly qualitative studies using interviews or experiments, again, your chances of success are probably slim because your paper represents a poor 'fit' there.

An excellent place to start is by looking through the reference list in your paper. Often, journals that are not featured there might imply a bad fit or that you need to look harder for articles in that journal and cite them. Since citations to papers in their journal would increase its impact factor, if you have not mentioned any papers in your target journal, it might discourage the editor from treating the submission seriously.

Another way to begin the process of selecting a target journal is to start with the AJG list for Accounting or Finance. Both field lists are incredibly long but quite exhaustive as the overwhelming majority of known journals are on the list. Although I would not advocate the Guide as providing a definitive ranking or using it as the only criterion upon which to make your choice, it is useful in acting as a pointer to some possible outlets about which you might not otherwise have been aware. The AJG also provides a rough gauge of how each journal is perceived by many researchers in the community and even by potential employers since it is widely used by university managers and other non-specialists on hiring and promotions committees.

When you have a shortlist of target journals, look at a few issues of them to get a feel for whether your work might fit there in terms of whether the subject matter and style seem to match. Has the topic you are working on been published there? Is your work more or less ground-breaking than those studies? While deciding on the first pick journal to which you will send the paper first, you can also develop a 'plan B' ordered list of alternative journals so that you are prepared in the likely event that the first choice rejects your work (see below).

Some researchers deliberately choose very highly rated journals to which first to submit their work since not only does it then give them an albeit tiny chance of success, but it is also often the case that the quality of referee reports is higher at the more prestigious journals. Therefore, even though the work is very likely to be rejected, such authors submit their work there as a deliberate strategy to get good feedback to improve it before resubmitting it to a more realistic target. Even though the leading journals in finance (and some in accounting) charge a submission fee, they consider it good value to get detailed comments from a field expert. As discussed below, however, it is increasingly common for the leading journals to reject some papers without sending them for review, in which case you might pay the submission fee to a prestigious journal but unfortunately not receive any feedback at all aside from a two-line response that the paper is not suitable.

It is also the case that the higher-rated journals tend to be better organised and better resourced so that they provide decisions quickly, whereas the lower-rated journals tend to be run on a shoestring with the editors getting no administrative support. So they struggle to cope with the volume of submissions they receive, and they are often very slow and inefficient at dealing with the papers. Here are some other considerations when choosing a journal:

- As always, your supervisor might have ideas, and, as discussed in section 14.4, if they are a co-author on your paper, they might submit the article for you and handle the process. If your supervisor has previously had success in getting work accepted at that journal and is a co-author, it is a good sign of your case's chances

- Each journal will have a main web page containing information about it and the submission process. In particular, check out the 'aims and scope' and the 'author guidelines'. The former will help you to ensure that your paper would fit there and is within the realms of the kind of study that it publishes. The latter will allow you to check that your piece will fit the style requirements. In particular, sometimes journals have a word or page limit for submitted papers, and if yours significantly exceeds this, it will be immediately returned to you for trimming or rejected

- Have a look at the editorial board for the journal. Are the main editor and associate editors predominantly from a single country or affiliated with prestigious schools? The status of the board in terms of its members' affiliations can be a reasonable indication of the prestige that the editors attach to the journal, so if they are all from the world's 'elite' universities, you can expect the bar for paper acceptance to be set very high

- The affiliations of members of the editorial board might also give you an indication of the locations of the core readership of the journal. You are likely to find more interest in your work, both in terms of getting the paper accepted and the readership subsequently, if your country focus in the study matches the audience's location

Don't consider completely unknown journals, which are usually published on an open-access basis so that authors pay an 'article processing fee' amounting to several hundred pounds, but readers can freely download the article without paying a journal subscription. The readership for unknown and unrated journals will likely be minimal, rendering all the work you did largely pointless. Sometimes, this is known as vanity publishing, where in essence you would be paying just to get your work in print.

Never be tempted to submit a specific piece of work to more than one journal concurrently. This process is considered extremely unethical and could cause you significant trouble if you are caught out. Such a practice would be a waste of the referees' and editor's time. Furthermore, if the paper is accepted for publication, you would need to sign a 'Transfer of Copyright' form before the journal will publish it, and evidently, you cannot assign the copyright to your paper to more than one outlet.

14.3.4 How to prepare your thesis chapters for publication

The discussion in this sub-section focuses on the situation where the PhD candidate elects to submit the chapters to journals rather than as a research monograph, although the ideal format for a book chapter is likely to be quite similar to that of a journal article. The required format and structure for a whole book will obviously be quite different.

The first consideration is what to prepare for publication. Usually, a thesis will contain three investigative chapters, and these will be the obvious starting point. It might be that you decide not all of your investigative chapters are sufficiently strong for it to be worth aiming to publish them so that you will only seek to obtain one or two papers from the thesis and spend any future research time working on new (non-thesis) projects.

It is also possible to publish literature a review chapter as a journal article since, as discussed in subsection 8.3.4, some journals welcome these as a way to boost their impact factors. But such a review needs to be novel (i.e., either on a topic that has not been the subject of a journal-published literature survey already or where existing reviews are dated or deficient in some way), timely, focused, and very polished. To have a reasonable shot at being accepted, it needs to synthesise the literature, contextualise and classify the subject matter, and suggest future research directions. Since most thesis literature reviews do not meet these exacting standards, they are usually hard to publish.

Relatedly, some journals (such as *Critical Perspectives on Accounting*) will welcome purely theoretical or conceptual studies that include no empirical work or data applications, and hence it might be possible to publish a conceptual chapter as a journal paper. But such outlets are relatively small in number, with most preferring empirical studies backed by a solid theoretical framework.

It might be preferable to work on one paper at a time, completing one piece's submission before beginning work on others. That way, ideally, you would have several pieces at various stages of preparation and review, which will maximise the chances that you will get an accepted output in the shortest time. If you try to process two or three papers concurrently, you will not have any completed initially, hence losing time when one of them could have already been under review.

If the PhD document is structured as a set of largely independent papers, this will make the process of carving up the thesis considerably more straightforward. Papers submitted to journals must be stand-alone so that it is not necessary for someone to have read your paper X before being able to understand what you are writing about in paper Y. The need for independence between papers can be problematic if you develop a theoretical or conceptual model in one chapter that you then implement empirically in the following chapter. Once in paper form for submission, the empirical work cannot refer to another unpublished paper that you have drafted, so you would need to find some way to describe the theoretical framework briefly in the empirical work but without explaining it in its entirety. More generally, you need to avoid any substantial overlaps between your papers.

Another aspect of each paper being stand-alone is that they will all need to contain a literature review, and this would entail some reorganisation of the material from your thesis if you had hived off the review into a separate chapter. Of course, each paper also needs its own abstract, data description, results, reference list, and so on. If you have used the same data source or methods for several empirical chapters, you will need to use different words to describe the same thing: strenuously avoid copying and pasting from one to another, which could be construed as an act of self-plagiarism.

Prior to submitting them to journals, each paper must be polished and in the correct format for the chosen journal. There are several aspects of this to consider:

- The length – some journals have a maximum length specified either in terms of numbers of pages or numbers of words. If your draft paper significantly exceeds this, it will likely be rejected straight away. On the other hand, papers that are too short might also fail to impress as the reader might consider that it would not be possible to develop your arguments and analysis in sufficient depth while using so few pages. A length of, perhaps, 25–40 pages including everything would be standard for a paper submitted to a journal
- The level of mathematics – some journals publish very technical papers, including detailed derivations of formulae, while others rely more on narratives and strong arguments. The style of your writing should fit that of the journal you are aiming for
- The number of references – some journals publish articles that are very heavily referenced where the list is several pages long, while typical papers in other journals have only a handful of citations. Again, the style of your work should match that of your target journal
- The number of tables or figures – it is common for theses to include vast numbers of tables or figures that repeat the core analysis for many countries or modify the model slightly and report the analysis. A paper for journal submission must have a good balance between the scale of each element (introduction, literature review, methods, tables, discussion of results, conclusions and tables or figures) If the latter takes up half of the space, the paper would be boring and unreadable, and so it is likely that the editor would simply reject it. The key message is to ensure that you don't have too many tables or figures in your paper: if you have a lot of results, identify the most important ones and either delete the rest or put them in a 'not for publication appendix' that can be made available on-line alongside the paper
- Citation of relevant studies from that journal – self-citations (that is, a paper published in Journal X citing other studies published previously in Journal X) will contribute to raising the impact factor of that journal. Therefore, editors will be more disposed to a submission that cites papers already accepted there. Consequently, you should look particularly hard for relevant work published in your target journal and mention it.

Non-native speakers might wish to consider employing a professional proof-reader to improve the standard of writing up to publication standard. The examiners might have been willing to overlook poor sentence structure or grammatical errors in a thesis, but these will usually not be acceptable in a journal publication and therefore making the writing as strong as it can be is an easy win.

Also, pay close attention to the motivation for the study – the 'so what' question. It is vital to explicitly state what the contribution is, why the work is important and for whom. This aspect is not sufficiently strong in many papers and a common reason they are rejected.

If your supervisor or another established academic is a co-author for the work, they should be able to provide detailed guidance on getting it into a suitable format to maximise the chances of success. They might even take on this aspect entirely, although it is important that you closely track the changes they make as part of your training so that you would be able to do something similar yourself in the future.

If you get the chance to present working papers derived from the thesis at seminars or conferences, do take up the opportunity as the feedback could help you to further refine the study before submission to a journal. Also, send the paper to others working in the field (or ask your supervisor to do that if they know each other) to gain further suggestions for improvement. Having an impressively long list of people who have read the paper and places it has been presented in the acknowledgements section on the front page of the article will give the editor the view that the work has been through a substantial development period, and it should now be in good shape.

14.3.5 Getting a paper ready for submission

Each journal will have a webpage with several sub-pages, including one on 'aims and scope' that will identify the subject areas where the journal would welcome submissions. Check that your work fits within this remit, and if not, it would probably be advisable to submit the paper elsewhere as your chances of success will be low. The journal will also have a webpage of 'instructions for authors', which usually contains a long list of style requirements for papers. You must read through these and comply with the substantive issues that they raise. For instance, most journals operate a 'double blind' refereeing process, which means that neither will you learn the identity of your referee(s) nor will they know who the authors are. Consequently, journals usually ask submitting authors to upload a 'blinded' version of the paper with author names and other identifying information removed and a separate cover sheet containing that material.

Other journals are single-blind, where the authors' names remain on the front cover, so the referees will know who wrote the paper, but the authors will not be able to identify the referees. In any case, it is common for researchers to upload their completed studies onto working paper repositories before submitting them to journals, in which case that, or the citations or other aspects of the methods, can reveal the identity of the author.

A second important issue might relate to line spacing (with some specifying that double-line is required), page limits, and whether US or UK spelling is required. There are sometimes also requests to place the references into a particular style, although most journals are unconcerned about these aspects at the initial submission stage.

Some journals require the author to draft a cover letter uploaded with the paper, although this is also an option for most others. If you have to write such a letter, prepare it on electronic university-headed paper, keep it short (perhaps two to three paragraphs or half a page), explaining what is exciting and new about your paper and why it is relevant for that journal. Address the letter to the journal's main editor. Avoid copying directly from the paper's abstract, which is likely to be in a slightly drier, more formal style than you might use in a cover letter, otherwise, you may appear lazy. End by saying that you hope the paper might be suitable for publication in the journal, and you look forward to hearing from them.

14.3.6 The process after journal submission

Once you have uploaded your paper onto the target journal's web site, along with any other required information (for instance, some journals also require a cover letter, author biographies, a statement of the contribution of each author, short summary 'highlights', etc.), it will be considered by the journal's editor. They will check that the subject matter fits within the journal's scope and that the paper is of sufficient quality (structure, investigative methods, standard of writing, and so on) and novelty. If the article does not pass this first test, it will be 'desk rejected', and usually, the authors have no opportunity to resubmit the same work to that journal again. If this outcome occurs, it will usually happen quickly – typically within a couple of weeks, enabling the work to be turned around and sent elsewhere without much delay.

If the submitted paper passes through the editor initial evaluation, it will be sent to one or more referees. Sometimes editors will handle this process themselves, but in other journals, the editor will delegate responsibility to an associate editor. The number of referee reports that the journal seeks to support the editor's decision-making varies between journals. Interestingly, the strongest and weakest journals both seem to use one reviewer: the former because they have absolute confidence in the people selected as referees that they will do a good job, and the latter because they find it so hard to identify even one person willing to review a paper that getting two such people would be an impossible dream.

Other journals will seek to obtain the views of between two and four independent readers. In theory, the referees should be acknowledged experts in the submitted research area who have already published on that topic. But in practice, it is often challenging for the editor to find people who are suitably qualified and willing to review the work, so referees are often relatively inexperienced generalists. Referees are usually unpaid, or if they are compensated, the sum will be derisory such as USD100, which is not in proportion to the time, skill and experience required to complete the task adequately.

The waiting game

Journals typically take three or four months to provide the first response if a paper is not desk rejected and goes out to review, but it could be much longer (nine months or even a year). The aspect determining how long it takes is whether the editors chase up reviewers who are slow in submitting their reports and replacing them if they fail to deliver; if not, the process can drag on for a very long time. Adding the time it takes authors to complete revisions, allowing for two rounds of review, and then the period until the publisher typesets the paper and prints it, altogether the process takes a year and possibly two.

This waiting period can feel like an eternity for those with just one paper completed and under review, and where the outcome could imply a major difference in their chances of securing a job. These extensive delays mean that you need to be even more efficient in getting work completed, polished and submitted well before the end of your PhD registration to have a reasonable chance of getting an accepted paper prior to going on the job market.

Avoid the temptation to chase up the editor weekly after submission to see if they have any news regarding your paper. Hassling the editor will rapidly cause irritation, and if you want an instant answer, it will be a rejection. Provided that the submission is made through an electronic system, you can be confident that your paper has been received and is under consideration rather than having been lost in the post, so I would wait at least four months before contacting the editorial office with a polite request to provide an update on the current status of your work.

14.3.7   The possible outcomes for your paper

The referees will read the work and draft a report for onward submission to the authors. The former will also provide a recommendation to the editor about what to do with the submission. Once the editor has all of the referee reports, they will decide what to do with the paper based on the referees' views. The editor might also read the article themselves and provide additional comments or a covering letter explaining which of the referees' suggestions are the most pertinent. In general, there are three possible outcomes:

1. 'Accept' – the paper is accepted for publication in its present form
2. 'Revise and resubmit' – the authors are asked to undertake further work on the article in light of the referees' and editor's comments
3. 'Reject' – the paper will not be considered further at this journal

The first of these outcomes is very unlikely at the first submission. Editors will seldom accept a paper without obtaining referee reports (for fear of being accused of favouritism), and referees will feel the need to justify their role by making some suggestions for improvement even if they believed that the work was outstanding.

While the third possibility is the same outcome as a 'desk rejection', if the editor had sent the paper out for review, you would receive the referee's comments. Even though you cannot send the piece back to that journal, the reviewers' reports might help you improve the work before you submit it elsewhere.

Unfortunately, the overwhelmingly most likely outcome is that your paper will be rejected by the journal you send it to. In general, the more prestigious the journal, the higher the rejection rate, and the leading journals have rejection percentages of 90 or more. Rejection appears to be the default outcome at most journals, and usually when there is more than one referee, all of them must agree that the paper is worth pursuing for the editor to select option 2 in the list above. Only one rejection recommendation from a referee will usually be required for that to be the option the editor selects. Sometimes the editor will still recommend rejection when two referees both seem to quite like the paper.

If this happens to you, try not to be too despondent. I remember my PhD supervisor telling me that if you don't get rejections, you are not aiming high enough. Refusals hurt, particularly for those lacking experience of them. Where the researcher does not yet have a portfolio of other work at various stages of the process, the potential for professional damage can be even greater as they needed a hit, not a miss, to get a job. It is worth remembering that almost every study is publishable, it just needs to find the right 'level' so you will get there eventually.

If the outcome is a rejection with no referee reports, the conclusion is that you perhaps selected an inappropriate journal to which to send the paper. If this happens, don't waste time, but pick another outlet and resubmit the paper as soon as possible, although you might decide to aim at a lower-rated journal next time where expectations are more modest, and therefore the chances of a successful outcome are higher.

I have written numerous papers that I thought were very strong, only to face repeated rejections. I interpreted this outcome not as implying that the work was weak or flawed but rather that it was not what the field was looking for at that time. Dealing with these rebuffs and the resubmissions to alternative journals is mentally draining and time-consuming. In such circumstances, there has to come a point where you send the paper to a considerably lower rated journal where you believe the chances of success are much higher just to get some closure and to allow you to concentrate on new work that will hopefully be better received.

Equally, consider the reasons why the editor has decided to reject the paper. If the letter is a 'fob off' that 'the journal receives large numbers of submissions and they need to make difficult decisions and reject many good papers etc...' or that the paper is out of the scope of work of interest to them, then the article can be quickly submitted elsewhere.

On the other hand, if the editor identifies important flaws in the work as the reason for rejection (e.g., the paper is badly written, poorly structured, or too long), it is essential to address these issues before submitting elsewhere, otherwise, the outcome will likely be the same again.

If you did receive one or more referee reports, then take time to reflect on the comments and see whether there are some 'easy wins' where you can improve the chances of success in the future without spending many months redoing the work. It is vital to take a balanced approach to dealing with referee comments: unlike the situation discussed below, where you have the opportunity to resubmit the paper, here it was rejected, so you do not need to do everything that the referees suggest. It might be that many of their comments are a matter of personal taste and style or will take too long to implement, in which case they might be best ignored.

But do correct any errors they spot, and in particular, if they were not able to identify the contribution or positioning of the work, this should be improved before submission elsewhere. Different referees will likely make wildly varying technical comments on the methods and results but homogeneous remarks on the writing quality and novelty. This situation is where a discussion with a more experienced published academic would be valuable, but as for the case where your work is rejected without a referee report, don't leave it on the shelf for many months – get any modifications completed quickly and send the paper to another outlet as soon as possible.

Before moving on, it is worth commenting that some 'elite' journals have started to occasionally offer a fourth outcome that they term 'reject and resubmit'. Usually, a revise and resubmit paper will be sent back to the original referees in the second round and therefore has a reasonable chance of eventual acceptance. But a reject and resubmit occurs when the editor expects the author(s) to undertake the revisions requested by the referee(s) but with the intention of treating it as a fresh submission when it comes back in, so it is sent to new referees who may or (more plausibly) may not like the paper. Therefore, a reject and resubmit paper has barely a higher chance of success in the second round than a newly submitted paper would in the first, yet authors are often so desperate for a shot at publishing in such journals that they will go through the process anyway.

Revise and resubmit

The second outcome in the above list requires some detailed discussion. Sometimes, the authors will have an opportunity to resubmit the paper, but they might decide not to because the amount of work involved is very substantial or because they have been asked to make changes to the document that they do not want to (for example, cutting out significant sections that the authors feel are a crucial aspect of the story). Also, sometimes the editor might offer the opportunity to send the paper in again even though there are very negative referee reports where they seem to fundamentally dislike the study based on aspects that could not be remedied in a revision. In that case, undertaking the additional work might be risky, with the likely outcome that the paper will still be rejected in the next round.

If the authors choose to take up the challenge to revise and resubmit their work, they will prepare a response to each of the referees' and editor's comments, line-by-line, explaining what they had changed or politely explaining why they had not undertaken a particular action that had been requested. Usually, there is little point in resubmitting the paper if an author is unwilling and able to undertake most of the changes or additions requested by the editors and referees.

Once the revisions are completed, and the paper sent back to the journal, it will usually go out to the same reviewers who had read it in the first round. The referees might recommend accepting this revised version, request another round of modifications, or suggest that the editor rejects the paper. The latter outcome is harsh for authors when they have put in a considerable additional effort to change their paper, perhaps many months have been lost, and they are back to square one. While this situation is rare, it does occur. Usually, two rounds with referees and the editor are sufficient for the paper to be accepted (if that is indeed the end result), although there could be more.

When authors receive referee reports, particularly if accompanied by a rejection decision, the first response upon reading them is that 'the referee is an idiot who didn't understand or didn't bother to read the paper.' Sometimes this statement would be accurate since referees are usually busy, unpaid for the role, and they might be inclined to be sloppy, and occasionally, downright spiteful for no apparent reason.

If this situation happens to you, also remember that a referee can provide an independent, dispassionate perspective on your research, and so the comments that they made might be fair. If they did not understand some parts of the paper, it might be because you didn't explain those aspects sufficiently clearly. Ultimately, the editor has the finals say about whether the article is accepted for publication or not, and they will generally side with the reviewers (whom they chose) in the event of a disagreement between the referee and author.

The closer relationship between editor and referee than author and referee means that it is only worth following up on a 'revise and resubmit' if you are willing to do most of what the referee asks. If the referees have asked for the impossible (e.g., they wanted to see a theoretical paper on this topic but yours is purely empirical, or they wanted unstructured interviews and you have used a survey), or if you are not willing to undertake what is requested, it is probably wiser to withdraw the paper at that stage and submit it to a different journal.

If the reviewers request substantive changes, such as new empirical work with different data, it is essential to engage with the suggestions if you intend to send the paper back to the same journal. Invariably, the editors will post the study back to the original referees, and they will be expecting you to have done what they asked. While it is not necessary to do precisely what is requested under every point, on balance, you need to do most of it to stand a good chance of getting past the next rounds. Don't think that some minor tinkering (such as redrafting or additional footnotes) will be sufficient to address a substantive point (e.g., a request to add additional control variables to the model) as the referee will see through the smokescreen and realise that you have not done what was asked.

If the referee requests additional empirical work, but you decide that it is not worth including it in the revised paper (perhaps because it would make the number of tables too large or because the new results are weaker than the old ones), you should still include the new tables of results in your response to the referees and editor to demonstrate that you did indeed complete the requested work.

Revising and resubmitting an article is a valuable option to hold because you are already over the first hurdle, and while the probability of eventual acceptance of your paper is much higher now than when you first submitted it, this probability is not one. There is still a non-trivial chance that the work will be rejected at the next round, or even worse, at the round after that. Sometimes, editors leave the referees to do all the work in the first two rounds and then only read the work thoroughly themselves after that, at which time they might decide upon closer inspection that they don't like it at all.

Hence, undertaking revisions is always a risky activity, and in the worst-case scenario, you could do a vast amount of extra work as required by the reviewers that, in your view, does not improve the study, and the paper is still rejected at the next round leaving you to start all over again with a different journal.

Preparing your resubmission

If you decide to resubmit the paper, never criticise the referees, question their knowledge or try to score points from them: always let them down gently. If a particular comment they make is genuinely unfounded or incorrect, point that out very delicately, or say that you believe you might have misunderstood their point, and so could they explain it differently. Similarly, if the referee asks for a particular change to the paper that you are loathed to make or would require an inordinate amount of additional work, politely explain why you believe that the study is better the way it is but say that you are, of course, willing to make the changes if the referee considers it particularly important to do so. That way, you are signalling a willingness to make the changes in a future round if necessary, but often when faced with a soft rebuttal, the referee will not ask for it in another round. On the other hand, a flat refusal or a suggestion to the reviewer that their advice is stupid is likely to offend and could even lead them to recommend that the paper is rejected at the second round. So tread carefully.

It is also important not to criticise referees in your cover letter to the editor: the latter selected the former, who probably provided their services for free, so such criticism will likely not be well taken. It might be possible to request a different referee but faced with such a request, the editor could deliberately select somebody who will be tough, leading to a bad outcome for the authors. Therefore, when you are unhappy with the comments made by a referee, it is perhaps best to cut your losses, formally withdraw the paper form that journal and send it elsewhere.

If you are asked to revise and resubmit your paper, the modifications could include requests to:

- Restructure the paper, moving parts around if the editor or reviewer believes that the material in the current version is not ideally ordered
- Reduce the length of the article by removing elements that they think are redundant
- Add more explanation of aspects that they found particularly interesting or not sufficiently clear in the previous draft
- Undertake additional empirical work where they doubt the claims you have made, or they feel that it is currently not sufficiently robust

A particular challenge is when there is more than one referee and each of them is making directly opposing requests. For instance, one reviewer might suggest that the paper is too long and material that they consider superfluous needs to be removed, while the other asks for more detail in parts or an additional strand of the literature to be reviewed. In such cases, clearly, you cannot make the paper shorter while adding more material, so you will need to prioritise but tread carefully to avoid upsetting one of the referees. Sometimes the editor will provide some overlaying commentary that could indicate which of the referees' comments you should focus on. It is not always the case that all of the referees have the same weight in the editor's mind, particularly if one is far more senior and experienced than the other. You might be able to gauge which referee the editor is focused on from the tone of their comments.

Another issue occurs when the editor or the entire editorial team changes after you received a revise and resubmit decision. The new editor may be more or less disposed towards your paper than the old one. In an ideal world, the new editor(s) ought to honour the refereeing process instigated by their predecessor(s), but they may or may not do that in reality. Sometimes the new editor will set the bold ambition to raise the journal's stature and plan to achieve that by rejecting a larger proportion of submissions, including some of those encouraged by the previous editor. Unfortunately, there is little that you can do if you find yourself in that situation.

When sending the paper back to the journal, include a cover letter to the editor thanking them for the opportunity to resubmit the study, and tell them how valuable their comments and those of the referees were and how much better it now is as a result. For example, you could write something like:

Dear Professor X

Thank you for providing us with the opportunity to revise and resubmit our paper entitled XXXXXXX. We very much appreciate the thorough and insightful comments by both reviewers, and we are also grateful for the time and effort you have put in to providing additional detailed suggestions and highlighting further relevant literature.

We have made extensive revisions to the paper in light of these comments. Below, we report each of your comments and those of the referees, followed by our responses to the points in italics. We hope that the paper might now be publishable in YYYY and look forward to hearing from you in due course.

< Detailed replies to each of the editor's comment (if they made any in addition to those of the referee(s))>

Before responding to each point the referee made line-by-line, you could include something like the following header statement:

We would like to thank the reviewer for her/his insightful and detailed comments on the previous version of this paper. We have significantly revised the paper in the light of these suggestions, those of the other reviewer and the Editor, and we believe that the work is much improved as a result. We hope that the paper might now be recommended for publication in YYYY.

A dirty business

You should write these polite preambles even if you believe that the referee or editor has provided unhelpful or ill-informed comments. Ultimately, the editor will make the decision as to whether to publish your paper or not, usually following the recommendation of the referees, so they have all the power in this association, and if you do not feel willing or able to do that, it would be better to cut your losses and send the study to another journal. Moreover, even if you feel very aggrieved by the way the process has been handled – for instance, if the referee has been downright rude or provided comments that demonstrate a total lack of understanding or that they did not read the paper, while in theory you probably have the right to complain formally, or to request a different referee, there is rarely any point in doing so. Again, withdraw the paper and try your hand elsewhere.

I have personally experienced some practices at journals that I found truly shocking. In one instance, a paper I had submitted to a finance journal was rejected with a report from one referee who evidently did not like the work. This would have been fair enough, but it later became apparent that another referee who was a contact of my co-author had also submitted a report, this time a favourable one and recommending a revise and resubmit. Rather than sending out both reports, which had conflicting opinions and requiring the editor to do their job and form a judgement, they decided to send only the negative report out to us and bury the other one.

Another journal in finance that I have had dealings with appears to routinely allow authors to resubmit their papers following very negative referee reports even though they have virtually no chance of eventually success simply to obtain another round of submission fees that the editor keeps. Journal submission fees can be shocking, particularly in the finance field – for instance, at the time of writing (mid-2021), the *Journal of Financial Economics* charges $1,000 for non-subscribers, and it is extremely likely that the small proportion of papers not rejected at the first stage will have to pay additional rounds of fees at resubmission.

It is challenging for those outside of the world elite schools to break into the top journals, particularly in finance, where editors have the opportunity to select referees according to their own views on how much they would like to publish the paper. Scholars outside of this magic circle often feel aggrieved and that their research is not given due consideration, and I have heard that this led two of the leading journals in finance, the *Journal of Finance* and *Journal of Financial Economics* to be sometimes referred to as the Journal of Friends and the Journal of Friends of the Editor. But the rewards for those who succeed are substantial: just a single paper in one of the journals of distinction together with a handful of publications in lower rated outlets can quickly lead to promotion to a full professorship. These are the rules of the game in journal publishing, particularly in finance, and you have no choice but to either play to them or choose a career not involving academic research. The other side of the coin is that one day, you might be a referee or journal editor and be able to make whimsical decisions on dubious grounds, but in the mean time, there is no choice but to dance to their tune.

14.4 Will your articles be co-authored with your supervisor?

Most PhD students aim to produce one or more journal articles or book chapters from their thesis. Creating such pieces is valuable for their career development for several reasons discussed in subsection 14.3.1. An essential question to consider and discuss with your supervisor is whether your working papers arising from the thesis for possible journal publication will be co-authored with them or sole-authored. In the sciences, almost all student-generated work is co-authored, whereas, in the arts and humanities, the overwhelming majority is authored by students alone. Accounting and finance are somewhere between the two, but still, most articles are co-authored with supervisors. Deciding which path to follow is tricky, and there are several issues to consider, but the ultimate choice should be yours since you are the lead investigator in your research:

- Supervisors should not and would not expect to be co-authors if they did not contribute to the work
- While the majority of the total time spent on the paper will be from the student, it might be that the supervisor had an important high-level role in its development. For example, it might be the case that while you did all of the data collection, empirical work, analysis and the first draft of the writing, your supervisor provided the initial idea, suggested the hypotheses and research methods, and did a substantial amount of rewriting. That being the case, they have made an intellectual contribution that probably warrants joint authorship
- Your supervisor will probably know the journal publishing 'game' well and be able to identify the appropriate outlet for the work that provides the optimal trade-off between journal prestige and the likely chance of success. You could make this decision yourself, but there is an increased danger of making an inappropriate choice
- Your supervisor would probably handle the submission of the paper to the journal. Although in an ideal world, the quality of the work would speak for itself, in reality, your supervisor's seniority might increase the chance that the paper is taken seriously and given genuine consideration rather than summarily dismissed
- If you get past the first stage of the review process (see subsection 14.3.7), the likely outcome is that you will be asked to undertake some modifications to the research and possibly conduct additional investigative work before resubmitting the paper. Your supervisor will be experienced in handling comments from the referees and knowing how to respond to the points they have made. Doing this appropriately is essential for maximising the chance that the paper will be accepted when sent back to the journal
- Learning how to handle the various stages of the journal submission, review

and publication process is part of your training to become a fully-fledged academic. Therefore, it is highly instructive if your first experience of this procedure is through working with someone who has been through it numerous times themselves.

- On the other hand, some scholars might argue that a joint paper for which you are one of two or three authors is worth less to you in terms of prestige than where you are the sole author. In that vein, although it would be unfair, it is nonetheless sometimes the case that some people seeing a co-authorship could question your role in the work, believing that the supervisors had done the creative stuff while you had merely pressed the buttons

Even if work from your thesis is co-authored with your supervisor, once the PhD is finished, it is best not to continue to work only with your former supervisor for fear of giving those examining your CV the incorrect impression that you had not made the transition to being an independent researcher capable of generating your own research agenda. Having one or two sole-authored papers is a valuable signal that you were able to master all aspects of the research and publication process without needing to rely on anyone else's input. For that reason, some PhD students choose to have one single-authored paper from their thesis even if the others are joint.

Over the longer term, co-authoring with a wider range of people is also helpful to demonstrate that you have built a network and that you can work as part of a variety of teams, possibly undertaking different roles in each case. There are many problems that would be difficult for a single scholar working alone to tackle, and indeed, engaging in interdisciplinary work would be extremely challenging as it would necessitate being an expert in two or more distinct fields.

In summary, the choice of whether work arising from your thesis should be co-authored is a delicate situation, but it is best to have an early and informal discussion with your supervisor about it to avoid any subsequent misunderstandings. It might be that they simply have insufficient time to be involved in co-publishing with you, especially if they have a high administrative load or are semi-retired, in which case the choice will be made for you.

Co-author name order

If you and your supervisor(s) decide that co-authorship is the way forward, a secondary issue is the order of author names. There are two conventions in common usage regarding this matter. One approach is to retain an alphabetical authoring wherever the student's surname would naturally place them. A benefit of this ordering is that it comes with no signal about the division of work between the co-authors, and some supervisors may feel more comfortable with this. An alternative is to allow the student to place their name first in the ordering, whatever it would have been according to the alphabetical listing. Putting PhD student names first has usually been my favoured approach to allow them more prominence as they need the publicity more than I do but perspectives on this vary between supervisors. Again, an open and frank discussion about this is the best way to avoid any confusion or embarrassment.

14.5   Writing for other audiences

14.5.1   Writing for practitioner magazines and newspapers

Alongside writing scholarly articles for publication in journals and books, many academics also write popular articles for newspapers, magazines or 'trade journals'. While career development is primarily determined by more academic articles, publishing work aimed at practitioners or the general public can also be valuable for several reasons:

- It gets your work in front of a different and potentially much bigger audience
- Your work is more likely to influence policy or practice. Unfortunately, the overwhelming majority of practitioners, let alone the general population, never read academic journal articles. Therefore, to reach these groups, it is vital to use some other means
- Popular articles are often quick and easy to write since they are far shorter, with less depth and little, if any, referencing
- Such work is also often quick and easy to publish as the newspaper or magazine editor will make a rapid decision without resorting to referees. At most, there could be one short round of revisions where you are asked to 'drop the paragraph on X' or 'say a bit more about Y'. Whereas the time from submission to acceptance will be measured in months or even years for scholarly journals and publishers, it will be days for newspapers and trade journals
- Popular pieces can often be spin-offs or summaries of full-length academic articles. Care is needed about copyright issues, but typically, popular magazines allow authors to retain the copyright to their work, allowing the academic to obtain two benefits from one piece of work. It's still essential to avoid self-plagiarism, though
- It is increasingly important for academics to be seen to do 'useful' research, and there is value for an academic's CV in demonstrating that their work is relevant for external audiences and that they have made an effort to communicate with those groups

The short length, timeliness of feedback, and high probability of success when writing practitioner articles makes them fun and easy to write. In the past, it was reasonable to ask magazines or trade journals for an author fee of, perhaps, £300-£1,000 for each article but nowadays they will likely expect to receive the content for free.

Stylistically, articles written for newspapers, magazines and other popular outlets differ significantly from scholarly outputs in several important respects:

- Length – academic papers are typically 8,000–10,000 words or 25+ pages long, whereas an article for a magazine could be anything from 500–2,000 words depending on the outlet

- Mathematical difficulty – academic articles sometimes, but not always, contain a considerable about of mathematical detail, including equations; practitioner and popular pieces will usually have none
- References – academic articles are typically heavily referenced with pages of citations to existing work; practitioner pieces might include up to two or three of the most vital references but usually none at all
- Presentation – academic articles tend to be written in a rather dry, formal style, whereas practitioner pieces need to be more journalistic and entertaining, perhaps referring to other unrelated contemporary or historical events as a way to generate interest
- Emphasis – academic pieces will emphasise the methodological details (indeed, the entire study could be developing a new method) and their rigour; practitioner articles will focus on the 'so what' question such as the additional profits or risk management benefits together with the implications for their readership
- Practitioner articles and those in newspapers and magazines tend to be visually appealing with sophisticated graphs and diagrams or even including stock photos on a vaguely relevant theme
- Most academic studies begin with a long preamble, and aside from the abstract, the paper might not get to the key findings or implications for many pages. On the other hand, for newspaper articles, the 'inverted pyramid' structure is often preferred. This ordering begins with the essential information so that the main facts should be in the first paragraph
- The piece will then continue with the rest of the material in declining order of pertinence, and the least important information should be at the end
- The writing style should be kept plain with brief sentences and short paragraphs (of possibly only one or two sentences)
- Newspaper articles do not express opinions, although quotes could be used to express your opinion through someone else's words. Note that it is preferable in the interests of balance to include opposing quotes
- There is no need to draw conclusions at the end or save the punchline until last

14.5.2 Drafting a press release

As well as writing practitioner articles, once you have a completed working paper, you might consider drafting a press release, which is often a good first step to outside engagement. It could lead to your research being mentioned in a newspaper or an invitation to chat about the work with a journalist, radio, or TV broadcaster. Press releases are short summaries (typically 200 words) of the research, but they cannot be a copy-and-paste of the abstract as they need to be written in a journalistic style.

Universities have communications teams that are very experienced in marketing research and gaining maximum publicity for it, and many business schools will have their own press office that might employ former journalists who have good contacts in the industry so that they are able to 'place' stories. It is worth chatting with them about your research, perhaps before you even begin to draft a press release. If you are really fortunate, they will be willing to write it for you.

Evidently, some topics are inherently more newsworthy than others, but timing is everything, and press releases are much more likely to be successful if they are linked with an important current news story. For instance, if your research is focused on auditing failures and the news story regarding Deloitte being investigated for its role at Lookers, the car showroom firm, is in the media, there could be considerable popular interest in your research, which would be timely. Journalists want a story that people will be excited to read about now, and surprising or contrary findings or opinions are particularly valued.

Many of the rules of the game for producing a press release are the same as those for an article in a practitioner magazine, although there are also a few extra points to bear in mind:

- Keep it very simple by avoiding technical language with no equations and no references
- Try to give the appearance of objectivity in what you write, even if your findings firmly fall on one side of a debate
- Be careful regarding any legal or controversial aspects and stick to provable facts unless you are stating opinions explicitly
- Make sure that the press-release is self-contained and could be fully understood by someone who has not read your research: a non-specialist should be able to follow it in its entirety even if they could not understand the underlying research
- Have the entire paper written and available to download before you circulate a press release, as some journalists might want to see this even if they don't understand it all
- The title should be attention-grabbing, so be creative
- Write in the third person (as if someone else is writing about your work)
- Newspaper articles and press releases always start with the key messages and then fill in the details. This structure means that the first couple of lines should be almost stand-alone as a summary of all your research
- It can build interest if you add a quote or two from someone about the work (not a 'classic' quote, though, a tailor-made statement about your research)
- Avoid cliché words such as 'world-class', 'breakthrough', 'outstanding'
- Include contact details (yours or possibly the press office's) and general information about the school after the end of the press release

14.5.3 Writing a referee report

Why review?

By the time you complete your thesis, you will have read a vast amount of literature and gained a good sense of what you think constitutes high-quality research. If you have also submitted a piece to a journal or publisher, you might have also received a review. Refereeing other researchers' papers is an integral part of academic life, and we all routinely provide suggestions and critical evaluations of each other's work. Such reviews are widely used to assess papers for publication and grant proposals as well as to make hiring, probation and promotion decisions.

You might be given the opportunity to write a review of a journal article, book or grant proposal, especially if you have already published a paper. It might also be the case that your supervisor asks you to be a referee, particularly if they hold editorial roles and need somebody to draft a report at short notice because someone that they had previously asked did not deliver.

Writing a referee report and making a decision can be quite daunting for those who have never done so before, as your recommendation could end up having a profound implication for someone's career. Therefore, it is an honour and responsibility that should be taken seriously and an opportunity not to be missed if it comes your way for several reasons:

- It is a scholarly activity, and the continuing functioning of the academy relies on such community-spirited actions
- Since, sooner or later, you will be submitting your work to journals, it seems reasonable to expect to do the same, *quid pro quo*. There is a danger that potential reviewers who persistently decline requests to review could be prohibited by the journal from submitting papers there in the future
- Acting as a referee allows you the chance to learn something about the latest research on the subject and sharpen your critical skills

There are some fascinating live issues around the peer-review process – for instance, the question as to whether those asked to produce reports are always experts. Most editors find it challenging to obtain high-quality referee reports – indeed, this is an issue I have faced on numerous occasions in my time as associate editor and guest editor of various journals. As a result, it is occasionally the case that the editor needs to find anyone competent to write something, even if they lack the credibility or even experience to act in that role.

Should as yet unpublished faculty or PhD students peer review? There is not an easy answer to that question. With the proper guidance, it would be a valuable part of their training as academics, and everybody has to start somewhere. But there are dangers if they have no prior experience of reviewing and are not provided with any support so that they might deliver an ill-informed judgement that is unfair on the writer of the submitted paper, whose own career development might depend on the outcome.

There are also serious questions about whether peer review can detect hoaxes and fakes. Unless the referee is an expert on the topic and goes through the work extremely careful, these could slip through the review screening system. Clark and Wright (2007) document a case where a team of psychology academics made minor modifications to already published papers and resubmitted them. Out of 12 such pieces, that they were identical was detected in only three cases, one paper was accepted, but eight were rejected, which is quite shocking given that they had been deemed sufficiently good when they were originally submitted. This example highlights the frailty and inherent randomness in the refereeing process.

How to draft a referee report for a journal

The first step in the process is obviously to read the paper carefully, possibly more than once. You can assume that the subject matter and overall style and structure match the journal's characteristics, otherwise the editor should have already rejected the paper before it would have been sent to you. Therefore, you can focus on the details.

Once you have read the paper, there are two tasks to complete: writing the report and the recommendation for the editor. The report will be seen by both the editor and the authors, while the advice regarding whether to publish the paper is for the editor only. Editors prefer it if the report is written with a neutral tone and not hinting at your recommendation, irrespective of whether you thought the work was tremendous or dreadful. Such neutrality allows them some flexibility to make a decision that is consistent with your views but also their own and those of any other referees or an associate editor who might have reviewed the paper in case there are stark differences of opinion.

The possible recommendations you can make for the editor were discussed above in the context of receiving a journal response: acceptance, conditional acceptance, revise and resubmit with either major or minor revisions, or reject. When trying to arrive at a decision, reflect on the journal's stature and the submitted paper's quality relative to other work published in that journal. There would be no point in being excessively harsh and recommending rejection of the submitted paper if most others in that journal are weaker. On the other hand, if the journal is of very high standing, you would need to establish a high threshold consistent with that, and if the paper you are reviewing is mediocre, you would probably recommend it is rejected.

The most important aspects to consider are the novelty and significance of the work. If the paper scores very highly on one of these measures (or quite highly on both), it would be appropriate to suggest that the editor offers the authors at least a revise and resubmit or even a conditional acceptance if you thought it was outstanding. If the paper is 'a diamond with a fixable flaw', it would be inappropriate and unfair to the authors if you recommend rejection. In that case, tell them what the issues are and ask that these problems are addressed in a revision. Matters that can be addressed would include relatively minor problems with the data or methods possibly requiring re-estimation, missing studies in the review, flawed arguments, sub-optimal ordering of the material, excessively long introduction, some instances of bad grammar or typos, and so on. Problems that cannot be fixed would include a lack of contribution or the use of inappropriate methods to address the research questions, in which case a rejection would be a plausible outcome.

How to write the report

The report for the authors will again comprise two elements: first, a summary of the work and second, a list of comments and suggestions. You might question why you need to draft an overview of the work when the authors have already written one (the abstract), but this convention helps the editor and author to confirm that you understood the paper at least to a minimum level and can identify the key features.

The summary should be only a paragraph or two and certainly need not be longer than half a page. Some referees who have little to add by way of comments fill their review with a very extensive precis of the work, but this is unnecessary and not what is expected. Don't copy the abstract; instead, summarise the paper in your own words, bringing out what you see as the main contributions and most important findings.

There should then be a list of comments and suggestions for the authors. These could be in order of importance with the most important first, or in their sequence of occurrence in the paper, or in no particular order at all. Focus on the most salient issues, and minor points such as individual typos are best left in a separate list at the end. Try to be constructive so that you point out flaws in the work and provide suggestions as to how the authors could fix them.

Even if your view of the paper is overwhelmingly negative, it is good practice to try to identify parts that the authors have done well and discuss those too in your report. In almost all cases, they will have tried their best to produce good work, and even if they have failed in that objective, very severe and nasty comments will not provide encouragement to do better. Not only would that upset the authors, but they are also more likely to discard your report, not making any of the changes, and concluding that you were unbalanced or had some ulterior motive justifying your excessive degree of negativity. In that case, the time and effort you put into writing the report would have been wasted. Therefore, whatever your views, keep the report polite and devoid of general judgements about the paper's quality.

The report must be completely anonymous so that you cannot be identified. Therefore, do not add your name or any other identifying information and check the document properties. Not revealing your identity also means that it is best to avoid asking the authors to cite your new, unpublished working papers.

Chapter takeaways – top tips for success

⊛ Your conference budget will be severely limited so choose carefully and it might be better to attend several events close to home rather than one in an exotic location

⊛ Maximise opportunities for networking. Presenting will increase your exposure, but also attend coffee breaks, lunch and dinner sessions

⊛ Thoroughly practice your talk in advance of delivering it, especially if you are inexperienced or nervous

Chapter takeaways – continued

* Don't prepare too many slides and limit the amount of literature review on them
* Aim to send a paper drawn from your thesis out for possible journal publication as soon as it is ready
* Decide in advance whether journal articles from the thesis will be co-authored with your supervisor and agree on the name ordering
* Select an appropriate journal that optimally trades off prestige with likelihood of success
* Consider writing practitioner articles or blogs alongside academic papers
* Seek out opportunities to review for journals or publishers

15. YOUR POST-PHD CAREER

Learning outcomes: this chapter covers

✓ Applying for academic posts
✓ Making a job application
✓ Preparing for job presentations and interviews

15.1 Do you want to continue with research as a career?

An important question to ask yourself as you are proceeding through the process of conducting and completing the PhD is whether you are enjoying the experience and if so, how much. Every researcher has bad days where they lose faith in their own abilities and begin to doubt whether they want to continue, but for most students these thoughts will be fleeting. Averaging over the good days and the bad, could you see yourself as a career researcher, doing essentially what you are currently doing for a living after graduation? Or perhaps you might be interested in a job involving some research but interspersed with other activities? A final possibility could be that while you are committed to finishing the doctoral programme that you have started, the idea of doing anything remotely like this in the future fills you with feelings of utter horror. This chapter aims to provide support to students who are contemplating a career in the academy and who would therefore need to apply for academic posts.

If you undertake further research, even though the topic will likely be different from the one you chose for your PhD, the raw ingredients of the process and the final output type will be the same. The skills that you have already developed will stand you in good stead for the next research project. This experience will mean that you will probably enjoy it more: you will be more confident, you will make progress much more quickly, you will become increasingly self-reliant and able to resolve more of the issues yourself without hitting a wall. All of the tasks that took a lot of time and effort to master – where to look for ideas and material, how to write a review, how to conduct empirical work, how to approach drafting an abstract and an introduction – will all come more naturally the second time around. In essence, you can use the best aspects of how you did things for the previous research as a template for how to proceed next time.

While research never becomes effortless, the more you have already conducted, the easier it becomes to do it again. The research journey becomes a never-ending mountain-climbing tour. Once you have ascended to a mountain peak, the trip to the next one begins. Each project is different, with new experiences and new skills learned each time, and all the while, you will be contributing to the body of knowledge. The production of research generates ideas for further research in a never-ending cycle. Life as an academic researcher allows you to master your own destiny, set your own agenda of inquiry, and take it in whatever direction you choose.

There are broadly three career options open to PhD graduates in accounting and finance who do decide that they would like to continue with research in some capacity:

1. Traditionally, a PhD was considered required training to become an academic researcher, possibly starting as a post-doc (post-doctoral research assistant) followed by a lecturer (assistant professor), senior lecturer or reader (associate professor) and then a (full) professor. Indeed, this is still the case, and it is virtually impossible to obtain an academic post without having completed or being close to completing a PhD

2. A researcher in a bank, consultancy or accountancy firm. In finance particularly, such roles were common and extremely lucrative before the global financial crisis, with hedge funds taking large numbers of PhD graduates as 'quants' (quantitative analysts), although the number of such roles has significantly diminished more recently

3. A researcher in a central bank, professional association or regulator (e.g., the Financial Conduct Authority or European Central Bank). Such organisations employ PhD graduates in quasi-academic roles that are mainly project-based and involve conducting research to address the organisation's specific needs. The research output might be published in a report or working paper format.

Although many PhD graduates will be applying for roles in central banks, regulators or the private sector, the remainder of this chapter focuses on applying for academic roles, since this is where my expertise and experience lies. As well as having applied and been appointed to various academic roles over time, I have also been a member of and chaired interview panels.

15.2 Applying for academic jobs

The work that you conducted for your thesis will have provided ample opportunity to determine whether a career involving scholarly research is for you. Once you have completed, or you are close to finishing, your PhD, three types of roles would be open in the academy:

1. A research-only role
2. A teaching and research role
3. A teaching-only role

The first of these would be a post-doc or research fellowship. The number of such opportunities in accounting and finance is quite limited, owing to the lack of funded projects that would employ people in post-doc roles. These are generally entry-level positions for those who are just starting out after getting their PhD, and they are almost invariably fixed-term posts (of one to five years' duration).

The second possibility would be to apply for a lectureship, which would constitute both the second and third items in the list. Most lecturers are employed on a 'T&R' basis, implying that the post-holders undertake both teaching and research, probably in roughly equal proportions, often alongside an academic administration role such as admissions tutor, exams officer, or programme director.

Alternatively, an increasing number of positions have become available for teaching-intensive (TI) lecturers who would not have any contractual requirement to undertake research but would probably have roughly double the teaching load of a T&R post, plus administrative duties. In both cases, having or being near completion of a PhD would be an absolute job requirement.

Whether a T&R or TI post is right for you depends on the relative strengths of your skills and interests between teaching and research and, of course, the availability of positions at the time you are looking. In general, T&R posts are more sought after, as the majority of academics prefer a balance between the two activities rather than a pure teaching focus.

Securing a first university post in accounting or finance has always been challenging but now increasingly so. In the past decade, the number of taught students in these fields grew substantially, particularly at the master's level, which generated both a need for greater faculty numbers to teach them and the funding to pay for the academic posts. Recently, however, taught student numbers have plateaued, leading academic staff recruitment to fall while PhD graduate numbers have remained high. Moreover, since the global financial crisis of c.2008, the number of opportunities for people with doctorates in the financial markets, particularly in London but also in many other financial centres, has declined. Overall, these factors have combined to lead the demand for PhD graduates in universities to diminish when the supply of applications for these posts has gone up. As a result, competition for positions is fierce, and universities might now expect 50-80 applicants for a single job. Against this job market backdrop, you need to do everything you can to stand out from other applicants.

Where to apply

The US job market model tends to be that every candidate applies for every job, but European universities are mostly not geared up for that as the recruitment process is less well-resourced and more personalised. Therefore, if you are going on the UK or European academic job market, apply widely, but don't bother applying for jobs where you have virtually no chance of success or where you have no intention of going even if you were offered the post. If you are studying for a PhD at a mid-ranking UK university, there is no point in applying for a position at Wharton or Yale. Whimsical applications are a waste of your time, your referees' time and the recruiter's time. But don't routinely dismiss jobs where you might be a good fit because the location isn't quite what you wanted or the place is less prestigious than you have hoped for – you might land your ideal job in a month, or it might never be advertised and you will end up with nothing.

You might initially think that the odds of job success are heavily stacked against you since other applicants could be established lecturers, who already have their PhD in the bag, a publication or two, and a year's experience across the full range of teaching and assessment duties. While such applicants might look stronger than you on paper, all is not lost because universities are looking not only at achievement but also at potential. So you need to be able to convince the recruiter – through your application and your interview responses – that even though the other candidate is currently way out in front, if you are given the opportunity, then in two years you will be ahead because you are progressing so much faster.

Don't be concerned by rejections since these are bound to happen frequently when there are 50+ applicants per post. Feedback will not be provided automatically, but it is worth asking for some, and this ought to be provided when you reached the interview stage. Even if not, the recruiter might be willing to supply a couple of statements that will indicate whether you could improve your application style or what you write.

In the UK, the application will usually comprise three parts: a completed form, a CV, and a covering letter. You might also have the opportunity to submit a sample of your work. Unlike the US and some parts of Europe, references will not be sent in with the application and instead will be requested by the university for short-listed candidates only. Each of these aspects will now be discussed.

The cover letter or supporting statement

To have a reasonable chance of success with so few openings, it is essential that you tailor the application to the place to which you are applying. This specialised information gathering and drafting can be very time-consuming, especially for the first couple of instances that you do so, but it will be worthwhile. A generic submission headed, 'Dear Recruitment Committee' with a standard statement about your CV and experiences will not impress or stand out from the others.

Instead, browse through the university's and department's websites where you are applying and draft your statement or covering letter around them as well as you.

For instance, you could explain:

- Why you would relish the opportunity to work with them because of their expertise and strength in financial accounting since you also research in this area and you want to collaborate with and learn from their senior faculty
- How innovative you find their new programme in fintech and cryptocurrencies, and you have ideas for a couple of additional modules that they could consider offering and which you could develop and teach
- How you visited the department once and were impressed by its facilities and location

Also, examine the person criteria and job specification that will have been made available to applicants on the university website and try to align your cover letter with some of the points they are looking for. It is unnecessary to mention each one in a tick-box exercise or even refer to the criteria at all by name; instead, ensure that your application materials discuss as many as you can of the aspects that they want the applicant to have.

An application where this amount of effort has been made will flatter and impress the recruiting university and stand out from the crowd.

15.2.1 The CV

This should be brief and probably of around two pages in length for an applicant at the start of their career. It should include:

- Standard details such as your name, address, e-mail and phone number
- A short statement (2–3 lines) explaining your background, research interests and career ambitions
- Your qualifications with grades
- Expected date of submission of your thesis (if you have not already submitted it)
- Any work experience you have
- A list of the papers you have produced with status (published papers or book chapters, working papers, papers under review with journals, work in process). You can include work that is not yet finished, but don't list anything you have not even started.
- Conferences you have attended
- Any prizes or other achievements
- Some people include a list of their wider skills or familiarity with software or databases; others state their hobbies. My view is neither of these is worthwhile mentioning unless you have something particularly unique to say. For example, if you have designed websites (which would be a valuable skill for a colleague to have) or you are a runner at the county-level (which provides an exciting talking point).

15.2.2 The presentation and interview
The presentation

If you are short-listed for a post, you will likely be asked to give a presentation to staff members in the department, followed by an interview with a smaller senior faculty group. How to conduct an effective research presentation was discussed in section 14.2, and those rules still apply in this different context. However, you should beware that, rather than asking you simply to present one of your research papers in 20 minutes, often you will be given a specific brief to discuss something different. For instance, you could be asked to 'Outline your research agenda for the next five years', or 'Explain how your research is relevant for external user groups', or even something teaching-related (e.g., 'Explain how you would design a new module on Social Accounting for masters students'). In such cases, ignoring the instructions and giving a standard research presentation will go down very badly and will probably rule you out from further consideration.

The guidance for giving interview presentations is similar to that for presenting at conferences as discussed in the previous chapter. But in this situation, keep in mind that the primary purpose is to secure you a post, not to get detailed feedback on your research. So pay particular attention to the time allotted, and ensure that your slides are not too esoteric for non-specialists. The audience will be assessing you on your generic presentational skills and how you might perform as a teacher too. Therefore, ensure that you speak clearly, look at the audience and try to grab their attention with an entertaining as well as informative talk.

The importance of being sociable

If you have the opportunity to attend a lunch or dinner with staff members or even other job candidates, it is essential that you attend and try to make some intelligent, polite conversation even if you dislike such events. The department will want to get to know applicants a little to see whether they would be a good 'fit' and see whether they are really as they present themselves in their application materials. The department will also be trying to gauge whether candidates would be good citizens if appointed – in other words, will they get involved with wider activities such as attending seminars, student recruitment fairs or student social events? Do they seem ambitious and hard-working or lazy and slow? Sometimes it is easier to get an idea of how someone measures up on these attributes via an informal chat than through a formal interview where the candidate is on their best behaviour for 20 minutes and manages to say what the recruiting committee wants to hear.

If the department does not organise such an opportunity, contact the Head and ask to meet with them and other colleagues informally. This conversation will not only provide you with more opportunities to impress than are available to other candidates, it will also help you to decide whether this would be a great place to work or not. How does the Head treat you and the other candidates – would you like them to be your line manager?

Hiring a new person is a considerable risk for a department, especially if it is a small group. Once a person is appointed, even if there is formally a probationary period, it is difficult to remove them from their post even if they perform exceptionally poorly. Therefore, the hiring committee will want to minimise these dangers, which is why internal candidates (e.g., students completing their theses at that institution) often have a higher chance than outsiders.

The interview

Most candidates will unsurprisingly be nervous when approaching a job interview. In the UK, academic interviews tend to last 20–40 minutes and there will usually be at least three or four people on the panel: the Head of Department or Dean of the Business School (or both), a representative from HR, and a subject specialist from the the department. It is possible there could also be a senior member of the university management structure present, such as a pro-vice chancellor, but this is more likely for senior posts. In the latter case, there will also probably be an external panel member (i.e., a senior academic from another university), whose role will be to provide another, independent input into the decision-making and also to ensure a comparability of standards across universities.

As for a PhD viva exam, preparing fully is difficult since it is impossible to predict exactly what the questions will be, but many of the tips given in section 13.2 for preparing and conduct during the viva also apply here:

- Think about your strengths as a candidate, and be prepared to summarise your research and also outline your plans and ideas for future projects
- Dress formally
- Read through all of your application materials again, particularly if you wrote them some time before the interview as it is highly likely that there will be some follow-on questions arising from them
- Do some research about the department and the university, and be prepared to say what excites you about the place and the people
- Use formal titles for panel members unless you already know them well
- Use the right amount of detail in your answers, avoiding one-word responses to questions but also trying not to ramble so that the interviewers become bored and interrupt you. Remember that they will have several candidates to talk to and a fixed amount of time for each one
- If you don't understand a question that you have been asked, you can request that the panel member repeats it. But if you really don't know the answer, then it is fine to say that or hazard a guess once or twice
- Try to focus your answer to a particular question at the person who asked it, but it is important to try to build a rapport with everyone in the room as they will be making a joint decision about who to appoint

Usually, each panel member will select a particular area and ask two or three questions on that before passing on to the next person. For instance, the panel chair (usually the Head of Department or most senior person there) will open the questioning with general items about your skills and motivations. Then another person might focus on research before a third discusses matters related to teaching. If there is time, a fourth person might ask about citizenship or come back to any issues thrown up by your previous responses. Although the precise questions will vary from one interview panel to the next, they will of course cover some common themes and hence overlap to an extent. A few possible interview questions are as follows:

- What skills and attributes will you bring to the department?
- What attracted you to apply for this post?
- What is your research agenda for the next few years?
- Of which piece of your research are you most proud?
- Professor X sitting over there is from another school. Can you explain this technical concept to them, bearing in mind they have no background in the subject?
- When do you expect to submit your thesis?
- When you co-author research with others, what is your typical role?
- How do you select the journals to which to send your papers?
- What are the most prominent recent contributions in your subject area?
- Whose research do you admire the most and why?
- What are the characteristics of research in the top field journals such as the *Journal of Finance* and the *Journal of Accounting and Economics*, and why are so few academics successful in publishing there?
- How do you decide what topics to work on and whom to work with (apart from your supervisor)?
- Where do you see your career going in ten years?
- Is research funding essential, and where would you apply for it?
- How would you reach out to possible external users of your research?
- What is the primary audience for your work – other academics or external users?
- What teaching specialisms can you offer?
- How would you go about setting up a new module from scratch that has not been taught here before?
- How would you approach teaching an extensive group?
- Is a different approach required when teaching executives compared with undergraduates?
- Which aspects of our range of programmes impressed you the most? Are there any gaps in what we offer?
- Do you think that new learning technologies valuable for teaching or have they made students too passive compared with a 'chalk and talk'?
- Has the financial crisis changed the way we teach accounting and finance? Should it have done?
- Is there a trade-off between rigour and popularity in teaching?
- What skills make an effective university teacher?

- Tell me about your teaching experience – what did you learn, and what would you improve?
- Do you feel ready to co-supervise a PhD student? What would be your approach?
- How would you feel about taking an administrative role, such as organising the research seminars or being undergraduate admissions tutor?
- How would you integrate new technologies into your teaching?
- What are the relative advantages and disadvantages of on-line versus face-to-face delivery?
- What are the characteristics of good on-line teaching materials?
- Do you have any questions you would like to ask the interview panel?

This list is by no means exhaustive, and the range of questions you could be asked is limited only by the imaginations of those on the panel. But the above does cover many of the items that are likely to come up in UK-style academic interviews. I will refrain from providing suggestions for these questions since the responses, in most cases, will need to be unique to you based on your background and experiences.

But the final question is worth some comment. It is perhaps not ideal, but reasonable to reply, 'No, I am happy that we covered everything I expected during the interview. Thanks for offering me the opportunity to come in and talk to you.' An inappropriate response would be to have a long list of detailed questions relating to minor issues or, even worse, information that is displayed on the school's web site. It is common to ask questions about workloads, research resources, and support available or when the candidate will hear the outcome of the application process. It is best to refrain from asking about the salary since this could cause awkwardness among panel members and is better discussed discretely with the Head of Department if you are offered the post. Similarly, avoid the temptation to try to outwit the panel by asking them a challenging interview-style question, the response to which you are not really interested in anyway, such as, 'what is the department's strategy to generate more research funding and impact?' The danger would be that the panel would not conclude you to be brilliant; rather, they would think you were smug and not a person with whom they would like to work.

The interview outcome

After the interview, send the panel chair an e-mail to thank them for providing you with the interview and say that you are very much looking forward to hearing from them in due course. Identify an aspect of your visit or the process that you were impressed with or pleasantly surprised by and mention that. The hiring committee will probably have already made up their minds whom to hire by then but leaving them with a good feeling about you is still worthwhile in case there are further opportunities there in the future.

Once the interview panel has seen all of the short-listed applicants (usually four to eight for one post), they will deliberate and first identify the candidates who are not appointable because they do not meet the criteria. Those individuals will usually be notified almost immediately that they have not made it. The remaining candidates will be ranked from the most suitable to the least (but still above the threshold to be appointed), with the first choice being informed straight away. The number two, three, ... choices will be left on hold until the first tells the panel whether they will accept the offer or not.

If you do not hear from the interview panel chair during the timeframe within which they had suggested they would inform candidates of the outcome, the most likely explanation is that you were a second or third choice. Unfortunately, if the first choice candidate procrastinates in making a decision about whether to accept the post or not, you could be left hanging for several weeks. If you have heard nothing a week or so after the interview, you could send a polite reminder to your key contact there (probably the Head of Department), although this is unlikely to speed up the process.

Try not to be too disheartened if your first few job applications ultimately result in rejections. If you get to the interview stage, in the current environment it would probably place you within the top 10% of applicants so that would be an achievement in itself. Undergoing these interviews will have been excellent experience, and you would no doubt have realised that they are quite similar in terms of the format, style and kinds of questions asked. Hopefully, you will have a better outcome next time, but if you repeatedly get to the interview stage with no job offer, it is worth reflecting on your technique and whether there is anything you could do to increase your chances of success. It could simply be that there were candidates with more experience and stronger track records, but is there anything you could have said (or not said) at the presentation or interview to push the odds in your favour? If you get a call or e-mail to say that you have been unsuccessful, ask for feedback on how you did, why you didn't get the role, and how you could improve your profile and interview technique for future applications.

Chapter takeaways – top tips for success

⊛ Don't waste your time and that of the recruitment panels by applying for posts you have no interest in taking even if you are successful

⊛ Rather than sending the same generic application, tailor each one to the institution to which you are applying

⊛ If you are called for interview, think carefully beforehand about how you will reply to standard questions such as what skills you would bring to the post and why you applied there, what are your research plans, etc.

⊛ Do your homework by looking carefully at the website of the departments to which you are applying. This will help you to answer questions about why you want to work there and where you would fit

Chapter takeaways – continued

- ⊛ It is essential to take up any opportunities to meet informally with members of the department to which you are applying
- ⊛ Try to get feedback from any unsuccessful applications, especially if you got to the interview stage

REFERENCES

Bailey, S. (2017) *Academic Writing: A Handbook for International Students* Routledge, Oxford, 5th edition.

Bartunek, J.M., Rynes, S.L., & Ireland, R.D. (2006) What makes management research interesting? *Academy of Management Journal* 49(1), 9–15.

Bell, A.R., Brooks, C. & Dryburgh, P.R. (2007) *The English Wool Market* c.1230–1327 Cambridge University Press, Cambridge, UK.

Birks, M. & Mills, J. (2015) *Grounded Theory: A Practical Guide* Sage, London.

Booth, A., Sutton, A. & Papaioannou, D. (2016) *Systematic Approaches to a Successful Literature Review* Sage, London, 2nd edition.

Brooks, C. (2019) *Introductory Econometrics for Finance* 4th edition, Cambridge University Press, Cambridge, UK.

Brooks, C., Chen, Z. & Zeng, Y. (2018) Institutional cross-ownership and corporate strategy: the case of mergers and acquisitions *Journal of Corporate Finance* 48, 187–216.

Brooks, C., Fenton, E., Schopohl, L., & Walker, J. (2014) Gender and the evaluation of research *Research Policy* 46(6), 990–1001.

Brooks, C., Fenton, E., Schopohl, L., & Walker, J. (2019) Why does research in finance have so little impact? *Critical Perspectives on Accounting* 58, 24–52.

Brooks, C., Prokopczuk, M. & Wu, Y. (2015) Booms and busts in commodity markets:

bubbles or fundamentals? *Journal of Futures Markets* 35 (10), 916–938.

Carroll, J. (2012) *Effective Time Management in Easy Steps* In Easy Steps Limited, Leamington Spa.

Cassell, C. (2015) *Conducting Research Interviews for Business and Management Students* Sage, London.

Clark, T. & Wright, M. (2007) Reviewing journal rankings and revisiting peer reviews: editorial perspectives *Journal of Management Studies* 44, 612–621.

Coleman, H. (2019) *Polish Your Academic Writing* Sage, London.

Comte, A. (1880) *A General View of Positivism*, Reeves & Turner, London.

Creswell, J.W. & Creswell, J.D. (2018) *Research Design: Qualitative, Quantitative, and Mixed Methods Approaches* Sage, London.

Curzer, H. & Santillanes, G. (2012) Managing conflict of interest in research: some suggestions for investigators *Accountability in Research* 19, 143–55.

Day, T. (2018) *Success in Academic Writing* Palgrave, London, 2nd edition.

Deer, B. (2011) How the case against the MMR vaccine was fixed *British Medical Journal* 342, c5347.

Denscombe, M. (2019) *Research Proposals* Open University Press, London, 2nd edition.

Dooley, D. (1995) *Social Research Methods* Prentice Hall, Englewood Cliffs, New Jersey.

Evans, D. (2013) *Don't Trust Your Spell Check: Pro Proofreading Tactics and Tests To Eliminate Embarrassing Writing Errors* Createspace, Scotts Valley, California.

Fink, A.G. (2016) *How to Conduct Surveys: A Step-by-Step Guide*, Sage, London, 6th edition.

Fowler, F.J. (2013) *Survey Research Methods* Sage, London, 5th edition.

Frankfurter, G.M. & McGoun, E.G. (2001) Anomalies in finance: what are they and what are they good for? *International Review of Financial Analysis* 10, 407–429.

Frankfurter, G.M. & McGoun, E.G. (1999) Ideology and the theory of financial economics *Journal of Economic Behavior and Organization* 39, 159–177.

Friedman, M. (1953) *Essays in Positive Economics* University of Chicago Press, Chicago.

Gippel, J. (2012) A revolution in finance? *Australian Journal of Management* 38(1) 125–146.

Glaser, B.G. & Strauss, A.L. (1967) *The Discovery of Grounded Theory: Strategies for Qualitative Research* Aldine, New York.

Greener, I. (2006) Nick Leeson and the collapse of Barings Bank: Socio-technical networks and the 'rogue trader' *Organization* 13(3), 421–441.

Greetham, B. (2020) *How to Write Your Literature Review* Macmillan, London.

Hammersley, M. & Traianou, A. (2012) *Ethics in Qualitative Research: Controversies and Contexts* Sage, London.

Hampton, A.R. (2019) *Proofreading Power: Skills & Drills* Cornerstone, Little Rock, Arcansas.

Hillenbrand, C., Saraeva, A., Money, K. & Brooks, C. (2021) Saving for a rainy day … or a trip to the Bahamas? How the framing of investment communication impacts retail investors *British Journal of Management*, forthcoming.

Hinnink, M., Hutter, I. & Bailey, A. (2020) *Qualitative Research Methods* Sage, London, 2nd edition.

Holland, J., Henningsson, J., Johanson, U., Koga, C. & Sakakibara, S. (2012) Use of IC information in Japanese financial firms *Journal of Intellectual Capital* 13(4), 562–581.

Hollis, M. (1994) *The Philosophy of Social Science, An Introduction* Cambridge University Press, Cambridge.

Howell, K. (2012) *An Introduction to the Philosophy of Methodology* Sage, London.

Hussey, J. & Hussey, R. (1997) *Business Research: A Practical Guide for Postgraduate Students* Macmillan Business, Basingstoke, UK.

Ide, K. (2013) *Proofreading Secrets of Best-Selling Authors* Lighthouse, Raleigh, North Carolina.

Johnstone, C. (2019) *Seven Ways to Build Resilience: Strengthening Your Ability to Deal with Difficult Times* Robinson, London.

Judge, TA, Cable, D.M., Colbert, A.E. & Rynes, S.L. (2007) What causes a management article to be cited: article, author or journal? *Academy of Management Journal* 50(3), 491–506.

Keasey, K. and Hudson, R. (2007) Finance theory: a house without windows *Critical Perspectives on Accounting* 18, 932–951.

Kuhn, T.S. (1962) *The Structure of Scientific Revolutions* University of Chicago Press, Chicago.

Lancaster, T. (2019) *Avoid Plagiarism* Sage, London.

Laughlin, R. (1999) Critical accounting: nature, progress and prognosis *Accounting, Auditing & Accountability Journal* 12(1), 73–78.

Loughran, T. & McDonald, B. (2011) When is a liability not a liability? Textual analysis, dictionaries, and 10-Ks *Journal of Finance* 66, 35–65.

Lovell, H. & MacKenzie, D. (2011) Accounting for carbon: the role of accounting professional organisations in governing climate change *Antipode* 43(3), 704–730.

Macdonald, S. & Kam, J. (2007) Ring a Ring o' Roses: Quality Journals and Gamesmanship in Management Studies *Journal of Management Studies* 44(4), 640—655.

Mattessich, R. (1989) Accounting and the input-output principle in the prehistoric and ancient world *Abacus* 25, 74–84.

Mill, J.S. (1881) *A System of Logic* Harper, New York.

Oldroyd, D. (1995) The role of accounting in public expenditure and monetary policy in the first century AD Roman empire *Accounting Historians Journal* 22, 117–129.

O'Leary, Z. (2018) *Research Proposal: Little Quick Fix* Sage, London.

Paterson, A., Leung, D., Jackson, W., MacIntosh, R. & O'Gorman, K. (2016) *Research Methods for Accounting and Finance* Goodfellow, Oxford.

Popper, K.R. (1959) *The Logic of Scientific Discovery* Hutchinson, London.

Punch, K.F. (2016) *Developing Effective Research Proposals* Sage, London.

Redfield, G. (2020) *Stop Procrastinating: Complete Step by Step Guide on How to Avoid Procrastination and Motivate Yourself Back on Track* Garrett Redfield.

Rendall, S., Brooks, C. & Hillenbrand, C. (2021) The impacts of emotions and personality on borrowers' abilities to manage their debts *International Review of Financial Analysis* 74, 101703.

Ridley, D. (2012) *The Literature Review: A Step-By-Step Guide For Students* Sage, London.

Ritchie, J., Lewis, J., Nicholls, C.M. & Ormston, R. (2013) *Qualitative Research Practice: A Guide for Social Science Students and Researchers* Sage, London, 2nd edition.

Sandberg, J. & Alvesson, M. (2011) Ways of constructing research questions: gap-spotting or problematization? *Organization*, 18(1), 23–44.

Smith, M. (2020) *Research Methods in Accounting* Sage, London, 5th edition.

Tanggaarrd, L. & Wegener, C. (2016) *A Survival Kit for Doctoral Students and Their Supervisors: Traveling the Landscape of Research* Sage, London.

Tao, R. Brooks, C. & Bell, A.R. (2020) When is a MAX not the MAX? How news resolves information uncertainty *Journal of Empirical Finance* 57, 33–51.

Tucker, B. & Parker, L. (2014) In our ivory towers? The research-practice gap in management accounting *Accounting and Business Research* 44(2), 104–143.

Urquhart, C. (2012) *Grounded Theory for Qualitative Research: A Practical Guide* Sage, London.

Wakefield, A.J., Murch, S.H., Anthony, A., Linnell, J., Casson, D.M., Malik, M., Berelowitz, M., Dhillon, A.P., Thomson, M.A., Harvey, P., Valentine, A., Davies, S.E. & Walker-Smith, J.A. (1998) Ileal-lymphoid-nodular hyperplasia, non-specific colitis, and pervasive developmental disorder in children *The Lancet* 351(9103), 637–641.

Williams, K. & Davis, M. (2017) *Referencing and Understanding Plagiarism* Palgrave, London.

Williams, M. (2016) *Key Concepts in the Philosophy of Social Research* Sage, London.

Willmott, H. (2011a) Journal list fetishism and the perversion of scholarship: reactivity and the ABS list *Organization,* 18, 429–442.

Willmott, H. (2011b) Listing perilously *Organization*, 18(4), 447–448.

Wilson, K. (2020) *How to Build a Healthy Brain: Reduce Stress, Anxiety and Depression and Future-proof Your Brain* Yellow Kite, London.

Yin, R.K. (2018) *Case Study Research and Applications: Design and Methods* Sage, London, 6th edition.

Index

www.ingramcontent.com/pod-product-compliance
Lightning Source LLC
Chambersburg PA
CBHW051203200326
41519CB00025B/6994